The Cognitive Neuroscience of Social Behaviour

The Cognitive Neuroscience of Social Behaviour

edited by
Alexander Easton and Nathan J. Emery

Psychology Press
Taylor & Francis Group
HOVE AND NEW YORK

First published 2005 by Psychology Press
27 Church Road, Hove, East Sussex BN3 2FA

Simultaneously published in the USA and Canada
by Psychology Press
270 Madison Avenue, New York NY 10016

Psychology Press is a part of the Taylor & Francis Group, an Informa business

Copyright © 2005 Psychology Press

Transferred to digital printing 2009

Typeset in Times by RefineCatch Limited, Bungay, Suffolk
Printed and bound in Great Britain by the MPG Books Group

Cover design by Hybert Design

All rights reserved. No part of this book may be reprinted or reproduced or utilized in any form or by any electronic, mechanical, or other means, now known or hereafter invented, including photocopying and recording, or in any information storage or retrieval system, without permission in writing from the publishers.

The publisher makes no representation, express or implied, with regard to the accuracy of the information contained in this book and cannot accept any legal responsibility or liability for any errors or omissions that may be made.

This publication has been produced with paper manufactured to strict environmental standards and with pulp derived from sustainable forests.

British Library Cataloguing in Publication Data
A catalogue record for this book is available from the British Library

Library of Congress Cataloguing-in-Publication Data
The cognitive neuroscience of social behaviour /
[edited by] Alexander Easton and Nathan Emery.—1st ed.
    p. cm.
  Includes bibliographical references and index.
  ISBN 978-1-84169-349-1 (hard cover)
  1. Cognitive neuroscience. 2. Social psychology.
I. Easton, Alexander, 1975– II. Emery, Nathan, 1971–

  QP360.5.C6395 2005
  153—dc22
                              2004013308

ISBN 978-1-84169-349-1

Contents

Acknowledgements vii
List of contributors ix

1 Introduction: What is social cognitive neuroscience (SCN)? 1
NATHAN J. EMERY AND ALEXANDER EASTON

PART I
Neural substrates of social interactions 17

2 The neurobiology of social-emotional cognition in nonhuman primates 19
JOCELYNE BACHEVALIER AND MARTINE L. MEUNIER

3 Behavioural flexibility, social learning, and the frontal cortex 59
ALEXANDER EASTON

4 Neural basis for the perception of goal-directed actions 81
TJEERD JELLEMA AND DAVID I. PERRETT

PART II
Cognitive neuroscience of social cognition 113

5 The evolution of social cognition 115
NATHAN J. EMERY

6 Functional anatomy of human social cognition 157
ANDREA S. HEBERLEIN AND RALPH ADOLPHS

7 The self and social perception: Three kinds of questions in social cognitive neuroscience 195
MATTHEW D. LIEBERMAN AND JENNIFER H. PFEIFER

PART III
Human disorders of social behaviour and cognition 237

8 **Autism and the origins of social neuroscience** 239
SIMON BARON-COHEN

9 **The neurobiology of social cognition and its relationship to unipolar depression** 257
ZOË KYTE AND IAN GOODYER

10 **The neurobiology of antisocial behaviour and psychopathy** 291
R. JAMES R. BLAIR

Index 325

Acknowledgements

Figure 2.1 Adapted from Figure 6–5A (p. 603), Figure 6–7A (p. 605), Figure 6–9A (p. 607), from *The Temporal Lobe and Limbic System* by Pierre Gloor. © 1997 by Oxford University Press, Inc. Used by permission of Oxford University Press, Inc.

Figure 2.2 Adapted from 'Orbitofrontal sulci of the human and macaque monkey brain', Chiavaras and Petrides (2000), *The Journal of Comparative Neurology*, 422, 35–54. © 2000 by John Wiley & Sons, Inc. Reprinted with permission of Wiley-Liss, Inc. a subsidiary of John Wiley & Sons, Inc.

Figure 2.3 Adapted from 'Influence of amygolactomy on social behaviour in monkeys', Rosvold et al (1954), *The Journal of Comparative and Physiological Psychology*, 47, 173–178. © 1954 by John Wiley & Sons, Inc. Reprinted with permission of Wiley-Liss, Inc. a subsidiary of John Wiley & Sons.

Figure 4.2 Adapted from *Brain and Cognition*, 44, Jellema, et al., 'Neural representation for the perception of the intentionality of actions', 280–302, © 2000, with permission from Elsevier.

Figure 4.3 Adapted from 'Single cell integration of animate form, motion, and location in the superior temporal sulcus of the macaque monkey', Jellema, et al. (2004), *Cerebral Cortex*, 14, 781–790. © 2004 by Oxford University Press, Inc. Used by permission of Oxford University Press, Inc.

Figure 4.5 Adapted from Jellema and Perrett (2003b). 'Cells in monkey STS responsive to articulated body motions and consequent static posture: A case of implied motion?' *Neuropsychologia*, 41, 1728–1737. © 2003, with permission from Elsevier.

Figure 4.6 Adapted from Jellema and Perrett (2003b). 'Cells in monkey STS responsive to articulated body motions and consequent static posture: A case of implied motion?' *Neuropsychologia*, 41, 1728–1737. © 2003, with permission from Elsevier.

Figure 4.7 Adapted from Jellema and Perrett (2003a). 'Perceptual history influences neural responses to face and body postures', *Journal of Cognitive Neuroscience*, 15:7 (October 2003), 961–971.

© 2003 by the Massachusetts Institute of Technology, used with permission of MIT.

Figure 4.8 Adapted from Jellema and Perrett (2003a). 'Perceptual history influences neural responses to face and body postures', *Journal of Cognitive Neuroscience, 15:7 (October 2003)*, 961–971. © 2003 by the Massachusetts Institute of Technology, used with permission of MIT.

Figure 4.9 Adapted from Baker, et al. (2001), 'Neuronal representation of disappearing and hidden objects in temporal cortex of the macaque', *Experimental Brain Research, 140(3)*, 375–381. © 2001 by Springer-Verlag, used with permission from Springer-Verlag.

Contributors

Ralph Adolphs, University of Iowa, College of Medicine, Dept of Neurology, 200 Hawkins Drive, Iowa City, IA 52242, USA.

Jocelyne Bachevalier, Professor Department of Psychology and Yerkes National Primate Research Center, Emory University, 954 Gatewood Road, Atlanta, GA 30329, USA.

Simon Baron-Cohen, Autism Research Centre, University of Cambridge, Departments of Experimental Psychology and Psychiatry, Downing St, Cambridge CB3 9JL, UK.

R. James R. Blair, Unit on Affective Cognitive Neuroscience, Mood and Anxiety Disorders Program, National Institute of Mental Health, 15K North Drive, Room 206, MSC 2670, Bethesda, MA 20892-2670, USA.

Alexander Easton, School of Psychology, University of Durham, Science Site, South Road, Durham DH1 3LE, UK.

Nathan J. Emery, Sub-department of Animal Behaviour, University of Cambridge, Madingley CB3 8AA, UK.

Ian Goodyer, Douglas House, Developmental Psychiatry Section, University of Cambridge, 18b Trumpington Road, Cambridge CB2 2AH, UK.

Andrea S. Heberlein, University of Pennsylvania, Centre for Cognitive Neuroscience, 3815 Walnut St, Philadelphia, PA 19104-6196, USA.

Tjeerd Jellema, Department of Psychology, University of Hull, Cottingham Road, Hull HU6 7RX, UK.

Zoë Kyte, Douglas House, Developmental Psychiatry Section, University of Cambridge, 18b Trumpington Road, Cambridge CB2 2AH, UK.

Matthew D. Lieberman, Franz Hall, University of California, Los Angeles, CA 90095-1563, USA.

Martine Meunier, CNRS UPR 9075, Institut Des Sciences Cognitives, 67 Bd Pinel, 69675 Bron Cedex, France.

David I. Perrett, School of Psychology, University of St. Andrews, Fife KY16 9JU, UK.

Jennifer Pfiefer, Department of Psychology, University of California, Los Angeles, CA 90095-1563, USA.

1 Introduction: What is social cognitive neuroscience (SCN)?

Nathan J. Emery and Alexander Easton

Understanding the neural mechanisms of cognitive processes, such as thought, perception, and language, or *cognitive neuroscience*, has been a rapidly progressing discipline for the last two decades. This expansion has been driven primarily by significant advances in the development of technology to observe the activity of the living human brain in action. Revolutionary techniques such as positron emission tomography (PET), event-related potentials (ERP), and functional magnetic resonance imaging (fMRI) have been at the heart of this revolution, and we now know much about how the human brain processes sensory information, plans and controls movement, perceives and produces speech, and experiences emotions.

Although we know infinitely more about the neural basis of human psychology than we did 20 years ago, the problems facing us in the future are immense. We highlight two main problems. First, the questions themselves are huge. For example, visual processing is a relatively minor component in the overall story of how the brain functions to give rise to complex human cognitive processes, but, in itself, vision is a horrendously complicated process involving over 50 cortical areas, and billions of neurons. Therefore, major advances must be made before we can even contemplate solving relatively "simple" processes, such as perception. Second, not all aspects of traditional psychology can be easily combined with the tools of cognitive neuroscience. This second problem applies especially to *social cognitive neuroscience* (SCN).

SCN is the study of the neural mechanisms of social cognition and social interactions in humans and animals, particularly nonhuman primates. It is also concerned with deficits of sociocognitive processes in humans, particularly those which have a dedicated neural basis, such as autism, schizophrenia, sociopathy, and depression. This branch of cognitive neuroscience is directed towards understanding complex aspects of social behaviour, such as mentalizing (understanding another's mental states), empathy, attractiveness, self-awareness, moral reasoning, intentionality, and imitation. As such, it is slightly different from *social neuroscience*, or the study of the neurobiology of social behaviour from a comparative perspective. This branch of neuroscience is concerned with the neurobiology of motivational systems, such as aggression, sexual and parental behaviour, and play. These behaviours appear to be controlled by the interaction of neural and endocrine systems, particularly the amygdala, hypothalamus, brainstem, and basal ganglia, and are largely devoid of cognitive processing. These behaviours are displayed by virtually all vertebrates, from amphibians and reptiles to birds and mammals. In contrast, the topics covered by SCN are restricted to higher-order cognitive processes, which are 1. mainly controlled by association cortical areas, such as the prefrontal cortex, 2. not under the influence of hormones, 3. party to disruption by psychopathological disorders or discrete brain lesions, and 4. found almost predominantly (although not exclusively) in human and nonhuman primates.

Traditional social psychology is inferential or relies on pseudo-natural experimental situations, neither of which lend themselves to the tools of cognitive neuroscience, which requires tightly controlled variables. There are also other problems in applying the techniques of cognitive neuroscience to social psychology. For example, functional imaging studies (which are a common tool of cognitive neuroscientists) are difficult to apply in situations that require interaction between subjects. Such studies are very much in their infancy. Similarly, animal studies which may shed light on the neural basis of social behaviour can be problematic because human social behaviour is extremely complex, very much more so than in any of the animals that might be used in such experiments. Indeed, those animals that most closely resemble humans, the great apes, cannot be used for invasive research. Therefore, SCN has been slow to get started (see below). However, in the last few years, there has been a sudden and dramatic increase in the number of studies in the field, and technological problems are finally not only being addressed, but are also being overcome.

In this introductory chapter, we will attempt to introduce the field of SCN, first from a historical perspective, focusing particularly on the recent development of the field and its specialization within cognitive neuroscience. Then we discuss what we predict might be the major research themes of the future, and finally we address Adolphs' (2003) 10 questions for SCN, putting it into context.

A brief history of SCN

The field of SCN has had a long gestation with two parents—cognitive neuroscience and social psychology. Attempts to understand the neural basis of cognition have a history longer than modern cognitive neuroscience, with their foundation in studies of brain-lesioned patients, such as soldiers sustaining gunshot wounds to the head during battle. However, the development of cognitive neuroscience as an experimental science was dependent on the invention of a new methodology—functional neuroimaging. Developed in the 1980s, these techniques, particularly PET and the subtraction method, provided researchers with the capability of localizing function to specific brain areas. These early studies were crude, largely replicating simple cognitive experiments in the scanner; however, the technology has become more complex, using sophisticated experimental designs to remove noise from the system. The formation of cognitive neuroscience was therefore driven primarily by improvements in technology rather than producing an entirely new theoretical approach.

Within cognitive neuroscience, studies in nonhuman primates were more sophisticated and elegant than those performed in humans. Of particular relevance to SCN was the finding, in the early 1980s, that neurons in the anterior temporal cortex of rhesus monkeys are selectively responsive to biologically important stimuli, such as faces (Bruce, Desimone, & Gross, 1981; Perrett, Rolls, & Caan, 1982). Later studies revealed that different neurons in this region are responsive to facial expressions, facial identity, gaze direction, facial movements, walking, and even intentional actions (for reviews, see Emery & Perrett, 2000; Jellema & Perrett, this volume).

Perhaps the most significant paper in the establishment of SCN as a tangible field of study was "The Social Brain: A Project Integrating Primate Behaviour and Neurophysiology in a New Domain" by Leslie Brothers (1990). This paper introduced the idea that it was possible to investigate the neurobiology of social interaction by integrating studies of neurophysiology, behaviour, and psychopathological disorders which specifically affect social behaviour, such as autism. What was particularly significant about this paper was the focus on a specific neural circuit essential to processing social information, which Brothers called the "social brain". This circuit included the anterior temporal cortex and temporal pole, the nuclei of the amygdala and the orbitofrontal cortex. As we will discover throughout this book, these areas and others connected to them play a central role in social behaviour.

A fundamental process which functions during social interaction is the ability to read another individual's mental states ("theory of mind" [ToM]). This "mind-reading" ability develops in human infants around 3–4 years of age, and is affected strikingly in various psychopathological disorders, such as autism, Asperger's syndrome, and schizophrenia. The first functional neuroimaging studies to address this issue of social problem solving were focused specifically on the neural basis of mental attribution (Baron-Cohen, Ring, Moriarty, Schmitz, Costa, & Ell, 1994; Fletcher, et al., 1995). These two studies found that different parts of the prefrontal cortex were activated during a story-comprehension ToM task. We now know that ToM is a suite of abilities (Emery, this volume) that are likely to be based on the integration of different neural systems (Heberlein & Adolphs, this volume). From the seeds sown by these two neuroimaging studies, similarly complex aspects of social interaction are now being investigated by this technique, such as self-knowledge, moral behaviour, empathy, stereotyping, gender or racial biases, attractiveness, and humour appreciation.

Earlier in this section, we made the claim that perhaps the most significant paper in the history of SCN was that of Brothers (1990). To investigate the claim that SCN has developed primarily in the years since this paper, we searched the PubMed on-line citation reference database (MEDLINE; www.ncbi.nlm.nih.gov/PubMed/) from 1990 to 2003, using the keywords "social" AND "brain". This produced a total of 5645 documents. As many of these papers were either not related to SCN or reported studies in social neurobiology, a more refined search using the keywords "social" AND "cognitive" AND "brain" was performed, producing 1013 documents. The titles and abstracts of the papers in the second search were examined for the following criteria. The papers were either theoretical, review, or experimental. The experimental papers used traditional methods of cognitive neuroscience (neuroimaging, lesion analysis, transcranial magnetic stimulation, and electrophysiology) and reported research performed on humans and nonhuman primates. The theoretical focus of the papers included the neurobiology of social interaction, ToM, imitation, empathy, facial attractiveness, self-awareness, moral cognition, cooperation, deception, humour, and gaze processing. Papers on the processing of emotion, including facial expressions, were not included if they did not focus on the role of social communication. Papers on language and face perception (with respect to visual processing) were not included. Finally, papers on disorders of social cognition were included only if they addressed both the social aspects of the disorder and the neural basis. Additional searches using other related criteria ("social" AND "amygdala"; "social" AND "prefrontal cortex"; "empathy" AND "brain"; "imitation" AND "brain", etc.) were also performed to determine whether any papers had failed to be selected with the search terms of the earlier searches.

We found a total of 312 documents that fulfilled these criteria. These documents were sorted by date, and the totals for each year from 1990 to 2003 are represented in Figure 1.1. As can be seen in Figure 1.1, throughout the 1990s, research in SCN was slowly increasing; however, there was an explosion of research at the beginning of the twenty-first century.

There are many possible explanations for this explosion of interest in the neural basis of social interaction. We make three suggestions. First, mental health has become a research priority for funding councils and government agencies. This increase in funding has grown steadily across the 1990s, the so-called Decade of the Brain. Second, cognitive neuroscience has become mainstream, using sophisticated methods for observing the brain in action, and techniques for extracting the huge amounts of information produced. Third, cognitive neuroscientists and social psychologists have started talking to one another, and they are now collaborating. This final point is crucial. For SCN to work, it is vital that there is collaboration between cognitive scientists (such as linguists, computer scientists, philosophers, and cognitive psychologists), neuroscientists, ethologists, and social psychologists. The requisite skills for the successful completion of projects in this area can be achieved only by a strong interdisciplinary approach.

What is social cognitive neuroscience? 5

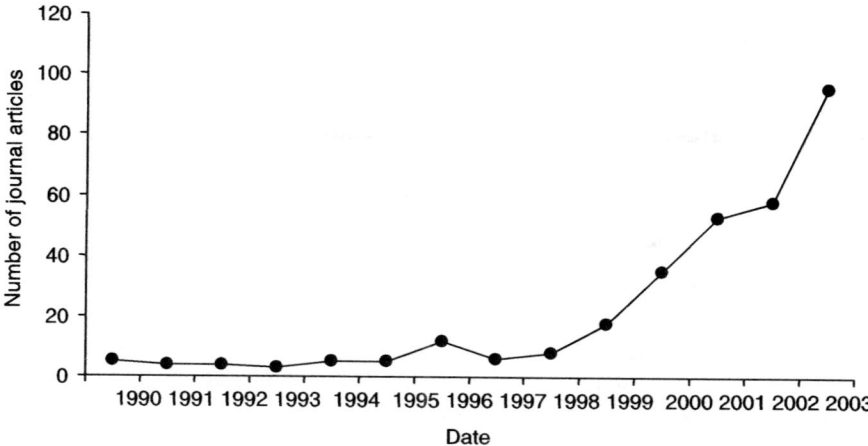

Figure 1.1 Number of journal articles directly related to social cognitive neuroscience (SCN) published every year between 1990 and 2003. Results were produced by an on-line PubMed (MEDLINE) and PsychInfo search, initially using the search criteria "social" AND "brain", and then "social" AND "cognitive" AND "brain". The titles and abstracts were studied to determine whether the papers were relevant to SCN. Other more refined searches were then made, using more specific search criteria, such as "empathy", "theory of mind", "self-awareness", "imitation", etc. There has been a steady increase in the number of papers published, with a dramatic increase after 2000.

What are the methods of SCN?

Although SCN was founded on work performed in animals, particularly nonhuman primates, is there still a place for this type of research? As will be seen in Chapters 2–5, animal studies remain vitally important to the neurobiology of social interaction. We see three main reasons why animal research is still essential. First, functional neuroimaging technology, although greatly advanced in the last 10 years, is still limited in how it can be applied to situations in which two or more protagonists are physically interacting. At present, our investigations are based on how individuals (constrained within a scanner or attached to electrodes) respond to static or moving video images of faces, hands, and bodies, and on questionnaires and self-report. Neuropsychological studies in human patients are equally constrained by the presentation of "simple" social stimuli, rather than involvement in real-life social scenarios. There are fewer methodological constraints with nonhuman animals. Animals can be observed during social interactions, or socially relevant cognitive tests can be presented after or during invasive manipulation. Techniques such as selective neurotoxic and reversible lesions, multiunit electrophysiology, microdialysis, psychopharmacology, and genetic knockouts have been used successfully for a number of years, providing a level of analysis currently impossible in studies of human beings. Some of these techniques, such as experimental lesions and genetic knockouts, can be used only in animals.

Second, a comparative approach to SCN may inform us about the evolutionary history of social interaction, and how certain neurocognitive processes may function similarly to or differently from those in humans. For example, there is increasing convergent evidence that western scrub-jays may possess an avian analogue to human ToM (Emery & Clayton, 2001). This is particularly striking because the common ancestor of scrub-jays and humans lived over 300 million years ago, and the brains of birds and mammals are completely different in structure. The medial prefrontal cortex appears to be the primary structure involved in the attribution of mental states in humans (Heberlein & Adolphs, this volume); however, birds do not have a prefrontal cortex (Emery & Clayton, 2003). Understanding the neural basis of "ToM" in corvids by using neurophysiology, lesions, and network models may inform us about whether understanding another's mental states is dependent on similar neural circuitry in terms of efficiency of coding, or whether completely different mechanisms are employed in distantly related species.

Third, the development of behavioural tests in nonhuman animals may be used in human populations which are impaired in their use of language, such as preverbal infants, patients with aphasia, the mentally handicapped, or autistics.

The physical and analytical techniques currently employed in human SCN studies are increasing in complexity. fMRI, in particular, may be the most revolutionary method available to help us understand the human brain. However, with respect to SCN, there are still many problems and limitations in applying these techniques to understand social behaviour. First, social behaviour involves the interaction of two individuals. Although presentation of images on a monitor provides us with information about how we perceive and categorize social stimuli, into different facial expressions, races, or genders, the interactive component essential to social cognition is missing. Currently, a number of laboratories have developed methods by which an individual interacts with either another person or a computer in a cooperative game (McCabe, Houser, Ryan, Smith, & Trouard, 2001; Rilling, Gutman, Zeh, Pagnoni, Berns, & Kilts, 2002), or two individuals in two separate MRI scanners interact in various deceptive games while their brains are scanned simultaneously (Montague et al., 2002). In both cases, the participants cannot see one another; however, with the implementation of web cams and the Internet, this does not seem too difficult to implement. Outside the realms of science fiction and portable MRI scanners, this new technology appears to have incredible potential, if the equipment is made available through collaborative effort.

These newly developed technologies should bring about unique opportunities to investigate previously difficult or impossible problems. As we described earlier, it has been impossible to investigate the neurobiology of human social interaction with the technology currently available, so that we rely instead on studies of social perception, particularly responses to facial stimuli. In the future, we see extensive use of video images (live and prerecorded) to present social stimuli, possibly with the use of "actors". This advance would directly utilize the methods of social psychological research. In this instance, images with sound could be presented as scenarios in the "real world" (for example, from popular soap operas), or live images of an actor in an adjacent room, or facial images of another individual also in a scanner by hyperscanning (Montague et al., 2002).

The future of SCN will be driven by advances not only in technology but also in sociocognitive theory. Most studies in SCN, to date, have focused on: 1. social perception, resulting from electrophysiological studies of face-responsive neurons in rhesus monkeys; 2. ToM, resulting from studies on autism; 3. social emotions. What is starting to occur, as will be highlighted in Chapters 6 and 7, is explicit collaboration between cognitive neuroscientists and social psychologists to investigate particular problems in social cognition, such as social exclusion (Eisenberger, Lieberman, & Williams, 2003), self-conscious emotions (Beer, Heerey, Keltner, Scabini, & Knight, 2003), social evaluation (Cunningham, Johnson, Gatenby, Gore, & Banaji, 2003), self-knowledge (Kelley, Macrae, Wyland, Caglar, Inati, & Heatherton, 2002), and social versus object knowledge (Mitchell, Heatherton, & Macrae, 2002).

Addressing Adolphs' 10 questions

In a recent review paper, Adolphs (2003) attempted to define the field of SCN within a framework of 10 questions to be addressed if it is to be taken seriously. In this section, we will discuss these questions, and try to provide some instances where they have been addressed in the literature.

1. How can we measure social behaviour?

It is incredibly important to be able to quantify social interactions, so that the components of such interactions can be correlated with the activity of specific patterns of neural activation. Is it sufficient to establish an ethogram of human social behaviour along similar lines to those established for nonhuman animals? Cross-cultural ethological studies of human social behaviour have been attempted, most notably by Eibl-Eibesfeldt (1970) and Morris (1967), but were largely problematic in their unusual interpretations and lack of appreciation of contextual variables. This is not to say that an ethogram of human social behaviour is not possible, but only that it needs careful consideration of the multiple factors involved. The complexity inherent in the components of any ethogram of human behaviour may be essential for correlating with specific neural activity, such as found in studies of nonhuman primate social behaviour; however, this complexity may also make this an impossible endeavour.

2. How should social stimuli be categorized?

Adolphs (2003) suggests that social stimuli are currently classified either by their physical properties (such as different facial expressions) or by a priori specified categories derived from a particular social psychological theory with high ecological validity (such as untrustworthy faces). As Adolphs suggests, it is almost impossible not to begin a study without having classified stimuli into some prior category—for example, classifying faces as category 1 and cars as category 2.

Recent work on human facial expressions has found that even traditional categories are sometimes blurred. For example, Young, Rowland, Calder, Etcoff, Seth, & Perrett (1997) (see also Calder, Young, Rowland, & Perrett, 1997) used computer morphing techniques to morph two facial expressions together with different intensities of each expression; for example, 50% fear and 50% disgust. When presented with a series of faces with different levels of intensity of each emotion (such as 10% disgust and 90% fear, and then 20% disgust and 80% fear, etc.), subjects were asked to state which emotion they saw in each morph. This study is a clear example of the problems involved in classifying complex biological stimuli, even those based on a priori categories.

3. How can we best use data to guide theory?

Adolphs also raised an important issue that is not specific to SCN, namely, whether we should include nonsignificant data as well as significant data in the interpretation of experiments, and particularly in the formulation of new theories. This may be particularly relevant to studies on social behaviour, where it may be impossible to eliminate all irrelevant variables without disrupting the main effects. Certainly, reporting only effects where $p<0.05$ may be meaningless. Adolphs makes the useful suggestion that reporting effect sizes, confidence intervals, or even raw data rather than significance based on an arbitrary choice of alpha level may overcome some of these problems.

4. What is the most appropriate way to interpret the data?

There may be many nonsignificant results in studies of SCN because there are many factors affecting social behaviour that cannot be controlled (see above). This may have particularly significant effects in lesion and neuroimaging studies where the intent is to localize a particular function to a specific brain area.

5. How can we best establish the reliability and generalizability of our results?

Of vital importance is the convergence of findings from different studies using different techniques: neuropsychological studies (lesions) in humans, experimental lesions in animals, and neuroimaging. A good example of where this approach has been successful is the social evaluation of trustworthy faces. Adolphs, Tranel, & Damasio (1999) presented a series of 50 faces which had been previously rated by normal control subjects as trustworthy, and a series of 50 faces rated as untrustworthy, to patients with bilateral amygdala lesions, patients with other brain lesions, and normal controls. The normal subjects and patients with other brain lesions rated the two sets of faces appropriately, whereas the amygdalectomized patients rated all faces as trustworthy. In a similar study using functional neuroimaging, the amygdala of normal people was activated when viewing untrustworthy faces, independently of emotional expression, gaze direction, and gender (Winston, Strange, O'Doherty, & Dolan, 2002). These two studies suggest that the amygdala is essential for making judgements about the social attributes of faces. Convergent evidence for this finding comes from a study of amygdala lesions in rhesus monkeys (Emery, Capitanio, Mendoza, Mason, Machado, & Amaral, 2001). When normal adult, male rhesus monkeys meet for the first time, they either fight or remain at a distance from one another, evaluating the other's strengths and weaknesses. This distance is reduced over time. Emery et al. (2001) found that monkeys with amygdala lesions directed high levels of affiliative behaviour towards novel monkeys on their first encounter. This suggests that the monkey amygdala is also essential for the appropriate evaluation of faces.

6. How theoretical should SCN be?

Is it too early to produce a theory of how the brain computes social problems from current knowledge? There is abundant evidence that a distinct neural circuit, including the anterior temporal lobes, the nuclei of the amygdala, and the medial/orbital prefrontal cortex, functions in perceiving social stimuli and producing appropriate behavioural responses. Although other brain areas have been included in this circuit (see Heberlein & Adolphs, this volume), consistent activation in response to social stimuli has been reported in these three brain areas. Although we know little about how these areas are functionally related, this preliminary theory is a useful starting point for framing future research questions. It may be premature to produce theories of more complex aspects of social cognition, such as a sense of self or moral reasoning, but it is likely that such theories will have to be derived from current states of knowledge concerning "simpler" neurocognitive systems.

7. What should be the language of SCN?

As SCN is the child of cognitive neuroscience and social psychology, what should be its language? Should it use a proprietary vocabulary which has been developed specifically for SCN; should it use an existing one, say, from experimental social psychology; or should it be bilingual? This is an especially important issue when we use terms which are exclusively related to a particular field, such as terms used in social psychology (for example, "trustworthy", "dominance", or "empathy"), or terms which are used only in relation to the brain, such as anatomical areas. One additional problem is that social psychology relies on the discussion of domain-specific processes, such as schemata, attitudes, scripts, and stereotypes, whereas cognitive psychology is based on general processes which can be social or nonsocial in nature, such as perception, memory, and attention. It may be possible to reconcile these differences only by training the next generation of social cognitive neuroscientists in both languages.

8. Are social cognitive processes reducible to nonsocial processes?

This is perhaps the most fundamental question facing SCN. Are there neural systems which are specialized for the processing of social stimuli or the production of social behaviour, or can general neural systems be cajoled into processing both social and nonsocial stimuli? For example, what is the evidence (if any) that the temporal-amygdala-prefrontal circuit described earlier is involved exclusively in processing social stimuli?

For example, in this book, we have restricted our view of sociality to processes that are not based primarily on emotion (unless the emotions are social and interact with cognitive processes). There is an intimate relationship between emotion and social behaviour, and between emotion and cognition. One function of facial expressions of emotion, for example, may be in social communication; to inform others of one's current emotional state. Facial expressions may also be inhibited or produced voluntarily with the purpose of deceiving others about one's true emotional state (Ekman, 2003). An alternative explanation for the evolution of facial expressions may be that they are by-products of the output of neural systems involved in the emotion that is currently being experienced. For example, contorting the facial muscles after eating something which tastes disgusting may produce the classic facial expression of disgust. This expression may then have evolved into the expression associated with experiencing disgust in other contexts, such as viewing disgusting images. There is abundant evidence that the amygdala processes facial expressions of fear (Heberlein & Adolphs, this volume); however, what is not clear is whether the amygdala is performing a perceptual role (processing the physical attributes of fear expressions) or an evaluative role (processing the emotional-communicative attributes of fear expressions). It is very unlikely that the former explanation is true, as this would mean that the amygdala is an extremely specialized perceptual processor, rather than one involved in the experience of emotion (as the large majority of contemporary evidence suggests). Therefore, when answering the question of whether specific neural circuits process social stimuli independently of nonsocial stimuli, we need to be certain of what we mean by social.

This question may also welcome an evolutionary approach. The "social intelligence hypothesis" (see Emery, this volume) states that the enhanced intelligence of primates evolved to solve social problems (rather than physical problems, such as finding and extracting food). Some theorists have suggested that sociocognitive processes may be an adaptive specialization to social living in some species, particularly those which live in large social groups (e.g. Bond, Kamil, & Balda, 2003), whereas other theorists have suggested that animals in complex societies will generally perform better in both social and nonsocial tasks (e.g. Humphrey, 1980). Therefore, one possible line of research is to test closely related social and solitary (or less social) species on the same social and nonsocial tasks. The adaptive specialization view predicts that the social species will outperform the nonsocial species only on the social tasks, whereas the social intelligence view predicts that social species will outperform the nonsocial species on both social and nonsocial tasks.

A different approach to the question is to ask whether all social processes are just specialized cases of nonsocial processes, such as memory, attention, or perception of complex stimuli. Perhaps the best-known research on this is the neural basis of face perception, and whether the "fusiform face area" (FFA) really responds only to facial stimuli, or whether it is involved in the categorization of all perceptually salient learned stimuli (such as "greebles"; Tarr & Gautier, 2000). There is no space here to discuss this question in detail. However, one issue which should be addressed is that neurobiological studies of face processing in monkeys have used techniques which are infinitely more subtle than those currently used in humans, and this may have clouded the issue somewhat. Neuroimaging still suffers from the problem of localizing activation to the same level of specificity as single- or multiunit electrophysiology uses in animals. Therefore, the presentation of faces and objects may both appear to activate the same area of the human fusiform gyrus; however, this does not mean that the activity for each category of visual stimuli is not specific to a particular area within the fusiform gyrus. This issue may be resolved only after refinement of scanner resolution.

9. How will we be able to understand a future SCN?

What will an understanding of the neural basis of social behaviour actually tell us that we do not already know from our "folk psychology" of how and why others behave the way they do? If such information is at odds with our folk psychology, where does this leave us? We think that the problem which Adolphs is addressing here is not what is the ultimate benefit of SCN to society, as this is clear with respect to understanding and treating psychopathological or neurological disorders of social cognition, but rather the more fundamental issue of whether this information will change the way we interpret one another's behaviour in our day-to-day lives. This problem may be related to question 7, in that we already use a language to describe one another's behaviour and intentions, but we are unlikely to adopt explanations of their behaviour and intentions based on knowledge of the underlying neural mechanisms. Many folk psychological concepts which are currently being investigated, such as moral cognition, self-awareness, and ToM may never map onto distinct neural systems, largely because we still do not know precisely what these concepts actually mean, but only what our intuitive sense tells us. This may be akin to recent attempts to study the neural basis of consciousness, without actually knowing what consciousness is and what it is not.

10. How integrative should SCN be?

What studies should be included as SCN? Earlier, we suggested that studies of the neurobiology of socially motivated behaviour (social neuroscience), such as aggressive, sexual, and parental behaviour, should not be included in SCN, but SCN should include analysis at all three levels—social, cognition, and neuroscience (Ochsner & Lieberman, 2001)—and so studies on only motivated behaviour are not likely to include the cognitive component. The question becomes more difficult when discussing emotion. However, if we follow Ochsner and Lieberman's criteria, only studies of the neurobiology of social emotions or facial expressions used within a social context should be included. The case for including studies on the neural basis of language is perhaps the most difficult because it includes all three levels of analysis. We would argue that the study of language is covered by a specific area of cognitive science, with its own vocabulary, which may be alien to those outside the field, and so difficult to integrate with other areas of SCN.

Overview of the book

This book attempts to review some of the main areas in which SCN has progressed over the last few years. In Part I, we are shown how understanding specific aspects of emotion (Chapter 2), memory (Chapter 3), and vision (Chapter 4) can provide fascinating insights into the mechanisms that are required to function normally in a social environment. All of these have led us to understand more fully what the neural basis of social behaviour might be.

Chapter 2 outlines studies that have been carried out on socioemotional processing in animals, with particular emphasis on the amygdala and orbitofrontal cortex. When these structures are surgically disrupted in monkeys, their emotional behaviour changes and they typically become tamer and less fearful. There is an intrinsic link, however, between emotion and social behaviour; therefore, animals with these changes in emotional behaviour also show abnormal social interactions. Recent studies have linked the tools of cognitive neuroscience with sophisticated behavioural methods used in primatology that are beginning to show how damage to these structures affects animals within social situations.

Chapter 3 explores recent work on the way in which the frontal cortex interacts with temporal lobe visual areas in retrieving visual memories. In this model, the frontal cortex is seen to play a part in the recall of memories (and the implementation of behaviour) only in circumstances where there is no fixed reward outcome for a learning condition. This is very similar to social situations in which the outcome of behaviour is not fixed, but, rather, depends on the social context in which it is carried out. Therefore, the cognitive neuroscience investigation of memory can also lead us to an understanding of the processes involved in social behaviour.

Chapter 4 examines the way in which studies of visual processing are also providing insights into the neural basis of social behaviour. To understand how to interpret the social world (in order to interact with others, or make decisions), we need to understand the aims and intentions of other people. For most of us, this requires interpreting the visual world, and Chapter 4 presents a series of studies in which specific aspects of visual processing give a clear insight into how we interpret others' goals.

Although social psychology is a difficult issue to apply the tools of cognitive neuroscience to, Part I shows us that social behaviour is just the result of combining lots of different processes in the brain. When we interact with one another, we need to understand the sensory world around us (to interpret the social situation we are in), we need memories of past situations that are similar, and we need to have emotive responses to those situations in order to guide our behaviour appropriately. Therefore, the first step in SCN is to understand how we can apply the research of many different areas of cognitive neuroscience to problems in social psychology.

Of fundamental importance to the SCN approach is the integration of cognitive neuroscience with social cognition. At the heart of this endeavour is research aimed to understand the neural basis of our intuitive *folk psychology*, which is used to categorize individuals into social categories (stereotyping), predict another's intentions, beliefs, and desires (ToM), form predispositions to evaluate people favourably or unfavourably (attitudes), categorize the actions of others (person perception), and determine self-knowledge (Ochsner & Lieberman, 2001).

Understanding others' mental states (ToM) is a high-level cognitive process which appears to depend on the same network of brain regions described in the preceding chapters; that is, the anterior temporal cortex, amygdala, and prefrontal cortex. As with the discovery of the important role of these brain areas in social behaviour, the concept of ToM was derived, from work not in humans, but in nonhuman primates (Premack & Woodruff, 1978). Chapter 5 reviews and evaluates the wealth of comparative evidence that nonhuman primates, dogs, and corvids may possess some appreciation of mental states in other beings, for example, their intentions, visual perspectives, knowledge states, and beliefs.

Chapter 6 covers the neurobiology of social cognition from the perspective of cognitive neuroscience. It covers a wide range of studies in the cognitive neuroscience of human social behaviour from the attribution of intentions to objects and people, emotional states, personality, and ToM. In so doing, Heberlein and Adolphs provide clear evidence for the importance of the temporal-amygdala-prefrontal neural circuit in human social behaviour, as in that of nonhuman primates (Chapter 2).

Chapter 7 approaches the neurobiology of social cognition from the perspective of social psychology, specifically whether an understanding of the self can be illuminated by an understanding of others, particularly the role of the self within a social group. This chapter differs quite significantly from the others in its approach, providing a framework for investigating some of the major questions concerned with the neurobiology of the self.

Part III of this book deals with human disorders of social behaviour or social cognition, and how the understanding of the mechanisms outlined in Parts I and II can allow us to understand these disorders and produce appropriate treatments.

Chapter 8 discusses the neural basis of autism, a developmental disorder that results in complex changes in cognition, including poor social interaction and knowledge. The hypothesis is outlined that empathy is required in order to have good social interaction, and that this is dysfunctional in autistic subjects. Much of our understanding of the neural basis of such dysfunction comes from work such as that outlined in Chapter 2 showing that monkeys with damage to the amygdala can superficially resemble human children with autism. Humans with damage to the amygdala also show problems with ToM and empathy, problems that seem so crucial in autism, and so strongly support a link between amygdala dysfunction and the social behavioural impairments in autistic subjects.

Chapter 9 outlines recent work on depression. Although depression is not normally considered a disorder relating to social behaviour or cognition, this chapter presents the hypothesis that social cognition, and in particular self-perception, is crucial to the pathogenesis of the disorder. Dysfunction in the pathways discussed in detail in Chapter 7, therefore, could provide crucial insights into the neural basis of depression.

Finally, Chapter 10 discusses the neural basis of psychopathy and antisocial behaviour. With increasing concern about antisocial behaviour in society, understanding the neural basis of this behaviour is of the utmost importance, but the issue is a complex one. Not only are there different types of antisocial behaviour, but there also appear to be different neural mechanisms for these different types. Such disorders, then, provide one of the greatest challenges to SCN, but Chapter 10 outlines how many differences between hypotheses are now starting to be integrated into a coherent understanding of a complex set of disorders.

Acknowledgements

Nathan J. Emery would like to thank Nicky Clayton for comments and discussion, and David I. Perrett for getting him interested in the neurobiology of social behaviour in the first place. Alexander Easton would like to thank Androulla for her constant support and David Gaffan for his guidance from the beginning. NJE was supported by a Royal Society University Research Fellowship, and his research by the Royal Society, the Biotechnology and Biological Sciences Research Council, and the University of Cambridge. AE was supported in his research by the Royal Society, the Medical Research Council, and the University of Nottingham.

References

Adolphs, R. (2003). Investigating the cognitive neuroscience of social behavior. *Neuropsychologia, 41*, 119–126.

Adolphs, R., Tranel, D., & Damasio, A. R. (1999). The human amygdala in social judgement. *Nature, 393*, 470–474.

Baron-Cohen, S., Ring, H., Moriarty, J., Schmitz, B., Costa, D., & Ell, P. (1994). Recognition of mental state terms. Clinical findings in children with autism and a functional neuroimaging study of normal adults. *British Journal of Psychiatry, 165*, 640–649.

Beer, J. S., Heerey, E. A., Keltner, D., Scabini, D., & Knight, R. T. (2003). The regulatory function of self-conscious emotion: Insights from patients with orbitofrontal damage. *Journal of Personality and Social Psychology, 85*, 594–604.

Bond, A. B., Kamil, A. C., & Balda, R. P. (2003). Social complexity and transitive inference in corvids. *Animal Behaviour, 65*, 479–487.

Brothers, L. (1990). The social brain: A project for integrating primate behavior and neurophysiology in a new domain. *Concepts in Neuroscience, 1*, 27–51.

Bruce, C., Desimone, R., & Gross, C. G. (1981). Visual properties of neurons in a polysensory area in superior temporal sulcus of the macaque. *Journal of Neurophysiology, 46*, 369–384.

Calder, A. J., Young, A. W., Rowland, D., & Perrett, D. I. (1997). Computer-enhanced emotion in facial expressions. *Proceedings of the Royal Society of London. Series B: Biological Sciences, 264*, 919–925.

Cunningham, W. A., Johnson, M. K., Gatenby, J. C., Gore, J. C., & Banaji, M. R. (2003). Neural components of social evaluation. *Journal of Personality and Social Psychology, 85*, 639–649.

Dunbar, R. I. M. (1998). The social brain hypothesis. *Evolutionary Anthropology, 6*, 178–190.

Ekman, P. (2003). Darwin, deception and facial expression. *Annals of the New York Academy of Sciences, 1000*, 205–221.

Emery, N. J., & Clayton, N. S. (2001). Effects of experience and social context on prospective caching strategies in scrub jays. *Nature, 414*, 443–446.

Emery, N. J., & Clayton, N. S. (2003). Comparing the complex cognitive abilities of birds and primates. In L. J. Rogers & G. Kaplan (Eds.), *Comparative vertebrate cognition: Are primates superior to non-primates?* (pp. 3–55). New York: Kluwer.

Emery, N. J., & Perrett, D. I. (2000). How can studies of the monkey brain help us understand "theory of mind" and autism in humans? In S. Baron-Cohen, H. Tager-Flusberg, & D. Cohen (Eds.), *Understanding other minds: Perspectives from developmental cognitive neuroscience* (2nd ed., pp. 279–310). Oxford: Oxford University Press.

Emery, N. J., Capitanio, J. P., Mendoza, S. P., Mason, W. A., Machado, C. J., & Amaral, D. G. (2001). The effects of bilateral lesions of the amygdala on dyadic social interactions in rhesus monkeys (*Macaca mulatta*). *Behavioral Neuroscience, 15*, 515–544.

Eibl-Eibesfeldt, I. (1970). *Ethology: The biology of behavior*. New York: Holt, Rinehart & Winston.

Eisenberger, N. I., Lieberman, M. D., & Williams, K. D. (2003). Does rejection hurt? An fMRI study of social exclusion. *Science, 302*, 290–292.

Fletcher, P. C., Happe, F., Frith, U., Baker, S. C., Dolan, R. J., Frackowiak, R. S. J., et al. (1995). Other minds in the brain: A functional neuroimaging study of "theory of mind" in story comprehension. *Cognition, 57*, 109–128.

Humphrey, N. J. (1980). Nature's psychologists. In B. Josephson & V. Ramachandran (Eds.), *Consciousness and the physical world* (pp. 57–80). London: Pergamon Press.

Kelley, W. M., Macrae, C. N., Wyland, C. L., Caglar, S., Inati, S., & Heatherton, T. F. (2002). Finding the self? An event-related fMRI study. *Journal of Cognitive Neuroscience, 14*, 785–794.

McCabe, K., Houser, D., Ryan, L., Smith, V., & Trouard, T. (2001). A functional imaging study of cooperation in two-person reciprocal exchange. *Proceedings of the National Academy of Sciences of the USA, 98*, 11832–11835.

Mitchell, J. P., Heatherton, T. F., & Macrae, C. N. (2002). Distinct neural systems subserve person and object knowledge. *Proceedings of the National Academy of Sciences of the USA, 99*, 15238–15243.

Montague, P. R., Berns, G. S., Cohen, J. D., McClure, S. M., Pagnoni, G., Dhamala, M., et al. (2002). Hyperscanning: Simultaneous fMRI during linked social interactions. *NeuroImage, 16*, 1159–1164.

Morris, D. (1967). *The naked ape*. London: Jonathan Cape.

Ochsner, K. N., & Lieberman, M. D. (2001). The emergence of social cognitive neuroscience. *American Psychologist, 56*, 717–734.

Perrett, D. I., Rolls, E. T., & Caan, W. (1982). Visual neurons responsive to faces in monkey temporal cortex. *Experimental Brain Research, 47*, 329–342.

Premack, D., & Woodruff, G. (1978). Does the chimpanzee have a theory of mind? *Behavioural and Brain Sciences, 4*, 515–526.

Rilling, J. K., Gutman, D. A., Zeh, T. R., Pagnoni, G., Berns, G. S., & Kilts, C. D. (2002). A neural basis for social cooperation. *Neuron, 35*, 395–405.

Tarr, M. J., & Gautier, I. (2000). FFA: A flexible fusiform area for subordinate-level visual processing automatized by expertise. *Nature Neuroscience, 3*, 764–769.

Winston, J. S., Strange, B. A., O'Doherty, J., & Dolan, R. J. (2002). Automatic and intentional brain responses during evaluation of trustworthiness of faces. *Nature Neuroscience, 5*, 277–283.

Young, A. W., Rowland, D., Calder, A. J., Etcoff, N. L., Seth, A., & Perrett, D. I. (1997). Facial expression megamix: Tests of dimensional and category accounts of emotion recognition. *Cognition, 63*, 271–313.

Part I
Neural substrates of social interactions

2 The neurobiology of social-emotional cognition in nonhuman primates

*Jocelyne Bachevalier and
Martine Meunier*

Summary

This chapter presents an overview of the evidence accumulated so far regarding the neural bases of social skills and emotional behavioural responses in monkeys. Special emphasis is put on findings from decades of lesion studies substantiating the idea that social-emotional cognition in primates critically depends on a fronto-temporal network linking the amygdala and orbital frontal cortex, and possibly including the anterior cingulate and temporopolar cortices as well. The review is intended to inform and stimulate research in this area, and, more particularly, to foster future studies that aim at elucidating the cooperative or competitive interactions underlying the contribution of this temporal-frontal network to social-emotional cognition in primates. Such animal models may offer a new foundation for determining the neuropathological bases of several psychopathologies in humans and, ultimately, for developing therapeutic tools to alleviate these disorders.

To survive, humans and other animals must navigate their species-specific social environment. Doing so requires an appreciation of the significance of others' social and emotional behaviour for oneself, so that socially relevant behaviours can be appropriately self-regulated. Another individual's behaviours can not only provide information to guide the actions appropriate to a specific instance, but can also offer more general guides to action, such as awareness of relationships between interacting members. Thus, social cognition (broadly construed) rests upon the ability to detect and interpret information about other individuals that is relevant to regulating one's own behaviour according to the current emotional and social context. In the case of humans, the use of social information to self-regulate behaviour is highly complex, reflecting not only emotional but also cognitive and cultural factors. Human social cognition will include not only the ability to understand and reason about the cognitive mental states of other individuals, but also the ability to identify emotional states, intentions, desires, attitudes, etc., and to use this information to guide behaviour (Baron-Cohen et al., 1999).

Only recently have researchers begun to appreciate the importance of studying the neurobiology of social cognition (Ochsner & Lieberman, 2001).

Reports of clinical cases with circumscribed lesions, as well as the results of neurostimulation, neurorecording, and neuroimaging of normal and damaged brain, have all indicated that there exists a specific neural substrate involved in processing social skills (for review, see Adolphs, 2001, as well as Chapter 6 in the present volume by the same author). In addition to this renewed research interest in humans, animal studies are also critical to refine our knowledge of the neurobiology of social cognition. Nonhuman primates that live in highly structured social organizations, such as macaque monkeys, provide an excellent animal model to reach this goal.

This chapter presents an overview of data from nonhuman primate research showing that a neural network linking the anterior medial temporal lobe to the ventromedial aspect of the frontal lobes is critical for emotional regulation and the establishment and maintenance of social bonds. We will begin with a brief description of nonhuman primate social behaviour, followed by an outline of the anatomical organization of four key brain regions implicated in social-emotional cognition, the amygdala and the orbital frontal, temporopolar, and anterior cingulate cortices. Next, the nonhuman primate studies that have addressed the role of these neural regions in normal social skills will be reviewed together with our current knowledge on the neural mechanisms by which these neural structures participate in a system essential for the maintenance of intraspecific social bonding. The final part will relate these nonhuman primate data to what is known on the neural substrate of social and emotional cognition in humans. It will be concluded that pursuing our effort to gain more refined knowledge on the neural system implicated in social cognition in nonhuman primates may bring critical progress in understanding human psychopathological states that specifically affect the ability to maintain appropriate social skills and emotional regulation.

Nonhuman primate social cognition

Investigations of the social skills of nonhuman primates in natural or seminatural settings have revealed that several monkey species, including various macaque species, live, like humans, in social groups that are characterized by complex and dynamic social organizations maintained through a variety of specific, long-term relationships between individual group members (Cheney & Seyfarth, 1990; DeWaal, 1989). It is now clear that each member of a monkey troop establishes and maintains numerous long-term relationships with many other group members, and that the nature, intensity, and stability of each relationship vary according to the specific ages, genders, and kinship bonds of that particular pair of monkeys. To maintain these relationships, monkeys must perceive and use information about other individuals in the troop and adapt their behaviour to function adequately within the social environment. Indeed, the presence of a stable social hierarchy within a troop indicates that the individuals that make up the social group recognize one another and respond differentially depending upon with whom they are interacting. Finally, although the ability to interpret mental states of others is still controversial in nonhuman primates (Cheney & Seyfarth, 1990), some studies have suggested that they, too, possess a rudimentary cognitive capacity for assessing intentions and motivations in others (Brothers, 1989, 1995; Byrne & Whiten, 1988). One cannot deny that the ability to communicate social intentions is likely to be far less complex in nonhuman primates than in humans. Nevertheless, it seems that the similarities between species in many phenotypic displays and basic behavioural processes outweigh the differences, suggesting that the neural mechanisms underlying social communication are likely to share common features across these species (Machado & Bachevalier, 2003).

Anatomy of the neural structures implicated in social cognition

As originally proposed by Papez (1937) and further elaborated by MacLean (1949), social-emotional cognition is orchestrated by a complex neural network of interconnected structures, including brain regions in the frontal and temporal lobes, as well as their interconnections with the hypothalamus and brainstem. Two of the key brain structures that appear to be essential for normal social skills and emotional behaviour in adult primates are the amygdala and the orbital frontal cortex (Adolphs, 2001; Amaral, 1992; Barbas, 1993, 1995, 2000; Cavada, Company, Tejedor, Cruz-Rizzolo, & Reinoso-Suarez, 2000; Dombrowski, Hilgetag, & Barbas, 2001; Emery & Amaral, 1999; Kling & Steklis, 1976; Öngür & Price, 2000; Petrides, 1994). However, these two structures are unlikely to constitute the sole substrate of social-emotional cognition. Although limited, some evidence exists that closely related regions, such as the temporopolar and cingulate cortices, do contribute to this functional domain as well.

Amygdala

The amygdala is located in the anterior portion of the medial temporal lobe, and comprises a set of 13 interconnected nuclei with different connectional features (Figure 2.1). The lateral nucleus receives an enormous array of highly processed sensory information, including visual information from faces and facial expressions, gaze direction, body postures, and movements, as well as auditory information from specific vocal sounds and intonations, and it reciprocally, via the basal nucleus, provides a route by which the amygdala can modulate the cortical processing of sensory stimuli (McGaugh, Ferry, Vazdarjanova, & Roozendaal, 2000). Interestingly, because these feedback projections to cortical sensory areas are widespread, reaching not only the higher-order areas but also the primary sensory areas, the amygdala is able to influence sensory inputs at very early stages in their processing. The basal nucleus in turn serves as an interface between sensory-specific cortical

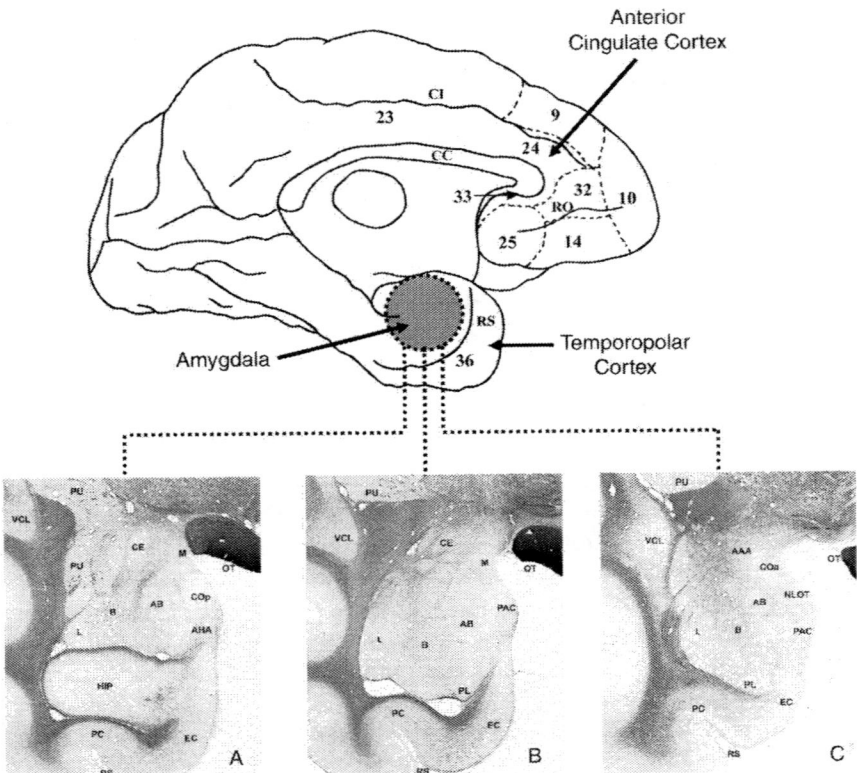

Figure 2.1 Medial view of the macaque brain (top) illustrating the architectonic areas of the medial prefrontal and medial temporal cortex, and depicting the anterior cingulate cortex (areas 24, 32, 33, and 25) and the temporopolar cortex (rostral to perirhinal area 36). The amygdala, a deep structure buried in the medial temporal lobe, is represented in grey in this medial view. Panels A–C (bottom) display myelin-stained coronal sections from the posterior, middle, and anterior thirds of the amygdala, respectively. Note the fibres from temporal cortical areas coursing around and through the amygdaloid nuclei and commonly destroyed by aspiration or electrolytic lesions of the amygdala. AAA: anterior amygdaloid area; AB: accessory basal nucleus; AHA: amygdalohippocampal area; B: basal nucleus; CE: central nucleus; CI: cingulate sulcus; CO: cortical nucleus; COa: anterior cortical nucleus; COp: posterior cortical nucleus; EC: entorhinal cortex; HIP: hippocampus; L: lateral nucleus; M: medial nucleus; NLOT: nucleus of the lateral olfactory tract; OT: optic tract; PAC: periamygdaloid cortex; PC: perirhinal cortex; PL: paralamellar part of the basal nucleus; PU: putamen; RO: rostral sulcus; RS: rhinal sulcus; VCL: ventral claustrum. This figure has been adapted from Machado and Bachevalier (2003).

inputs and the central nucleus that constitutes a relay to the brainstem and hypothalamus through which the amygdala is thought to influence the autonomic and endocrine manifestations of emotion. The basal and accessory basal nuclei project substantially to the ventral striatum, thereby providing a potential access to subcortical elements of the motor system, and so affect actions, including the modulation of facial and vocal expressions, body postures, and movements. In addition, the amygdala significantly interacts with the hippocampal formation, and can thus act upon and modulate stored information in cortical areas (such as past experience with an individual) (Amaral, 1992; Saunders & Rosene 1988; Saunders, Rosene, & Van Hoesen, 1988).

Orbital frontal cortex

The orbital region of the frontal cortex (Figure 2.2) is a mesiocortical area which occupies the ventral surface of the frontal lobe. The orbital cortex shares great similarities among primates and has been subdivided into distinct cortical areas (for review, see Barbas, 1993; Carmichael & Price, 1994; Cavada et al., 2000; Öngür & Price, 2000; Petrides & Pandya, 2002; Semendeferi, Armstrong, Schleicher, Zilles, & Van Hoesen, 1998). Like the amygdala, the orbital frontal cortex receives highly processed information from all sensory modalities (visual, somatosensory, visceral, olfactory, and gustatory) and, by the pattern of connectivity, has been divided into medial and lateral networks. The medial network of the orbital frontal cortex, for example, area 14, has strong connections with the hippocampus and associated areas of the cingulate, retrosplenial, and entorhinal cortices. The lateral network has been further subdivided into a caudal sector, such as areas 12 and 13, that is mainly interconnected with the amygdala, midline thalamus,

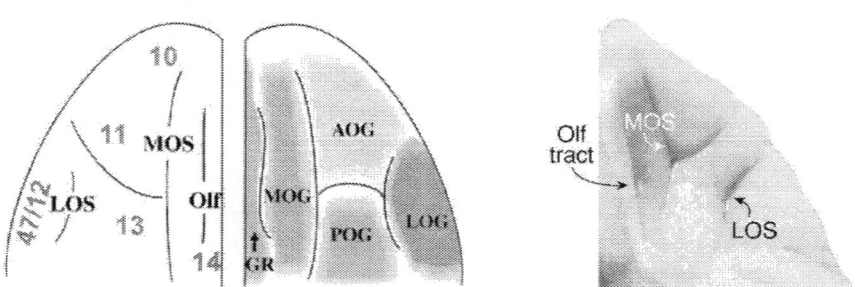

Figure 2.2 Ventral views of the macaque brain illustrating the different cytoarchitectonic areas (10, 11, 12, 13, 14, and 47) composing the orbital frontal cortex. AOG: anterior orbital gyrus; GR: gyrus rectus; LOG: lateral orbital gyrus; LOS: lateral orbital sulcus; MOG: medial orbital gyrus; MOS: medial orbital sulcus; Olf: olfactory sulcus; POG: posterior orbital gyrus (adapted from Machado & Bachevalier, 2003).

and temporal pole, and a rostral sector, such as areas 11 and 12, that has more pronounced connections with the insula, mediodorsal nucleus of the thalamus, inferior parietal lobule, and dorsolateral prefrontal cortex. Interestingly, the orbital frontal cortex differs in many ways from the most dorsolateral prefrontal region. For example, unlike the dorsolateral prefrontal area, which receives projections primarily from the mediodorsal nucleus of the thalamus, the orbital frontal area receives projections primarily from midline and intralaminar nuclei (Barbas, 1995). In addition, the orbital frontal cortex receives robust projections from both the amygdala and the temporopolar area, whereas the rest of the prefrontal cortex appears to have few, if any, links with the amygdala and temporal pole (Ghashghaei & Barbas, 2002; Kondo, Saleem & Price, 2003). Thus, unlike the dorsolateral aspect of the prefrontal cortex, the orbital frontal area receives information about all aspects of the external and internal environment, from thalamic nuclei involved in associative aspects of memory, and from the amygdala and temporal pole, which are thought to be implicated in the regulation of emotion. Thus, the connections between the amygdala and orbital frontal cortex may permit the modulation and self-regulation of emotional behaviour in relation to rapid changes in a social situation or context (as in dominance relationships and situational features). Finally, the orbital frontal cortex also sends inputs to brain regions, such as the preoptic region of the lateral hypothalamus, that are critical for hormonal modulation of emotions, and to motor centres, such as the head of the caudate and the ventral tegmental area, that are critical for motor control of emotions (Selemon & Goldman-Rakic, 1985).

Temporopolar cortex

The temporopolar cortex covers the rostral tip of the temporal pole (Figure 2.1) and consists of a mesiocortical area that corresponds to a great extent to Brodmann's area 38 (Chabardès, Kahane, Minotti, Hoffmann, & Benabid, 2002; Kondo et al., 2003). It provides a site for convergence of highly processed sensory inputs arising from sensory cortical areas and limbic inputs from the amygdala and orbital prefrontal cortex (Gloor, 1997; Moran, Mufson, & Mesulam, 1987). Strong mutual connections exist between the temporopolar cortex and the orbital frontal and medial prefrontal surfaces (via the uncinate fasciculus), whereas only weak connections have been found between the temporopolar cortex and the anterior cingulate cortex. The temporopolar cortex also projects to the lateral hypothalamus and sends unidirectional descending connections to the dorsolateral thalamic nucleus. This cortical region represents a discrete temporal area where integration of both internal and external inputs could occur, and which has been associated with the regulation of autonomic functions and emotions (Chabardès et al., 2002).

Anterior cingulate cortex

The anterior cingulate cortex is an agranular cortical area which lies on the medial surface of the frontal lobe, around the genu of the corpus callosum (Figure 2.1). This cortical area is interconnected with the amygdala (basal and accessory basal nuclei). It receives dense projections from the midline and intralaminar nuclei of the thalamus but few direct cortical projections from the frontal pole and lateral prefrontal cortex; from the temporopolar, parahippocampal, and entorhinal cortices; or from the posterior parietal cortex (Bachevalier, Meunier, Lu, & Ungerleider, 1997; Baleydier & Mauguière, 1980; Vogt, Rosene, & Pandya, 1979). The anterior cingulate cortex has been implicated in the production of vocalizations in monkeys (Jürgens & Ploog, 1970; Ploog, 1986; Robinson, 1967) and in the initiation of speech in humans (Barris & Schuman, 1953; Jürgens & von Cramon, 1982). Thus, the pathway connecting the amygdala to the anterior cingulate cortex may be crucial for the emotional modulation of vocalizations and speech. In addition, because the anterior cingulate cortex is involved in effector and executive functions, that is, in controlling visceromotor, endocrine, or skeletomotor outputs, it is likely that this area controls emotional outputs not only for speech but also for all body postures and movements, and for internal emotional changes (Devinsky, Morrell, & Vogt, 1995; Vogt, Finch, & Olson, 1992). That is, as the organism evaluates the affective significance of something experienced, the anterior cingulate may be involved in selecting specific responses that are consistent with the situation as evaluated (such as fight or flight?). Another function attributed to the anterior cingulate cortex is the control of the mechanisms underlying exploratory behaviour and attention to sensory stimuli. Thus, this cortical area may be important to direct the subject's vigilance to events that are of emotional or motivational significance.

To sum up, the reciprocal anatomical relationship between the amygdala and the temporopolar, orbital frontal, and cingulate cortices implies that these brain regions may share a close functional relationship within a system essential for the maintenance of intraspecific social bondings. However, the mechanisms by which these neural structures participate in social cognition are still poorly understood, and it is unknown whether the specific mechanisms related to each structure can be distinguished or whether these neural structures function as a unitary "system". The behavioural lesion, stimulation, and electrophysiological recording studies that have linked these four neural structures to social-emotional behaviours will be reviewed next, and an attempt will be made to provide some insights into the role that each structure might play in the control of social cognition.

The primate amygdala and social-emotional cognition

The historical foundation of our current understanding of temporal functions is typically traced back to Heinrich Klüver and Paul Bucy's behavioural observations (1938, 1939) of monkeys with bilateral resections of the entire temporal lobe. These seminal observations subsequently led to the identification of the inferior temporal cortex as a visual region and of the amygdala as an important substrate for social-emotional cognition (see Gross, 1994, for a detailed historical account). However, whereas inferior temporal cortex research has closely intertwined lesion studies and single-cell recordings, amygdala research in monkeys has predominantly relied on the lesion approach. Hence, progress in this field has been tightly linked to technical refinements of surgical and histological procedures. Two periods can be distinguished. The most recent one encompasses the last 15 years, which has seen the application to the monkey of selective, neurotoxic lesions (a technical impossibility in the pre-MRI era because of the interindividual variability of monkey brain anatomy). This surgical procedure has brought a great advance by narrowing the spectrum of amygdala functions to the social-emotional domain, but too few studies are available as yet to ascertain the exact nature of the amygdala contribution to this vast domain. By contrast, early studies used various nonselective lesion techniques now known to disrupt perceptual/mnemonic functions that depend on adjacent medial and inferior temporal areas rather than on the amygdala proper (Baxter & Murray, 2000; Easton & Gaffan, 2000). Yet, these early studies contain a wealth of behavioural observations that we will review in some detail below, before turning to recent data, for they offer insights into the brain control of social-emotional functions that remain of great value.

Bilateral temporal lobectomies and the Klüver–Bucy syndrome

It was in the course of unsuccessful attempts to locate the brain site of the action of mescaline that Klüver and Bucy made the serendipitous discovery of the complex syndrome that now bears their names[1]. Their first report provided a detailed behavioural description of a single female rhesus monkey (Klüver & Bucy, 1938), and was quickly followed by an extensive study reproducing the results in 15 additional subjects from three different monkey species (Klüver & Bucy, 1939). Histology was, by contrast, poorly documented. The removal was produced by a first cut "just below and parallel to the sylvian vessels", followed by a transerve cut removing the entire temporal lobe in a single block. It was described, for one case, to have included most of the lateral and medial temporal cortex together with the amygdala, most of the hippocampus, and the tail of the caudate nucleus. In hindsight, the

---

1 In fact, an accurate description of the syndrome had been made earlier in one monkey by Brown and Schäfer in 1888, but this finding was forgotten until Klüver rediscovered it in 1948, 10 years after the publication of his own studies. Brown and Schäfer had focused on their monkey's intact hearing, and viewed its general behaviour as mimicking "idiocy", thus failing to detect the combination of visual agnosia and emotional disorder later emphasized by Klüver and Bucy (for detail, see Gross, 1994).

removal must have, at the very least, disrupted all the visual functions now associated with the inferior temporal cortex, interfered with the social and emotional functions now attributed to the amygdala, and produced the dense anterograde amnesia now known to follow damage to the hippocampal and parahippocampal regions. Remarkably, Klüver and Bucy's careful observations missed little, except the amnesia that was later discovered by Scoville and Milner (1957), and which they only alluded to in 1938 by stating that "even though some of the objects had been presented previously, the monkey, nevertheless, examines such objects as if they were being presented for the first time" (p. 50).

Typically, the Klüver–Bucy syndrome is viewed as comprising six symptoms. The first two include visual agnosia (or "psychic blindness") and its corollary, hyperorality. Visual agnosia is the inability to detect the meaning of objects by sight only, despite the lack of gross defects in visual perception. Hyperorality is the tendency to explore all stimuli, whether objects, other monkeys, or humans, by mouthing (and smelling) them, often directly, without prior attempt to use the hands. The third symptom was termed "hypermetamorphosis", after Wernicke, to describe the animals' compulsive impulse to attend and react to every stimulus. For example, when faced with a rotating platform providing alternatively, at 30-s intervals, a piece of banana or a nail, the first operated female kept taking both banana and nail, eating the former while examining the latter by mouth before discarding it, ending up after 140 trials with the cage floor "practically covered by nails" which she "again and again picked up to examine them by mouth" (by comparison, normal monkeys would simply ignore the nail after a few trials). The remaining three symptoms characteristic of the Klüver–Bucy syndrome are often presented as a loss of emotional reactions, dietary changes including meat eating and coprophagia, and excessive and aberrant sexuality[2]. As these common formulations probably constitute inaccurate overgeneralizations, it is important to note here some original qualifications provided by Klüver and Bucy. The loss of emotional reactions they described referred selectively to fear and anger, whose absence or drastic reduction was all the more striking because it occurred in animals that had been specifically selected for their "viciousness" prior to surgery. The authors nevertheless noted that vocalizations and facial expressions of emotions were only transiently suppressed by the lesions, that the first operated female frequently engaged in hindquarter presentations (a submission display presumably devoid of sexual content since she had had both the uterus and ovaries removed), and that some

---

2 Note that hypersexuality will not be discussed in the present chapter (although, unlike changes in dietary habits, it was included in Klüver and Bucy's original list of symptoms in 1939). Sexual disturbances in animals with temporal lobe or amygdala damage have been reviewed by Kling and Brothers, 1992; see also Aggleton, 1992, for a comparison between monkeys and humans.

animals could become aggressive, in particular when attempts to examine an object were thwarted. Thus, the lesions transformed fierce wild monkeys into overly tame animals, but not into emotionless beings. As for dietary changes, the authors did report in a footnote (Klüver & Bucy, 1939) that three males were willing to eat animal foods (made of meat or fish) that they had never seen a normal monkey accept, but nonetheless stressed (Klüver & Bucy, 1938) that the first operated female never swallowed inedible items (whether nails or faeces), and appropriately refused pieces of fruit soaked in quinine. Thus, food/nonfood discrimination was never impaired by the lesion, nor were global palatability judgements.

The Klüver–Bucy syndrome and social behaviour

Social behaviour was not specifically investigated in the original Klüver and Bucy studies, which were carried out in a laboratory setting and in individually housed animals. Social disturbances were therefore not included in the original list of symptoms. Yet, as monkey testing was considerably more casual at that time, the authors did mention several social improprieties in their animals' behaviour. When turned loose in a room containing objects as well as two other (leashed) monkeys and two experimenters, the first operated female never retreated into a safe corner as most normal monkeys would. Instead, she compulsively examined all stimuli, indiscriminately touching or mouthing both the inanimate objects and alive beings. She ignored social signals from her conspecifics, whether antagonistic or affiliative, and showed no retaliatory reaction to another monkey that had attacked her, or to humans (familiar or unknown) handling or even slapping her. The authors (Klüver & Bucy, 1939) also noted that animals that at times initiated an attack on the experimenter would abruptly interrupt it to switch to oral exploration of the experimenter's mouth (a similar peculiar switch from aggression to oral examination was noted by Horel, Keating, and Misantone, 1975, after ablation of the amygdala region in a monkey presented with "a gloved hand").

Social disturbances were explicitly added to the constellation of symptoms listed by Klüver and Bucy after the first systematic study of the social consequences of temporal lobe damage was carried out in monkeys by Rosvold, Mirsky, and Pribram in 1954. These authors monitored the dominance hierarchy within a group of eight male rhesus monkeys, housed in a large cage, over 9 months, before and after operating on the three top-ranking animals (one animal at a time, with a 2-month interval between animals). In addition, they regularly assessed each subject's behaviour when placed in an individual cage and faced with an experimenter offering food. The lesions were made by aspiration and included the anterior portion of the temporal lobe (temporal pole, amygdala, and subjacent rhinal cortical areas) but spared most of the hippocampus, thus extending far less laterally and caudally than the removals produced by Klüver and Bucy. The original illustrations depicting social relationships at the beginning and near the end of the experiment are reproduced in Figure 2.3. When reintroduced in the group cage after their operation, the first (Dave) and second (Zeke) operated monkeys both lost their leadership position in a matter of days. Although they transiently retained preeminence over the lowest ranking animal, they both eventually reached the bottom of the hierarchy and, once there, withdrew from all social contacts. The third and last operated monkey (Riva), on the contrary, did not fall in dominance at any time during the experiment, and any manipulation of the space or food available to the group served only to increase his aggressiveness. Yet, when alone and offered food by the experimenter, all three monkeys appeared less fearful or more assertive after the surgery than before. These early data thus provided the first clear-cut evidence of the temporal lobe involvement in the control of social behaviour in monkeys. In addition, they underscored one point that is often overlooked in today's research, namely, that the symptoms following temporal damage can take more variable forms than can be predicted from the seminal work by Klüver and Bucy. First, although all three monkeys developed social disturbances after the lesion, the direction of the changes differed across individuals, appearing as a switch either to hypoaggression and excessive social fear or, on the contrary, to hyperaggression and decreased social fear. The authors emphasized that Dave and Zeke, which both fell in dominance, were returned after surgery to a group containing one or more aggressive animals, whereas Riva, who retained his top-ranking position, was returned to a less challenging group that had been deprived of its most assertive individuals by Dave and Zeke's operations. Thus, the specific social environment with which the operated animal is confronted (and perhaps also its own premorbid temperament) probably affects the social consequences of temporal damage. Second, the two operated animals that were withdrawn and fearful when placed in the social situation nevertheless appeared more assertive after than before surgery when observed individually. Thus, for the same individual, the behavioural manifestations of temporal damage can vary with the testing situation. In light of this interindividual and intraindividual variability, Rosvold and colleagues made an early cautionary statement that may remain useful today: "Unless the effects of an operation on behaviour is studied in a variety of situations, the findings are at best of limited generalizability."

Identification of the amygdala region as the core temporal substrate for emotional functions

In their second study, Klüver and Bucy (1939) had included animals with removals limited to the lateral temporal cortex or with disconnections of the temporal lobe from either the frontal or occipital lobe, but had failed to reproduce with these more restricted lesions the constellation of symptoms observed after complete bilateral temporal lobectomies. Consequently, they

(a) Presurgical social hierarchy

(b) Postsurgical social hierarchy

suggested that these symptoms form a unitary syndrome, and encouraged future research to determine whether they reflect disruption of "higher" visual functions or, alternatively, "merely represent disturbances in the affective sphere" (Klüver & Bucy, 1939). Studies carried out in the late 1950s and early 1960s provided an answer to that question by suggesting that both explanations may hold true. On the one hand, a series of lesion studies laid the foundation for the large body of data that was accumulated thereafter on the "higher" visual functions of the middle and inferior temporal gyri, that is, the region now known as the inferior temporal cortex (Gross, 1994). On the other hand, Weiskrantz (1956) demonstrated that ablations restricted to the anterior medial temporal lobe, which includes the amygdala, are sufficient to yield the tameness, and tendency to explore all objects, including previously aversive ones, described earlier in monkeys with drastic temporal lobectomies. The importance of the amygdala region was further stressed by Downer (1961) in split-brain monkeys with removal of this region in one hemisphere and suture of the eye contralateral to the lesion. In this condition, which deprived the intact amygdala region of visual input, the monkey was unresponsive to visual threat, although not to auditory or somatosensory stimulation. By contrast, when the ipsilateral eye was sutured, instead of the contralateral one, the animal recovered its normal aggressive responses to visual threat. These studies, together with that by Rosvold and colleagues (1954) already mentioned, established the importance of the amygdala region for both social and emotional functions in monkeys. To this day, however, it remains unclear whether the undeniable functional differences existing between the anterior medial (amygdalar) and inferior temporal regions mean that the Klüver–Bucy syndrome can be fractionated into two separate disorders, one visual and one affective (if one overlooks amnesia). Indeed, unlike Klüver and Bucy, Horel and colleagues (Horel & Misantone, 1974; Horel et al., 1975; see also Iwai, Nishio, & Yamaguchi, 1986) did find some evidence of hyperorality, hypermetamorphosis, or decreased aggressiveness after extensive ablations or disconnections of the inferior temporal cortex. Thus, how much these "affective" symptoms owe to visual difficulties remains an open question.

Figure 2.3 Artistic drawings representing the dominance status within a group of eight adult male monkeys before surgery (a) and after the three top-ranking animals had undergone bilateral removal of the amygdala region (b). Dave was operated first, followed by Zeke, and then by Riva, with 2-month intervals between animals. The first two monkeys eventually fell to the bottom of the hierarchy (in a final stage not depicted here, Dave was removed from the group; Zeke then became the outcast and no longer displayed any aggressiveness). By contrast, the third operated monkey claimed and retained the top rank of the group as modified by Dave and Zeke's surgeries. Adapted from 'Influence of amygdalectomy on social behaviour in monkeys', Rosvold, Mirsky and Pribram (1954), *The Journal of Comparative Physiological Psychology*, 47, 173–178.

The amygdala region and social behaviour: early studies

Findings from the late 1950s firmly anchored the idea of the amygdala region as the core temporal substrate for affective functions in monkeys (and other species such as rats and cats) (Schreiner & Kling, 1953, 1956). One of the consequences of this idea was to spur further investigation of the social consequences of amygdala lesions over the next two decades. Lesions were then generally produced by aspiration, and histological control was less refined than that practised today, and sometimes simply impossible to obtain (in field studies). Thus, the term "amygdalectomy" will be used below to describe nonselective removal of the anterior medial temporal lobe, likely to include the amygdala together with, at least, some of the anterior rhinal cortex and variable amounts of the temporopolar cortex.

In 1960, Mirsky built upon Rosvold and colleagues' (1954) findings. Using the same experimental approach, this author showed that if amygdalectomized rhesus monkeys were placed during the 6 weeks following surgery with unchallenging youngsters, they did not fall in rank when later returned to their original adult group; rather, upon rejoining their original group, all three amygdalectomized animals displayed an increase in aggressiveness (albeit a transient one). Plotnik (1968) extended these results by observing social interactions in a group of four male squirrel monkeys in two situations—in one, the food-deprived animals had to compete to retrieve food; in the other, they had to compete to avoid electrical shocks (only one out of the four animals being allowed to avoid shock per trial). The decrease in aggressiveness produced by amygdalectomy was more pronounced during the negatively reinforced competition than during the positively reinforced one, thereby providing additional evidence of the context influence on the behavioural outcome of the lesion. In addition, Plotnik underlined that although all operated monkeys exhibited a decrease in aggression and social rank, anger was not totally suppressed by amygdalectomy, for the animals could also, occasionally, "respond with direct rage".

During the 1960s and 1970s, Kling and colleagues complemented the above studies by testing the consequences of amygdalectomy in many different situations and several animal species. Regarding monkeys, the fundamental contribution of this author has been to investigate for the first time the social effects of the lesion in animals living in naturalistic settings (Steklis, 1998). This large body of data has been reviewed in detail in Kling and Steklis (1976) and Kling and Brothers (1992); therefore, only a brief account will be provided here. Klüver and Bucy (1939) had surmised that "a monkey which approaches every enemy to examine it orally will conceivably not survive longer than a few hours if turned loose in a region with a plentiful supply of enemies" (p. 996). Kling and colleagues tested this hypothesis by assessing the effects of amygdalectomies in different social contexts, including large laboratory cages, the seminatural Cayo Santiago colony, and a completely natural African setting. As foreseen by Klüver and Bucy, amygdalectomized monkeys released to their natural, wild troop failed to readapt, and most eventually died. However, this downfall was not brought by inconsiderate oral examination of enemies; on the contrary, it was due to a reaction of complete social withdrawal, even from positive signs from their peers, eventually leading the animal to leave the troop altogether (Kling, 1972). A decrease in aggression and social rank was common to all settings (although the opposite was also observed in some individuals), but Klüver–Bucy signs, such as hyperorality and hypersexuality, occurred only in laboratory group cages (Kling & Mass, 1974). In fact, the same animals that showed the typical syndrome when singly caged immediately after the lesion failed to display it when released in a complex group. This puzzling effect of the social environment remains unexplained. Kling and Mass (1974) proposed an interpretation akin to visual agnosia; that is, after amygdalectomy, the monkey would be unable to comprehend its visual world. In impoverished artificial environments, hyperexploration could be a way to overcome this problem that would fail when the animal is confronted with a natural environment and its constant flood of information. However, Kling and Brothers (1992) underlined that another possibility has yet to be ruled out, namely, that, had their wild animals sustained complete temporal lobectomy, rather than amygdalectomy, they might have displayed the classical Klüver–Bucy syndrome even after their release.

The amygdala proper and social-emotional cognition: recent studies

Because, in primates, the amygdala is buried within the anterior medial temporal lobe, its aspiration or resection was necessarily accompanied by removal of some of the surrounding cortex. The first attempts to produce more selective lesions employed stereotaxic, radiofrequency lesions, whose vertical approach to the amygdala avoided direct damage to the surrounding cortex. This lesion technique was used in two studies by Aggleton and Passingham (1981, 1982; see also Zola-Morgan, Squire, Alvarez-Royo, & Clower, 1991), which reported an exaggerated tendency to approach and examine objects, and a willingness to eat meat; coprophagia was mentioned in some cases, but it is unclear whether the animals simply mouthed or actually ate faeces. Notwithstanding, the animals demonstrated clear food/nonfood discrimination, retained their preoperative spontaneous preferences among several highly palatable items, and, like normal monkeys, worked harder (in terms of number of lever presses) for large than for small amounts of reward. Thus, radiofrequency lesions already outlined an "amygdala syndrome" much less dramatic than the Klüver–Bucy syndrome, an idea which, as detailed below, has recently been confirmed by selective, neurotoxic lesions.

Important contingents of nonamygdaloid fibres extend near or through the amygdala. Among them are fibres originating in the inferior temporal, temporopolar, and rhinal (that is, entorhinal and perirhinal) areas, en route to the medial thalamus and orbital frontal cortex (Baxter, Saunders, & Murray,

1998; Goulet, Doré, & Murray, 1998), as well as projections from the basal forebrain to the inferior temporal and perirhinal areas (Easton & Gaffan, 2000). These nonamygdaloid fibres are inevitably disrupted by aspiration and radiofrequency lesions alike. The importance of such indirect damage had been first demonstrated in the rat by using stereotaxic injections of neurotoxins, such as ibotenic acid, which destroys neural cells, but spares fibres of passage (see Everitt & Robbins, 1992). Likewise, when MRI availability allowed transposition of the technique to monkeys, many of the deficits previously attributed to amygdala damage, including impairments in recognition memory, and stimulus–stimulus and stimulus–reward associations, were shown to result instead from unintended disruption of the frontal, thalamic, and/or basal forebrain connections of adjacent medial and inferior temporal cortical areas (Baxter & Murray, 2000, 2002; Easton & Gaffan, 2000). This re-evaluation of amygdala functions by neurotoxic lesions is not yet complete, however, and has mainly focused on memory; therefore, to date, only a handful of studies are available as regards social-emotional functions.

In one of these studies, we carried out a direct comparison of the effects of aspiration and neurotoxic amygdala lesions (Meunier, Bachevalier, Murray, Málková, & Mishkin, 1999). Monkeys were observed individually in the presence of four items, two bearing a social component, the experimenter wearing a face mask (serving as an unfamiliar human) and a taxidermic monkey head (serving as a conspecific stimulus), and two inanimate items, one positive (an object concealing a reward) and one negative (a toy snake[3]). The two types of lesion had common effects, including, for the "social" items, overly affiliative/ hypoaggressive responses (albeit with unchanged fear), and for inanimate items decreased fear/excessive touching and mouthing. Differences were nevertheless evident in that 1. "social" changes, that is, aggression attenuation and submission enhancement, were clear-cut after aspiration lesions, but less marked or absent after total or subtotal neurotoxic damage; 2. hypermetamorphosis and hyperorality were more pervasive after aspiration removals than after neurotoxic lesions (they were even absent in one case, although its cell loss encompassed most of the amygdala; Figure 2.4). These findings therefore demonstrated that, unlike memory functions, social-emotional behaviour can be disrupted by selective damage to the amygdala proper. Nevertheless, they indicated that the affective changes following amygdala aspiration are likely to be exacerbated by the attendant insult to medial and/or inferior temporal cortex. Since ablations restricted to the rhinal cortex did not produce Klüver–Bucy-like symptoms in the same paradigm (the animals appearing, on the contrary, more withdrawn or fearful; Figure 2.4), this

---

3 Monkeys, like humans, show a potent fear of snakes. This fear is, in part, learned through experience in wild-reared monkeys but rests upon an innate bias strong enough to be detectable even in laboratory-reared monkeys (for detail, see Nelson, Shelton, & Kalin, 2003; Öhman & Mineka, 2003).

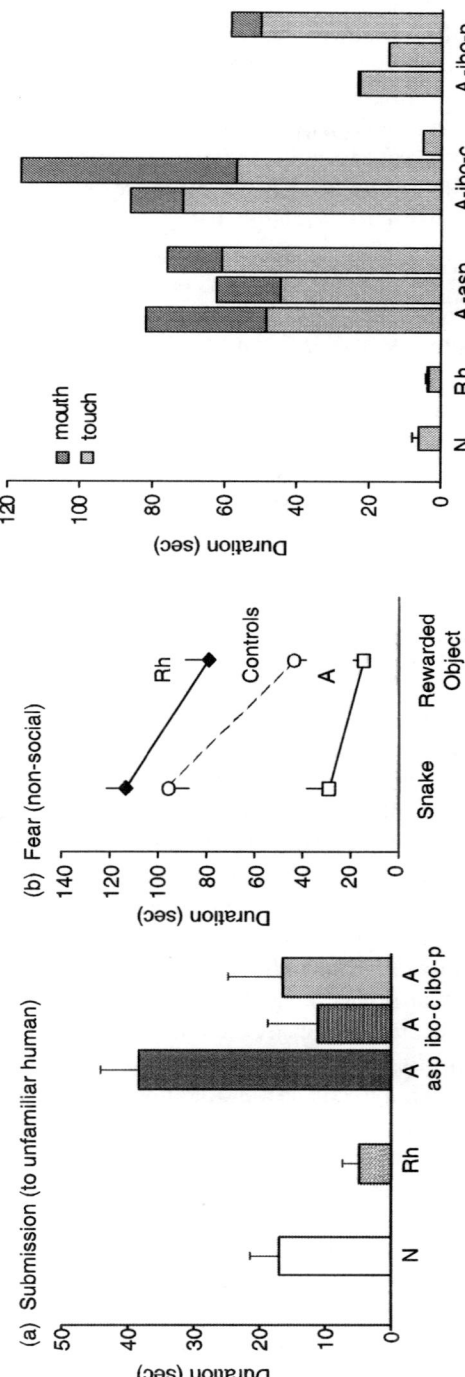

Figure 2.4 Socio-emotional changes in (individually observed) adult monkeys after bilateral amygdala versus rhinal cortex damage (adapted from Meunier et al., 1999; Meunier & Bachevalier, 2002). (a) Cumulated duration (group means ± S.E.M.) of the submissive responses (that is, lip smack, grimace, or hindquarter presentation) recorded during three 20-s presentations of an unfamiliar human. Relative to normal controls (N, $n = 6$), rhinal cortex ablations (Rh, $n = 6$) tended to decrease submission, whereas amygdala aspiration lesions (A-asp, $n = 3$) produced a clear-cut increase in affiliative behaviours. This increase was absent after neurotoxic amygdala lesions, whether complete (A-ibo-c, $n = 3$), or partial (A-ibo-p, $n = 3$). (b) Cumulated duration (group means ± S.E.M.) of the defensive responses (that is, piloerection, eye aversion, startle, moving away, or freezing) recorded during three 20-s presentations of either a toy snake or a junk object concealing a food reward. These nonsocial items elicited little or no fear in all three A groups (which were therefore pooled). By contrast, Rh monkeys, although appropriately less fearful of the positive object than of the snake, were consistently more defensive/withdrawn than controls. (c) Cumulated duration of the manual (touch, light grey) or oral (mouth, dark grey) exploration directed towards the toy snake, rewarded object, and taxidermic monkey-head (three 20-s presentations per stimulus). Scores are means (± S.E.M.) for groups N and Rh. For the nine animals with amygdala damage, individual scores are given to illustrate the interindividual variability of two of the cardinal Klüver–Bucy signs, hypermetamorphosis and hyperorality. The two signs, present in all the A-asp animals, were absent in one A-ibo-c monkey (despite near complete cell loss in the amygdala), but present in one A-ibo-p monkey (despite partial, bilaterally asymmetrical cell loss in the amygdala).

exacerbation may stem from an interaction of the many visual "agnostic" deficits, now known to follow rhinal cortex insult, with the "affective" defects produced by amygdala damage (Meunier & Bachevalier, 2002).

Another noteworthy finding of Meunier and colleagues' study (1999) was that animals with extensive amygdala lesions, aspiration and neurotoxic alike, were not indifferent but, on the contrary, strongly reacted to the absence of an expected food reward. This finding provides further evidence that amygdala damage has much less impact on food-related behaviours than was once thought. It is now evident that monkeys with such damage learn many food-motivated tasks normally (e.g. Málková, Gaffan, & Murray, 1997), distinguish food from nonfood items, and exhibit normal preferences for highly palatable foods (e.g. Aggleton & Passingham, 1982; Bachevalier & Machado, 2001; Horel et al., 1975; Murray, Gaffan, & Flint, 1996). Changes in food preferences after amygdala neurotoxic lesions appear to be limited to an exaggerated tendency to pick up and mouth inedible items, and an increased willingness to eat unfamiliar food (Bachevalier & Machado, 2001; Málková et al., 1997; Murray et al., 1996), both of which might result from the loss of neophobia associated with hypermetamorphosis. A reduced sensitivity to reinforcer devaluation has been reported in one study, which required the animals to displace objects to obtain the reinforcer (Málková et al., 1997; for a detailed description of the task, see section entitled *Orbital frontal cortex involvement in the control of response selection* below). In this task, failure to adapt to satiation may mean that the amygdala is necessary to update information about the current value of a particular reward (Baxter & Murray, 2000). However, this hypothesis is inconsistent with electrophysiological data showing that taste-related activity in the amygdala, unlike that in orbital frontal cortex, does not efficiently reflect shifts in reward value (Rolls, 2000). Consequently, the lack of reaction to satiation observed by Málková and colleagues (1997) could simply represent yet another manifestation of hypermetamorphosis, that is, the animals' compulsive impulse to react to objects. In line with this idea, preliminary data obtained with a reinforcer devaluation paradigm allowing direct choice between visible food treats indicate that monkeys with neurotoxic amygdala lesions appropriately refuse, in this situation devoid of intermediate object, the food item that has been provided earlier to satiation (Bachevalier & Machado, 2001). Thus, there is now compelling evidence that amygdala lesion does not interfere with monkeys' inner drives or hedonic preferences for food items, and may have little or nothing to do with the establishment and subsequent adjustments of stimulus–reward associations (for further debate on this issue, see Baxter & Murray, 2002; Easton & Gaffan, 2000).

A second investigation of the socioemotional consequences of neurotoxic amygdala lesions in individually observed monkeys was performed by Kalin and colleagues (2001; see also Benca, Obermeyer, Shelton, Droster, & Kalin, 2000). In that study, the operated animals were faster than controls to retrieve a treat placed close to a real or a toy snake, although they did so less readily than when the treat was near a neutral object. In addition, they were less reactive than controls when placed in the proximity of a threatening, unfamiliar adult monkey. These findings converge with earlier results by Meunier and colleagues (1999) to indicate that neurotoxic amygdala lesions are sufficient to both diminish (though perhaps not abolish) snake fear and disrupt behavioural responses to conspecifics. However, unlike in the earlier study, the operated animals' responses to a human intruder were unchanged. This discrepancy further cautions against hasty generalization of symptoms across testing situations, however similar they may seem. Indeed, a total of three studies have now used a human intruder paradigm, and reported exaggerated submission (Meunier et al., 1999), increased aggression (Machado & Bachevalier, 2000), or no change at all (Kalin et al., 2001). Interestingly, however, Kalin and colleagues (2001) interpreted their data as reflecting altered fear responses but intact inner individual anxiety traits after amygdala damage, an idea which converges with that of the spared inner drives and preferences for food already mentioned (see previous paragraph).

To date, only one study has investigated the effects of neurotoxic amygdala lesions on actual social interactions between adult monkeys (Emery, Capitanio, Mason, Machado, Mendoza, & Amaral, 2001). Operated middle-ranking male monkeys underwent a series of 10–20-min sessions during which they were first placed near and, then, together with a relatively unfamiliar partner. In all conditions, the operated subjects appear socially disinhibited, that is, they showed no aggression, and were instead overly affiliative with an excess of social and sociosexual approach behaviours. No aberrant sexual behaviours were noted, but hyperorality was present. This unbridled approach was positively received by the other member of the pair, whether operated or control. The difference, however, was that, in controls, this increase in social interactions was selectively directed toward operated animals, whereas the latter appear to indiscriminately approach operated and normal peers alike. Operated animals thus globally demonstrated none of the initial tension or wariness that monkeys usually show when confronted with an unfamiliar, and hence potentially dangerous, conspecific. These findings constitute the first evidence that selective amygdala damage is sufficient to disrupt actual social interactions. The authors acknowledge, however, that in light of the marked differences seen earlier by Kling and collaborators across social contexts, the specific change they observed during these brief dyadic encounters (decreased social fear) may not generalize to more demanding social situations. Future studies will need to determine whether selective amygdala lesions can, like nonselective ones, eventually lead to the opposite change, that is, complete social withdrawal, when the animals are faced with the long-lasting challenge of a complex social environment.

Electrophysiological studies of amygdala involvement in social-emotional cognition

Although the emphasis has been placed on neuropsychology in the present chapter, neurophysiology has also made an important contribution to research on the amygdala and social functions. Early studies showed that electrical stimulation of the amygdala in monkeys living in social groups yields significant changes in vocalization in both rhesus (Robinson, 1967) and squirrel (Jürgens, 1982; Jürgens & Ploog, 1970) monkeys, suggesting amygdala involvement in the regulation of vocal social communications (see also Newman & Bachevalier, 1997). Kling and colleagues also conducted radio-telemetry recordings of neuronal activity in the amygdala during social interactions. They showed that amygdala activity in the normal monkey differentiates threatening situations, such as threat face display, from tension-lowering behaviours, such as grooming and huddling (Kling, Steklis, & Deutsch, 1979). In addition, their findings suggested that amygdala activity reflects the degree of ambiguity of the socioemotional context, the greatest activity being recorded in situations of high uncertainty, such as a conspecific behaving in an unpredictable manner or a setting associated with unpredictable shocks (Kling, Lloyd, & Perryman, 1987; Lloyd & Kling, 1991).

More recently, single-cell recording studies have investigated the role of the amygdala in the discrimination of face identity, facial expressions, and body movements (for review, see Rolls, 1986, 1994, 2000). Thus, amygdala neurons code not only for several aspects of a face, such as dimension (Yamane, Kaji, & Kawao, 1988), hairline, eyes, and mouth (Desimone, Albright, Gross, & Bruce 1984; Leonard, Rolls, Wilson, & Baylis, 1985; Perrett, Rolls, & Caan, 1982), but also for identity of a face (Baylis, Rolls, & Leonard, 1985; Perrett et al., 1984) and for facial expressions (Hasselmo et al., 1989a, 1989b; Perrett et al., 1984). Some of the amygdala neurons respond specifically to body movements, such as direction of rotation of head or direction of gaze, but not to movements of inanimate objects (Perret & Mistlin, 1990; Perrett et al., 1985). Finally, amygdala recordings in monkeys viewing short videoclips of social interactions in a natural setting (Brothers, 1995; Brothers, Ring, & Kling, 1990) showed neurons firing specifically to the identity of the individual or to active movements of a specific area of the face, such as the eyebrow region. It is thus clear from these studies that the amygdala appears to code and process facial movements, body postures, and gestures that are potent signals for the production and modulation of appropriate social and emotional responses to other individuals.

The nonhuman primate amygdala and social-emotional cognition: progress and perspective

Klüver and Bucy's cornerstone studies (1938, 1939) established very early the idea of a link between the primate temporal lobe and both vision and emotion, an idea that was later complemented by Scoville and Milner's (1957) discovery of a third temporal lobe function, memory. Subsequent lesion studies in monkeys, based on nonselective ablation or radiofrequency techniques, were instrumental in identifying broad regional functional specializations within the temporal lobe. Thus, the inferior temporal cortex became associated with "higher" visual functions, and the posterior medial temporal lobe (including the hippocampus) with the formation of new memories. By contrast, for the anterior medial temporal region (comprising the amygdala), ablation studies unveiled a wide spectrum of disorders (encompassing emotion and social behaviour, but also many forms of learning and memory), a finding which was hardly compatible with a single, unitary, view of amygdala functions. Decisive progress was made on this issue after the recent introduction of neurotoxic lesions in monkey research. This technique demonstrated that most, if not all, the mnemonic functions previously attributed to the amygdala, were in fact dependent on adjacent temporal cortical areas. Conversely, it clearly established that this was not the case regarding emotional and social functions.

The contour of amygdala functions having thus been considerably clarified, time is now ripe for progress on a still elusive issue, namely, how best to synthesize the amygdala contribution to social-emotional cognition in monkeys. Recent studies using neurotoxic lesions converge with earlier results after temporal lobectomy or amygdalectomy to indicate that the disorders most frequently seen in adult laboratory monkeys (mostly males, observed alone or in dyads) are characterized by reduced fear and aggression, together with excessive and indiscriminate object exploration (manual and/or oral) and social affiliation. However, as repeatedly emphasized above, generalization of these specific changes as the hallmark effects of amygdala damage is inaccurate. Selective lesions, like conventional ones, can yield shifts in the opposite direction, depending on the subject and the testing situation. Such opposite changes (such as increased as compared with reduced fear) are likely to be more frequent in naturalistic, complex social environments, although this remains to be tested. This variability suggests that the amygdala is not the generator of specific emotional responses, such as fear; rather, it may act as a control device ensuring that emotional responses are both appropriate to and adequate for the external stimuli and social context.

In the near future, pursuing the comparison between the effects of selective amygdala damage and those of lesions restricted to specific medial temporal, inferior temporal, or orbital frontal areas, will be necessary to elucidate the cooperative or competitive interactions underlying the contribution of this temporal-frontal network to social-emotional cognition. Reversible lesions produced by intracerebral injection of agents transiently blocking neural activity may constitute an invaluable tool in this new endeavour. As a first step, a preliminary report indicates that unilateral $GABA_A$ receptor blockade of the amygdala suffices to produce a temporary breakdown of dyadic social interactions (Málková, Barrow, Lower, & Gale, 2003).

The primate orbital frontal cortex and social-emotional cognition

In reviewing the literature on prefrontal cortex functions in nonhuman primates, it is clear that much more emphasis has been placed on cognitive aspects of behaviour, learning and memory, and attention, with far less interest in the prefrontal cortex involvement in social aspects of behaviour.

The orbital frontal cortex and social behaviour

In one of the first studies, Butter and colleagues (1968, 1970) examined the effects of orbital frontal lesions on aversive and aggressive reactions when the animals were exposed to an experimenter's stare. These lesions yielded a transitory increase in avoidance responses associated with a more persistent decrease in aggressive behaviours. In addition, these changes in emotional responses seemed more evident when the cortical damage was centred within the posteromedial sector of the orbital frontal cortex (the sector densely interconnected with the amygdala) and occurred more predominantly in some situations than in others. Interestingly, as indicated for amygdala lesions, these authors clearly cautioned readers against using an overgeneralization in the description of the frontal lesion effects (that is, tameness or placidity) since these lesions produce a variety of different changes depending on the particular behavioural response investigated, on the situation during which the behavioural response is initiated, and on the animals' species, gender, and age (Peters & Ploog, 1976; Raleigh, Steklis, Ervin, Kling, & McGuire, 1979). Butter and Snyder (1972) also observed monkeys' agonistic behaviour before and after receiving orbital frontal lesions, when they were introduced singly into an established group of four normal male monkeys. Before surgery, the to-be operated animals, being older and heavier than the four members of the group, always rapidly acquired a dominant hierarchical status. Immediately after the orbital frontal lesions, when the operated monkeys were reintroduced in the group, they exhibited a higher degree of aggressivity, and initially achieved the top position. However, since this reintroduction procedure was repeated every 2 months, the authors were also able to observe that with time the operated monkeys eventually lost their ability to reclaim their dominant status. Thus, high levels of aggression in monkeys with orbital frontal lesions appear to progressively result in a loss of dominant status.

While these earlier studies were carried out in a laboratory setting, it is possible that different behavioural outcomes might follow lesions of the orbital frontal cortex if the animals were observed in a more naturalistic situation resembling their natural habitat. Such a study was carried out on a well-known colony of rhesus monkeys on the island of Cayo Santiago (Puerto Rico) by Franzen and Myers (1973) and Myers and colleagues (1973). Social behaviour was investigated in groups of free-ranging monkeys before and after several members of each group had received either a frontal lobotomy that included the anterior sector of the orbital frontal cortex or a sham operation. Monkeys with frontal lesions exhibited a generalized reduction in behavioural activities that tend to maintain social bonds, such as grooming, huddling, near-body contact, and socially communicative facial, vocal, and postural actions. Coincident with these behavioural changes appeared a seeming loss of social awareness demonstrated by inappropriate advances and interactions with other group members. Although most of the behavioural deficits were permanent, and normal behaviours failed to reappear in the animals' repertoire, other emotional changes, such as increased fear grimaces, were only transitory and slowly decreased with time. Thus, taken together, the results suggest that the orbital frontal cortex plays a critical role in the control and regulation of social behaviour in the primate. The ultimate question that needs to be addressed, however, is what are the processes that underlie these dramatic social changes. The orbital frontal cortex has been implicated in many different functions, including the processing of facial cues and the modulation of responses based on changes in reinforcement contingencies (for review, see Zald & Kim, 1996), that if disrupted could result in striking changes in social-emotional behaviour.

The orbital frontal cortex involvement in the processing of facial cues

Recent electrophysiological studies in monkey behaviour have reported that both the inferior lateral convexity of the prefrontal cortex and the orbitofrontal cortex comprise neurons that selectively respond to faces (Klopp, Marinkovic, Chauvel, Nenov, & Halgren, 2000; O'Scalaidhe, Wilson, & Goldman-Rakic, 1997; Rolls, 1990, 1994; Wilson, O'Scalaidhe, & Goldman-Rakic, 1993). Thus, the orbital frontal cortex, like the amygdala, seems to detect and interpret facial movements, body postures, and gestures that provide important information for the production and modulation of appropriate social and emotional responses to other individuals.

The orbital frontal cortex involvement in the control of response selection

Like the amygdala, the orbital frontal cortex appears of little importance for identifying the reward value (significance or valence) of stimuli, but rather is involved in correcting behavioural responses when the reward values of stimuli have changed. In one of the first studies investigating oral tendencies after orbital frontal lesions, Butter and colleagues (1969) demonstrated that these lesions enhanced the animal's selection and assessment of reinforcement value of a nonfood item but did not alter their preference behaviour. Interestingly, several behavioural studies in monkeys suggest that the orbital frontal cortex is critical for the control of response selection to ensure the best potential outcomes in a given situation. Thus, monkeys with damage to the orbital frontal cortex continue to respond in the no-go trials of go/no-go task performance (Iversen & Mishkin, 1970), and continue to respond to an object that is no longer rewarded in object reversal and extinction tasks (Butter & Snyder, 1972; Dias, Robbins, & Roberts, 1996; Jones & Mishkin, 1972; Meunier, Bachevalier, & Mishkin, 1997; Rolls, Hornak, Wade, & McGrath, 1994). Similar findings were obtained in a recent disconnection study using a reinforcer devaluation procedure (Baxter, Parker, Lindner, Izquierdo, & Murray, 2000). Monkeys received two successive surgical interventions and were tested in a reinforcer devaluation task prior to and after the second surgical procedure. One group of monkeys first received a unilateral lesion of the amygdala and then removal of the orbital frontal cortex in the contralateral hemisphere, together with a forebrain commissurotomy. The second group of monkeys first received the unilateral orbital frontal lesions and commissurotomy, and then a contralateral amygdalectomy. In the devaluation task, the monkeys were first trained to learn a series of 60 object pairs in which the rewarded object of each pair was associated with one of two preferred food items. They were then given four critical test sessions consisting of choices between pairs of the 30 positive objects of the discrimination task. Two of the critical sessions occurred after having satiated the monkeys with one of the food items, whereas the other two were not preceded by satiation of the animal. The later sessions provided a choice behaviour baseline for each monkey. Thus, the two sessions given just after satiation challenged the monkey to make adaptive responses to compensate for the altered value of the outcome. Following the first operation, all operated monkeys, like normal control animals, tended to avoid choosing objects that were paired with the devalued (satiated) food item compared with their own choice behaviour during the baseline sessions. This normal behavioural tendency for avoiding the objects associated with the satiated food item was drastically reduced after the second surgical procedure. This demonstrates that cooperative interaction between the amygdala and orbital frontal cortex is critical for making choices associated with the best outcomes. Interestingly, preliminary data (Bachevalier & Machado, 2001) indicate that, in the reinforcer devaluation paradigm devoid of intermediate object mentioned above (see section entitled *The amygdala proper and social-emotional cognition: recent studies*), monkeys with orbital ablations, unlike those with amygdala neurotoxic lesions, keep failing to react to satiation. This dissociation strengthens the idea that it is the orbital cortex, rather than the amygdala, which is chiefly responsible for rapid, flexible re-evaluation of changing reward value.

The role of the orbital frontal cortex in modulating goal-directed behaviour in response to changing stimulus–reward contingencies is also supported by electrophysiological recording of monkeys. Thus, in the extinction task, orbital frontal neurons have been shown to respond immediately after a response was made to a visual stimulus which had previously been associated with reward, and, in the object-reversal task, immediately after the monkey has responded to the previously rewarded visual stimulus, but has obtained punishment rather than reward (Thorpe, Rolls, & Maddison, 1983). These neural responses thus occur when expected rewards were omitted in certain situations. Accordingly, taste-related activity in orbital frontal neurons was found to efficiently reflect changes in reward value, being, in particular, abolished by satiety (Rolls, 2000). Furthermore, Schultz and colleagues (Schultz, Tremblay, & Hollerman, 2000) showed that orbital frontal neurons displayed three principal forms of reward-related activity during the performance of delayed-response tasks, namely, responses to reward-predicting instructions, activation during the expectation period immediately preceding reward, and responses following reward. These activations discriminated between different rewards, often on the basis of the animal's preferences. Thus, the failure to respond normally after damage to the orbital frontal cortex by adapting behaviour when reinforcers have changed may be a fundamental deficit that underlies impulsiveness, disinhibition, misinterpretation of others' moods, and inadequate self-regulation of social-emotional behaviour.

Other cortical areas and social-emotional cognition

The temporopolar and anterior cingulate cortex are among the brain regions that are the most intimately interconnected with the amygdala and orbital frontal cortex. This anatomical proximity suggests a close functional relationship which has been little studied in monkey research. Thus, the following paragraphs will be dedicated to a brief overview of the few studies that have reported impairments in emotion and social behaviour following damage involving either the temporopolar or the anterior cingulate region.

The temporopolar cortex

To date, there are no observations on socioaffective changes after lesions involving exclusively the temporopolar cortex. Nevertheless, in a few studies in which this area was damaged together with more lateral temporal cortical areas, but in which the amygdala was left intact, changes in social behaviour and affect were noted (Akert, Gruesen, Woolsey, & Meyer, 1961; Myers, 1958, 1975; Myers & Swett, 1970). The monkeys with such lesions displayed all symptoms of the Klüver–Bucy syndrome (see above). They also showed abnormal social interactions as well as a lack of vocal and facial communications. Those operated animals that were released in the field never rejoined their social group, although there was no evidence that they were rejected by their peers. When attacked by strangers, they displayed no aggressive responses. Conversely, bilateral lesions of temporal visual areas located more posteriorly, but which spared the temporopolar area, resulted in no changes in social behaviour. Thus, this pattern of results indicates that the behavioural deficits in socioaffective behaviour following anterior temporal lesions are dependent on rostral temporal cortical removal and can occur without incidental damage to the medial temporal lobe structures, such as the amygdala. In a more recent study, Kling and colleagues (1993) used microdialysis to investigate neurochemical changes in the amygdala and hypothalamus after bilateral lesions of the temporal pole area in monkeys. The results indicated that, after the lesions, the animals displayed many of the symptoms described in the Klüver–Bucy syndrome, that is, loss of fear, hyperorality, loss of social rank, and social withdrawal. In addition, there were concomitant neurochemical changes observed in the amygdala and hypothalamus. In the amygdala, levels of dopamine (DA) metabolites, 5-hydroxytriptamine (5-HIAA), glutamate, and aspartate decreased, but levels of norepinephrine (NE) increased. Similar neurochemical changes were also noted in the hypothalamus, except for the decrease in DA. The authors concluded that the profound socioemotional changes displayed by animals with temporopolar cortex lesion may have in fact resulted from partial deafferentation of the amygdala from the temporopolar cortex. Thus, although further investigation of the specific role played by the temporopolar region is clearly needed, this region does appear to contribute to the maintenance of affiliative behaviour and emotions, either by itself or in conjunction with the amygdala and orbital frontal cortex.

The anterior cingulate cortex

The effects of anterior cingulate lesions on social bondings have been conflicting. Bilateral damage to this cortical area in monkeys has been associated with transient behavioural changes, such as increased tameness, lack of social sense (Glees, Cole, Whitty, & Cairns, 1950; Kennard, 1955; Pechtel, MacAvoy, Levitt, Kling, & Masserman, 1958; Smith, 1944; Ward, 1948), and loss of fear of humans (Mirsky, 1960; Mirsky, Rosvold, & Pribram, 1957), although no changes in social behaviour were reported by others (Myers, 1975; Pribram & Fulton, 1954). A transient increase of vocalizations has also been associated with bilateral anterior cingulotomy in monkeys (Jürgens, 1982; Kennard, 1955; Ploog, 1986; Smith, 1944). This difference in results is not surprising given the heterogeneity of cortical areas contained in the anterior cingulate cortex and their respective functions. A more recent study assessed the effects of the bilateral anterior cingulate cortex, including the subcallosal cortex (Hadland, Rushworth, Gaffan, & Passingham, 2003). Operated monkeys showed a decrease in social interactions and vocalizations, indicating that the cingulate cortex clearly has a role in the regulation of affiliative behaviour. In addition, electrical stimulation of the anterior cingulate cortex is known to produce autonomic effects similar to the spontaneous vegetative correlates of emotion, that is, changes in blood pressure and heart rate, respiratory arrest, dilation of the pupils and piloerection (Dunsmore & Lennox, 1950; Kaada, Pribram, & Epstein, 1949; Showers, 1959; Smith, 1945; Ward, 1948). These autonomic effects lend further support to the hypothesis of an involvement of the cingulate gyrus in affective behaviour.

As compared to the temporopolar region, the organization and contribution of the anterior cingulate cortex to behaviour have received a great deal of attention in both experimental and human literature (for review, see Bush, Luu, & Posner, 2000; Devinsky et al., 1995). More specifically, the anterior cingulate cortex has been divided into two subcomponents; that is, an "affective" subdivision (areas 25 and 33, and rostral area 24) and a "cognitive" subdivision (caudal areas 24 and 32). The "cognitive" subdivision appears to mediate attention and executive functions, such as the detection of response conflict or errors via strong interconnections with the dorsolateral prefrontal cortex, parietal cortex, and premotor and supplementary motor areas. By contrast, the "affective" subdivision, which has connections with the limbic and paralimbic areas, appears to play a critical role in the assessment of the salience of emotional and motivational information, and could also regulate emotional responses during the monitoring of response conflict or errors (Dickman & Allen, 2000; Laurens, Ngan, Bates, Kiehl, & Liddle, 2003; Luu, Collins, & Tucker, 2000). Thus, the anterior cingulate cortex is part of a large complex of structures engaged in the assessment of the motivational content of internal and external stimuli, and it regulates context-dependent behaviour. Given the recent discovery that the anterior cingulate area can be divided into subregions with specific functions, it will be fruitful to initiate new behavioural lesion studies involving more restricted damage to each of these subregions to establish which subregion is important for the regulation of social behaviour. In the monkey, neurotoxic lesions or reversible inactivations of cingulate subdivisions will be mandatory tools in this endeavour because, like the amygdala, the cingulate cortex contains important contingents of fibres of passage coursing through the cingulum bundle. Indeed, extraneous transection of this bundle by aspiration or radiofrequency lesions has been shown to profoundly alter the outcome of cingulate damage in rodents (Aggleton, Neave, Nagle, & Sahgal, 1995; Meunier & Destrade, 1997).

Relevance of nonhuman primate data to human social-emotional cognition

On the basis of the evidence reviewed here, it would appear that the amygdala, orbital frontal cortex, temporopolar region, and anterior cingulate cortex constitute an anatomical interconnected system for the maintenance of affiliative bonds in nonhuman primates. Interestingly, a similar interconnected system appears to be operating in humans as well.

The amygdala and social-emotional cognition in humans

As reviewed by Halgren (1992) and Aggleton (1992), changes in emotional responses akin to those described in nonhuman primates have been found in humans with amygdala dysfunction, such as patients with viral encephalitis and those who received bilateral temporal resections as a treatment either for psychosis or for otherwise untreatable epileptic seizures (see also Adolphs et al., 1999; Broks et al., 1998; Schmolk & Squire, 2001). Recent case studies of patients with more restricted amygdala damage have reported inappropriate and irrational social behaviour and social disinhibition (Adolphs & Tranel, 2000; Broks et al., 1998; Nahm, Tranel, Damasio, & Damasio, 1993; Tranel & Hyman, 1990). In addition, when patients with bilateral amygdala damage were asked to make social judgements of approachability and trustworthiness when presented with faces of unfamiliar people (Adolphs, Tranel, & Damasio, 1998), they abnormally rated as trustworthy faces of people who were judged untrustworthy by control subjects. Interestingly, the deficit appeared to be even greater with the most negative ratings of unapproachable and untrustworthy-looking faces. Thus, amygdala lesions do trigger social disturbances in human patients reminiscent of those seen in monkeys (for review, see Adolphs & Tranel, 2000).

The orbital frontal cortex and social-emotional cognition in humans

The effects of orbital frontal lesions in monkeys are also in line with some of the most striking deficits reported after damage to this cortical area in humans. Thus, in humans, prefrontal damage lesions encroaching onto the orbital frontal sector result in dramatic emotional changes, such as euphoria, irresponsibility, and lack of affect (for review, see Damasio, 1994; Rolls, 1999). These patients also manifest impairment in real-life decision making, associated with changes in their autonomic responses (Bechara, Damasio, Damasio, & Anderson, 1994) and in the ability to generate expectations of others' negative emotional reactions (Blair & Cipolotti, 2000). Damage to the orbital frontal cortex has also been associated with a reduction in the production of facial expressions of emotions and in the recognition of emotional expression from the face, voice, or gesture (Damasio, Tranel, & Damasio, 1990; Hornak, Rolls, & Wade, 1996; Kolb & Taylor, 1981, 1990; Ross, Harney, Delacosta-Utsamsing, & Ourdy, 1981; Ross & Mesulam, 1979). In addition, as in monkeys, orbital frontal neurons in humans are selectively activated by faces (Klopp et al., 2000). Finally, recent neuroimaging studies have indicated that activation of the left orbital frontal cortex occurs in humans listening to stories including both intentional or unintentional violations of social norms (Berthoz, Armony, Blair, & Dolan, 2002).

Other cortical areas and social-emotional cognition in humans

The temporopolar region has also been linked to social-emotional behaviour in humans (for review, see Dupont, 2002). For example, activation of the left temporopolar region has been found in healthy volunteers performing face-recognition tasks, whereas activation of the right temporopolar region has been reported when normal volunteers processed stories with emotional and affective content (Beauregard, Chertkow, Bub, Murtha, Dixon, & Evans, 1997). In addition, direct electrical stimulation of the temporal pole in patients with drug-resistant temporal lobe epilepsy elicits psychic, viscerosensitive, autonomic, and visceromotor responses (Ostrowsky, Desestret, Ryvlin, Coste, & Mauguière, 2002). Similarly, rostral anterior cingulate cortex activation has generally been found when human subjects view emotionally arousing images (Blair, Morris, Frith, Perrett, & Dolan, 1999; Lane, Chua, & Dolan, 1999; Whalen et al., 1998), engage in anxious situations (Ploghaus et al., 1999), or make attributions about the thoughts and beliefs of others (Frith & Frith, 1999; Gallagher, Happe, Brunswick, Fletcher, Frith, & Frith, 2000).

Thus, the amygdala, orbital frontal cortex, temporopolar region, and anterior cingulate cortex appear to be part also of an interconnected system for the establishment and maintenance of affiliative bonds in humans. The critical problem that remains is the discovery of the specific neural mechanisms by which each of these brain structures mediates social-emotional cognition in primates.

Conclusion

The review presented above focuses on a circuit linking the amygdala, orbital frontal cortex, temporopolar polar cortex, and anterior cingulate cortex in nonhuman primates that appears to be critical for social-emotional cognition. However, it is clear that the regulation of social cognition is orchestrated by a multitude of interconnected structures, including other structures that have not been discussed here. The complexity of this neural system shows that studies of nonhuman primates will be needed to further our understanding of the neural processes subserving social cognition. Because of the many similarities in the ways social signals are perceived and modulated across primate species, research in monkeys and humans should proceed in parallel, each informing and complementing the other with theoretical and empirical contributions. Thus, we stress the urgent need to initiate joint clinical (human) and animal research explorations, in order to specify the contribution of the amygdala and other related brain regions to the regulation of well-adapted social behaviour. These clinical and experimental studies will require multiple levels of analysis (brain, behaviour, genetic, and environmental factors), given that well-adapted social skills are the result of a dynamic process linking neural structures with environmental influences and one's own self-regulatory activity across life. Such a multidisciplinary research approach has the potential to revise and expand our current understanding of brain structures linked to basic behavioural processes, such as social cognition and social-emotional self-regulation. We believe that it also may offer a new foundation for determining the neuropathologic bases of several psychopathologies in humans and, ultimately, for developing therapeutic tools to alleviate these disorders (Bachevalier & Loveland, 2003; Machado & Bachevalier, 2003).

Acknowledgements

The research described in this chapter was supported in part by grants (MH58846 (NIMH), HD35471 (NICHD) and the National Alliance for Autism Research) to J.B. and a grant from the Centre National de la Recherche Scientifique to M.M. We are grateful to Christopher J. Machado for valuable comments on an earlier version of this chapter.

References

Adolphs, R. (2001). The neurobiology of social cognition. *Current Opinion in Neurobiology, 11*, 231–239.

Adolphs, R., & Tranel, D. (2000). Emotion, recognition, and the human amygdala. In J. P. Aggleton (Ed.), *The amygdala: A functional analysis* (2nd ed., pp. 587–630). New York: Oxford University Press.

Adolphs, R., Tranel, D., & Damasio, A. R. (1998). The human amygdala in social judgement. *Nature, 393*, 470–474.

Adolphs, R., Tranel, D., Hamann, S., Young, A. W., Calder, A. J., Phelps, E. A., et al. (1999). Recognition of facial emotion in nine individuals with bilateral amygdala damage. *Neuropsychologia, 37*, 1111–1117.

Aggleton, J. P. (1992). The functional effects of amygdala lesions in humans: A comparison with findings from monkeys. In J. P. Aggleton (Ed.), *The amygdala: Neurobiological aspects of emotion, memory, and mental dysfunction* (pp. 485–503). New York: Wiley-Liss.

Aggleton, J. P., Neave, N., Nagle, S., & Sahgal, A. (1995). A comparison of the effects of medial prefrontal, cingulate cortex, and cingulum bundle lesions on tests of spatial memory: Evidence of a double dissociation between frontal and cingulum bundle contributions. *Journal of Neuroscience, 15*, 7270–7281.

Aggleton, J. P., & Passingham, R. E. (1981). Syndrome produced by lesions of the amygdala in monkeys (*Macaca mulatta*). *Journal of Comparative and Physiological Psychology, 95*, 961–977.

Aggleton, J. P., & Passingham, R. E. (1982). An assessment of the reinforcing properties of foods after amygdaloid lesions in the rhesus monkey. *Journal of Comparative and Physiological Psychology, 96*, 71–77.

Akert, K., Gruesen, R. A., Woolsey, C. N., & Meyer, D. R. (1961). Klüver–Bucy syndrome in monkeys with neocortical ablations of temporal lobe. *Brain, 84*, 480–497.

Amaral, D. G. (1992). Anatomical organization of the primate amygdaloid complex. In J. P. Aggleton (Ed.), *The amygdala: Neurobiological aspects of emotion, memory, and mental dysfunction* (pp. 1–66). New York: Wiley-Liss.

Bachevalier, J., & Loveland, K. (2003). Early orbitofrontal-limbic dysfunction and autism. In D. Ciccchetti & E. F. Walker (Eds.), *Neurodevelopmental mechanisms in the genesis and epigenesis of psychopathology* (pp. 215–236). Cambridge: Cambridge University Press.

Bachevalier, J., & Machado, C. J. (2001). Food choice strategies are altered differently by amygdala and orbital frontal cortex lesions in macaques. *Society for Neuroscience Abstract, 27*, online retrieval 2003.

Bachevalier, J., Meunier, M., Lu, M., & Ungerleider, L. G. (1997). Thalamic and temporal cortex input to medial prefrontal cortex in rhesus monkeys. *Experimental Brain Research, 115*, 430–444.

Baleydier, C., & Mauguière, F. (1980). The duality of the cingulate cortex in monkey: Neuroanatomical study and functional hypothesis. *Brain, 103*, 525–554.

Barbas, H. (1993). Organization of cortical afferent input to orbitofrontal areas in the rhesus monkey. *Neuroscience, 56*, 841–864.

Barbas, H. (1995). Anatomic basis of cognitive-emotional interactions in the primate prefrontal cortex. *Neuroscience and Biobehavioral Reviews, 19*, 499–510.

Barbas, H. (2000). Connections underlying the synthesis of cognition, memory and emotion in primate prefrontal cortices. *Brain Research Bulletin, 52*, 158–165.

Baron-Cohen, S., Ring, H. A., Wheelwright, S., Bullmore, E. T., Brammer, M. J., Simmons, A., et al. (1999). Social intelligence in the normal and autistic brain: An fMRI study. *European Journal of Neuroscience, 11*, 1891–1898.

Barris, R. W., & Schuman, H. R. (1953). Bilateral anterior cingulate gyrus lesions: Syndrome of the anterior cingulate gyri. *Neurology, 3*, 44–52.

Baxter, M. G., & Murray, E. A. (2000). Reinterpreting the behavioural effects of amygdala lesions in non-human primates. In J. P. Aggleton (Ed.), *The amygdala: A functional analysis* (2nd ed., pp. 545–568). New York: Oxford University Press.

Baxter, M. G., & Murray, E. A. (2002). The amygdala and reward. *Nature Neuroscience Review, 3*, 563–573.

Baxter, M. G., Parker, A., Lindner, C. C. C., Izquierdo, A. D., & Murray, E. A. (2000). Control response selection by reinforcer value requires interaction of amygdala and orbital prefrontal cortex. *Journal of Neuroscience, 20*, 4311–4319.

Baxter, M. G., Saunders, R. C., & Murray, E. A. (1998). Aspiration lesions of the amygdala interrupt connections between prefrontal cortex and temporal cortex in rhesus monkeys. *Society for Neuroscience Abstract, 24*, 1905.

Baylis, L. L., Rolls, E. T., & Leonard, C. M. (1985). Selectivity between faces in the responses of a population of neurons in the cortex in the superior temporal sulcus of the monkey. *Brain Research, 342*, 91–102.

Beauregard, M., Chertkow, H., Bub, D., Murtha, S., Dixon, R., & Evans, A. (1997). The neural substrates of concrete, abstract and emotional word lexica: A positron emission tomography study. *Journal of Cognitive Neuroscience, 9*, 441–461.

Bechara, A., Damasio, A. R., Damasio, H., & Anderson, S. W. (1994). Insensitivity to future consequences following damage to human prefrontal cortex. *Cognition, 50*, 7–15.

Benca, R. M., Obermeyer, W. H., Shelton, S. E., Droster, J., & Kalin, N. H. (2000). Effects of amygdala lesions on sleep in rhesus monkeys. *Brain Research, 879*, 130–138.

Berthoz, S., Armony, J. L., Blair, R. J. R., & Dolan, R. J. (2002). An fMRI study of intentional and unintentional (embarrassing) violations of social norms. *Brain, 125*, 1696–1708.

Blair, R. J. R., & Cipolotti, L. (2000). Impaired social response reversal: A case of acquired sociopathy. *Brain, 123*, 1122–1141.

Blair, R. J., Morris, J. S., Frith, C. D., Perrett, D. I., & Dolan, R. J. (1999). Dissociable neural responses to facial expressions of sadness and anger. *Brain, 122*, 883–893.

Broks, P., Young, A. W., Maratos, E. J., Coffey, P. J., Calder, A. J., Isaac, C. L., et al. (1998). Face processing impairments after encephalitis: Amygdala damage and recognition of fear. *Neuropsychologia, 36*, 59–70.

Brothers, L. (1989). A biological perspective on empathy. *American Journal of Psychiatry, 146*, 10–19.

Brothers, L. (1995). Neurophysiology of the perception of intention by primates. In M. S. Gazzaniga (Ed.), *The cognitive neurosciences* (pp. 1107–1117). Cambridge, MA: MIT Press.

Brothers, L., Ring, B., & Kling, A. (1990). Response of neurons in the macaque amygdala to complex social stimuli. *Behavioural Brain Research, 41*, 199–213.

Brown, S., & Schafer, A. (1888). An investigation into the functions of the occipital and temporal lobes of the monkey's brain. *Philosophical Transactions of the Royal Society of London. Series B: Biological Sciences, 179*, 303–327.

Bush, G., Luu, P., & Posner, M. I. (2000). Cognitive and emotional influences in anterior cingulate cortex. *Trends in Cognitive Sciences, 4*, 215–222.

Butter, C. M., McDonald, J. A., & Snyder, D. R. (1969). Orality, preference behavior, and reinforcement value of nonfood object in monkeys with orbital frontal lesions. *Science, 164*, 1306–1307.

Butter, C. M., Mishkin, M., & Mirsky, A. F. (1968). Emotional responses towards humans in monkeys with selective frontal lesions. *Physiology and Behavior, 3*, 213–215.

Butter, C. M., & Snyder, D. R. (1972). Alternations in aversive and aggressive behaviors following orbital frontal lesions in rhesus monkeys. *Acta Neurobiologica Experimentalis, 32*, 525–565.

Butter, C. M., Snyder, D. R., & McDonald, J. A. (1970). Effects of orbital frontal lesions on aversive and aggressive behaviors in rhesus monkeys. *Journal of Comparative and Physiological Psychology, 72*, 132–144.

Byrne, R., & Whiten, A. (1988). *Machiavellian intelligence: Social expertise and the evolution of intellect in monkeys, apes, and humans.* Oxford: Clarendon Press.

Carmichael, S. T., & Price, J. L. (1994). Architectonic subdivision of the orbital and medial prefrontal cortex in the macaque monkey. *Journal of Comparative Neurology, 15*, 366–402.

Cavada, C., Company, T., Tejedor, J., Cruz-Rizzolo, R. J., & Reinoso-Suarez, F. (2000). The anatomical connections of the macaque monkey orbitofrontal cortex. A review. *Cerebral Cortex, 10*, 220–242.

Charbadès, S., Kahane, P., Minotti, L., Hoffmann, D., & Benabid, A.-L. (2002). Anatomy of the temporal pole region. *Epileptic Disorders (Suppl. 1), 4*, 9–16.

Cheney, D. L., & Seyfarth, R. M. (1990). *How monkeys see the world.* Chicago: University of Chicago Press.

Damasio, A. R. (1994). *Descartes' error.* New York: Avon Press.

Damasio, A. R., Tranel, D., & Damasio, H. (1990). Individuals with sociopathic behavior caused by frontal damage fail to respond autonomically to social stimuli. *Behavioral Brain Research, 41*, 81–94.

Desimone, R., Albright, T. D., Gross, C. G., & Bruce, C. (1984). Stimulus-selective properties of inferior temporal neurons in the macaque. *Journal of Neuroscience, 4*, 2051–2062.

Devinsky, O., Morrell, M. J., & Vogt, B. A. (1995). Contributions of anterior cingulate cortex to behaviour. *Brain, 118*, 279–306.

DeWaal, F. (1989). *Peacemaking among primates.* Cambridge, MA: Harvard University Press.

Dias, R., Robbins, T. W., & Roberts, A. C. (1996). Dissociation in prefrontal cortex of affective and attentional shifts. *Nature, 380*, 69–72.

Dickman, Z. V., & Allen, J. J. (2000). Error monitoring during reward and avoidance learning in high- and low-socialized individuals. *Psychophysiology, 37,* 43–54.

Dombrowski, S. M., Hilgetag, C. C., & Barbas, H. (2001). Quantitative architecture distinguishes prefrontal cortical systems in the rhesus monkey. *Cerebral Cortex, 11,* 975–988.

Downer, J. L. de C. (1961). Changes in visual gnostic functions and emotional behavior following unilateral temporal pole damage in the split brain monkey. *Nature, 191,* 50–51.

Dunsmore, R. H., & Lennox, M. A. (1950). Stimulation and strychninization of supracallosal anterior cingulate gyrus. *Journal of Neurophysiology, 13,* 207–214.

Dupont, S. (2002). Investigating temporal pole function by functional imaging. *Epileptic Disorders (Suppl. 1), 4,* 17–22.

Easton, A., & Gaffan, D. (2000). Amygdala and the memory of reward: The importance of fibers of passage from the basal forebrain. In J. P. Aggleton (Ed.), *The amygdala: A functional analysis* (2nd ed., pp. 545–568). New York: Oxford University Press.

Emery, N. J., & Amaral, D. G. (1999). The role of the amygdala in primate social cognition. In R. D. Lane & L. Nadel (Eds.), *Cognitive neuroscience of emotion* (pp. 156–191). Oxford: Oxford University Press.

Emery, N. J., Capitanio, J. P., Mason, W. A., Machado, C. J., Mendoza, S. P., & Amaral, D. G. (2001). The effects of bilateral lesions of the amygdala on dyadic social interactions in rhesus monkeys (*Macaca mulatta*). *Behavioral Neuroscience, 115,* 515–544.

Everitt, B. J., & Robbins, T. W. (1992). Amygdala-ventral striatal interactions and reward-related processes. In J. P. Aggleton (Ed.), *The amygdala: Neurobiological aspects of emotion, memory, and mental dysfunction* (pp. 401–429). New York: Wiley-Liss.

Franzen, E. A., & Myers, R. E. (1973). Neural control of social behavior: Prefrontal and anterior temporal cortex. *Neuropsychologia, 11,* 141–157.

Frith, C. D., & Frith, U. (1999). Interacting minds: A biological basis. *Science, 286,* 1692–1695.

Gallagher, H. L., Happe, F., Burnswick, N., Fletcher, P. C., Frith, U., & Frith, C. D. (2000). Reading the mind in cartoons and stories: An fMRI study of theory of mind in verbal and non-verbal tasks. *Neuropsychologia, 38,* 11–21.

Ghashghaei, H. T., & Barbas, H. (2002). Pathways for emotion: Interactions of prefrontal and anterior temporal pathways in the amygdala of the rhesus monkeys. *Neuroscience, 115,* 1261–1279.

Glees, P., Cole, J., Whitty, C. W. M., & Cairns, H. (1950). The effects of lesions of the cingular gyrus and adjacent areas in monkeys. *Journal of Neurology, Neurosurgery, and Psychiatry, 13,* 178–190.

Gloor, P. (1997). *The temporal lobe and limbic system.* Oxford: Oxford University Press.

Goulet, S., Doré, F. Y., & Murray, E. A. (1998). Aspiration lesions of the amygdala disrupt the rhinal corticothalamic projection system in rhesus monkey. *Experimental Brain Research, 119,* 131–140.

Gross, C. G. (1994). How inferior temporal cortex became a visual area. *Cerebral Cortex, 4,* 455–469.

Hadland, K. A., Rushworth, M. F. S., Gaffan, D., & Passingham, R. E. (2003). The effect of cingulate lesions on social behaviour and emotion. *Neuropsychologia, 41,* 919–931.

Halgren, E. (1992). Emotional neurophysiology of the amygdala within the context of human cognition. In J. P. Aggleton (Ed.), *The amygdala: Neurobiological aspects of emotion, memory, and mental dysfunction* (pp. 191–228). New York: Wiley-Liss.

Hasselmo, M. E., Rolls, E. T., & Baylis, G. C. (1989a). The role of expression and identity in the face-selective responses of neurons in the temporal visual cortex of the monkey. *Behavioural Brain Research, 32*, 203–218.

Hasselmo, M. E., Rolls, E. T., Baylis, G. C., & Nalwa, V. (1989b). Object-centered encoding by face-receptive neurons in the cortex in the superior temporal sulcus of the monkey. *Experimental Brain Research, 75*, 417–429.

Horel, J. A., Keating, E. G., & Misantone, L. J. (1975). Partial Klüver–Bucy syndrome produced by destroying temporal neocortex and amygdala. *Brain Research, 94*, 347–359.

Horel, J. A., & Misantone, L. J. (1974). The Klüver–Bucy syndrome produced by partial isolation of the temporal lobe. *Experimental Neurology, 42*, 101–112.

Hornak, J., Rolls, E. T., & Wade, D. (1996). Face and voice expression identification in patients with emotional and behavioural changes following ventral frontal lobe damage. *Neuropsychologia, 34*, 247–261.

Iversen, S., & Mishkin, M. (1970). Perseverative interference in monkeys following selective lesions of the inferior prefrontal convexity. *Experimental Brain Research, 11*, 376–386.

Iwai, E., Nishio, T., & Yamaguchi, K. (1986). Neuropsychological basis of a K–B sign in Klüver–Bucy syndrome produced following total removal of inferotemporal cortex of macaque monkeys. In Y. Oomura (Ed.), *Emotion—neural and chemical control* (pp. 299–311). Tokyo: Japan Scientific Society Press.

Jones, B., & Mishkin, M. (1972). Limbic lesions and the problem of stimulus–reinforcement associations. *Experimental Neurology, 36*, 362–377.

Jürgens, U. (1982). Amygdalar vocalization pathways in the squirrel monkey. *Brain Research, 241*, 189–196.

Jürgens, U., & Ploog, D. (1970). Cerebral representation of vocalization in the squirrel monkey. *Experimental Brain Research, 10*, 532–554.

Jürgens, U., & von Cramon, D. (1982). On the role of the anterior cingulate cortex in phonation: A case report. *Brain Language, 15*, 234–248.

Kaada, B., Pribram, K. H., & Epstein, J. (1949). Respiratory and vascular responses in monkeys from temporal pole, insula, orbital surface and cingulate gyrus. *Journal of Neurophysiology, 12*, 347–356.

Kalin, N. H., Shelton, S. E., Davidson, R. J., & Kelly, A. E. (2001). The primate amygdala mediates acute fear but not the behavioral and physiological components of anxious temperament. *Journal of Neuroscience, 21*, 2067–2074.

Kennard, M. A. (1955). The cingulate gyrus in relation to consciousness. *Journal of Nervous and Mental Diseases, 121*, 34–39.

Kling, A. S. (1972). Effects of amygdalectomy on social-affective behavior in nonhuman primates. In Y. Eleftheriou (Ed.), *The neurobiology of the amygdala* (pp. 511–537). New York: Plenum.

Kling, A. S., & Brothers, L. (1992). The amygdala and social behavior. In J. P. Aggleton (Ed.), *The amygdala: Neurobiological aspects of emotion, memory, and mental dysfunction* (pp. 353–377). New York: Wiley-Liss.

Kling, A. S., Lloyd, R. L., & Perryman, K. M. (1987). Slow wave changes in amygdala to visual, auditory, and social stimuli following lesions of the inferior temporal cortex in squirrel monkey (*Saimiri sciureus*). *Behavioral and Neural Biology, 47*, 54–72.

Kling, A. S., & Mass, R. (1974). Alterations of social behavior with neural lesions in nonhuman primates. In R. L. Holloway (Ed.), *Primate aggression, territoriality, and xenophobia* (pp. 361–386). New York: Academic Press.

Kling, A. S., & Steklis, H. D. (1976). A neural substrate for affiliative behavior in nonhuman primates. *Brain Behavior and Evolution, 13*, 216–238.

Kling, A. S., Steklis, H. D., & Deutsch, S. (1979). Radiotelemetered activity from the amygdala during social interactions in monkeys. *Experimental Neurology, 66*, 88–96.

Kling, A. S., Tachiki, K., & Lloyd, R. (1993). Neurochemical correlates of the Klüver–Bucy syndrome by *in vivo* microdialysis in monkey. *Behavioural Brain Research, 56*, 161–170.

Klopp, J., Marinkovic, K., Chauvel, P., Nenov, V., & Halgren, E. (2000). Early widespread cortical distribution of coherent fusiform face selective activity. *Human Brain Mapping, 11*, 286–293.

Klüver, H., & Bucy, P. (1938). An analysis of certain effects of bilateral temporal lobectomy in rhesus monkeys. *American Journal of Physiology, 5*, 33–54.

Klüver, H., & Bucy, P. (1939). Preliminary analysis of functioning of the temporal lobes in monkeys. *Archives of Neurology and Psychiatry, 42*, 979–1000.

Kolb, B., & Taylor, L. (1981). Effective behaviour in patients with localized cortical excisions: Role of lesion site and side. *Science, 214*, 89–91.

Kolb, B., & Taylor, L. (1990). Neocortical substrate of emotional behaviour. In N. L. Stein, B. Leventhal, & T. Trabasso (Eds.), *Psychological and biological approaches to emotion* (pp. 115–144). Hillsdale, NJ: Lawrence Erlbaum Associates, Inc.

Kondo, H., Saleem, K. S., & Price, J. L. (2003). Differential connections of the temporal pole with the orbital and medial prefrontal networks in macaque monkeys. *Journal of Comparative Neurology, 465*, 499–523.

Lane, R. D., Chua, P. M., & Dolan, R. J. (1999). Common effects of emotional valence, arousal and attention on neural activation during visual processing of pictures. *Neuropsychologia, 37*, 989–997.

Laurens, K. R., Ngan, E. T. C., Bates, A. T., Kiehl, K. A., & Liddle, P. F. (2003). Rostral anterior cingulate cortex dysfunction during error processing in schizophrenia. *Brain, 126*, 610–622.

Leonard, C. M., Rolls, E. T., Wilson, F. A. W., & Baylis, G. C. (1985). Neurons in the amygdala of the monkey with responses selective for faces. *Behavioural Brain Research, 15*, 159–176.

Lloyd, R. L., & Kling, A. S. (1991). Amygdaloid electrical activity in response to conspecific calls in squirrel monkeys (*S. sciureus*): Influence of environmental settings, cortical inputs and recording site. In J. O. Newman (Ed.), *Physiological control of mammalian vocalization*. New York: Plenum.

Luu, P., Collins, P., & Tucker, D. M. (2000). Mood, personality, and self-monitoring: Negative affect and emotionality in relation to frontal lobe mechanisms of error monitoring. *Journal of Experimental and Psychological Genetics, 129*, 43–60.

Machado, C. J., & Bachevalier, J. (2000). Selective lesions to the amygdala, hippocampus or orbital frontal cortex alter reactivity to a human intruder in monkeys. *Society for Neuroscience Abstract, 26*, on line retrieval 2003.

Machado, C., & Bachevalier, J. (2003). Nonhuman primate models of childhood psychopathology: The promise and the limitations. *Journal of Child Psychology and Psychiatry: Annual Research Review, 44*, 1–24.

MacLean, P. D. (1949). Psychosomatic disease and the "visceral brain": Recent developments bearing on the Papez theory of emotion. *Psychosomatic Medicine, 11*, 338–353.

Málková, L., Barrow, K. V., Lower, L. L., & Gale, K. (2003). Decreased social interactions in monkeys after unilateral blockade of $GABA_A$ receptors in the basolateral amygdala. *Annals of the New York Academy of Science, 985*, 540–541.

Málková, L., Gaffan, D., & Murray, E. A. (1997). Excitotoxic lesions of the amygdala fail to produce impairment in visual learning for auditory secondary reinforcement but interfere with reinforcer devaluation effects in rhesus monkeys. *Journal of Neuroscience, 17*, 6011–6020.

McGaugh, J. L., Ferry, B., Vazdarjanova, A., & Roozendaal, B. (2000). Amygdala: Role in modulation of memory storage. In J. P. Aggleton (Ed.), *The amygdala: A functional analysis* (2nd ed., pp. 391–424). New York: Oxford University Press.

Meunier, M., & Bachevalier, J. (2002). Comparison of emotional responses in monkeys with rhinal cortex and amygdala lesions. *Emotion, 2*, 147–161.

Meunier, M., Bachevalier, J., & Mishkin, M. (1997). Effects of orbital frontal and anterior cingulate lesions on object and spatial memory in rhesus monkeys. *Neuropsychologia, 35*, 999–1015.

Meunier, M., Bachevalier, J., Murray E. A., Málková, L., & Mishkin, M. (1999). Effects of aspiration *vs* neurotoxic lesions of the amygdala on emotional responses in monkeys. *European Journal of Neuroscience, 11*, 4403–4418.

Meunier, M., & Destrade, C. (1997). Effects of radiofrequency versus neurotoxic cingulate lesions on spatial reversal learning in mice. *Hippocampus, 7*, 355–360.

Mirsky, A. F. (1960). Studies of the effects of brain lesions on social behaviors in *Macaca mulatta*: Methodological and theoretical considerations. *Annals of the New York Academy of Science, 85*, 785–794.

Mirsky, A. F., Rosvold, H. E., & Pribram, K. H. (1957). Effects of cingulectomy on social behavior in monkeys. *Journal of Neurophysiology, 20*, 588–601.

Moran, M. A., Mufson, E. J., & Mesulam, M. M. (1987). Neural inputs into the temporopolar cortex of the rhesus monkey. *Journal of Comparative Neurology, 256*, 88–103.

Murray, E. A., Gaffan E. A., & Flint, R. W. Jr. (1996). Anterior rhinal cortex and amygdala: Dissociation of their contributions to memory and food preference in rhesus monkeys. *Behavioral Neuroscience, 112*, 1291–1303.

Myers, D. P. (1958). Some psychological determinants of sparing and loss following damage to the brain. In H. F. Harlow & C. N. Woolsey (Eds.), *Biological and biochemical bases of behavior* (pp. 173–192). Madison, WI: University of Wisconsin Press.

Myers, R. E. (1975). Neurology of social behavior and affect in primates: A study of prefrontal and anterior temporal cortex. In K. J. Zulch, O. Creutzfeldt, & G. C. Galbraith (Eds.), *Cerebral localization* (pp. 161–170). New York: Springer-Verlag.

Myers, R. E., & Swett, C. (1970). Social behavior deficits of free-ranging monkeys after anterior temporal cortex removal: A preliminary report. *Brain Research, 1*, 551–556.

Myers, R. E., Swett, C., & Miller, M. (1973). Loss of social group affinity following prefrontal lesions in free-ranging macaques. *Brain Research, 64*, 257–269.

Nahm, F. K. D., Tranel, D., Damasio, H., & Damasio, A. R. (1993). Cross-modal associations and the human amygdala. *Neuropsychologia, 31*, 727–744.

Nelson, E. E., Shelton, S. E., & Kalin, N. H. (2003). Individual differences in the response of naïve rhesus monkeys to snakes. *Emotion, 3*, 3–11.
Newman, J. D., & Bachevalier, J. (1997). Neonatal ablations of the amygdala and inferior temporal cortex alter the vocal response to social separation in rhesus macaques. *Brain Research, 758*, 180–186.
Ochsner, K. N., & Lieberman, M. D. (2001). The emergence of social cognitive neuroscience. *American Psychologist, 56*, 717–734.
Öhman, A., & Mineka, S. (2003). The malicious serpent: Snakes as a prototypical stimulus for an evolved module of fear. *Current Directions in Psychological Science, 12*, 5–9.
Öngür, D., & Price, J. L. (2000). The organization of networks within the orbital and medial prefrontal cortex of rats, monkeys and humans. *Cerebral Cortex, 10*, 206–219.
O'Scalaidhe, S. P. O., Wilson, F. A. W., & Goldman-Rakic, P. S. (1997). Areal segregation of face-processing neurons in prefrontal cortex. *Science, 278*, 1135–1138.
Ostrowsky, K., Desestret, V., Ryvlin, P., Coste, S., & Mauguière, F. (2002). Direct electrical stimulations of the temporal pole in human. *Epileptic Disorders* (Suppl. 1), *4*, 23–27.
Papez, J. W. (1937). A proposed mechanism of emotion. *Archives of Neurology and Psychiatry, 38*, 725–744.
Pechtel, C., MacAvoy, T., Levitt, M., Kling, A. S., & Masserman, J. H. (1958). The cingulates and behavior. *Journal of Nervous and Mental Diseases, 126*, 148–151.
Perrett, D. L., & Mistlin, A. J. (1990). Perception of facial characteristics by monkeys. In M. Berkeley & W. Stebbins (Eds.), *Comparative perception* (pp. 53–71). New York: Wiley.
Perrett, D. L., Rolls, E. T., & Caan, W. (1982). Visual neurons responsive to faces in the monkey temporal cortex. *Experimental Brain Research, 47*, 329–342.
Perrett, D. L., Smith, P. A. J., Potter, D. D., Mistlin, A. J., Head, A. S., Milner, A. D., et al. (1984). Neurones responsive to faces in the temporal cortex: Studies of functional organization, sensitivity to identity and relation to perception. *Human Neurobiology, 3*, 197–208.
Perrett, D. L., Smith, P. A. J., Potter, D. D., Mistlin, A. J., Head, A. S., Milner, A. D., et al. (1985). Visual cells in the temporal cortex sensitive to face view and gaze direction. *Proceedings of the Royal Society of London (Biology), 223*, 293–317.
Peters, M., & Ploog, D. (1976). Frontal lesions and social behavior in the squirrel monkey (*Saimiri*): A pilot study. *Acta Biologica Medicine Germani, 35*, 1317–1326.
Petrides, M. (1994). Frontal lobes and behaviour. *Current Opinion in Neurobiology, 4*, 207–211.
Petrides, M., & Pandya, D. N. (2002). Comparative cytoarchitectonic analysis of the human and the macaque ventrolateral prefrontal cortex and corticocortical connection patterns in the monkey. *European Journal of Neuroscience, 16*, 291–310.
Ploghaus, A., Tracey, I., Gati, J. S., Clare, S., Menon, R. S., Matthews, P. M., et al. (1999). Dissociating pain from its anticipation in the human brain. *Science, 284*, 1979–1981.
Ploog, D. (1986). Biological foundations of the vocal expressions of emotions. In R. Plutchik & H. Kellerman (Eds.), *Emotion: Theory, research, and experience* (Vol. 3, pp. 173–197). New York: Academic Press.
Plotnik, R. (1968). Changes in social behavior of squirrel monkeys after anterior temporal lobectomy. *Journal of Comparative Physiological Psychiatry, 66*, 369–372.

Pribram, K. H., & Fulton, J. F. (1954). An experimental critique of the effects of anterior cingulate ablations in monkey. *Brain, 77*, 34–44.

Raleigh, M. J., Steklis, H. D., Ervin, F. R., Kling, A. S., & McGuire, M. T. (1979). The effects of orbitofrontal lesions on the aggressive behavior of vervet monkeys (*Cercopithecus aethiops sabaeus*). *Experimental Neurology, 66*, 158–168.

Robinson, B. W. (1967). Vocalization evoked from forebrain in *Macaca mulatta*. *Physiology and Behavior, 2*, 345–354.

Rolls, E. T. (1986). A theory of emotion, and its application to understanding the neural basis of emotion. In Y. Oomura (Ed.), *Emotions* (pp. 325–344). Tokyo: Japan Scientific Society.

Rolls, E. T. (1994). A theory of emotion and consciousness, and its application to understanding the neural basis of emotion. In M. S. Gazzaniga (Ed.), *The cognitive neurosciences* (pp. 1091–1106). Cambridge, MA: MIT Press.

Rolls, E. T. (1999). *The Brain and Emotion*. Oxford: Oxford University Press.

Rolls, E. T. (2000). Neurophysiology and function of the primate amygdala, and the neural basis of emotion. In J. P. Aggleton (Ed.), *The amygdala: A functional analysis* (2nd ed, pp. 545–568). New York: Oxford University Press.

Rolls, E. T., Hornak, J., Wade, D., & McGrath, J. (1994). Emotion-related learning in patients with social and emotional changes associated with frontal lobe damage. *Journal of Neurology, Neurosurgery and Psychiatry, 57*, 1518–1524.

Ross, E. D., Harney, J. H., Delacoste-Utsamsing, C., & Ourdy, P. D. (1981). How the brain integrates affective and propositional language into a unified behavioral function. *Archives in Neurology, 38*, 745–748.

Ross, E. D., & Mesulam, M. M. (1979). Dominant language functions in the right hemisphere. *Archives in Neurology, 36*, 144–148.

Rosvold, H. E., Mirsky A. F., & Pribram, K. H. (1954). Influence of amygdalectomy on social behavior in monkeys. *Journal of Comparative and Physiological Psychology, 47*, 173–178.

Saunders, R. C., & Rosene, D. L. (1988). A comparison of the efferents of the amygdala and the hippocampal formation in the rhesus monkey. I. Convergence in the entorhinal, prorhinal, and perirhinal cortices. *Journal of Comparative Neurology, 271*, 153–184.

Saunders, R. C., Rosene, D. C., & Van Hoesen, G. W. (1988). Comparison of the efferents of the amygdala and the hippocampal formation in the rhesus monkey. II. Reciprocal and non-reciprocal connections. *Journal of Comparative Neurology, 271*, 185–207.

Schmolk, H., & Squire, L. R. (2001). Impaired perception of facial emotions following bilateral damage to the anterior temporal lobe. *Neuropsychology, 15*, 30–38.

Schreiner, L., & Kling, A. S. (1953). Behavioral changes following rhinencephalic injury in cat. *Journal of Neurophysiology, 16*, 643–659.

Schreiner, L., & Kling, A. S. (1956). Rhinencephalon and behavior. *Acta Neurovegetativa, 26*, 12–34.

Schultz, W., Tremblay, L., & Hollerman, J. R. (2000). Reward processing in primate orbitofrontal cortex and basal ganglia. *Cerebral Cortex, 10*, 272–284.

Scoville, W. B., & Milner, B. (1957). Loss of recent memory after bilateral hippocampal lesions. *Journal of Neurology, Neurosurgery, and Psychiatry, 20*, 11–21.

Selemon, L. D., & Goldman-Rakic, P. S. (1985). Longitudinal topography and interdigitation of corticostriatal projections in the rhesus monkey. *Journal of Neuroscience, 5*, 776–794.

Semendeferi, K., Armstrong, E., Schleicher, A., Zilles, K., & Van Hoesen, G. W. (1998). Limbic frontal cortex in hominoids: A comparative study of area 13. *American Journal of Physiological Anthropology, 106*, 129–155.

Showers, M. J. C. (1959). The cingulate gyrus: Additional motor area and cortical autonomic regulator. *Journal of Comparative Neurology, 112*, 231–301.

Smith, W. K. (1944). The results of ablation of the cingular region of the cerebral cortex. *Federation Proceedings, 3*, 42–43.

Steklis, H. D. (1998). Arthur S. Kling: A pioneer of the primate social brain. *American Journal of Primatology, 44*, 227–230.

Thorpe, S. J., Rolls, E. T., & Maddison, S. (1983). The orbitofrontal cortex: Neuronal activity in the behaving monkey. *Experimental Brain Research, 49*, 93–115.

Tranel, D., & Hyman, B. T. (1990). Neuropsychological correlates of bilateral amygdala damage. *Archives of Neurology, 47*, 349–355.

Vogt, B. A., Finch, D. M., & Olson, C. R. (1992). Functional heterogeneity in cingulate cortex: The anterior executive and posterior evaluative regions. *Cerebral Cortex, 2*, 435–443.

Vogt, B. A., Rosene, D. L., & Pandya, D. N. (1979). Thalamic and cortical afferents differentiate anterior from posterior cingulate cortex in the monkey. *Science, 204*, 205–207.

Ward, A. A. (1948). The cingular gyrus: Area 24. *Journal of Neurophysiology, 11*, 13–24.

Weiskrantz, L. (1956). Behavioral changes associated with ablation of the amygdaloid complex in monkeys. *Journal of Comparative and Physiological Psychology, 49*, 381–391.

Whalen, P. J., Bush, G., McNally, R. J., Wilhelm, S., McInerney, S. C., Jenike, M. A., et al. (1998). The emotional counting Stroop paradigm: A functional magnetic resonance imaging probe of the anterior cingulate affective division. *Biological Psychiatry, 44*, 1219–1228.

Wilson, F. A. W., O'Scalaidhe, S. P. O., & Goldman-Rakic, P. (1993). Dissociation of object and spatial processing domains in the primate prefrontal cortex. *Science, 260*, 1955–1958.

Yamane, S., Kaji, S., & Kawao, K. (1988). What facial features activate face neurons in the inferotemporal cortex of the monkey? *Experimental Brain Research, 73*, 209–214.

Zald, D. H., & Kim, S. W. (1996). Anatomy and function of the orbital frontal cortex. II. Function and relevance to obsessive-compulsive disorder. *Journal of Neuropsychiatry, 8*, 249–261.

Zola-Morgan, S., Squire, L. R., Alvarez-Royo, P., & Clower, R. P. (1991). Independence of memory function and emotional behavior: Separate contributions of the hippocampal formation and the amygdala. *Hippocampus, 1*, 207–220.

3 Behavioural flexibility, social learning, and the frontal cortex

Alexander Easton

Introduction

Humans, like all primates, are extremely social animals. The social context we are in is dependent on many interconnecting factors, many of which we learn to understand over the course of our lives. Understanding our own position in this social context, then, is extremely complicated and requires us to constantly follow the ever changing social group around us. Despite the complexity of the social context, however, we are adept at adapting to new and constantly changing social contexts, and our behaviour itself is modified by the social setting we find ourselves in, even though we may not be consciously aware of such changes in our behaviour.

In this chapter, I review the evidence that many aspects of social behaviour require "behavioural flexibility" (the ability to quickly and constantly modify our behaviour on the basis of an ever changing environment), and that many of the neural structures implicated in social behaviour are required to allow behavioural flexibility to occur. In particular, I will review a series of studies examining the role of the frontal cortex in a variety of tasks, which demonstrate its involvement in learning, only when the learning can not be performed by using fixed reward associations. The frontal cortex, then, and in particular the ventral prefrontal cortex, is crucial to normal adaptations to changing social contexts, precisely the sort of social impairments displayed in psychiatric disorders such as schizophrenia.

What is behavioural flexibility?

Events in day-to-day life rarely have exactly the same effect on an individual's behaviour if they recur. Many factors influence our responses to these events, such as our mood, or other events that happen simultaneously. In the same way, social context can modify our behaviour to events. A typical example might be our response to the telling of a joke. If it is a particularly funny joke, we will probably laugh in response to it. However, our response to the joke changes depending on the social context we are in. For example, if our new boss is the joke's teller, we may laugh a little harder and a little louder than we otherwise might in an attempt to impress. Alternatively, someone telling you the joke at a friend's funeral will probably mean you will not laugh at all, and may indeed be upset at the apparent inappropriateness. The important aspect of these three scenarios is that the joke has the very same inherent funniness in each situation. If our behaviour was simply a response to a stimulus of a given value, then we might imagine that the inherent value or "funniness" of the joke would lead to an identical response in every situation. This inflexibility in response, however, is clearly not the case. Rather, our behaviour appears highly adaptable, responding quickly and unconsciously to the social context we find ourselves in. Throughout this chapter, I will refer to this type of behavioural modification as *behavioural flexibility*.

Without behavioural flexibility, our social interactions would be severely limited. Social interactions typically rely on hierarchical structures within a group of individuals. People's position within the hierarchy then determines the behaviours they will express within that social context. However, other individuals may come or go from that particular social group, or a person may enter an entirely different social setting. In these conditions, that person's own position in the hierarchy will change. If one's position in the hierarchy changes, one's behaviour within that context should also change. This will mean different behavioural patterns appropriate to one's current social context. Behavioural flexibility allows precisely this sort of change in behaviour.

Although social psychology has provided many insights into the complexities of such behaviour in humans, human social behaviour is so complex, and is modulated by so many different (and often only partially understood) and interacting factors, that an understanding of this type of behavioural flexibility and its mechanisms would be difficult to achieve in these studies. However, primate societies provide a useful alternative. Primate societies are often complex, with a range of factors determining status and other things. However, the modulating factors (and the behaviours being exhibited) are often fewer and simpler than in human society. For example, behavioural studies in animals often take the form of an ethogram, in which exact behavioural patterns can be identified and recorded in a limited number of behaviour categories. To develop a comprehensive ethogram for human studies would be near impossible. Therefore, primates provide a useful model for understanding the mechanisms underlying social behaviour, and behavioural flexibility in humans. However, before we consider the investigation of behavioural flexibility in primates, we must demonstrate that such behavioural flexibility does indeed exist within the primate species we wish to study.

A recent series of experiments provided good evidence of such behavioural flexibility in a social context in macaque monkeys. Christine Drea and Kim Wallen carried out a series of studies examining how monkeys performed on a colour-discrimination task when tested as part of a large group. When the monkeys learnt the discrimination in a large group, in which both dominant and subordinate animals were present, the subordinate animals appeared to learn the discrimination at a slower rate than dominant animals (Drea & Wallen, 1999). However, when these animals were split into groups where animals were among others of their own social status (that is, typically dominant animals, or typically subordinate animals), all animals learned discriminations at a similar rate. This led Drea and Wallen to propose that the subordinate animals were "playing dumb". In the presence of many dominant animals, there is a distinct disadvantage to making correct responses and collecting food rewards, as the dominant animals will become aggressive in an attempt to get as much of the available food for themselves as possible. When the social context changes, however, to a group of animals of similar status, such competition becomes much less, and so behavioural responses are no longer inhibited, and the animals display the learning behaviour more readily. Such behaviour is a good example of behavioural flexibility in nonhuman primates, in that animals are making judgements about what behaviours are appropriate in a given social context. However, such behavioural flexibility might not be made on the basis of judgements about social context, but rather they could be influenced by stress levels. Subordinate animals might have substantially higher stress where dominant animals are present. Stress hormones are known to inhibit learning (Lupien & Lepage, 2001), and this might explain the poorer learning in this condition. Therefore, displays of behavioural flexibility in animals that cannot be explained simply by stress levels would be useful in helping to understand how such behavioural flexibility is modulated in humans.

One such example in birds is covered by Emery and Clayton (2001, Ch 5). There are clear examples in primates, too, particularly in the great apes. A series of studies has explored how chimpanzees understand each other's perceptions of the world, and this perception is measured by examining the changes in behaviour brought about by this understanding of the social environment. Two chimpanzees are placed in cages either side of a large test cage, which can be seen clearly from the individual cages. The dominance status of the chimpanzees is known before the start of the experiment, and one is labelled dominant, and the other subordinate. Food is then placed in the large cage, either in a location visible to both animals, or only to the subordinate, or with one piece visible to both animals and one piece visible only to the subordinate. Both animals are subsequently allowed to enter the large test cage, but the subordinate animal is allowed to enter before the dominant animal, forcing the subordinate animal to make a choice over which (if any) food to take.

When one piece of food is placed in the test cage, and in sight of both animals, the subordinate animal does not eat the food on entering the test cage, instead opting to leave the food for the dominant animal (Hare, Call, & Tomasello, 2000). However, if the food is visible to the subordinate, but not to the dominant animal, the subordinate will take the food on entering the test cage, presumably making a judgement that the dominant animal will not miss food about which it knows nothing (Hare et al., 2000). Similarly, when two pieces of food are placed in the test cage, both visible to the subordinate, but only one visible to the dominant animal, the subordinate animal will take only the food which the dominant animal can not see (Hare, Call, Agnetta, & Tomasello, 2000). On top of this, subordinate animals do not take food out of sight of the dominant animals if they have seen that the dominant animal saw where the food was hidden (Hare et al., 2001), presumably making the judgement that the dominant animal now expects to find the food in that location, even though it is out of sight.

This series of experiments clearly shows behavioural flexibility in nonhuman primates. In each of the experimental situations, the food has the same intrinsic reward value, and the stress of being in the presence of the dominant animal is constant in all conditions. However, the behaviour of the subordinate animal changes in a flexible way dependent on what we might term the "understanding" that the chimpanzee has of the situation it is in. So, if from the work in chimpanzees (Hare et al., 2000, 2001) and macaques (Drea & Wallen, 1999) we can assume that primates are indeed able to express behavioural flexibility in respect to their social environment, the next stage is to understand the neural mechanisms behind this flexibility.

The role of the amygdala in behavioural flexibility

The amygdala is a collection of nuclei in the medial temporal lobe, just anterior to the hippocampus. Lesion studies of amygdala function in monkeys have long suggested a role in emotional processing (Horel, Keating, & Misantone, 1975; Klüver & Bucy, 1939; Weiskrantz, 1956), and also in normal social behaviour (Bachevalier, 1996; Emery, Capitanio, Mason, Machado, Mendoza, & Amaral, 2001; Prather et al., 2001). Large temporal lobe lesions, including the amygdala, but also damaging the hippocampus and inferior temporal cortex, were shown to produce abnormal food preference and sexual behaviour, hyperorality (exploring objects with the mouth, whether food items or not) and a reduction in fear responses (Klüver & Bucy, 1939). More restricted lesions of the amygdala (though still removing the overlying cortex) showed similar, if milder, changes in behaviour (Weiskrantz, 1956).

One particular function of the primate amygdala that has been extensively studied is the learning of object–reward associations, that is, learning the link between an object and its value. However, bilateral lesions of the amygdala in monkeys have varied effects on the learning of such object–reward associations, ranging from significant impairment (Barrett, 1969; Schwartzbaum & Poulos, 1965) to almost no impairment at all (Douglas, Barrett, Pribram, & Cerny, 1969; Horel et al., 1975). However, when learning is about the association between an object and a secondary reinforcer, it is severely impaired by lesions of the amygdala in monkeys (Gaffan & Harrison, 1987). In this task, the monkey learns which of two objects is rewarded, but the immediate feedback on each trial is one of two tones, indicating a correct or incorrect response. Only after a predetermined number of consecutive correct responses have been made does the animal get rewarded with food delivery. In this task, within-trial learning is not dependent on the primary reinforcing values of the food (such as taste), but rather on the secondary reinforcer (the tone), which in itself is inherently reinforcing, but has no primary reinforcing properties. This led to the proposal that the amygdala is crucially involved in associating objects with their *intrinsic* reward value (Gaffan, 1992; Gaffan & Harrison, 1987).

Knowing about objects' *intrinsic* reward value (rather than simply an absolute reward value) could be crucial to behavioural flexibility. Changing our responses to the same item in a way determined by ever changing social context implies that responses are not guided simply by the absolute and fixed reinforcing properties of the stimulus. For example, in the series of experiments in chimpanzees described earlier (Hare et al., 2000, 2001), the food has the same *primary* reinforcing properties in each of the experimental conditions, and yet the animal's responses are determined by whether the food is visible or not to a more dominant animal. Therefore, if the amygdala is crucial for learning about more than simple primary reinforcement values, it may also be crucial for modulating the behaviour in such social interactions.

Two lines of evidence, however, imply that the amygdala on its own is not sufficient to allow behavioural flexibility. Firstly, once satiated with a particular reinforcer, the motivational value of that reinforcer diminishes, while the motivation for other reinforcers can remain high (Rolls, Rowe, & Rolls, 1982). Therefore, although the primary reinforcement properties of the reinforcer remain constant (that is, things such as the food's taste do not change with decreasing motivation), an animal's responses change to reflect the altered motivation (Malkova, Gaffan, & Murray, 1997; Rolls et al., 1982). Cells in the orbitofrontal cortex respond to such changes in the motivational value of a reward (Critchley & Rolls, 1996), but the amygdala is generally much less responsive to such changes in the motivational significance of a reward (Rolls, 1999). This change in behaviour in response to changing motivational significance is similar to the behavioural flexibility seen in social behaviour. The subordinate chimpanzee does not go for food that is visible to a dominant animal (Hare et al., 2000) because, although the food's taste and so on remain the same, the motivation for the food is reduced by the social situation and the "knowledge" that the dominant animal will fight for access to that food. If cells in the amygdala do not respond to changes in the motivational value of a reward, how could it modulate behaviour on the basis of different motivational values within different social contexts?

Secondly, although Gaffan and Harrison (1987) saw significant impairments in learning for secondary reinforcement with aspiration lesions of the amygdala, these lesions also damage fibres of passage through the amygdala, and not just cell bodies of the amygdala. A more recent study using excitotoxic lesions of the amygdala on the same auditory secondary reinforcement task (Malkova et al., 1997) failed to find any impairment. This would imply that fibres of passage through the amygdala, and not the amygdala itself, are crucial to this type of reward learning. One group of fibres passing through and close to the amygdala that could be important for this type of reward learning are those from the cholinergic cells of the basal forebrain to the inferior temporal cortex. The communication between the cholinergic basal forebrain and inferior temporal cortex can be interrupted by sectioning the white-matter pathways themselves in the temporal stem, amygdala, and fornix (Gaffan, Parker, & Easton, 2001); by disrupting the basal forebrain activity with lesions of the medial forebrain bundle (Easton & Gaffan, 2000a, 2001); or by inducing immunotoxic lesions which specifically target the cholinergic cells of the basal forebrain themselves (Easton, Ridley, Baker, & Gaffan, 2002b). All these interruptions of the pathway between the cholinergic basal forebrain and inferior temporal cortex impair many types of memory task, including object–reward association learning. It seems likely, therefore, that it was damage to these fibres projecting through and near the amygdala that gave rise to the variety of object–reward association impairments (including the impairment in secondary reinforcement learning) from aspiration lesions of the amygdala (Easton & Gaffan, 2000b).

It appears, therefore, that the amygdala itself might not be crucial to the behavioural flexibility that is seen in social situations. However, excitotoxic lesions of the amygdala, which do not damage fibres of passage, do significantly change the social behaviour of monkeys (Emery et al., 2001), and so one might still imagine that it has some role in behavioural flexibility. Indeed, there is some evidence for this in monkeys with excitotoxic lesions of the amygdala. The same monkeys that were not impaired at secondary reinforcement learning were impaired at a task of reinforcer devaluation (Malkova et al., 1997).

In this reinforcer-devaluation task, monkeys were initially taught a list of object–reward associations whereby two objects are presented, but only one is rewarded. However, unlike conventional tests of object–reward learning, different rewards were given for different objects; half the rewarded objects were associated with a peanut reward, while the other objects were associated with a fruit reward. Once the object–reward associations had been learnt, the nonrewarded items were removed and then pairs of objects were presented to the animal whereby *both* objects were rewarded, but one was rewarded with a peanut and the other with a fruit snack. Therefore, at this stage, the task is similar to a food preference task, in that the animal tends to pick the object associated with the food it prefers. Once a reward preference has been determined, the reinforcer-devaluation task can begin. Let us imagine that the monkey prefers peanuts and has been mainly choosing objects associated with peanuts rather than those associated with fruit. In this situation, the motivational value of the peanut can be reduced by encouraging the animal to satiate itself on peanuts, simply by providing the animal (before the test procedure) with free access to peanuts until it has eaten its fill. At this stage, the animal is then placed in the test apparatus, and is once again given a choice between pairs of objects when one is rewarded with peanut and one with fruit snacks. As mentioned above, sensory specific satiety means that although the animal has satiated itself with peanuts (and so should have reduced motivation for peanut rewards), it should still be motivated for fruit (Rolls et al., 1982). This is reflected in the performance of normal animals, who will change their responding from choosing objects associated with their preferred (but now devalued) reward type (in this case, peanuts) to choosing objects associated with their normally less preferred (but now more motivating) reward (in this case, fruit). However, animals with bilateral, excitotoxic lesions of the amygdala do not change their responding. If they have been satiated with their preferred reward, they will still choose it preferentially in the task where they have a choice of reward.

In terms of the behavioural flexibility related to social behaviour, this is extremely important. These animals with amygdala lesions do not modify their behaviour on the basis of changing motivational significance. This is exactly the sort of behavioural modification that is needed in social interactions, where stimulus value is not in itself sufficient to determine appropriate behaviour, but instead the behaviour should reflect the stimulus value given the social context. Animals with bilateral amygdala lesions, then, do not appear to show behavioural flexibility. Where, then, are the changes in motivational values of reinforcers represented, and does this area interact with the amygdala to allow behavioural flexibility?

The role of the orbitofrontal cortex in behavioural flexibility

One area which might be ideally suited for such behavioural flexibility is the orbitofrontal cortex. Situated on the ventral surface of the frontal polar region, it receives input from cortical sensory areas (especially those areas where the sensory signal is well refined), the amygdala, dopaminergic regions of the midbrain, and memory regions such as the hippocampus and perirhinal cortex (for review, see Cavada, Company, Tejedor, Cruz-Rizzolo, & Reinoso-Suarez, 2000).

Damage to the orbitofrontal cortex (and other ventral and medial aspects of the prefrontal cortex) in humans results in severe alterations in both emotional and social behaviour. One example of this is patient E.V.R. (Eslinger & Damasio, 1985), who has bilateral damage to the ventral (including orbitofontal) and medial region of the prefrontal cortex. Although of normal intelligence, and without apparent impairment in memory or language, E.V.R. has distinct problems in emotional processing.

Other patients with lesions that include the orbitofrontal cortex also have problems with recognition of emotions (Hornak, Rolls, & Wade, 1996), and, interestingly, these same patients are impaired at tasks which require a degree of behavioural flexibility (Rolls, Hornak, Wade, & McGrath, 1994). When these patients learn an object–reward association task (where two objects are presented on a touchscreen, but only one is correct), they learn to choose the correct stimulus at a near normal rate. However, once the correct object has been learnt, the reward outcomes can be reversed; that is, the previously correct stimulus is now incorrect and the previously incorrect stimulus is now correct, without the subjects being told. In this reversal condition, normal control subjects learn to change their response to the previously incorrect object within one or two trials. Patients with damage to the orbitofrontal cortex, however, fail to alter their responses, continuing to respond to the previously (but not currently) rewarded object (Rolls et al., 1994). The ability to change response patterns in relation to a change in reward outcome is the type of behaviour discussed earlier as the behavioural flexibility that allows normal social interactions. If the orbitofrontal cortex is crucial for behavioural flexibility, then, perhaps through its connections with the amygdala, it allows the type of behavioural flexibility seen in the reinforcer-devaluation experiment of Malkova et al. (1997) described above.

One way to examine the importance of the interaction of amygdala and orbitofrontal cortex is to use a technique of crossed unilateral disconnection. In this style of surgery, asymmetrical lesions are made, that is, different structures are lesioned in each hemisphere of the brain. In examining the interactions of the amygdala and orbitofrontal cortex, one would produce a lesion of the amygdala in one hemisphere and the orbitofrontal cortex in the opposite hemisphere. In this pattern of lesions, the amygdala and orbitofrontal cortex will each be intact in one hemisphere. However, each hemisphere will have one or the other structure absent. As a result, the *only* disruption in *both* hemispheres will be to the interaction between the two structures. In one hemisphere, there can be no interaction between the two, as the amygdala is absent; and in the opposite hemisphere, there can be no interaction because the orbitofrontal cortex is absent. This pattern of lesions and its effect is outlined in Figure 3.1.

The reinforcer-devaluation experiment studied by Malkova et al. (1997) with bilateral amygdala lesions has been studied with this type of crossed unilateral disconnection, precisely to examine the role of the interaction between the amygdala and orbitofrontal cortex in solving this task (Baxter, Parker, Linder, Izquierdo, & Murray, 2000). Just like animals with bilateral lesions of the amygdala, animals in which the interaction between the amygdala and orbitofrontal cortex was prevented did not change their responses to differently rewarded objects when one of the rewards available had been devalued prior to the test (Baxter et al., 2000). This indicates that the interaction between these two structures is crucial to the sort of behavioural flexibility that allows one to change response patterns when reward values change.

This interaction between the amygdala and the orbitofrontal cortex explains why the amygdala might be involved in such behavioural flexibility. Cells in the orbitofrontal cortex clearly show this type of change in response to changing reward value (Critchley & Rolls, 1996). Neurons in the orbitofrontal cortex preferentially respond to different types of food reward

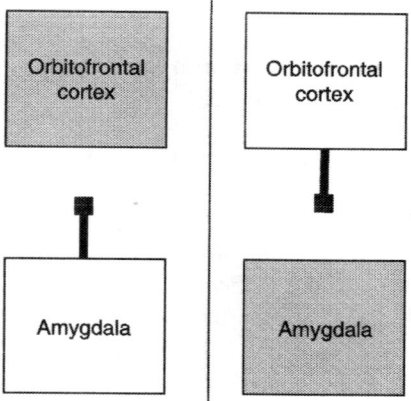

Figure 3.1 Crossed unilateral lesions of the amygdala and orbitofrontal cortex. The amygdala is removed in one hemisphere (shaded), and the orbitofrontal cortex is removed in the opposite hemisphere (shaded). This prevents all communication between these two structures in both hemispheres, although one of each structure remains intact.

(for example, they are activated by banana and grape, but not apple). If one of the rewards is devalued by satiation (as by allowing the monkey to eat its fill of banana), then the neuronal response to the devalued reward reduces, but the response to the nondevalued reward remains high (that is, the cells' response to the banana will reduce, but the response to the grape reward will be unaffected). This is exactly the type of change in neuronal response to changing reward values required for behavioural flexibility.

Further evidence supports the proposal that the orbitofrontal cortex is critically involved in responding to the current motivational value of rewards, rather than their absolute reward value. When a simple memory task (spatial delayed responding, in which a monkey sees a cue for a location and after a delay period has to choose that spatial location) is used and different food rewards are given (that is, each location has a different food reward associated with it), then the cells of the orbitofrontal cortex signal the preferred food reward, irrespective of the spatial location of that reward or the visual cue predicting it (Tremblay & Schultz, 1999). Importantly, the experiment tested the response of the same food reward in a condition where it was the unpreferred reward available and in a condition where it was the preferred available food reward. In this case, the neurons of the orbitofrontal cortex signal the motivational value of the reward, not the specific reward type; that is, if the cells did not respond to the reward when it was the unpreferred type, they would respond in the condition where it was the preferred reward type (Tremblay & Schultz, 1999). This again is the type of change in neural responding necessary for changing behaviour in a social context when the value of available rewards is dependent on the current social context.

The nature of frontal interactions with the inferior temporal cortex in learning tasks

I have so far discussed how behavioural flexibility is necessary for normal social behaviour, and how the amygdala and orbitofrontal cortex might be crucial neural structures underlying this type of behavioural flexibility. I now turn my attention to attempting to formalize the nature of the frontal cortex's role in this type of behavioural flexibility. The neuronal evidence for changing neuronal responses to changing motivational value of rewards, described above, could indicate that the orbitofrontal cortex has a crucial role to play in all aspects of reward learning, rather than especially in those situations in which behavioural flexibility is required.

Direct interaction between the frontal and inferior temporal cortex is essential in tasks that require memory for visual properties of objects and scenes, but interaction through the uncinate fascicle, the direct corticocortical pathway between them, appears to be required only for the learning of visually cued conditional tasks. A much wider range of tasks rely upon interaction between frontal and inferior temporal cortices within the same hemisphere. However, some tasks appear able to be performed normally even when these two structures can no longer communicate within the same hemisphere. From a series of studies that specifically examine the nature of frontotemporal interactions in learning, we can determine whether the frontal cortex is involved in all aspects of reward learning, or whether it is specifically involved when a variety of factors (such as rules and conditions) are applied, such as we might get in complex social environments.

Frontal interactions with the inferior temporal cortex in object–reward association learning

Object–reward association learning is simply learning that choice of a particular object results in reward. This is a never changing association: if object X is rewarded, it will be rewarded every time it is presented; if object Y is never rewarded, it will fail to produce reward any time it is chosen. Lesions of the inferior temporal cortex lead to severe impairments in object–reward association learning (Easton & Gaffan, 2000a; Gaffan, Harrison, & Gaffan, 1986a, 1986b; Meunier, Bachevalier, Mishkin, & Murray, 1993; Mishkin, 1954), as would be expected, because it is in the inferior temporal cortex that complex objects are represented (Tanaka, 1996). The frontal cortex, however, is also crucial for learning object–reward associations in the monkey, and bilateral disruption of frontal cortex activity (by lesion or inactivation) severely impairs performance on object–reward association tasks (Parker & Gaffan, 1998a; Voytko, 1985).

Although the frontal cortex and inferior temporal cortex are both essential for normal performance of object–reward association learning tasks, lesions of the direct corticocortical connection between the two areas (the uncinate fascicle) fail to impair such learning (Eacott & Gaffan, 1992; Gutnikov, Ma, Buckley, & Gaffan, 1997). Indeed, crossed unilateral lesions of the frontal cortex in one hemisphere and of the inferior temporal cortex in the opposite hemisphere (which serve to prevent *all* communication between these areas within the same hemisphere) also fail to impair object–reward association learning in monkeys (Gaffan, Easton, & Parker, 2002; Parker & Gaffan, 1998a). This implies that although both cortical areas are essential to normal performance of the task, they do not need to interact within the same hemisphere. There must, then, be some communication *between* the hemispheres between these two cortical areas.

Recent studies in the monkey have implicated the basal forebrain as the crucial route of communication between hemispheres by which the frontal and inferior temporal cortex communicate to learn visual tasks, including object–reward association learning (Easton et al., 2002; Easton & Gaffan, 2000a, 2000b, 2001; Easton & Parker, 2003; Gaffan et al., 2001, 2002). However, in all these cases, the basal forebrain is required for new learning, but not the retrieval of memories which have been previously learnt (Easton & Gaffan, 2000a; Gaffan et al., 2001, 2002). Object–reward associations, however, are not the only type of learning task that relies on frontotemporal interactions, and these other tasks can provide insight into the type of procedures that are invoked in complex social situations.

Frontal interactions with the inferior temporal cortex in tasks other than object–reward association learning

Although preventing communication between the frontal and inferior temporal cortices, by crossed unilateral lesions, does not impair object–reward association learning, it does impair a number of other tasks. Lesions of the frontal cortex in one hemisphere and inferior temporal cortex in the opposite hemisphere significantly impair conditional discrimination learning (Parker & Gaffan, 1998a), strategy learning (Gaffan et al., 2002), recognition memory (Parker & Gaffan, 1998b), and scene learning (Easton & Gaffan, 1999). All of these tasks, therefore, differ from object–reward association learning in the way in which frontal cortex and inferior temporal cortex interact. Although the route via the basal forebrain is important in these tasks (Easton et al., 2002a, 2002b; Easton & Gaffan, 2000a; Easton, Parker, & Gaffan, 2001; Gaffan et al., 2001, 2002), there must be some alternate route of interaction as well.

A clear example of this comes from a recent study on performance of a complex strategy by monkeys (Gaffan et al., 2002). In this study, monkeys were taught visual stimuli from two categories, and two stimuli would be presented to the animal simultaneously, one from each category. The categories were determined simply by when a response to the object would result in reward delivery. Objects from the "persistent" category would be rewarded only if there were four consecutive responses made to objects from this category. In contrast, objects from the "sporadic" category were rewarded from a single response, but only once a reward had been obtained from the "persistent" category of objects. There were, therefore, a number of response patterns an animal could make and achieve reward. However, there was only one optimally efficient way of achieving rewards, and that was to use a strategy of four consecutive responses to objects from the "persistent" category, followed immediately by a single response to an object from the "sporadic" category, and then four consecutive responses to objects from the "persistent" category, and so on. This would mean an animal making an average of 2.5 responses per reward attained. In normal monkeys, performance is very good, as they get very close to this optimal level of responding.

As one might expect from the complex nature of this task, the frontal cortex and inferior temporal cortex need to interact with each other for optimal performance of the strategy. Crossed lesions of the frontal cortex in one hemisphere and the inferior temporal cortex in the opposite hemisphere severely impair performance, almost reducing the animals to chance patterns of responding (Gaffan et al., 2002). However, unlike object–reward association learning, interrupting the route of communication between the frontal cortex and inferior temporal cortex (by section of the anterior temporal stem white matter, amygdala, and fornix, all of which carry projections from the basal forebrain to the inferior temporal cortex [Kitt, Mitchell, DeLong, Wainer, & Price, 1987; Seldon, Gitelman, Salamon-Murayama, Parrish, & Mesulan, 1998]) fails to alter the animal's pattern of optimal strategy performance (Gaffan et al., 2002). The projection via the basal forebrain does still play a part, as animals with this circuit interrupted are impaired at learning new objects within each category (Gaffan et al., 2002). Learning new stimuli for each category, however, is (like object–reward association learning) not dependent on interaction between the frontal and inferior temporal cortices *within the same hemisphere* (Gaffan et al., 2002). This double dissociation of stimulus learning and strategy performance indicates that there are clearly two routes of interaction between the frontal and inferior temporal cortices that are important in the learning and performance of this complex task.

Does behavioural flexibility determine whether the frontal and inferior temporal cortices interact within the same hemisphere?

It appears from these series of experiments, then, that a common route of communication between the frontal and inferior temporal cortices (sometimes between hemispheres) via the basal forebrain is important in all new learning. However, there appears to be another route of communication between these cortical areas *within the same hemisphere* which is not involved in learning object–reward associations or new stimuli for a category (Gaffan et al., 2002), but is involved in other, more complex tasks such as strategy *performance* (Gaffan et al., 2002), conditional discrimination learning (Parker & Gaffan, 1998a), and recognition memory (Parker & Gaffan, 1998b). What differs between these tasks and object–reward association learning that makes them reliant on communication between the frontal and inferior temporal cortices within the same hemisphere? One possibility is that the tasks that do not rely on interaction between these cortical areas within the same hemispheres (such as object–reward association learning) are so simplistic that they do not require the frontal cortex. An alternative explanation is that the way in which the tasks are solved determines whether or not interaction between these cortical areas within the same hemisphere is necessary.

Earlier in the chapter, I put forward the idea of behavioural flexibility, the notion that we are able to adjust our behaviour to the same stimulus depending on various factors, including social context. I also discussed how the amygdala shows relatively inflexible responses to rewards, while the orbitofrontal cortex is able to indicate the motivational value of a reward, and not just its absolute value. There is an important difference between object–reward association learning and tasks such as the strategy task discussed above (Gaffan et al., 2002), namely, behavioural flexibility. In object–reward association learning, an object is always either rewarded or unrewarded; the reward outcome for a response never varies, and there is no requirement for behavioural flexibility. However, in the strategy task described above (Gaffan et al., 2002), a response to an object from the "sporadic" category is appropriate only after a reward from responding to objects from the "persistent" category. Similarly, objects from the "persistent" category are not the appropriate objects to choose when one has received a reward from this category on the previous response. This provides an ambiguity as to the reward value of an object which is only resolved by cues such as what was the reward outcome on the previous trial. Therefore, behavioural flexibility (rather than simply task difficulty) might determine whether the frontal and inferior temporal cortices must interact within the same hemisphere.

This hypothesis has recently been tested by a complex task which does not require behavioural flexibility to be solved. If this task is impaired by crossed unilateral lesions of the frontal and inferior temporal cortices, it implies that task difficulty is all that is required to predict when the frontal and inferior temporal cortices are required to interact within the same hemisphere. However, if the task is unimpaired by this pattern of lesions, it implies that communication between these cortical areas within the same hemisphere is required only when behavioural flexibility is required to solve the task. The task used a biconditional discrimination task, similar to those developed in rats and pigeons by Trapold (1970) in the 1970s. In a normal conditional discrimination task, a cue object predicts which of two choice objects will be rewarded. For example, Figure 3.2a shows that the presence of cue object A predicts that choice object X is rewarded, while the presence of cue object B predicts that choice object Y is rewarded. In this type of task, behavioural

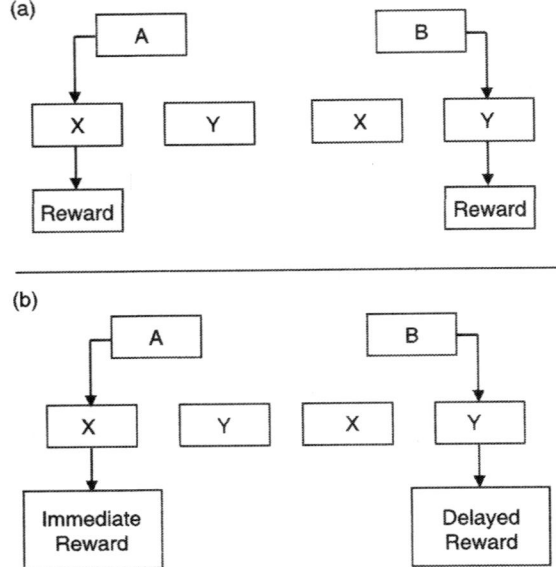

Figure 3.2 Outline of conditional- and biconditional-discrimination learning. (a) Conditional-discrimination learning. In the presence of cue A, only a response to object X produces a reward. In the presence of cue B, only a response to object Y produces a reward. The reward is the same in both conditions. (b) Biconditional-discrimination learning. Object X is rewarded only in the presence of cue A, and object Y in the presence of cue B. However, unlike conditional-discrimination learning, the reward outcomes for both cues are unique. Therefore, both cue A and object X are associated only with immediate reward, and never with delayed reward, while cue B and object Y are associated only with delayed reward, and never with immediate reward.

flexibility is required, as there is no fixed pattern of reward outcome for any of the cue or choice objects. For example, object X is both rewarded (in the presence of cue A) and unrewarded (in the presence of cue B). Similarly, cue A is either rewarded (if followed by a choice of object X) and unrewarded (if followed by a choice of object Y). Therefore, the pattern of responding to an object by an animal requires more than a simple, fixed object–reward association.

In a biconditional discrimination task, the same pattern of cue and choice objects is used, but there is a unique reward outcome for each condition. Figure 3.2B shows that once again cue A predicts that choice object X is rewarded while cue B predicts that choice object Y is rewarded. However, cue A followed by choice object X is rewarded by an *immediate* food reward, while cue B followed by choice object Y is rewarded by a *delayed* food reward. This difference in timing of the reward is enough to allow the task to be learnt differently (Carlson & Wielkiewicz, 1972). Now there is a fixed reward outcome for each stimulus. Cue A is only ever rewarded by *immediate* food reward, and never by delayed food reward. Similarly, choice object Y is only ever rewarded by *delayed* food reward, and never by immediate food reward. This direct association between each cue object or choice object and a specific reward outcome means that there is no requirement for behavioural flexibility. The task, however, is a complex one, certainly more complex than simple object–reward association learning, and so this is an ideal task with which to test whether task difficulty or behavioural flexibility is the factor that determines whether the frontal and inferior temporal cortices must interact with one another within the same hemisphere or not.

We found that animals that were perfectly well able to learn new biconditional discriminations before surgery were unaffected in their performance following crossed unilateral lesions of the frontal cortex in one hemisphere and the inferior temporal cortex in the opposite hemisphere (Easton & Gaffan, 2002). This strongly supports the hypothesis that it is not task difficulty that determines whether or not the frontal and inferior temporal cortices must interact within the same hemisphere. Rather, this complex task does not require interaction between the two cortical areas within the same hemisphere because there is no behavioural flexibility required.

The frontal cortex determines currently appropriate choices

The results from these studies of crossed unilateral lesions of frontal and inferior temporal cortices has allowed us to develop a hypothesis that predicts in which situations there will be communication between the frontal and inferior temporal cortices within the same hemisphere (Easton & Gaffan, 2002; Gaffan et al., 2002; Easton, Parker, & Gaffan, 2002a). This hypothesis is outlined in Figures 3.3 and 3.4. As shown in Figure 3.3, in a normal conditional-discrimination task (used as an example of a task requiring behavioural flexibility), the frontal cortex is required to determine the current condition of the task, which is what determines which choice object will be rewarded on that trial. It is clear that cells within the prefrontal cortex can respond to rules related to the current condition of a task (Asaad, Rainer, & Miller, 2000), and so are ideally suited to make such judgements about current task conditions. In Figure 3.3, it can be seen that the presence of cue object A determines that the task is in "condition A/X" (that is, cue object A, so choice object X should be chosen). This is communicated to posterior cortical areas, where the cells are themselves able to signal the current reward condition (Platt & Glimcher, 1999). This current condition of the task, as signalled by posterior cortical areas, can then be communicated to the visual areas of the inferior temporal cortex, where the object representations of the choice objects X and Y are stored. This posterior activation of inferior temporal cortex could then activate the representation of the appropriate object (object X) within the inferior temporal cortex. This type of selection process would be an example of an integrated competition system (Duncan, 1996). In

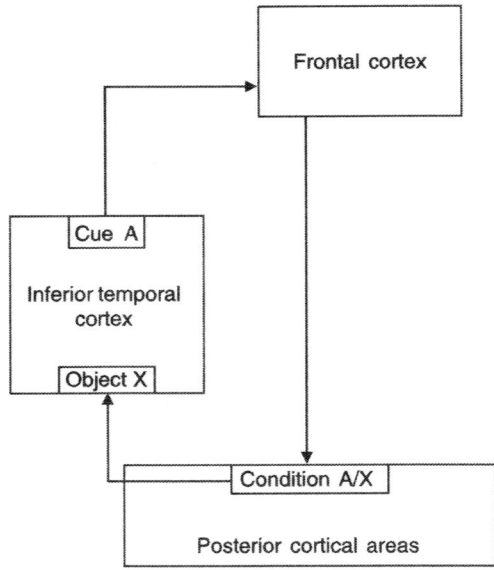

Figure 3.3 Neural interactions in conditional-discrimination learning. Cue A is represented in the inferior temporal cortex, and this is communicated to the frontal cortex, which determines that in the presence of cue A object X should be chosen. This is communicated to posterior cortical areas, where the current condition of the task (cue A and object X) is represented. These posterior cortical areas then interact with the inferior temporal cortex, where the object representations are stored, and enhance the representation of object X as it is rewarded on this particular trial.

this way, the frontal cortex communicates with the inferior temporal cortex within the same hemisphere in order to allow the choice of the appropriate choice object.

Figure 3.4 shows a similar outline of the interactions required to solve the biconditional-discrimination task. As in the outline for the more usual conditional discrimination in Figure 3.4, the presence of cue object A determines the appropriate choice object to be X. However, because the biconditional task has a direct relationship between both the cue object and the reward outcome and the choice object and the reward outcome, the cue object itself is all that is needed to determine the current condition of the task. This is because the current condition of the task is simply which reward type is available, and this can be known by means of a simple object–reward association between the reward and the cue object. Therefore, all that is needed to activate the appropriate condition (condition A/X) in the posterior cortical areas is the cue object itself, which is represented not in the frontal cortex, but in the visual areas of the inferior temporal cortex. The representation of the current condition in the posterior cortical areas then activates the appropriate

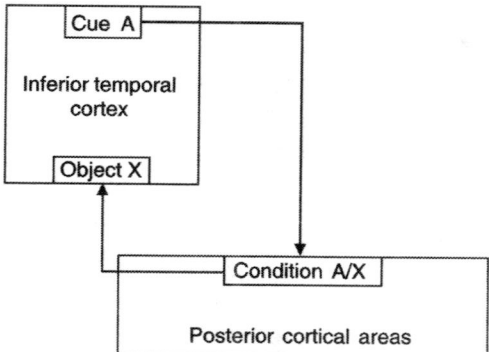

Figure 3.4 Neural interactions in biconditional-discrimination learning. Cue A is represented in the inferior temporal cortex. Because of the direct association between the cue and the outcome, the cue provides all the required information to select the current condition of the task. This is then communicated directly to posterior cortical areas, where the current condition of the task (cue A and object X) is represented. These posterior cortical areas then interact with the inferior temporal cortex, where the object representations are stored, and enhance the representation of object X as it is rewarded on this particular trial. The frontal cortex is not required in this interaction.

choice object (choice object X) representation in the inferior temporal cortex, as for the more usual conditional-discrimination task in Figure 3.3. Therefore, the entire task is solved by reciprocal interactions between the inferior temporal cortex and the posterior cortical areas. The frontal cortex is not required at all in solving this task (Easton & Gaffan, 2002).

This model of interactions between cortical areas makes a specific prediction; the frontal cortex and inferior temporal cortex must interact within the same hemisphere to solve problems that require behavioural flexibility, but need not interact where a problem has a fixed and inflexible reward outcome. This would clearly predict that the type of behavioural flexibility discussed at the beginning of this chapter in relation to social behaviour is likely to be dependent upon interactions between the frontal cortex and inferior temporal cortex.

Implications of the model for social behaviour

As discussed at the beginning of this chapter, social interactions (especially within a complex primate society) require behavioural flexibility in order to allow behaviour to be appropriate to social conditions. The model proposed above, which outlines a role for the frontal cortex in learning that requires behavioural flexibility, indicates that this region might also be critical for the types of behavioural flexibility required in social interactions. Although so far detailing only interactions between the frontal cortex and inferior temporal cortex in visual learning tasks, models such as this can (and should) be applied to more complex cognitive tasks.

One prediction of the model is especially testable. It is clear that object–reward association learning is not dependent on the interaction between frontal and inferior temporal cortices within the same hemisphere. However, we also know from such studies as Drea and Wallen's observation (1999) of monkeys "playing dumb" on this sort of task in a social group that the task can be subject to behavioural flexibility in a social setting. Therefore, the model proposed in this chapter would suggest that an animal's learning of object–reward associations in isolation should be spared after crossed lesions of the frontal and inferior temporal cortex (e.g. Gaffan et al., 2002; Parker & Gaffan, 1998a), but that the social modulation of this task (e.g. Drea, 1998; Drea & Wallen, 1999) should be impaired.

Social behaviour has long been regarded as too complex a situation to apply the rigours of scientific hypothesis testing. However, with modern techniques, this has become less true, and social behaviour has become a new focus of cognitive neuroscience research. As shown in this chapter, however, social behaviour should be regarded in the greater context of cognition and behaviour. Although undoubtedly complex, social behaviour relies on the same principal cognitive mechanisms as many other types of behaviour, such as learning and memory. There is good reason, then, to test the hypotheses generated by these other disciplines in order to lay the foundation of an understanding of the neural mechanisms of social behaviour.

References

Asaad, W. F., Rainer, G., & Miller, E. K. (2000). Task-specific neural activity in the primate prefrontal cortex. *Journal of Neurophysiology*, *84*, 451–459.

Bachevalier, J. (1996). Medial temporal lobe and autism: A putative animal model in primates. *Journal of Autism and Developmental Disorders*, *26*, 217–220.

Barrett, T. W. (1969). Studies of the function of the amygdaloid complex in *Macaca mulatta*. *Neuropsychologia*, *7*, 1–12.

Baxter, M. G., Parker, A., Lindner, C. C. C., Izquierdo, A. D., & Murray, E. A. (2000). Control of response selection by reinforcer value requires interaction of amygdala and orbital prefrontal cortex. *Journal of Neuroscience*, *20*, 4311–4319.

Carlson, J. G., & Wielkiewicz, R. M. (1972). Delay of reinforcement in instrumental discrimination learning in rats. *Journal of Comparative Physiology and Psychology*, *81*, 365–370.

Cavada, C., Company, T., Tejedor, J., Cruz-Rizzolo, R. J., & Reinoso-Suarez, F. (2000). The anatomical connections of the macaque monkey orbitofrontal cortex. A review. *Cerebral Cortex*, *10*, 220–242.

Critchley, H. D., & Rolls, E. T. (1996). Hunger and satiety modify the responses of olfactory and visual neurons in the primate orbitofrontal cortex. *Journal of Neurophysiology*, *75*, 1673–1686.

Douglas, R. J., Barrett, T. W., Pribram, K. H., & Cerny, M. C. (1969). Limbic lesions and error reduction. *Journal of Comparative Physiology and Psychology*, *68*, 437–441.

Drea, C. M. (1998). Status, age, and sex effects on performance of discrimination tasks in-group-tested rhesus monkeys (*Macaca mulatta*). *Journal of Comparative Psychology*, *112*, 170–182.

Drea, C. M., & Wallen, K. (1999). Low-status monkeys "play dumb" when learning in mixed social groups. *Proceedings of the National Academy of Sciences of the USA*, *96*, 12965–12969.

Duncan, J. (1996). Cooperating brain systems in selective perception and action. In T. Inui & J. L. McLelland (Eds.), *Attention and performance* (Vol. 16, pp. 549–578). Cambridge, MA: MIT Press.

Eacott, M. J., & Gaffan, D. (1992). Inferotemporal-frontal disconnection: The uncinate fascicle and visual associative learning in monkeys. *European Journal of Neuroscience*, *4*, 1320–1332.

Easton, A., & Gaffan, D. (1999). Interaction of frontal lobe and inferior temporal cortex in object-in-place memory. *Society for Neuroscience Abstracts*, *25*.

Easton, A., & Gaffan, D. (2000a). Comparison of perirhinal cortex ablation and crossed unilateral lesions of medial forebrain bundle from inferior temporal cortex in the rhesus monkey: Effects on learning and retrieval. *Behavioral Neuroscience*, *114*, 1041–1057.

Easton, A., & Gaffan, D. (2000b). Amygdala and the memory of reward: The importance of fibres of passage from the basal forebrain. In J. P. Aggleton (Ed.), *The amygdala: A functional analysis* (pp. 569–586). Oxford: Oxford University Press.

Easton, A., & Gaffan, D. (2001). Crossed unilateral lesions of the medial forebrain bundle and either inferior temporal or frontal cortex impair object–reward association learning in rhesus monkeys. *Neuropsychologia*, *39*, 71–82.

Easton, A., & Gaffan, D. (2002). Insights into the nature of fronto-temporal interactions from a biconditional discrimination task in the monkey. *Behavioural Brain Research*, *136*, 217–226.

Easton, A., & Parker, A. (2003). A cholinergic explanation of dense amnesia. *Cortex*, *39*, 813–826.

Easton, A., Parker, A., & Gaffan, D. (2001). Crossed unilateral lesions of medial forebrain bundle and either inferior temporal or frontal cortex impair object recognition memory in rhesus monkeys. *Behavioural Brain Research*, *121*, 1–10.

Easton, A., Parker, A., & Gaffan, D. (2002a). Memory encoding and retrieval: The nature of the interactions between the primate frontal lobe and posterior cortex. In A. Parker, E. L. Wilding, & T. J. Bussey (Eds.), *The cognitive neuroscience of memory: Encoding and retrieval* (pp. 173–196). Hove, UK: Psychology Press.

Easton, A., Ridley, R. M., Baker, H. F., & Gaffan, D. (2002c). Lesions of the cholinergic basal forebrain and fornix in one hemisphere and inferior temporal cortex in the opposite hemisphere produce severe learning impairments in rhesus monkeys. *Cerebral Cortex, 12*, 729–736.

Emery, N. J., & Clayton, N. S. (2001). Effects of experience and social context on prospective caching strategies by scrub jays. *Nature, 414*, 443–446.

Emery, N. J., Capitanio, J. P., Mason, W. A., Machado, C. J., Mendoza, S. P., & Amaral, D. G. (2001). The effects of bilateral lesions of the amygdala on dyadic social interactions in rhesus monkeys (*Macaca mulatta*). *Behavioral Neuroscience, 115*, 515–544.

Eslinger, P. J., & Damasio, A. R. (1985). Severe disturbance of higher cognition after bilateral frontal lobe ablation: Patient EVR. *Neurology, 35*, 1731–1741.

Gaffan, D. (1992). Amygdala and the memory of reward. In J. P. Aggleton (Ed.), *The amygdala: Neurobiological aspects of emotion, memory, and mental dysfunction* (pp. 471–483). New York: Wiley.

Gaffan, D., & Harrison, S. (1987). Amygdalectomy and disconnection in visual learning for auditory secondary reinforcement by monkeys. *Journal of Neuroscience, 7*, 2285–2292.

Gaffan, D., Harrison, S., & Gaffan, E. A. (1986a). Visual identification following inferotemporal ablation in the monkey. *Quarterly Journal of Experimental Psychology, 38B*, 5–30.

Gaffan, D., Parker, A., & Easton, A. (2001). Dense amnesia in the monkey after transection of fornix, amygdala and anterior temporal stem. *Neuropsychologia, 39*, 51–70.

Gaffan, D., Easton, A., & Parker, A. (2002). Interaction of inferior temporal cortex with frontal cortex and basal forebrain: Double dissociation in strategy implementation and associative learning. *Journal of Neuroscience, 22*, 7288–7296.

Gaffan, E. A., Harrison, S., & Gaffan, D. (1986b). Single and concurrent discrimination learning by monkeys after lesions of inferotemporal cortex. *Quarterly Journal of Experimental Psychology, 38B*, 31–51.

Gutnikov, S. A., Ma, Y., Buckley, M. J., & Gaffan, D. (1997). Monkeys can associate visual stimuli with reward delayed by 1 s even after perirhinal cortex ablation, uncinate fascicle section or amygdalectomy. *Behavioural Brain Research, 87*, 85–96.

Hare, B., Call, J., & Tomasello, M. (2001). Do chimpanzees know what conspecifics know? *Animal Behaviour, 61*, 139–151.

Hare, B., Call, J., Agnetta, B., & Tomasello, M. (2000). Chimpanzees know what conspecifics do and do not see. *Animal Behaviour, 59*, 771–785.

Horel, J. A., Keating, E. G., & Misantone, L. G. (1975). Partial Kluever–Bucy syndrome produced by destroying temporal neocortex or amygdala. *Brain Research, 94*, 347–359.

Hornak, J., Rolls, E. T., & Wade, D. (1996). Face and voice expression identification in patients with emotional and behavioural changes following ventral frontal lobe damage. *Neuropsychologia, 34*, 247–261.

Kitt, C. A., Mitchell, S. J., DeLong, M. R., Wainer, B. H., & Price D. L. (1987). Fiber pathways of basal forebrain cholinergic neurons in monkeys. *Brain Research, 406*, 192–206.

Klüver, H., & Bucy, P. (1939). Preliminary analysis of functions of the temporal lobes in monkeys. *Archives of Neurology and Psychology, 42*, 979–1000.

Lupien, S. J., & Lepage, M. (2001). Stress, memory, and the hippocampus: Can't live with it, can't live without it. *Behavioural Brain Research*, *127*, 137–158.

Malkova, L., Gaffan, D., & Murray, E. A. (1997). Excitotoxic lesions of the amygdala fail to produce impairment in visual learning for auditory secondary reinforcement but interfere with reinforcer devaluation effects in rhesus monkeys. *Journal of Neuroscience*, *17*, 6011–6020.

Meunier, M., Bachevalier, J., Mishkin, M., & Murray, E. A. (1993). Effects on visual recognition of combined and separate ablations of the entorhinal and perirhinal cortex in rhesus monkeys. *Journal of Neuroscience*, *13*, 5418–5432.

Mishkin, M. (1954). Visual discrimination performance following partial ablations of the temporal lobe. II. Ventral surface vs. hippocampus. *Journal of Comparative Physiology and Psychology*, *47*, 187–193.

Parker, A., & Gaffan, D. (1998a). Memory after frontal-temporal disconnection in monkeys: Conditional and nonconditional tasks, unilateral and bilateral frontal lesions. *Neuropsychologia*, *36*, 259–271.

Parker, A., & Gaffan, D. (1998b). Interaction of frontal and perirhinal cortices in visual object recognition memory in monkeys. *European Journal of Neuroscience*, *10*, 3044–3057.

Platt, M. L., & Glimcher, P. W. (1999). Neural correlates of decision variables in parietal cortex. *Nature*, *400*, 233–238.

Prather, M. D., Lavenex, P., Mauldin-Jourdain, M. L., Mason, W. A., Capitanio, J. P., Mendoza, S. P., et al. (2001). Increased social fear and decreased fear of objects in monkeys with neonatal amygdala lesions. *Neuroscience*, *106*, 653–658.

Rolls, B. J., Rowe, E. A., & Rolls, E. T. (1982). How sensory properties of food affect human feeding behaviour. *Physiology and Behavior*, *29*, 409–417.

Rolls, E. T. (1999). *The brain and emotion*. Oxford: Oxford University Press.

Rolls, E. T., Hornak, J., Wade, D., & McGrath, J. (1994). Emotion-related learning in patients with social and emotional changes associated with frontal lobe damage. *Journal of Neurology, Neurosurgery and Psychiatry*, *57*, 1518–1524.

Schwartzbaum, J. S., & Poulos, D. A. (1965). Discrimination behavior after amygdalectomy in monkeys: Learning set and discrimination reversals. *Journal of Comparative Physiology and Psychology*, *60*, 320–328.

Seldon, N. R., Gitelman, D. R., Salamon-Murayama, N., Parrish, T. B., & Mesulam, M.-M. (1998). Trajectories of cholinergic pathways within the cerebral hemispheres of the human brain. *Brain*, *121*, 2249–2257.

Tanaka, K. (1996). Inferotemporal cortex and object vision. *Annual Review of Neuroscience*, *19*, 109–139.

Trapold, M. A. (1970). Are expectancies based upon different positive reinforcing events discriminably different? *Learning and Motivation*, *1*, 129–140.

Tremblay, L., & Schultz, W. (1999). Relative reward preference in primate orbitofrontal cortex. *Nature*, *398*, 704–708.

Voytko, M. L. (1985). Cooling orbital frontal cortex disrupts matching-to-sample and visual discrimination learning in monkeys. *Physiological Psychology*, *13*, 219–229.

Weiskrantz, L. (1956). Behavioral changes associated with ablation of the amygdaloid complex in monkeys. *Journal of Comparative Physiology and Psychology*, *49*, 381–391.

4 Neural basis for the perception of goal-directed actions

Tjeerd Jellema and David I. Perrett

1. Summary

Natural body actions can be thought of as consisting of continuous and complex sequences of static postures, linked by motion. The first claim of this chapter is that cells in the anterior part of the superior temporal sulcus (STSa) in the macaque monkey are tuned to the visual analysis of such complex body actions. The neural representations constructed in the STSa first of all form a direct visual description of these actions. Some cell populations in the STSa go one step further in that they are sensitive to multiple, visually distinct stimuli, such as multiple views of the same animate object or action. Other cells are tuned to conceptually related visual stimuli, such as multiple body signals of directed attention. We postulate that these cells play a role in forming representations of socially relevant concepts, such as another's attention.

Recent findings from our recording studies, which form the bulk of this chapter, have made it increasingly clear that the sensitivity of cell populations in the STSa exceeds that which would be required to form merely a "pictorial" description of complex actions. The newly discovered cells respond, in intricate ways, to the sight of actions that occur either in conjunction or in sequence with other visual cues. The remarkable response characteristics that are created in this way have led us to suggest that the cells are tuned toward the goal-directedness, predictability, and even intention of the action. This brings us to the second, more speculative, claim of this chapter, which is that STSa cell populations constitute essential building blocks underlying the capacity of an observer to *understand* naturally occurring behaviour in terms of the goals and intentions of the actor, over and above the perceptual description of that behaviour. The cells we describe may facilitate coding of concepts that are associated with the *causes* or *consequences* of the observed actions, such as the intention of an action or the event most likely to follow it.

2. Background

Different streams for processing of the visual stimulus

Existing ideas about where in the brain the processing of the different features of a visual stimulus occurs are heavily influenced by the Ungerleider and Mishkin model (1982), and by a subsequent adaptation by Milner and Goodale (1995). The Ungerleider and Mishkin model basically envisages a separation of visual processing into two distinct cortical streams: a dorsal "where" stream, extending from V1 into the inferior parietal cortex, primarily dealing with the spatial relationships of objects; and a ventral "what" stream, extending from V1 into the inferior temporal cortex (IT), dealing with the shape and identity of objects (Desimone & Ungerleider, 1989; Haxby et al., 1991). Milner and Goodale questioned the strict "what–where" dichotomy, and suggested that space and form are processed in both parietal and temporal areas but for different purposes (Goodale, Milner, Jakobson, & Carey, 1991; Milner & Goodale, 1995). In their view, the ventral stream subserves visual "perception", that is, object and scene recognition, requiring allocentric spatial coding to represent the enduring characteristics of objects, while the dorsal stream subserves the visual control of "action", requiring egocentric spatial coding for short-lived representations (vision for perception *versus* vision for action). These ideas of joint processing of form and position have been substantiated by studies at the cellular level, with cells coding for object shape in parietal cortex (Murata, Gallese, Kaseda, & Sakata, 1996; Sereno & Maunsell, 1998), and cells coding for the object's spatial position in area V4 within the ventral stream (Dobbins, Jeo, Fiser, & Allman, 1998). The role of the ventral stream in the recognition of complex objects is supported by findings showing a gradual increase in the complexity of stimuli analysed by cells from V1 up to IT (Perrett & Oram, 1993; Ungerleider & Mishkin, 1982).

Recently, it has been proposed that the dorsal visual stream should be subdivided into two streams: a dorso-dorsal stream, encompassing the superior parietal lobule, and a ventrodorsal stream, encompassing the inferior parietal lobule (the "three visual system hypothesis": Matelli & Luppino, 2000; Turnbull, Carey, & McCarthy, 1997). The dorso-dorsal and ventrodorsal (V-D) streams are both thought to be involved in "vision for action", similar to Milner and Goodale's dorsal stream, but the V-D stream is also involved in the perception of space and action.

The anterior part of the superior temporal sulcus (STSa) in the monkey

The STSa in the macaque monkey, corresponding to area STPa (Bruce, Desimone, & Gross, 1981), is considered part of the ventral visual stream. STSa cells often maximally respond to the visual appearance of the face and body, and to body actions, most notably of conspecifics and humans. Gross, Rocha-Miranda, & Bender (1972) made the first startling finding of cells that responded selectively to the sight of a specific body part, such as a monkey's paw. Subsequent work in the STSa revealed populations of cells selective for the sight of faces and bodily actions, such as articulations of the limbs and torso, but also whole-body actions (such as walking) (Bruce et al., 1981; Desimone, Albright, Gross, & Bruce, 1984; Jellema, Baker, Oram, & Perrett, 2002; Jellema & Perrett, 2002; Perrett et al., 1984, 1985a, 1985b, 1989; Perrett, Rolls, & Caan, 1982; Perrett, Hietanen, Oram, & Benson, 1992). Because bodily actions are so complex in terms of the component postures and motions which make them up, coding for them is no mean feat. It implies that an individual cell responding to, for example, forward walking combines input from many cells coding for each of the constituent components with respect to both form and motion.

Other STSa cells are tuned to multiple views of the same animate object (Logothetis, Pauls, & Poggio, 1995; Perrett, Mistlin, & Chitty, 1987) or the same action (Jellema et al., 2002), or are tuned to conceptually related visual stimuli, such as multiple body signals of directed attention (Perrett et al., 1985a, 1992). This response selectivity is, again, probably obtained through pooling of the outputs of cells coding for separate, distinct, stimuli.

It is characteristic of many STSa cells that they integrate information about form and motion of animate objects (Oram & Perrett, 1994, 1996; Tanaka, Koyama, & Mikami, 1999) and, as has only recently become clear, integrate information about the spatial location of animate objects (Baker, Keysers, Jellema, & Perrett, 2000; Jellema, Maassen, & Perrett, 2004). The ventrodorsal path within the dorsal stream (Turnbull et al., 1997) seems well placed to contribute to the spatial object sensitivity we found in the STSa. STSa cells often generalize their sensitivity to complex shapes across changes in various other stimulus properties such as size, retinal position, orientation, the species (human or monkey), luminance, and colour (e.g. Ashbridge & Perrett, 1998; Ashbridge, Perrett, Oram, & Jellema, 2000; Perrett et al., 1984, 1989; Rolls & Baylis, 1986). The above summarized response characteristics suggest a role in object recognition and allocate the STSa to the ventral visual stream (Milner & Goodale, 1995), in particular its lower bank. The upper bank of the STS is thought to form an interface between the ventral and dorsal streams (Karnath, 2001).

The above findings in the macaque monkey have led to the idea that the STSa is primarily involved in the visual analysis of actions performed by other individuals (Perrett et al., 1989). This view is supported by recent brain-imaging studies, which show activation of the human posterior STS, which area is thought to be the homologue of the monkey STSa, for the perception of biologically significant stimuli. Examples of such stimuli are "biological motion" of human figures (Bonda, Petrides, Ostry & Evans, 1996), hand actions (Grafton, Arbib, Fadiga, & Rizzolatti, 1996; Rizzolatti et al., 1996a), static faces (Allison, Puce, & McCarthy, 2000), eye gaze and eye motion

(Hoffman & Haxby, 2000; Puce, Allison, Bentin, Gore, & McCarthy, 1998), and meaningful actions (Decety, Grezes, Costes, Perani, Jeannerod, & Procyk, 1997) (for reviews, see Allison et al., 2000; Puce & Perrett, 2003). A recent study explicitly showed that the human posterior STS represents goal-directed or intentional actions (Saxe, Xiao, Kovacs, Perrett, & Kanwisher, 2004).

General procedures

The findings presented in this chapter are based on different subsets of *visually* responsive STSa cells. All cells were located in either the upper or lower bank, or fundus, of the STSa, 20–12 mm anterior to the interaural plane. The experiments were performed on awake rhesus macaque monkeys (*Macaca mulatta*). A detailed description of the methods can be found elsewhere (e.g. Jellema, Baker, Wicker, & Perrett, 2000; Oram & Perrett, 1996). Stimuli, consisting of humans or monkeys, were presented either on film projected onto a screen at life size, or live (only for human stimuli) from behind a fast rise-time shutter. Most cells do not discriminate between these two species (Perrett et al., 1985b). About 75% of the visually responsive cells responded maximally when the visual stimulus consisted of a conspecific or a human (that is, an animate object) performing a particular action or assuming a particular body posture. Only these cells were subjected to detailed analysis. The remaining 25% of the cells responded less selectively to various bodily actions and postures.

PART I

3. Conjunctions of actions and head/eye gaze direction

A population of STSa cells responded to the sight of an actor making a reaching action with the arm, but only on the condition that the direction of head and eye gaze of the actor matched the direction of reaching (Jellema et al., 2000). In other words, the agent performing the action needed to attend to the target position of the reaching action in order to excite the cell. Such conditional selectivity can be generated from combining the properties of two distinct cell populations within the STSa: one cell population which responds selectively to face view and eye gaze, and another cell population which responds to directed arm movement. The combined analysis of direction of attention and body movements may well support the detection of whether an observed action was made intentionally or accidentally.

The responses of STSa cells to faces have often been interpreted as having a role either in the recognition of faces as a class of object, or in discriminating between individuals (Baylis, Rolls, & Leonard, 1985; Perrett et al., 1984; Young & Yamane, 1992). These ideas are in particular supported by findings

The perception of goal-directed actions 85

that a minority of cells respond to all possible head views (Hasselmo, Rolls, Baylis, & Nalwa, 1989; Perrett et al., 1985a, 1991). The majority of the cells, however, respond selectively to a particular view of a head (front view, left profile view, etc.). Cell sensitivity to just one view or orientation of an animate object may have a function in understanding an action sequence from momentary postures that constitute key components of that action (Byrne, 1995; Perrett, 1999). Another, particularly potent, use of view selectivity could be to infer the direction of attention of others (Perrett et al., 1992). Thus, a cell responding to the left profile, but not to the right, may code for the abstract notion of "attention directed to the observer's left", instead of coding for the geometric characteristics of the left side of the face. The finding that cells coding for the frontal face view are most frequently encountered may then reflect the importance of attention being directed at the observer in social interactions. The visual information arising from body cues appears to contribute to cell sensitivity in a way that is consistent with the cell's role in analysing the direction of attention. For example, cells tuned to the left profile view of the head are often also tuned to the left profile view of the body (Wachsmuth, Oram, & Perrett, 1994). However, the direction of another individual's head or body may not always be a reliable index of where that individual's attention lies (Perrett et al., 1992). Gaze direction seems a more powerful guide in this respect, and gaze may therefore also be expected to affect STSa cell responses. This is indeed the case. For example, cells inhibited by a frontal face looking at the subject, responded vigorously to the right and left profiles, and to the back of the head. When the gaze of the frontal face was directed away from the subject, the inhibition was lifted (Figure 4.1a). A plausible interpretation is that such cells contribute to the coding for attention

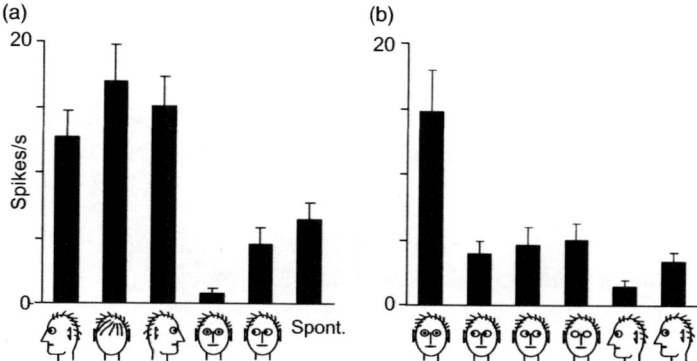

Figure 4.1 Responses of cells sensitive to head and gaze direction. (a) Responses of one cell to head and gaze (and attention) directed away from the subject. (b) Responses of a different cell to head and gaze (and attention) directed toward the subject. Mean responses (± s.e.) are shown. Spont. = spontaneous activity. The visual stimuli are schematically indicated at the bottom. Adapted from Jellema et al. (2000).

directed away from the subject (Jellema et al., 2000). By contrast, other cells (Figure 4.1b) responded maximally when the gaze was directed at the subject, and significantly less when the gaze was directed away to the left or right, or when the eyes were closed. Eye gaze compatible with head direction (such as both directed to the right) gave no response, but subsequently switching the gaze direction towards the subject did produce a response (Figure 4.1b). Such cells may code for attention directed at the subject. We do not claim that all cells in the STSa responsive to the sight of the face code for the direction of attention, but rather that this capacity is "constructed" within the STSa.

Despite the findings of cellular sensitivity to attention direction in macaques, it still remains a matter of debate whether Old World monkeys are able to use information about the gaze direction of others. For example, Anderson, Montant, & Schmitt (1996) report that macaque monkeys cannot be trained to use human gaze to locate hidden food. Behavioural assessments in our laboratory, however, have shown that macaques do spontaneously utilize the direction of attention of conspecifics to orient their own attention (Emery, Lorincz, Perrett, Oram, & Baker, 1997; Lorincz, Baker, & Perrett, 1999).

STSa cells that are selectively responsive to articulations of limbs or parts of the face or body, such as the mouth, eyes, head, torso, legs, arms, hands and fingers, have also been documented (Mistlin & Perrett, 1990; Perrett et al., 1985b, 1990). Cells may respond selectively to arm movements, and not to equivalent leg movements, or to leg movements, and not to equivalent arm movements (Jellema et al., 2000). We have yet to establish exactly which visual cues the STSa cells utilize to discriminate between arm and leg movements; whether it is the form, the kinematics of articulation, or both. Additionally, the cells often showed sensitivity to the direction of the motion; some are tuned to reaching toward the observer, others to reaching to the observer's left, etc. Movements directed away from the subject may acquire particular meaning in a given context. For example, if a food tray is kept out of sight to the subject's right, the sight of the experimenter reaching right can become salient, since this may bring the experimenter's hand to food that is subsequently given to the subject. The significance of such events may contribute to the cells' sensitivity to the distinction between arm and leg movements.

For a subset of the population of STSa cells responding to the sight of arm reaching, the response could be modulated by the direction of attention of the agent performing the action (Jellema et al., 2000). Figure 4.2 illustrates one such cell. A reaching action directed toward the subject evoked a vigorous response, provided the agent paid attention to the site the action was directed at (1.5 m in front of the subject; Figure 4.2a). Exactly the same reaching movement, but made while the agent constantly looked away to either the left or right, evoked a significantly smaller response (Figure 4.2b; $p < 0.001$). Note that the modulation was not confined to the actual reaching action, but persisted in the subsequent static phase during which the experimenter held

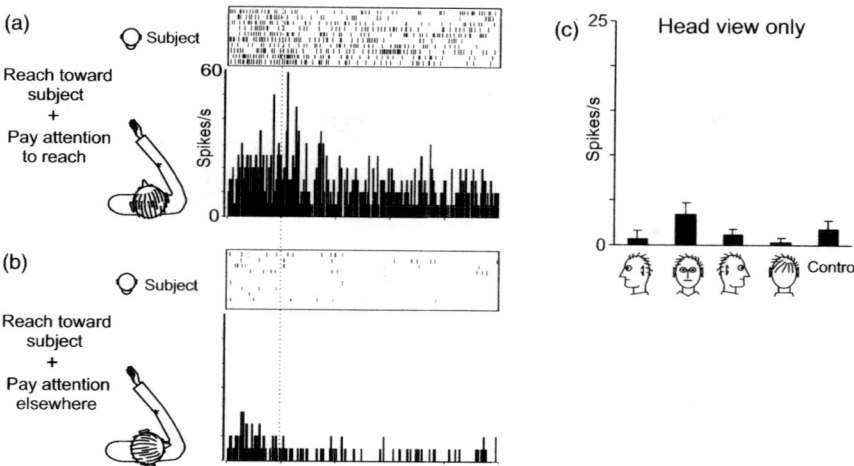

Figure 4.2 Responses of a cell discriminating between the sight of actions performed with and without congruent attention. (a) The experimenter reached his arm in the direction of the subject and constantly paid attention to his arm. The reaching action evoked a vigorous burst that was maintained after the arm became static in an outstretched posture (dotted line). (b) The experimenter performed an identical movement but continuously paid attention elsewhere. (c) The responses to different perspective head views were all relatively small. Peristimulus time histograms (bin width is 20 ms; total duration, 5 s), with spike rastergrams on top, are shown. The schematic drawings to the left of the panels show the experimenter and the subject (plan view), to indicate their relative position. Adapted from Jellema et al. (2000).

his arm stationary in the extended position. The only difference in the visual stimulus between the attended and unattended conditions (a and b) was the orientation of the head and gaze. In principle, this might explain the results, since it is known that STSa cells can respond differently to different head views. However, the responses of the reaching cells to just the different perspective views of the head (with gaze and head direction congruent) were all very small, effectively ruling out this possibility (Figure 4.2c).

This "modulation" of responses to reaching by the direction of attention has not been studied extensively. For seven cells (of nine tested) responsive to reaching, the mean response magnitude in the "attended" condition was more than twice that in the "unattended" condition. Body posture, which provides another potential cue to the direction of attention (Perrett et al., 1992; Wachsmuth et al., 1994), was found to further contribute to the "modulation" of the response to a reaching movement (Jellema et al., 2000).

We argue that by combining the appropriate outputs of cells that respond to directed attention with the outputs of cells that respond to directed limb movements, a third cell type with conjoint selectivity for congruent reaching and attention can be formed. In this manner, it is possible to generate cells selective for reaching and attention to the observer's left and different cells selective for reaching and attention directed high up, and so on.

The significance of someone's reaching toward an object while his/her attention is focused on the object clearly differs from an identical arm and hand action performed with attention directed elsewhere. In the former case, one is likely to infer that it was this person's intention to reach out for the object in order to pick it up or make contact with it. In the latter case, one may infer that the object was incidental to the arm extension. It is crucial that information about the reaching action, such as its direction and the possible presence of a reaching goal, is linked to information about the direction of attention of the performer. We propose that the responses of the cells are selective for movements of the agent that appear purposive and intentional.

4. Conjunctions of actions and spatial locations

The brain integrates different features of a visual stimulus, such as its form, colour, motion, and location, into a single coherent percept. The question of how the brain manages to do this is often referred to as the binding problem, and has been the subject of intense study and debate. Milner and Goodale suggested that space and form might be processed in both dorsal (parietal) and ventral (temporal) streams but for different purposes (e.g. Goodale et al., 1991; Milner & Goodale, 1995). Recently, we discovered cell populations in the STSa that are sensitive to the spatial location of animate objects after they moved out of sight behind a screen (Baker et al., 2000; Baker, Keysers, Jellema, Wicker, & Perrett, 2001; Jellema & Perrett, 1999). These findings corroborated the ideas put forward by Milner and Goodale, and prompted further investigation into the question of whether the single-cell sensitivity to form and motion in the STSa is combined with sensitivity to location. If it is, in what way could these stimulus characteristics be integrated in single cells, and for what purpose? We showed that spatial information is indeed integrated with form and motion information at the single-cell level, and we argue that this capacity enables STSa cell populations to form representations of goal-directed or socially relevant actions.

We tested 31 STSa cells responsive to sight of walking within the testing room, toward or away from the subject in a compatible manner (that is, forward walking, following one's nose) or in an incompatible manner (backward walking, head and body facing same way). The three features of the visual stimulus: motion, form, and location, each had two levels. The levels of the factor motion consisted of "motion away from the subject" and "motion toward the subject". For the factor form, they consisted of "front view of body" and "back view of body"; for the factor location, they consisted of "near to subject" and "far away from subject". The total walking distance per trial was 4.5 m (walking velocity 1 m/s), between the subject and the wall opposite. The walking space in the testing room (width: 4 m; length: 5 m) was pragmatically divided into three zones: "near" (1–2 m from subject), "middle" (2–3 m), and "far" (3–4 m) (see Figure 4.3a for a plan view of the testing room). Only the "near" and "far" locations were used in the analysis, resulting in $2 \times 2 \times 2 = 8$ conditions.

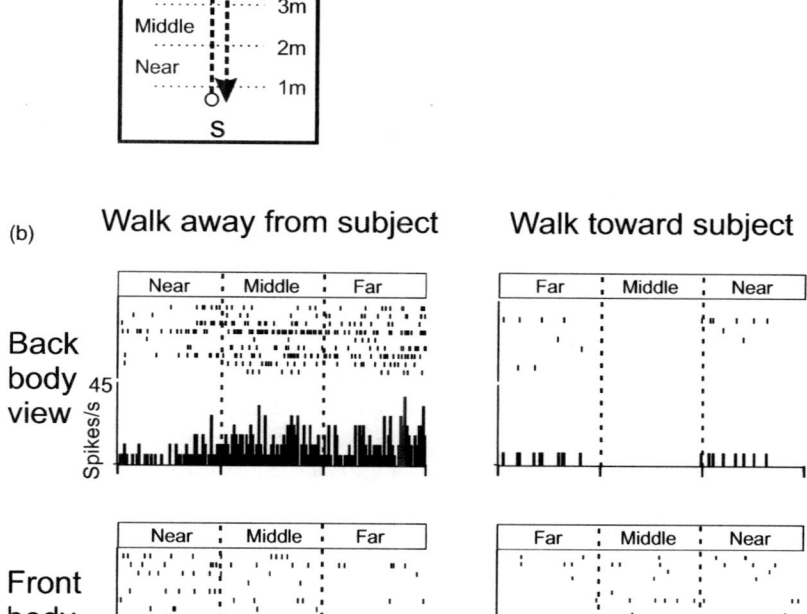

Figure 4.3 Cell response determined by the interaction between motion, form, and location cues. (a) Plan view of the testing room, in which the location of the subject (S) and agent (circle), and the agent's walking path (interrupted lines) are indicated. Walking was performed in either forward or backward manner. (b) Rastergrams and stimulus time histograms show the cell activity during 3-s stimulation periods. Responses are shown for the four combinations of the factors motion and form: motion away/back body view (top left); motion away/front body view (bottom left); motion toward/back body view (top right); motion toward/front body view (bottom right). Locations in the testing room (near, middle, and far) are indicated above the rastergrams. Adapted from Jellema et al. (2004).

Fifty-eight per cent of the cells (18/31) showed sensitivity to the spatial location of the agent. A typical example of a cell maximally sensitive to the walking agent at the "far" location, and significantly less so at the "near" location, is given in Figure 4.3b (top left). Crucially, for this cell, the location sensitivity was present only when the direction of motion of the agent was away from the subject, *and* the back view of the body was visible to the subject (that is, forward walking). Changing the levels of just one of the factors form and motion was enough to abolish the response to walking at the "far" location. Thus, the sight of the agent walking toward the subject, while maintaining the back view of the body to the subject (that is, backward walking; Figure 4.3b, top right), did not evoke a response at the "far" location. The sight of the agent walking away from the subject with the front body view directed to the subject (backward walking) also did not evoke a response at the "far" location (Figure 4.3b, bottom left). The response cannot be explained by assuming that the cell coded exclusively for one type of walking, in this case, forward walking, irrespective of the direction of motion. Such cells have been documented previously, and are said to use an object-centred frame of reference (Perrett et al., 1989). For the cell in Figure 4.3, however, walking forward at the far location toward the subject did not evoke a response (Figure 4.3b, bottom right). Thus, a walking action at the "far" location was effective only when the form consisted of the back view *and* the motion was away from the subject. In other words, the cell's location sensitivity was not absolute, but depended on the form and motion factors. The response magnitude was not related to the pattern of eye fixations. For other cells, significantly larger responses were obtained at the "near" location, while in the remaining 13 out of the 31 cells, no sensitivity for location was found.

For 31 cells, the main effects for the factors motion, form, and location, and the two-way and three-way interactions were analysed: (1) all 31 cells (100%) were significantly influenced by the factor form, either through a main effect and/or through an interaction with one or more of the other factors; (2) the vast majority of the cells (28/31, 90%) were significantly influenced by the factor motion (through a main and/or interaction effect); (3) 18/31 cells (58%) were influenced by the factor location, which consisted of a main effect in nine cells. For the other nine location-sensitive cells, a significant two-way or three-way interaction effect was found in absence of a main location effect.

The population of 31 cells turned out to be quite heterogeneous with respect to the particular combination of factors most effective in driving the cell. For each of the eight possible factor-level combinations, a cell could be found that was maximally excited by it. Certain combinations were, however, much more prevalent than others. A clear example was the motion–form interaction, found in 87% of cells. Close examination of these two-way interactions showed that 70% of these cells were sensitive to form–motion interactions indicating forward walking, while 30% responded to interactions indicating backward walking. The 3:1 ratio confirmed earlier reports (Oram

& Perrett, 1996; Perrett et al., 1985a, 1989), and might reflect the prevalence of forward walking in human, and to a somewhat lesser extent in monkey, society.

Previous studies reported integration of form and motion information at the single-cell level in the STSa (Oram & Perrett, 1994, 1996; Perrett et al., 1985a, 1989), but in these studies the factor location had not been manipulated. We demonstrated that in 58% of a population of cells sensitive to a walking agent, the location of the agent influenced the responses, often by means of intricate two- and three-way interactions with the factors form and motion.

We labelled the locations of the walking agent from the subject's perspective: near or far from the subject. This assumes an egocentric frame of reference, but, in principle, the cells could just as well have used an allocentric frame of reference (that is, spatial descriptions based on environmental landmarks rather than the subject's own position and orientation). Allocentric coding has been observed for STSa cells sensitive to goal-directed actions (Perrett et al., 1989), and for an STSa cell coding for occluded agents (Baker et al., 2001). The ego/allocentric question awaits further investigation. Irrespective of ego- or allocentric references, spatial coding in the STSa seems to be of the categorical type, that is, independent of the absolute positions of the agent and the object in space, but instead dependent on their relative positions (e.g. Kosslyn, 1987). Such relative positions are especially relevant in social interactions.

Our results suggest that spatial coding may indeed be widespread in the STSa, prompting the question of why it was not found before. One reason may be that due to the predominant view of the functions of the dorsal and ventral visual streams (Ungerleider & Mishkin, 1982), most studies on the ventral stream were biased toward investigating object processing, neglecting possible effects of position. But why would the ventral visual stream care about distance if its purpose were to perform object identification? One would rather expect it to ignore distance in order to achieve object constancy. Previously, we suggested that the STSa plays a role not only in animate object identification but also in the visual analysis of the intentions and goals of others' actions, which forms an important aspect of social cognition (Emery & Perrett, 1997; Jellema & Perrett, 2002). We propose that the significance of spatial coding in the STSa must be seen in this light. The spatial positions that individuals occupy with respect to each other, or with respect to objects, contain essential information for an observer when it comes to determining the goals and intentions of those individuals.

STSa cells have been shown to code for different congruent sets of body actions and postures, which convey information about the direction of others' attention (Perrett et al., 1992), or others' intentions (Jellema et al., 2000) and goals (Perrett et al., 1989). Such body actions/postures often relate to particular locations, such as reaching toward a location at which a food reward is kept, or walking toward the door. The previous studies, however, did not define the role of object location in that sensitivity. It is still an open question as to the extent to which STSa cells are sensitive to the spatial location where someone's attention, intention, or action is directed.

5. Conjunctions of actions and their target object

Some STSa cells seem to be sensitive to the causal relationship between an action and the object or goal of that action. This has been demonstrated most clearly in cells sensitive to purposeful hand–object interactions, such as reaching for, picking, tearing, and manipulating objects (Jellema et al., 2000; Perrett et al., 1989, 1990). These STSa cells are sensitive to the form of the hand performing the action, and are unresponsive to the sight of tools manipulating objects in the same manner as hands. Furthermore, the cells code the spatiotemporal interaction between the agent performing the action and the object of the action. For example, cells tuned to hands manipulating an object cease to respond if the object is removed, the hand action is made in a direction away from the object, or the hands and object move appropriately but remain spatially separated (Perrett et al., 1989). This selectivity ensures the cells are more responsive in situations where the agent's motion is *causally* related to the object's motion. Many such cells demonstrate response sensitivity to the relation between the action performed and the goal of the action. Figure 4.4 gives an example of a cell for which reaching toward a target position (where food objects were located) provoked a larger response than reaching in directions away from the target object, irrespective of the location in the testing room from where the reaching action was made. The response of this cell can be best understood by considering the direction of reaching relative to the target object/position. The premotor cortex (F5) shows striking similarities to the STSa in terms of cell responses to the sight of goal-directed hand actions. See Section 9 of this chapter for a discussion of the similarities and differences between these two areas.

PART II

6. Sequence of articulated actions leading to articulated body postures

Actions performed by most animals typically involve articulation. Purely nonarticulated actions, where the body moves solidly, are rare in the animal kingdom. To understand an articulated action performed by another individual, we do not necessarily have to witness the entire action sequence. A single momentary view is often enough to identify the action and possibly also the goal of the action. This is a very useful capacity since it allows us to understand others' actions in situations where the other is intermittently occluded from view, or when we get only one glimpse.

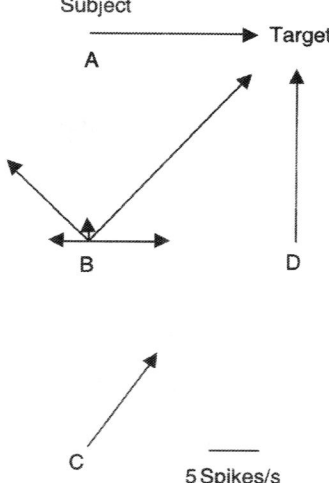

Figure 4.4 Neuronal response to reaching toward a target location. The figure illustrates a plan view of the position of the experimenter relative to the observing subject and the fixed target location. The experimenter stands immediately in front of the subject (A), 1 (B) or 2 m (C) away from the subject, or to the side (D) and reaches in different directions. The length of the lines indicates the magnitude of average neuronal response to one direction of reaching. The arrowheads indicate the direction of reaching. Reaching toward the target produces larger responses than other directions of reaching. Note that the target position or goal of reaching can be attained from multiple starting positions. Adapted from Perrett et al. (1989).

We have studied the sensitivity of STSa cells to body postures containing implied motion and to actual articulated body movements (Jellema & Perrett, 2003b). The underlying idea we wanted to test was that the neural representation of implied biological motion in the STSa might result from forming associations between particular posture and articulation present in actual biological motion. Articulated motion seems to be preferentially processed in the STS, as shown by Beauchamp, Lee, Haxby, & Martin (2003), who made a direct comparison between articulated and nonarticulated human motion, and found that the former activated the STS significantly more than the latter. We postulated that if the static articulated posture were to be presented in isolation (that is, in the absence of actual movement), the cell would respond as if the associated actual motion was presented. The nature of any association between sensitivity to posture and sensitivity to action could provide insight into the neural basis of the phenomenon of implied motion. We defined articulated actions as actions where one body part (such as a limb or head) moves with respect to the body(-part) it is attached to, which remains static; conversely, nonarticulated actions are actions where the equivalent body parts do not move with respect to each other but move as one. Similarly, articulated static body postures contain a torsion or rotation between parts, while nonarticulated postures do not (that is, the head, chest, and pelvis aligned and oriented in the same direction, typical of an "at rest" posture).

The procedure for testing the STSa cells started with presenting a wide variety of articulated body actions. When a cell was found to respond specifically to an articulated action, three further conditions were employed. Firstly, similar, but non- or less articulated, actions were presented. The nonarticulated actions were chosen such that the body part in question moved in the same way as in the articulated action. For example, if the articulated action consisted of a rotation of the head from right profile view to face view, with the trunk remaining static in the right profile view, then the nonarticulated action would be a similar head rotation from right profile to face view but with the trunk rotating along with the head (no torsion between head and trunk). Such nonarticulated rotational motion can easily be made by the experimenter when sitting on a rotating chair. Secondly, the nonarticulated starting point (such as right profile head and right profile chest) and the articulated end point of the action (such as front face view head and right profile chest) were presented in isolation (that is, presented immediately after opening of the shutter). Thirdly, static, nonarticulated postures similar to the effective articulated posture were presented (such as front view head and front view chest).

The main result is that 24 cells out of a sample of 44 cells (24/44, 55%) responded vigorously both to the articulated action and to the articulated static posture that formed the end point of the action presented in isolation. The cells did not respond to the sight of the nonarticulated static posture, which formed the starting point of the action. Moreover, the cells did not respond to static postures resembling the articulated end-point posture, but which were in a more relaxed muscular state (that is, nonarticulated). The cells also did not respond to other articulated body actions that were less often associated with the effective static articulated posture. The other 20 cells (20/44, 43%) did not discriminate between whole-body motions and articulations.

Responses to the articulated actions were often highly specific. For example, the cell illustrated in Figure 4.5 responded vigorously to a horizontal head rotation to the right shoulder, starting at the left profile view and ending with the back view of the head. The trunk did not rotate along with the head but remained static throughout (in the left profile view) (Figure 4.5a). Note that the cell continued to respond for several seconds when the presentation of the static articulated end posture was continued following the action. Other similar body actions, such as the mirror image of the action (Figure 4.5b) or a rotation of the whole upper body (that is, head and trunk) (Figure 4.5c), produced significantly smaller responses. The reverse of the action in Figure 4.5A, that is, a rotation of the head from back view to the left profile, also did not evoke a response (Figure 4.5d).

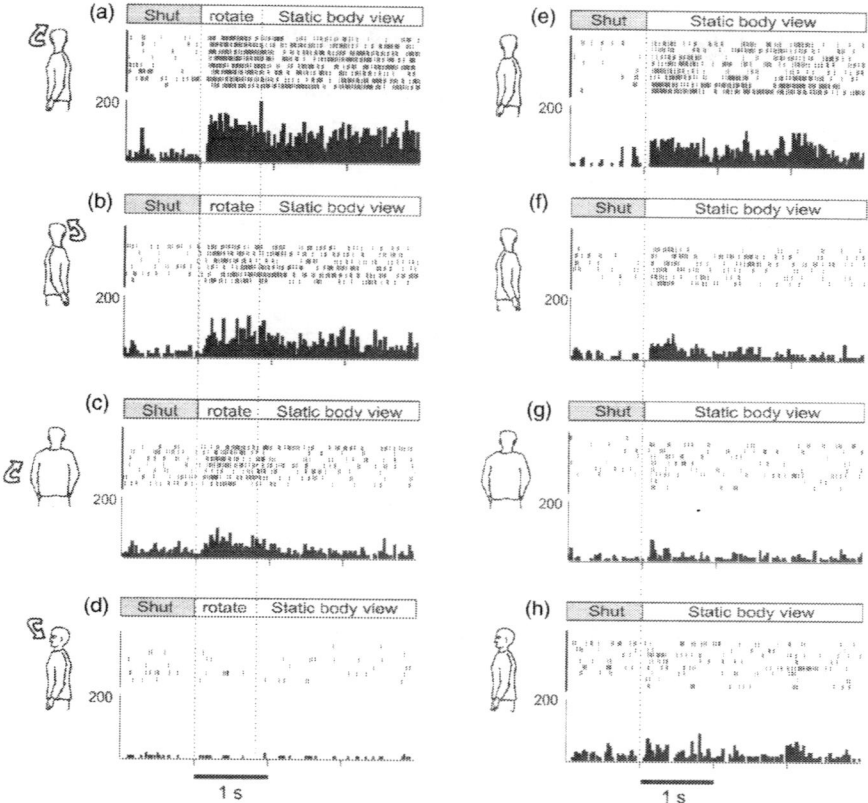

Figure 4.5 Cell responses to a specific articulated action and to the consequent static articulated posture. During the first second of each record, the shutter was closed ("shut"), and the rastergrams show the spontaneous cell activity. During the 2 s following opening of the shutter, the visual stimulus is presented. The direction of articulation of the body is indicated by arrows; the figures indicate the final body posture. Left-hand column (a–d): body actions followed by consequent static postures; right-hand column (e–h): only static body views. See text for details. Adapted from Jellema & Perrett (2003b).

The sight of the articulated static end posture in isolation (Figure 4.5e) evoked a response only slightly smaller than the response to the articulated action (Figure 4.5a). The mirror image of the posture in Figure 4.5e, however, produced a significantly smaller response ($p < .05$; Figure 4.5f). Other static postures that represented a body "at rest", such as the nonarticulated back view of the trunk and head (Figure 4.5g), and the nonarticulated starting posture of the action (Figure 4.5h) failed to produce a response. The response during the first second after shutter opening of the effective articulated action (Figure 4.5a) was significantly larger than the responses in all other conditions in the equivalent time period ($p < .00005$). Thus, the cell required torsion between trunk and head to respond, and did so in a strict manner: only a head rotated over the right shoulder was effective; a rotation over the left shoulder was much less effective (Figure 4.5f).

The population responses under the four main stimulus conditions are shown in Figure 4.6. Figure 4.6a shows a much greater effectiveness of articulated actions compared to the nonarticulated actions, during the action phase itself but also during the consequent static phase ($p < .0007$, comparison for the entire response period). Responses to the static body postures

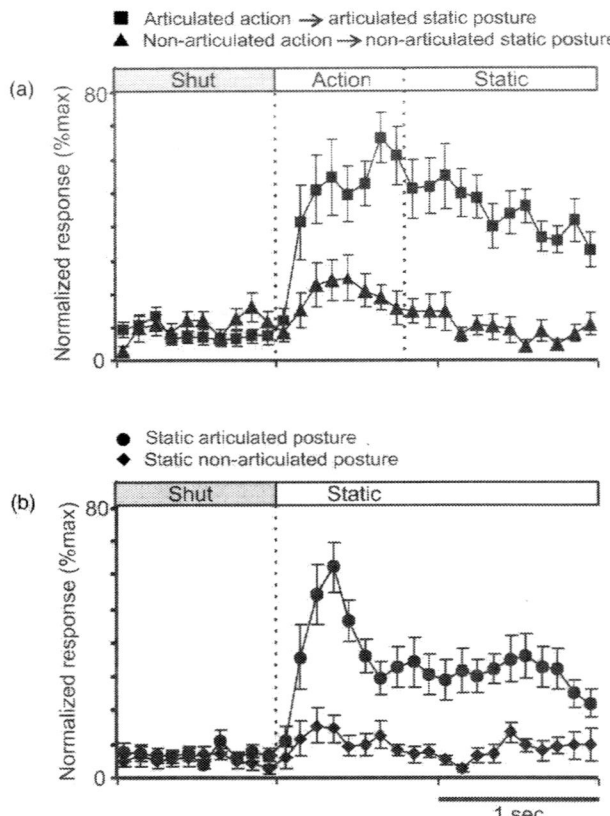

Figure 4.6 Population responses to the actions and resultant postures. Normalized cell responses (expressed as a percentage of the maximal response of the cell) are given for 100-ms time bins (± S.E.). (a) Population responses to the specific articulated action and end static articulated posture that each cell was tuned to (■). Responses to similar but nonarticulated whole body actions, and end static nonarticulated posture (▲). (b) Population responses to articulated static postures (●) and similar but nonarticulated static postures (♦), both without preceding actions. Adapted from Jellema & Perrett (2003b).

presented immediately after opening of the shutter are shown in Figure 4.6b, revealing a much greater effectiveness of the static articulated posture than the nonarticulated control postures ($p < .00001$). The responses to the articulated actions were significantly larger than to the static articulated postures ($p < .004$), demonstrating sensitivity to motion during articulation.

The above findings give rise to the intriguing possibility that STSa cells code for a particular articulated action both when actually presented and when implied in a still image. Previously, STSa cell responses were described that were tuned to the same perspective view of multiple parts of the body (such as left profile view of the trunk and left profile view of the head) (Wachsmuth et al., 1994). The cells described here required different perspective views of body segments (that is, torsion or twisting of body parts). We suggest that the cells code for the implied motion contained in the static articulated posture, or, in other words, code for the association of motion and posture, rather than for the articulated posture per se.

In principle, a static image of an animate object with implied motion can be associated with movements that are likely to have occurred before the time at which the static image was formed, but also with movements that are likely to follow. In our study, the association between motion and posture exhibited by cell responses involved movement that brought the body into the static articulated end-point postures. We did not find cell responses tuned both to articulated postures and to motions that followed these postures. This asymmetry may reflect a sample bias, or a more fundamental difference in organization.

A brain structure known to be particularly relevant to processing visual object motion is the medial temporal/medial superior temporal (V5(MT)/MST) complex. This complex plays a primary role in the analysis of the direction and speed of moving objects in the visual world (Maunsell & Van Essen, 1983; Shadlen, Britten, Newsome, & Movshon, 1996). Recently, it was shown that in humans the V5(MT)/MST complex is also involved in the processing of *implied* motion of objects (as in a snapshot of an athlete running) (Kourtzi & Kanwisher, 2000; Senior et al., 2000). This suggests that V5(MT)/MST can be activated in the absence of any direct visual motion experience. Furthermore, it suggests a top-down influence on V5(MT)/MST, since the object and context may first need to be identified, before the likely type of movement associated with the object in that context can be determined. Such object-recognition and knowledge-related processes suggest an involvement of areas in the ventral recognition stream that may play a role in registering the associations between particular forms and associated movements. These areas should represent knowledge of the repertoire of behaviours an animate object normally exhibits, allowing an observer to infer whether or not the object was moving at the time at which a fleeting glimpse was made (or a picture was taken), and its most likely previous/next position. We propose that the STSa forms an important source of feedback projections onto V5(MT)/MST in the case of biological implied motion. Direct and indirect anatomical connections between the two areas exist (e.g. Boussaoud, Ungerleider, & Desimone, 1990).

To conclude this section, we envisage that the neural representations in the STSa for *actual* biological motion may also extend to biological motion *implied* from static postures. These representations could play a role in producing the activity in the V5(MT)/MST areas reported in fMRI studies when subjects view still photographs of people in action. Our data show that the visual processing of static form may contribute to the comprehension of dynamic actions. Sensitivity to associations between image form and motion could form the basis of the ability of the nervous system to retrieve likely motion given entirely static images.

7. Sequences of actions and postures

Under natural viewing conditions, STSa cell responses to the sight of static body postures may be controlled by actions performed by that body in the 1 or 2 s immediately preceding the onset of the static posture (Jellema & Perrett, 2003a). In other words, the perceptual history can enable or prevent a cell's response to the current retinal input. For example, a cell may respond vigorously to the sight of a face when the face was preceded by action A, but fail to respond to the identical face when preceded by action B and fail to respond to the sight of a face when presented without any preceding action.

For 29 out of 54 cells (54%) sensitive to the static posture, we found that the nature of the movement preceding a static posture proved critical to the modulation of cell responses. The remaining 25 cells were not sensitive to the perceptual history. For example, the response of the cell illustrated in Figure 4.7 increased dramatically about 500 ms after the agent had stopped walking, and maintained high spiking activity for several seconds during which the agent maintained the static posture (Figure 4.7a). Note that the response of this cell during the action phase was no different from the spontaneous activity during the blank (Figure 4.7b, left side). Other actions leading up to the same static body view, such as walking backward followed by stopping, did not result in a response during the static phase. Thus, although the type of preceding motion was crucial for evoking a response during the static phase, the cells did not respond to the action itself. Front, side, and back views of the static body could all produce a response after cessation of forward walking in any direction, but not after cessation of backward walking (the cell thus displayed object-centred coding). The cell failed to respond to the identical static body posture when presented directly after opening of the shutter (Figure 4.7b), indicating that sight of the action was necessary. To ensure that the presence of the static body view was also strictly necessary, that is, that the response would not have happened anyway, irrespective of the type of stimulus that followed the "effective" action, a further condition was employed. In this condition, the static body view was

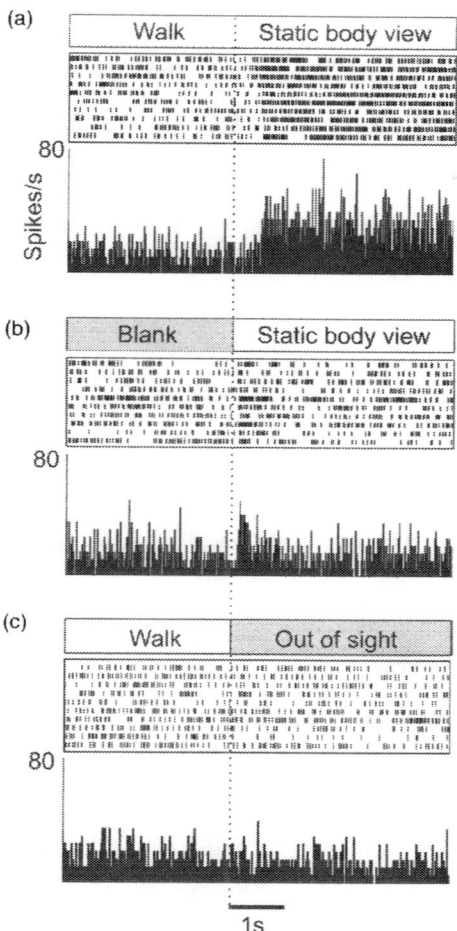

Figure 4.7 Cell responses sensitive to a walking–posture sequence, but not to the isolated walking and static elements. (a) Vigorous response to the static view of the agent once walking had stopped. (b) The identical static view evoked a small transient response when presented immediately after opening of the shutter. (c) The agent kept walking until he completely disappeared from view behind an occluding screen. The activity during full occlusion of the experimenter did not differ from the activity during walking ($p > .1$). Jellema & Perrett (2003a).

replaced by a static scene without the body (the agent had walked behind a screen), but such a situation did not enhance the cell's spiking activity (Figure 4.7c). This indicated that the response during the static phase required the presence of the particular static body view, and could not be explained by cessation of the visibility of the effective action or by a delayed, or continued response to the effective action.

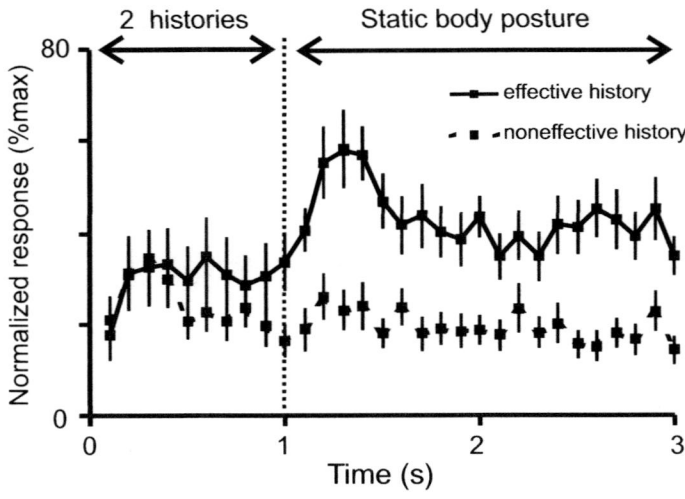

Figure 4.8 Population response to static body postures dependent on perceptual history. The responses of 25 cells sensitive to perceptual history were pooled. Cells were tested with two different perceptual histories, directly followed by the same static body posture. For each cell, the mean spike count in 100-ms time bins was expressed as a percentage of the maximal response of that cell during the 3-s recording period. Adapted from Jellema & Perrett (2003a).

The population response ($n=29$) is shown in Figure 4.8. Individual mean cell responses were entered for two different perceptual histories: an "effective" and an "ineffective" history. The responses to the static posture when preceded by the "effective" history were significantly larger than when preceded by the "ineffective" history, during s 1 ($p < .0002$) and s 2 ($p < .0005$) of the static phase. The responses during the two preceding histories did not differ ($p = .2$). It was surprising to find that the responses during the static phase when preceded by an "effective" action were often quite prolonged (see also Figure 4.7a), because the "classical" response of STSa cells to, for example, a static face, typically does not exceed 500 ms (Oram & Perrett, 1992). The sensitivity to perceptual history applied to virtually all types of action that were tested, stressing the pervasive influence that the immediate history has on perceptual processing.

These results show that the "vocabulary" of actions and body postures coded by single STSa cells is much larger than previously thought and encompasses specific action–posture sequences. We argue that temporal cortex cells can support the formation of expectations about impending behaviour of others, suggesting a role in the understanding of actions.

The interpretation of an observed action is profoundly influenced by the perceptual history, that is, events that have been witnessed in the immediate past. The traditional view is that in passive viewing situations the responses of visual temporal cortex cells are straightforwardly related to the current visual stimulation of the retina; the response selectivity is determined by the geometrical characteristics of the stimulus. However, studies employing learning paradigms, such as delayed matching-to-sample (Miller, Li, & Desimone, 1993; Miyashita, 1988) and paired-association tasks (Sakai & Miyashita, 1991), have shown that neurons in the macaque anterior temporal cortex can acquire stimulus selectivity through learning. These studies show that the cells are able to link the representations of temporally associated stimuli, even though the stimuli are geometrically dissimilar. The temporal cortex may therefore be involved in forming long-term visual associative memories during a lifetime (Booth & Rolls, 1998). The sensitivity to multiple stimuli that are temporally related, even though visually distinct, is echoed in the tuning of cells to multiple views of the same object (Jellema et al., 2002; Logothetis et al., 1995; Perrett et al., 1987).

Previous studies indicated that temporal cortex cells represent particular attributes of objects and are activated when these attributes are present and attended to in the visual scene, or are recalled from memory through associations. Such a description fails to predict the visual selectivity for prior events which we describe. We find that for a population of STSa cells there is an additional (second order) selectivity for the sequence of two stimuli. Classically, cells respond to a particular static stimulus X, and not to other static stimuli (Y, Z). For the cells we describe, a response to X occurs only when it follows movement A, and not movements B or C. Thus, images from the immediate past control the response to the current stimulus. We also show that both the preceding history and the static posture need to be present in order to get the response.

Our results are fundamentally different from those of delayed matching-to-sample tasks (Miller et al., 1993; Miyashita, 1988) and pair-association learning tasks (Sakai & Miyashita, 1991). The cells showing paired associate sensitivity show responses to one of the images from the pair when this is presented in isolation, while the cells we describe do not respond to component elements (the action alone or the posture alone). Moreover, in our data, all preceding actions "match" the static posture to the same degree, yet only one of them is able to enhance the response to the posture, whereas in the study of Miller et al. (1993), the degree of similarity between sample and test stimulus determined the response.

The association of representations of the different momentary views (that is, the spatiotemporal sequence) of a moving object, acquired via learning throughout a lifetime, is thought to form an integral part of the neural representation of that object (Földiák, 1991; Koenderink & Van Doorn, 1979; Wallis & Bülthoff, 2001). The neural representations for sequences of events may play a role in predicting or anticipating the next move or posture of the animate object. For example, the sight of a body that has just stopped walking forward may invoke an expectation that, should walking commence again, it is likely to resume a forward direction. The same view of a static body that has just stopped walking backward, by contrast, may be expected to move in a backward direction should walking resume.

8. Sequences of actions in which agents become hidden

The actions of others are not always fully visible; for example, people may become hidden from our sight as they move behind a tree, or their hands may not remain fully in view as they reach to retrieve an object. Within the STS, it is now apparent that specific cell populations are activated when the presence of a hidden agent can be inferred from the preceding visual events (that is, the agent was witnessed passing out of sight behind a screen and has not yet been witnessed re-emerging into sight—therefore, the agent is likely to remain behind the screen; Baker et al., 2001). The population response of STSa cells to this sequence of events is shown in Figure 4.9.

Figure 4.9 shows that STSa cells responded maximally when individuals were seen to "hide" behind an occluding screen. In the 3 s following disappearance from sight behind a screen, the population response was significantly larger than in the prior 3 s when the agent was visible and moving toward the screen. Some cells had no detectable response to visible movements but started responding 1–4 s after the agent had become completely hidden. The cells responding to occlusion also showed spatial sensitivity discriminating between locations at which the agent was hidden (at the left, right, or middle of the room) (Baker et al., 2001). Cell responses to the experimenter walking in sight were consistent with the out-of-sight responses. For example, if hiding behind a screen located at the right-hand side of the testing room evoked significantly larger responses than hiding behind a screen at the left-hand side, then walking toward the right-hand screen would also evoke a larger response than walking toward the left-hand screen, walking in both cases from left to right. These responses are consistent with the idea that the cells coded not only for the presence of the experimenter behind the right-hand screen, but also for the intention of the experimenter to go behind that screen. For this interpretation, we need assume only that walking toward the right screen reflects the intention to move behind that screen.

9. Comparison between cell responses in the STSa and the premotor cortex (F5)

The STSa cell populations coding body and hand actions appear to be exclusively visual, although information from the motor system does affect other STSa cell populations (Hietanen & Perrett, 1996) and modulates STS activity in humans (Iacoboni et al., 2001; Nishitani & Hari, 2001). Gallese and Goldman (1998) suggested that the "action-detecting" system in STSa could provide an initial "pictorial" description of the action, this information being then relayed to frontal motor planning systems. The manner in which temporal STS and frontal systems interact is not fully clear, but probably

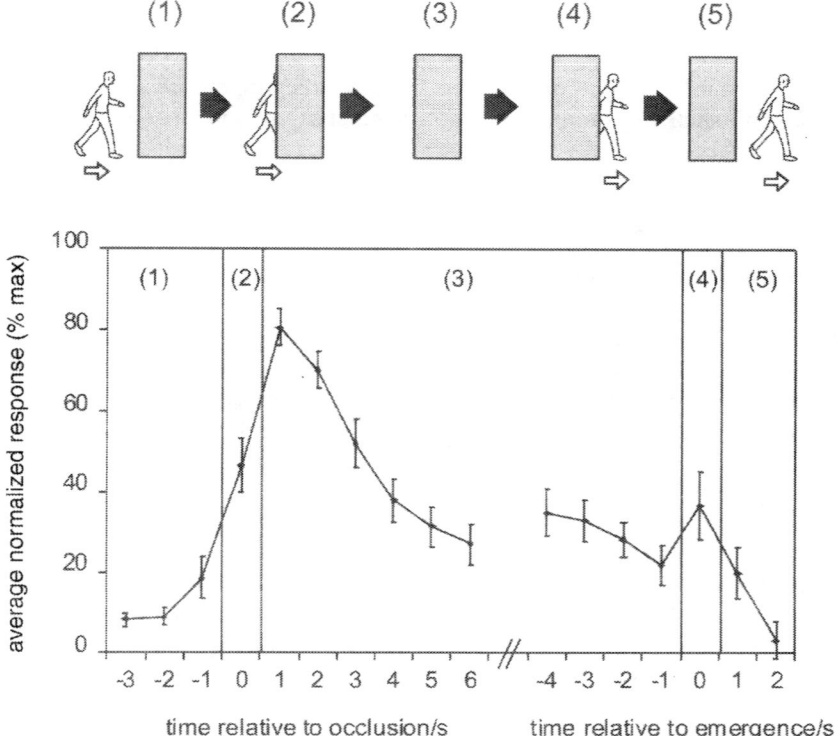

Figure 4.9 STS population response before, during, and after an occlusion from sight. Upper panel: periods of the visual stimulus. The experimenter moved towards the occluding screen (1), was gradually occluded (2), remained hidden from view with only the screen visible (3), and gradually re-emerged (4), until the object was once again fully in view (5). Filled arrows show the progression of events and outlined arrows the direction of movement. Lower panel: activity profile during the disappearance and subsequent emergence of the experimenter. The graph shows the average normalized population response of 26 cells recorded in STSa. On the left of the graph, responses are aligned with respect to the occlusion period (2). On the right, the responses are aligned with respect to the emergence period (4). Adapted from Baker et al. (2001).

involves intermediate processing steps mediated by parietal areas (Gallese, Fadiga, Fogassi, & Rizzolatti, 2002; Nishitani & Hari, 2000, 2001). The frontal region of primate cortex (inferior area 6) has long been known to be somatotopically organized for the representation and control of movements of the mouth and arm (Rizzolatti, Camarda, Fogassi, Gentilucci, Luppino, & Matelli, 1988). This area can be subdivided into areas F4 and F5 (Rizzolatti & Gentilucci, 1988). Neurons in F5 are activated during specific motor acts performed with the hand or mouth, such as grasping, holding, and tearing.

Cells with responses related to reaching movements of the arm are typically found in F4.

Cells in F5 discharge during the execution of a particular action and during the sight of the same action. For example, an F5 cell that responds selectively when the monkey executes a grasping action may also respond (like STS cells) to the sight of another monkey or the experimenter grasping an object, but not to the sight of different hand actions such as tearing (Di Pellegrino, Fadiga, Fogassi, Gallese, & Rizzolatti, 1992; Gallese, Fadiga, Fogassi, & Rizzolatti, 1996; Rizzolatti et al., 1996a; Rizzolatti, Fadiga, Gallese, & Fogassi, 1996b). An F5 cell selective for the execution of grasping would also respond when the monkey grasps an object in the dark, thereby demonstrating the motor properties of the response. These conjoint properties have led Rizzolatti et al. (1996a, 1996b) and Gallese et al. (1996) to postulate that the F5 neurons form a system for matching observation and executing actions for the grasping, manipulation, and placement of objects. These neurons have now been labelled "mirror" neurons. Cells with response selectivity similar to those in F5 have recently been reported in the inferior parietal lobule (Gallese et al., 2002; Williams, Whiten, Suddendorf, & Perrett, 2001).

The experiments in which actions are partially, or totally, occluded from sight have also highlighted the similarities of the STS and F5 systems in the processing of actions. F5 cells may respond, in a manner analogous to the STS cells, to the sight of the agent reaching to grasp an object. The same F5 cells are active when the experimenter places an object behind a screen and then reaches as if to grasp it (even though the object and hand are hidden from view; Umilta et al., 2001). The sight of equivalent reaching when there is no reason to believe an object is hidden from sight fails to activate the F5 cells. Thus, F5 and STS cells code the sight of actions on the basis of what is currently visible and on the basis of the recent perceptual history (Jellema et al., 2002; Jellema & Perrett, 2002, 2003a).

Thus, the visual properties of mirror neurons in F5 cell are strikingly similar to those described in STSa. Both F5 and STSa cells respond when the monkey observes the experimenter reaching and grasping an object, but will not respond to the sight of the experimenter's hand motion alone or to the sight of the object alone. In addition, the F5 cells respond to the execution of the corresponding motor act, and to the corresponding sound of actions (Kohler, Keysers, Umilta, Fogassi, Gallese, & Rizzolatti, 2002). Therefore, the F5 mirror system may provide a supramodal conceptual representation of actions and their consequences in the world. Crucially, the properties of the frontal mirror system suggest that we may understand actions performed by others because we can match the actions we sense through vision and audition to our ability to produce the same actions ourselves.

While STS and F5 cells have similar visual properties, they may subserve distinct functions; the frontal system perhaps serves to control the behaviour of the self particularly in dealing with objects (Rizzolatti et al., 1996a,

1996b), whereas the STS system is specialized for the detection and recognition of the behaviour of others (Hietanen & Perrett, 1996; Mistlin & Perrett, 1990; Perrett et al., 1989). The mirror neuron system might also complement the STSa description of the perceived action by adding information about the motor requirements of the perceived action, which could not easily be obtained from purely visual features. At a more speculative level, it has been proposed that the mirror neurons are involved in the ability to "read" others' minds. The cells may allow an observer to "experience" and understand an action performed by another through "simulating" that action (Gallese & Goldman, 1998).

10. General discussion

We reviewed recent data that indicate that neurons in the STSa of the macaque monkey code not only for the sight of others' bodily actions per se, but also for combinations of actions with other visual cues. These other visual cues derive from the body, such as head/eye gaze direction or articulated body postures, or from the environment, such as target objects of the action, and the spatial location of the actor. We have found two basic ways in which the sensitivity for actions is combined with the sensitivity for these other visual cues: (1) by means of spatial conjunctions of cues (that is, the cues are simultaneously present); (2) by means of temporal sequences of cues (that is, the cues are present consecutively). We argue here that combining the sensitivity to actions with sensitivity to other bodily or environmental cues puts the STSa in a position to form representations of the causality or goal-directedness of others' actions. As such, the STSa is thought to contribute to the understanding of actions.

In Part I, we described how sensitivity to *conjunctions* of actions and other visual cues might contribute to the forming of representations of the goal-directedness of actions. For instance, conjunctions of perceived actions with the perceived eye gaze direction of the agent performing the action may contribute to detecting the accidental or intentional outcome of the perceived action (Section 3). An obvious question is of course whether there is behavioural evidence that nonhuman primates indeed discriminate between intentional and nonintentional actions (Byrne & Whiten, 1988). A study by Call and Tomassello (1998) showed that nonhuman great apes preferentially followed intentional actions performed by the experimenter, rather than non-intentional actions. In our laboratory, it was shown that macaque monkeys spontaneously follow the direction of attention of conspecifics (Emery et al., 1997; Lorincz et al., 1999). The advantages of being able to determine others' intentions from their actions are clear. For instance, it allows the observer to quickly anticipate the nature of the future actions of the other individual, which may range from friendly and cooperative to hostile and threatening, and to adjust responses accordingly.

The relative spatial locations of the agent and the objects the agent interacts with (including the observer) may give important insight into what the agent's intention or goal might be. We described cells which seem especially equipped to keep track of such spatial relationships between (animate-)objects. They achieve this by means of integrating, in intricate ways, the spatial information with form and motion information (Section 4). Such integration may thus support the comprehension of animals and their actions.

The object toward which an action is directed is particularly important when it comes to interpreting the goal of the action (Section 5). Cells were described that code the spatiotemporal interaction between the agent performing the action and the target object of the action. Such selectivity ensures the cells are optimally responsive in situations where the agent's motion is causally related to the object's motion.

In Part II, we described how sensitivity to *sequences* of actions and other visual cues might contribute to the forming of representations of goal-directed actions. The formation of associations between an articulated action and the static articulated end posture of that action might well underlie the ability of the brain to infer impending or prior action from static postures (Section 6). The performance of dexterous manual tasks can easily be specified as a series of static pictures, each demonstrating particular subgoals or stages in the action sequence. Based on an understanding of momentary postures during an action sequence, individuals can infer the dynamics of how an action was performed.

Other cells seemed tuned to impending behaviours of others, based on the perceptual history (Section 7). Witnessing the perceptual history prior to viewing a static body allows one to predict the likelihood and nature of the body's future movement with more certainty than from a still image of a person performing a motor act (Section 6). Our data strongly suggest that the building blocks for the representations of complex action–static sequences are represented within the STSa, but *predictions* about actions are not necessarily computed in the STS. The relatively long onset latency (~500 ms) of some cells sensitive to perceptual history (see the cell in Figure 4.7) allows ample time for top-down inputs to exert their effects. Yet other cells show sensitivity to history without an obvious delay. The coding of sequences of events can help our understanding of natural body actions. Such natural actions are not isolated postures, but are continuous and complex sequences of postures with linking movements. We speculate that these cells play a role in predicting the most likely next stage or consequence of the action. They may also help recognize complex action sequences, which comprise component acts.

Sequences of events are also crucial for those cells that code for agents hidden behind a screen. The observer needs to witness the agent disappearing behind the screen in order for the cell to produce a response to the hidden agent (Section 8). The responses indicated that some cells coded not only for the presence of the agent behind the screen, but also for the intention of the agent to go behind the screen.

Determining the goal or intention of a visually perceived animate action involves not only the visual system but also the emotional (Adolphs, 1999) and motor (Gallese & Goldman, 1998) systems. The ability to determine others' intentions is thus likely to be generated in a widely distributed network, involving many brain areas. We argue that the role the STSa plays in this network is that it provides descriptions of others' actions in terms of goals, intentions, or causes. These descriptions are, however, still mechanistic in nature, presumably lacking the attribution of mental states, such as motivational drives and belief (Baron-Cohen, 1994; Saxe et al., 2004), to the agent performing the action. Interactions of the STS with the mirror-neuron systems in parietal and premotor areas, and with systems attaching emotional values to stimuli (such as the amygdala) (Brothers, Ring, & Kling, 1990), may produce the understanding of others' actions in mental states.

References

Adolphs, R. (1999). Social cognition and the human brain. *Trends in Cognitive Sciences, 3,* 469–479.

Allison, T., Puce, A., & McCarthy, G. (2000). Social perception from visual cues: Role of the STS region. *Trends in Cognitive Sciences, 4,* 267–278.

Anderson, J. R., Montant, M., & Schmitt, D. (1996). Rhesus monkeys fail to use gaze direction as an experimenter-given cue in an object-choice task. *Behavioural Processes, 37,* 47–55.

Ashbridge, E., Perrett, D. I., Oram, M. W., & Jellema, T. (2000). Effect of image orientation and size on object recognition: Responses of single units in the macaque monkey temporal cortex. *Cognitive Neuropsychology, 17,* 13–34.

Baker, C. I., Keysers, C, Jellema, T., & Perrett, D. I. (2000). Coding of spatial position in the superior temporal sulcus of the macaque. *Current Psychology Letters: Behaviour, Brain and Cognition, 1,* 71–87.

Baker, C. I., Keysers, C., Jellema, T., Wicker, B., & Perrett, D. I. (2001). Neuronal representation of disappearing and hidden objects in temporal cortex of the macaque. *Experimental Brain Research, 140,* 375–381.

Baron-Cohen, S. (1994). How to build a baby that reads minds: Cognitive mechanisms in mind-reading, *Current Psychology of Cognition, 13,* 513–552.

Baylis, G. C., Rolls, E. T., & Leonard, C. M. (1985). Selectivity between faces in the responses of a population of neurons in the cortex in the superior temporal sulcus of the monkey. *Brain Research, 342,* 91–102.

Beauchamp, M. S., Lee, K. E., Haxby, J. V., & Martin, A. (2003). Parallel visual motion processing streams for manipulable objects and human movements. *Neuron, 34,* 149–159.

Bonda, E., Petrides, M., Ostry, D., & Evans, A. (1996). Specific involvement of human parietal systems and the amygdala in the perception of biological motion. *Journal of Neuroscience, 16,* 3737–3744.

Booth, M., & Rolls, E. T. (1998). View-invariant representations of familiar objects by neurons in the inferior temporal cortex. *Cerebral Cortex, 8,* 510–523.

Boussaoud, D., Ungerleider, L. G., & Desimone, R. (1990). Pathways for motion analysis: Cortical connections of the medial superior temporal and fundus of the superior temporal visual areas in the macaque. *Journal of Comparative Neurology*, *296*, 462–495.

Brothers, L., Ring, B., & Kling, A. (1990). Responses of neurons in the macaque amygdala to complex social stimuli. *Behavioural Brain Research*, *41*, 199–213.

Bruce, C., Desimone, R., & Gross, C. G. (1981). Visual properties of neurons in a polysensory area in superior temporal sulcus of the macaque. *Journal of Neurophysiology*, *46*, 369–384.

Byrne, R. W. (1995). *The thinking ape: Evolutionary origins of intelligence*. New York: Oxford University Press.

Byrne, R. W., & Whiten, A. (1988). *Machiavellian intelligence: Social expertise and the evolution of intellect in monkeys, apes and humans*. Oxford: Clarendon Press.

Call, J., & Tomasello, M. (1998). Distinguishing intentional from accidental actions in orangutans (*Pongo pygmaeus*), chimpanzees (*Pan troglodytes*) and human children (*Homo sapiens*). *Journal of Comparative Psychology*, *112*, 192–206.

Decety, J., Grezes, J., Costes, N., Perani, D., Jeannerod, M., & Procyk, E. (1997). Brain activity during observation of actions. Influence of action content and subject's strategy. *Brain*, *120*, 1763–1777.

Desimone, R., Albright, T. D., Gross, C. G., & Bruce, C. (1984). Stimulus-selective properties of inferior temporal neurons in the macaque. *Journal of Neuroscience*, *4*, 2051–2062.

Desimone, R., & Ungerleider, L. G. (1989). Neural mechanisms of visual processing in monkeys. In F. Boller & J. Grafman (Eds.), *Handbook of neuropsychology* (Vol. 2, pp. 267–299). Amsterdam: Elsevier.

Di Pellegrino, G., Fadiga, L., Fogassi, V., Gallese, V., & Rizzolatti, G. (1992). Understanding motor events: A neurophysiological study. *Experimental Brain Research*, *91*, 176–180.

Dobbins, A. C., Jeo, R. M., Fiser, J., & Allman, J. M. (1998). Distance modulation of neural activity in the visual cortex. *Science*, *281*, 552–555.

Emery, N. J., Lorincz, E. N., Perrett, D. I., Oram, M. W., & Baker, C. I. (1997). Gaze following and joint attention in rhesus monkeys (*Macaca mulatta*). *Journal of Comparative Psychology*, *111*, 286–293.

Emery, N. J., & Perrett, D. I. (1999). How can studies of monkey brain help us understand "theory of mind" and autism in humans? In S. Baron-Cohen, H. Tager-Flusberg, & D. J. Cohen (Eds.), *Understanding other minds 2: Perspectives from autism and cognitive neuroscience* (pp. 279–310). Oxford: Oxford University Press.

Földiák, P. (1991). Learning invariance from transformation sequences. *Neural Computations*, *3*, 194–200.

Gallese, V., Fadiga, L., Fogassi, L., & Rizzolatti, G. (1996). Action recognition in the premotor cortex. *Brain*, *119*, 593–609.

Gallese, V., & Goldman, A. (1998). Mirror neurons and the simulation theory of mind-reading. *Trends in Cognitive Sciences*, *2*, 493–501.

Gallese, V., Fadiga, L., Fogassi, L., & Rizzolatti, G. (2002). Action representation and the inferior parietal lobule. In W. Prinz & B. Hommel (Eds.), *Attention and Performance XIX* (pp. 334–355). Oxford: Oxford University Press.

Goodale, M. A., Milner, A. D., Jakobson, L. S., & Carey, D. P. (1991). A neurological dissociation between perceiving objects and grasping them. *Nature*, *349*, 154–156.

Grafton, S. T., Arbib, M. A., Fadiga, L., & Rizzolatti, G. (1996). Localization of grasp representations in humans by positron emission tomography. II. Observation compared with imagination. *Experimental Brain Research*, *112*, 103–111.

Gross, C. G., Rocha-Miranda, C. E., & Bender, D. B. (1972). Visual properties of neurons in inferotemporal cortex of the macaque. *Journal of Neurophysiology, 35,* 96–111.

Hasselmo, M. E., Rolls, E. T., Baylis, G. C., & Nalwa, V. (1989). Object-centred encoding by face-selective neurons in the cortex in the superior temporal sulcus of the monkey. *Experimental Brain Research, 75,* 417–429.

Haxby, J. V., Grady, C. L., Horwitz, B., Ungerleider, L. G., Mishkin, M., Carson, R. E., et al. (1991). Dissociation of object and spatial visual processing pathways in human extrastriate cortex. *Proceedings of the National Academy of Sciences of the USA, 88,* 1621–1625.

Hietanen, J. K., & Perrett, D. I. (1996). Motion sensitive cells in the macaque superior temporal polysensory area: Response discrimination between self- and externally generated pattern motion. *Behavioural Brain Research, 76,* 155–167.

Iacoboni, M., Koski, L. M., Brass, M., Bekkering, H., Woods, R. P., Dubeau, M. C., et al. (2001). Reafferent copies of imitated actions in the right superior temporal cortex. *Proceedings of the National Academy of Sciences of the USA, 98,* 13995–13999.

Hoffman, E. A., & Haxby, J. V. (2000). Distinct representations of eye gaze and identity in the distributed human neural system for face perception. *Nature Neuroscience, 3,* 80–84.

Jellema, T., & Perrett, D. I. (1999). Coding of object position in the banks of the superior temporal sulcus of the macaque. *Society of Neuroscience Abstracts, 25,* 919.

Jellema, T., Baker, C. I., Wicker B., & Perrett D. I. (2000). Neural representation for the perception of the intentionality of actions. *Brain and Cognition, 44,* 280–302.

Jellema, T., Baker, C. I., Oram, M. W., & Perrett, D. I. (2002). Cell populations in the banks of the superior temporal sulcus of the macaque and imitation. In A. N. Meltzoff & W. Prinz (Eds.), *The imitative mind. Development, evolution, and brain bases* (pp. 267–290). Cambridge: Cambridge University Press.

Jellema, T., & Perrett, D. I. (2002). Coding of visible and hidden objects. In W. Prinz & B. Hommel (Eds.), *Common mechanisms in perception and action. Attention and performance XIX* (pp. 356–380). Oxford: Oxford University Press.

Jellema, T., & Perrett, D. I. (2003a). Perceptual history influences neural responses to face and body postures. *Journal of Cognitive Neuroscience, 15,* 961–971.

Jellema, T., & Perrett, D. I. (2003b). Cells in monkey STS responsive to articulated body motions and consequent static posture: A case of implied motion? *Neuropsychologia, 41,* 1728–1737.

Jellema, T., Maassen, G., & Perrett, D. I. (2004). Single cell integration of animate form, motion, and location in the superior temporal sulcus of the macaque monkey. *Cerebral Cortex, 14,* 781–790.

Karnath, H.-O. (2001). New insights into the functions of the superior temporal cortex. *Nature Reviews Neuroscience, 2,* 568–576.

Kohler, E., Keysers, C., Umilta, M. A., Fogassi, L., Gallese, V., & Rizzolatti, G. (2002). Hearing sounds, understanding actions: Action representation in mirror neurons. *Science, 297,* 846–848.

Kosslyn, S. M. (1987). Seeing and imagining in the cerebral hemispheres: A computational approach. *Psychological Reviews, 94,* 148–175.

Koenderink, J. J., & Van Doorn, A. J. (1979). The internal representation of solid shape with respect to vision. *Biological Cybernetics, 32,* 211–216.

Kourtzi, Z., & Kanwisher, N. (2000). Activation in human MT/MST by static images with implied motion. *Journal of Cognitive Neuroscience, 12*, 48–55.

Logothetis, N. K., Pauls, J., & Poggio, T. (1995). Shape representation in the inferior temporal cortex of monkeys. *Current Biology, 5*, 552–563.

Lorincz, E. N., Baker, C. I., & Perrett, D. I. (1999). Visual cues for attention following in rhesus monkeys. *Current Psychology of Cognition, 18*, 973–1001.

Matelli, M., & Luppino, G. (2000). Parietofrontal circuits: Parallel channels for sensory-motor integrations. *Advances in Neurology, 84*, 51–61.

Maunsell, J. H. R., & Van Essen, D. C. (1983). Functional properties of neurons in the middle visual temporal area of the macaque monkey. I. Selectivity for stimulus direction, speed, and orientation. *Journal of Neurophysiology, 49*, 1127–1147.

Miller, E. K., Li, L., & Desimone, R. (1993). Activity of neurons in anterior inferior temporal cortex during a short-term memory task. *Journal of Neuroscience, 13*, 1460–1478.

Milner, A. D., & Goodale, M. A. (1995). *The visual brain in action*. Oxford: Oxford University Press.

Mistlin, A. J., & Perrett D. I. (1990). Visual and somatosensory processing in the macaque temporal cortex: The role of 'expectation'. *Experimental Brain Research, 82*, 437–450.

Miyashita, Y. (1988). Neuronal correlate of visual associative long-term memory in the primate temporal cortex. *Nature, 335*, 817–820.

Murata, A., Gallese, V., Kaseda, M., & Sakata, H. (1996). Parietal neurons related to memory-guided hand manipulation. *Journal of Neurophysiology, 75*, 2180–2186.

Nishitani, N., & Hari, R. (2000). Temporal dynamics of cortical representation for action. *Proceedings of the National Academy of Sciences of the USA, 97*, 913–918.

Nishitani, N., & Hari, R. (2001). Sign language and mirror neuron system. *Neuroimage, 13*, S452.

Oram, M. W., & Perrett, D. I. (1992). Time course of neural responses discriminating different views of the face and head. *Journal of Neurophysiology, 68*, 70–84.

Oram, M. W., & Perrett D. I. (1994). Responses of anterior superior temporal polysensory (STPa) neurones to 'biological motion' stimuli. *Journal of Cognitive Neuroscience, 6*, 99–116.

Oram, M. W., & Perrett, D. I. (1996). Integration of form and motion in the anterior superior temporal polysensory area (STPa) of the macaque monkey. *Journal of Neurophysiology, 76*, 109–129.

Perrett, D. I., Rolls, E. T., & Caan, W. (1982). Visual neurones responsive to faces in the monkey temporal cortex. *Experimental Brain Research, 47*, 329–342.

Perrett, D. I., Smith, P. A. J., Potter, D. D., Mistlin, A. J., Head, A. S., Milner, A. D., et al. (1984). Neurones responsive to faces in the temporal cortex: Studies of functional organization, sensitivity to identity and relation to perception. *Human Neurobiology, 3*, 197–208.

Perrett, D. I., Smith, P. A. J., Mistlin, A. J., Chitty, A. J., Head, A. S., Potter, D. D., et al. (1985a). Visual analysis of body movements by neurons in the temporal cortex of the macaque monkey: A preliminary report. *Behavioural Brain Research, 16*, 153–170.

Perrett, D. I., Smith, P. A. J., Potter, D. D., Mistlin, A. J., Head, A. S., Milner, A. D., et al. (1985b). Visual cells in the temporal cortex sensitive to face view and gaze direction. *Proceedings of the Royal Society of London. Series B, 223*, 293–317.

Perrett, D. I., Mistlin, A. J., & Chitty, A. J. (1987). Visual cells responsive to faces. *Trends in Neurosciences, 10*, 358–364.

Perrett, D. I., Harries, M. H., Bevan, R., Thomas, S., Benson, P. J., Mistlin, A. J., et al. (1989). Frameworks of analysis for the neural representation of animate objects and actions. *Journal of Experimental Biology*, *146*, 87–113.
Perrett, D. I., Mistlin, A. J., Harries, M. H., & Chitty, A. J. (1990). Understanding the visual appearance and consequences of hand actions. In M. A. Goodale (Ed.), *Vision and action: The control of grasping* (pp. 163–180). Norwood, NJ: Ablex.
Perrett, D. I., Oram, M. W., Harries, M. H., Bevan, R., Hietanen, J. K., Benson, P. J., et al. (1991). Viewer-centred and object-centred coding of heads in the macaque temporal cortex. *Experimental Brain Research*, *86*, 159–173.
Perrett, D. I., Hietanen, J. K., Oram, M. W., & Benson, P. J. (1992). Organization and functions of cells responsive to faces in the temporal cortex. *Philosophical Transactions of the Royal Society of London. Series B*, *335*, 23–30.
Perrett, D. I., & Oram, M. W. (1993). Neurophysiology of shape processing. *Image and Vision Computing*, *11*, 317–333.
Perrett, D. I. (1999). A cellular basis for reading minds from faces and actions. In M. Hauser & M. Konishi (Eds.), *Behavioural and neural mechanisms of communication*. Cambridge, MA: MIT Press.
Puce, A., Allison, T., Bentin, S., Gore, J. C., & McCarthy, G. (1998). Temporal cortex activation in humans viewing eye and mouth movements. *Journal of Neuroscience*, *18*, 2188–2199.
Puce, A., & Perrett, D. I. (2003). Electrophysiology and brain imaging of biological motion. *Philosophical Transactions of the Royal Society of London. Series B*, *358*, 435–445.
Rizzolatti, G., Camarda, R., Fogassi, L., Gentilucci, M., Luppino, G., & Matelli, M. (1988). Functional organization of inferior area 6 in the macaque monkey. II. Area F5 and the control of distal movements. *Experimental Brain Research*, *71*, 491–507.
Rizzolatti, G., & Gentilucci, M. (1988). Motor and visual-motor functions of the premotor cortex. In P. Rakic & W. Singer (Eds.), *Neurobiology of the neocortex* (Vol. 42). New York: Wiley.
Rizzolatti, G., Fadiga, L., Matelli, M., Bettinardi, V., Paulesu E., Perani, D., et al. (1996a). Localization of grasp representations in humans by PET: I. Observation versus execution. *Experimental Brain Research*, *111*, 246–252.
Rizzolatti, G., Fadiga, L., Gallese, V., & Fogassi, L. (1996b). Premotor cortex and the recognition of motor actions. *Cognitive Brain Research*, *3*, 131–141.
Rolls, E. T., & Baylis, G. C. (1986). Size and contrast have only small effects on the responses to faces of neurons in the cortex of the superior temporal sulcus of the monkey. *Experimental Brain Research*, *65*, 38–48.
Sakai, K., & Miyashita, Y. (1991). Neuronal organization for the long-term memory of paired associates, *Nature*, *354*, 152–155.
Saxe, R., Xiao, D.-K., Kovacs, G., Perrett, D. I., & Kanwisher, N. (2004). Distinct representations of bodies, actions and thoughts in posterior superior temporal sulcus. *Neuropsychologia*, *42*, 1435–1446.
Senior, C., Barnes, J., Giampietro, V., Simmons, A., Bullmore, E. T., Brammer, M., et al. (2000). The functional neuroanatomy of implicit-motion perception or 'representational momentum'. *Current Biology*, *10*, 16–22.
Sereno, A. B., & Maunsell, J. H. R. (1998). Shape selectivity in primate lateral intraparietal cortex. *Nature*, *395*, 500–503.

Shadlen, M. N., Britten, K. H., Newsome, W. T., & Movshon, J. A. (1996). A computational analysis of the relationship between neuronal and behavioral responses to visual motion. *Journal of Neuroscience, 16*, 1486–1510.

Tanaka, Y. Z., Koyama, T., & Mikami, A. (1999). Neurons in the temporal cortex changed their preferred direction of motion dependent on shape. *Neuroreport, 10*, 393–397.

Turnbull, O. H., Carey, D. P., & McCarthy, R. A. (1997). The neuropsychology of object constancy. *Journal of the International Neuropsychological Society, 3*, 288–298.

Umilta, M. A., Kohler, E., Gallese, V., Fogassi, L., Fadiga, L., Keysers, C., et al. (2001). I know what you are doing: A neurophysiological study. *Neuron, 31*, 155–165.

Ungerleider, L. G., & Mishkin, M. (1982). Two cortical visual systems. In D. J. Ingle, M. A Goodale, & R. J. W. Mansfield (Eds.), *Analysis of visual behavior* (pp. 549–586). Cambridge, MA: MIT Press.

Wachsmuth, E., Oram, M. W., & Perrett, D. I. (1994). Recognition of objects and their component parts: responses of single units in the temporal cortex of the macaque. *Cerebral Cortex, 5*, 509–522.

Wallis, G., & Bülthoff, H. H. (2001). Effects of temporal association on recognition memory. *Proceedings of the National Academy of Science of the USA, 98*, 4800–4804.

Williams, J. H. G., Whiten, A., Suddendorf, T., & Perrett, D. I. (2001). Imitation, mirror neurons and autism. *Neuroscience and Behavioural Reviews, 25*, 287–295.

Young, M. P., & Yamane, S. (1992). Sparse population coding of faces in the inferotemporal cortex. *Science, 256*, 1327–1331.

Part II
Cognitive neuroscience of social cognition

5 The evolution of social cognition

Nathan J. Emery

Introduction

Although this book is focused on the cognitive neuroscience of *human* social behaviour, an understanding of social cognition in *nonhuman* animals is critical for unravelling the neural basis of social cognition in humans as well as the selective pressures that have shaped the evolution of complex social cognition. As the result of methodological limitations, we know little about the relationships between certain biochemical and electrophysiological properties of the human brain and how they compute the behaviour and mental states of other individuals. Traditional techniques for examining neural function in humans, such as event-related potentials (ERP), positron emission tomography (PET), and functional magnetic resonance imaging (fMRI), are constrained by the fact that subjects are either placed into an immoveable scanner with a lot of background noise or wired up with dozens of electrodes sensitive to slight movements. The possibility of scanning or recording brain waves from two individuals that are physically interacting socially is technically impossible at present (however, see Montague et al., 2002, for a new method for simultaneously scanning two individuals interacting via a computer).

The only way to understand the neurocognitive architecture of human social behaviour is to examine similar social processes in both human and nonhuman animal minds and make comparisons at the species level. An additional argument is that traditional human sociocognitive tasks are dependent on the use of stories, cartoons, and verbal cues and instructions (Heberlein & Adolphs, this volume) which themselves will elicit specific neural responses that have to be eliminated from neural responses specifically related to mind-reading. Therefore, the development of nonverbal tasks would provide a breakthrough for studies in nonlinguistic animals, preverbal human infants, and human cognitive neuroimaging.

Social cognition and evolution of the social brain

Before we discuss comparative approaches to social cognition, it is important to assess how such lines of thinking have developed and why such questions may be of interest to cognitive neuroscientists. In discussing the evolution of human intellect and by association the evolution of the human brain, both Humphrey (1976) and Jolly (1966) independently proposed that living in a social group and predicting the behaviour of conspecifics requires unprecedented levels of cognitive processing that are not displayed in nonprimates. This "social intelligence hypothesis," as it later became known, was proposed as an alternative to the more traditional candidates for the evolution of primate and human intelligence: tool use, hunting, enhanced spatial memory, or extractive foraging (Humphrey, 1976). Due to the anthropocentric bias of those working in this area at the time, who focused solely on the evolution of human intelligence, the experimental and theoretical work in the area was really concerned only with comparing nonhuman and human primates.

A classic example of these types of study was de Waal's observations of the social life of a group of chimpanzees at the Arnhem Zoo, which highlighted the Machiavellian strategies employed by certain male group members (de Waal, 1982). This study, in particular, developed the idea that there are benefits in understanding and remembering the previous interactions and relationships of conspecifics, and that this information could be used to predict or manipulate their behaviour in the future. de Waal observed that there are clear similarities between the complex social behaviour of the chimpanzees and the political shenanigans that are rife in human affairs of state, something which he subsequently called "chimpanzee politics".

Byrne and Whiten later encapsulated this idea as "Machiavellian intelligence" (Byrne & Whiten, 1988; Byrne, 1999), after Niccolò Machiavelli's *The Prince*, in which the prince of the title would use any deceptive and manipulative means possible to retain political power. They further suggested that the ability to "intentionally" deceive another individual, so-called tactical deception (TD), formed the basis of this form of social intelligence, relegating cooperative behaviour to the sidelines. Byrne and Whiten collected "evidence" for TD, not through rigorous experimentation, but through the collation of anecdotes from a wide variety of field primatologists. They found that TD appeared to be widespread throughout the primate order; however, it was most prevalent in the cercopithecine monkeys and the great apes (although this tended to be biased by the greater number of field studies performed in these species). Some examples of experimental studies of TD will be described in the relevant section below.

Other social mammals, such as dolphins, killer whales, wolves, wild dogs, horses, hyenas, lions, elephants, and social birds, such as corvids and parrots, appear to demonstrate many of the sophisticated traits of complex social behaviour, such as coalition and alliance formation, reciprocity and interchange, understanding of third-party relationships, and reconciliation (Connor, Heithaus, & Barre, 2001; Emery, Seed, & Clayton, 2003b; Feh, 1999; Grinnell, Packer, & Pusey, 1995; Smale, Holekamp, Weldele, Frank, & Glickman, 1995; see also papers in de Waal & Tyack, 2003). We therefore argue that the study of mental attribution in nonhuman animals should be extended to all social animals that demonstrate these traits.

Also relevant to this discussion (particularly for neuroscientists) is the finding that the size of the primate brain (Sawaguchi, 1990) and, more specifically, the neocortex as a ratio to the rest of the brain (Barton & Dunbar, 1997; Dunbar, 1992), are correlated with mean group size; that is, those primates with relatively larger brains are usually found in larger social groups. It was suggested that the larger the social group, the greater the number of potential relationships that can occur between individuals, and thus the size of the group may indicate the level of social complexity. However, the notion that group size may provide a useful indication of the social complexity of a species has recently been refuted, because there is no correlation between social learning, innovation, and group size in primates, although there is a significant correlation between social learning and neocortex size (Reader & Laland, 2002). No such relationship has been found between brain (or neocortex) size and various ecological variables, such as home range size or percentage of fruit in the diet. These findings are consistent with a link between the evolution of the primate neocortex (the seat of cognition) and social intellect, and, importantly, they are not based on the accumulation of anecdotes. However, the relationship between social intelligence and primate brain size at this stage was correlational, not causal. As we have already seen in Chapters 2–4, there is now significant evidence that distinct regions of the nonhuman primate brain are essential for social behaviour, and that these areas may also be important for social cognition (Brothers, 1990).

At the same time that the "social brain hypothesis" was being developed (Brothers, 1990; Dunbar, 1992, 1998), a mechanism for *how* primates (human and nonhuman) and other large-brained social animals perform such complex social operations was proposed by Premack and Woodruff (1978), which they named "theory of mind" (ToM). However, there was an immediate backlash from behavioural scientists, who suggested that interpretations of chimpanzee mentalizing abilities by the language-trained chimpanzee, Sarah, were nothing more than "mere" associative learning (Savage-Rumbaugh, Rumbaugh, & Boysen, 1978). This had the devastating effect of stifling studies on comparative social cognition for many years.

At the same time, however, more productive empirical lines of research into ToM were being developed by developmental psychologists (Frith & Frith, 2003; Perner, 1991; Premack & Premack, 2002). Some of this work will be reviewed in a later section. Of particular note, was the development of the "false-belief" task, which appeared to be a nail in the coffin of comparative social cognition. In brief, the false-belief task tests whether children understand that another individual can have different beliefs from themselves. A classic example of this is the Sally–Anne test. Here a child is presented with two dolls, Sally and Anne, who both witness candy being placed into one of two boxes. Anne is then removed from the room, but during this time the candy is moved to the second box in the presence of Sally and the child. Anne then re-enters the room, and the child is asked, "Where does Anne think the candy is?" or "Where will Anne search for the candy?" If the child has understood the question, and understands that because Anne did not witness the change in the candy's location she would believe that the candy is located in the first, rather than the second box, the child should say the first box. Wimmer and Perner (1983), who first developed a version of this test based on a suggestion by Dennett (1978), found that 4-year-old children answered correctly, whereas those of 3 years of age and younger based their response purely on their own knowledge that the candy had been moved. As we will see later, the development of an equivalent test for nonhuman animals has so far proved futile.

The false-belief task is believed by many developmental psychologists to be the benchmark test for ToM in human children (Wimmer & Perner, 1983), but it is highly dependent on the use of language. Does this therefore suggest that animals without the benefit of human language could never possess a ToM? There has been a recent backlash against the importance of the false-belief task for demonstrating ToM in children (and therefore, by necessity, in nonhuman animals), maintaining that it is too difficult a task (Siegal & Beattie, 1991) or that younger children demonstrate implicit understanding of belief (Clements & Perner, 1994). However, in a recent meta-analysis of all studies tackling the problem of false-belief development in human children, Wellman, Cross, and Watson (2001) found that the general consensus that false belief develops in human children around 4 years old is robust.

Theory of mind (ToM)

ToM, also called *folk psychology, mind-reading, mentalizing, metarepresentation*, or *secondary representation*, is the ability to understand the psychological or mental states of other individuals, such as their beliefs, desires, and knowledge (Premack & Woodruff, 1978).

The mechanics of mind-reading

It is important from an empirical and theoretical viewpoint to discuss how an understanding of animal mind-reading could translate to studies of neurobiology. Two concepts that are extremely important to an understanding of the mechanisms of mentalizing are "the intentional stance" (Dennett, 1983) and "intervening variables" (Whiten, 1996).

Many animals appear to act intentionally. However, the important questions are whether their behaviour is actually intentional or merely reflexive. If it is intentional, can they understand that the behaviour of others is also intentional? Dennett (1983) formulated a scheme based on different levels of intentionality which an agent (animal or human) may possess in relation to the presence and understanding of their own or another's mental states:

- *Zero-order intentionality*—an agent possesses no beliefs or desires, and therefore responds to events and stimuli in the environment through reflexes, as in producing a scream vocalization when frightened or running to evade a predator.
- *First-order intentionality*—an agent possesses beliefs and desire, but not beliefs about beliefs, as in producing an alarm call because it *believes* a predator is present, or *wants* others to run to the trees.
- *Second-order intentionality*—an agent possesses mental states about another's mental states, as in producing an alarm call because it *wants* others to *believe* there is a predator nearby.
- *Third-order intentionality*—an agent possesses mental states about others' mental states about its mental states, as in producing an alarm call because it *wants* others to *believe* that it *thinks* that they should run to the trees.

One difficulty with previous attempts to understand ToM is the fact that it is a "theory" based on unobservables (mental states) (Premack & Woodruff, 1978). For example, I do not know for sure what you feel or believe, but I can guess from your actions, your facial expression, and, in the human case, your language. (The use of language as a cue to internal states, however, is fraught with additional problems, as speakers may be intentionally deceptive, may speak a different language, or may be unable to transfer their thoughts and feelings into appropriately colourful language.) Whiten (1996) therefore suggested that a productive way to think about mental states is as intervening variables between causes and outcomes. For example, depriving an animal of water, injecting it with saline, and feeding it dry food will produce an animal that increases its rate of bar pressing to gain liquid—it will drink a large volume of liquid and it has a significant tolerance to quinine. To all intents and purposes, this animal can be said to be in a motivational state of thirst between the causes of its thirst and the outcomes of its thirst (Miller, 1959). Whiten suggests that a similar notion can be applied to mental states. For example, an individual A may behave as if it has the intention of gaining bananas (such as reaching toward them, moving toward them, affiliating with those that have bananas, begging toward those that already have bananas, etc.). In addition, the behaviour of other individuals may also provide clues to individual A's mental state in regard to the bananas, such as providing it with bananas, preventing its access to their bananas. This collection of behaviours, as a whole, may therefore be interpreted as that individual A "wants" or "desires" bananas (see Figure 5.1a). As such, mental states are intervening variables between behavioural causes and outcomes, and experiments designed to provide evidence for an understanding of mental states should be based on these types of variables. Importantly, only an examination of *multiple* intervening variables should be used as evidence for the existence of ToM.

Intervening variables may not only be useful for providing evidence for

ToM in animals, but may also provide a useful theoretical framework for investigating the neural basis of mind-reading. For example, neurons in the superior temporal sulcus (STS) of rhesus monkeys respond to particular social stimuli, such as faces, eye gaze direction, body postures, and movements (see Chapter 4). These neurons have been suggested to form the basis for a neurophysiological system coding for an understanding of another's intentions (Emery & Perrett, 2000; Perrett & Emery, 1994) (see Chapter 4). Using the example above, we can imagine a scenario in which the *same* ensembles of neurons code for: 1) actions used by individual A to reach a goal, such as walking and reaching toward bananas; 2) actions of individual B protecting the bananas from Individual A; 3) actions of individual A after attaining the goal, such as eating the bananas. From these three response profiles, we may state that the neural ensemble formed a representation that individual A *wanted* the bananas.

Mental states come in different forms; therefore, any investigation attempting to discover whether animals understand another's mental states should differentiate between the different types. Premack (1988) separated the different forms of ToM into three classes: perceptual (understanding seeing and attention), motivational (understanding desires, goals, and intentions), and informational (understanding knowledge and beliefs). I will attempt to discuss all previous studies on each of the three classes, and, where possible, compare an associative learning account of the data with a mentalistic account. This is important, as the ability to *read* behaviour may be a precursor to, but independent of, the ability to represent mental states.

Understanding attention: perceptual ToM 1

Gaze is an important social signal that may provide information about individuals' knowledge of the external environment and the state of their internal environment, such as their emotions (Emery, 2000). Social gaze is especially important for nonhuman primates and other social animals that rely on visual communication. Gaze cues may also function in complex forms of social cognition, such as visual perspective-taking, deception, empathy, and ToM.

Many animals appear to perceive that eye-like shapes, such as a small black circle within a larger white circle, represent "eyes". A number of prey species can also discriminate between two circles representing a forward-facing predator and a single circle representing a predator facing away, and therefore posing less of a threat (as all predators have forward-facing eyes) (Burger, Gochfield, & Murray, 1992; Coss, 1978; Hampton, 1994). A more complex use of another's eyes is that they provide an indication of what another can see, either reflexively in response to another's gaze direction (visual co-orienting [VCO]), or, more specifically, in tracing another's line of sight to interesting objects in the environment (gaze following). VCO has been demonstrated in a number of primates, such as stump-tailed macaques

(Anderson & Mitchell, 1999; however, see Itakura, 1996) and cotton-top tamarins (Neiworth, Burman, Basile, & Licktig, 2002), but not black lemurs (Anderson & Mitchell, 1999; see also Itakura, 1996). Note that lemurs and other prosimians do not have a visually based communication system.

Povinelli and Eddy (1996b) were the first to examine gaze following in nonhuman animals, in a group of young chimpanzees. The chimpanzees were first trained to produce a natural begging gesture toward an experimenter in order to receive food at the end of a trial. Once they were trained to do this, the experimenters produced specific attention cues for the subjects, either using the eyes only or the eyes and head directed toward various locations, such as behind and to the left or right of the subject, or behind a barrier, or, as a control, the experimenter made no change in the direction of their attention and remained focused on the subject. In the eyes and head condition, 50% of trials elicited a gaze-following response to the correct side, and in the eyes-only condition, 30% of trials elicited a correct response. From this, Povinelli and Eddy suggested that chimpanzees do not follow gaze with an understanding of the mental states of the individual whose gaze they followed; they follow gaze reflexively until they come across an object or event of interest within the line of sight (low-level explanation). However, the percentage of correct responses reported (30–50%) was not greater than chance, yet reflexive responding should surely produce results closer to 100%. So perhaps the chimpanzees can follow gaze with an understanding of the reasons why the individual looked at a particular point in space (see later).

Further evidence against the argument that chimpanzees follow gaze reflexively was reported by Tomasello, Hare, & Agnetta (1999). In this study, human experimenters gazed at objects hidden behind different types of barriers (gutter, board, another room, or around a wall). The chimpanzees could perceive what the experimenters were looking at by looking around the barrier. All subjects looked around all types of barrier. In an additional test, Tomasello et al. (1999) set up a situation in which an experimenter looked at a target object far behind the subject. In one condition, the target object only was present (target-only trials); in a second condition, a distractor object only was present between the chimpanzee and the target (distractor-only trials); and in a final condition, both the target and distractor were present (target plus distractor trials). If chimpanzees follow gaze reflexively, the subjects would attend only the distractor object in the distractor-only trials and in the target plus distractor trials. By contrast, a mentalistic account would predict that the subjects should attend the target in both the target-only and target plus distractor trials. Tomasello et al. found that although the target and distractor were equally salient in the target-only and distractor-only trials, the subjects looked at them both equally in the target plus distractor trials. Therefore, the distractor object was relatively salient to the chimpanzees, but was not entirely sufficient to distract the chimpanzees from the object of the experimenter's gaze. These results are comparable to those of 18-month-old human infants, who demonstrate "geometric" gaze following (Butterworth & Jarrett, 1991).

A further study examining the relative contributions of low-level versus high-level gaze processing was reported for rhesus monkeys. Monkeys' eye movements were recorded as they watched videotapes of conspecifics looking at one of two identical, moving objects (animal puppets). The rhesus monkeys appeared to respond specifically to the gaze direction of conspecifics, looking more toward the direction in space, and toward the specific object than to other locations and objects that were presented (Emery, Lorinez, Perrett, Oram, & Baker, 1997). However, when the attention cue was removed (that is, the monkey in the videotape disappeared while the objects remained), the observing monkeys looked at the two objects at the same frequency, suggesting that once the cue had been removed, the salience of the attended object disappeared. These two results seem at odds with one another. The first result that monkeys reliably look to the specific object of the conspecific's attention (compared to just looking in the general direction in which they were attending, as to the left) suggests a high-level interpretation, whereas the second result, that the monkeys do not continue to select the target object once the conspecific is removed, possibly suggests a low-level reflexive interpretation. However, the objects were present on screen, unchanging for almost 20 s, and so the subjects may have "decided" that the objects were not of interest. Interestingly, an additional analysis of the temporal pattern of inspections (eye movements) demonstrated that the observing monkeys consistently looked back to the conspecific after looking toward the attended object (Emery, unpublished observations), presumably in order to determine that the objects were still of interest.

Similar results in socially housed chimpanzees, sooty mangabeys, rhesus macaques, stump-tailed macaques, and pigtailed macaques using conspecifics as the sources of social information were reported by Tomasello, Call, & Hare (1998). The description of gaze following in monkeys is particularly interesting because neurons in the STS of the rhesus monkey brain are selectively responsive to faces and eye direction (Emery & Perrett, 2000). However, a subset of these neurons did not respond selectively to faces looking at objects compared to away from objects (Emery, 2000). This was a small population of cells and so requires further study (see Chapter 4, this volume for an overview of the neurophysiology of goal-directed behaviour in monkeys).

More complex processing of another's gaze may be that an individual with open eyes or eyes that are not occluded can perceive objects in the world. This cognitive level implies an understanding of the mental state; *seeing*. In a protracted series of experiments, Povinelli and Eddy (1996a) examined the ability of young chimpanzees (5–6 years old) to beg toward one of two experimenters with different types of visual occlusion; one that could see them versus a second that could not. In all cases, the chimpanzees were presented with a conditional discrimination problem; if the chimpanzee begged toward the experimenter that could see them, they were rewarded. One of the experimenters always had the eyes open or free from occlusion, in contrast to a second whose eyes were covered with different barriers, such as blindfolds, buckets, or tinted goggles, or whose back was turned, head was turned, or eyes were closed. In almost all cases, the chimpanzees did not differentiate between the two experimenters by their ability to see. The only discrimination the chimpanzees made was between an experimenter who was facing toward them and another whose back was turned. However, the chimpanzees failed to discriminate between two experimenters facing away, one of whom had once turned their head toward the subject. Povinelli and Eddy (1996a) concluded that chimpanzees may use a more sophisticated level of gaze-following than purely reflexive, but that their gaze following abilities do not extend to a concept of seeing or understanding another's mental states from their gaze cues.

There have been a number of criticisms of this study. Because Povinelli and Eddy tested the ability of chimpanzees to follow human eye gaze as opposed to conspecifics, one can argue that chimpanzees might have an understanding of seeing as a mental state, but one that does not generalize to people. Clearly, the experiment should be repeated using conspecifics. A second issue is age of the chimpanzees tested in these studies. It has been suggested that because the chimpanzees were only 5 years of age they were not old enough to have developed ToM. But subsequent tests when the same chimpanzees had reached adolescence have continued to show negative results, so even those individuals that were most adept at these tasks continued to use stimulus-based rules about the frontal orientation of the face and eyes rather than using the attribution of seeing (Reaux, Theall, & Povinelli, 1999).

A final test of whether animals understand another's mental states from gaze (understanding attention as a mental state or level-1 perspective-taking; Flavell, Everett, Croft, & Flavell, 1981) is the "object-choice" paradigm. In this paradigm, animals are first trained that food can be located under boxes or cups. An experimenter then baits one of two inverted cups behind a screen. When the cups are revealed, the experimenter looks at (or points at; see later) the cup covering the food. The animal is then required to displace the cup that hides the food. Many species of primates perform this task with ease or after training, and respond to different pointing cues, and head direction close to the correct choice, but do not use head direction far from the cup or eye gaze alone (Anderson, Montant, & Schmitt, 1996; Anderson, Sallaberry, & Barbier, 1995; Call, Hare, & Tomasello, 1998; Itakura & Anderson, 1996; Povinelli, Bierschwale, & Cech, 1999); however, see Peignot and Anderson (1999) for controversial results in gorillas, which appear to use all available human social cues, except glancing).

There are inconsistencies between the results of different laboratories, which are largely the consequence of positive findings in enculturated apes and domestic dogs (see later section on "the domestication of social cognition"). Itakura and Tanaka (1998), for example, found that human infants, an enculturated chimpanzee, and an enculturated orang-utan could use point, tap, distal and proximal gaze, and glancing (eyes only) cues with accuracy levels of 70–100% (all significantly above chance).

The basic failure of monkeys and apes to use distal head and eye gaze cues, but their general success in the use of proximal head and pointing cues, suggests that these species are probably basing their decisions on low-level, proximity-based social information, such as stimulus and local enhancement, to locate hidden food, rather than a high-level interpretation that a human experimenter is looking at one of the two cups because the human knows that the cup hides food. Additional behavioural cues or nuances of the experiment appear to enhance the ability of chimpanzees to locate hidden food. Itakura, Agnetta, Hare, and Tomasello (1999) found that producing a vocalization (chimpanzee-like food call or a human vocalization) to accompany gaze cues increased performance on the object-choice task. Did the vocalization enhance the effect of the gaze cues, or did it attract the subject to the experimental situation by providing an aid to use of the cues? Call, Agnetta, and Tomasello (2000) tested chimpanzees with the same paradigm as Itakura et al. (1999); however, the temporal order of the gaze and vocalization cues was manipulated, with either the gaze produced before vocalization, or vice versa. The chimpanzees produced above-chance performances on the object-choice task independently of when the gaze and call cues occurred. In addition, the type of call did not affect performance, and, amazingly, when other sounds were used, such as snapping the fingers, slapping the hand on the floor, or playing a recording of a bicycle horn, they also produced significant responses. Other important behavioural cues related to local enhancement, such as moving toward the correct container and staring at it, lifting the container and looking into it, and approaching the container (Call et al., 2000; Itakura et al., 1999), all enhance performance of chimpanzees on the object-choice task.

Finally, Call et al. (1998) examined whether the type of occluder influenced responses on this task. They found that chimpanzees could utilize the experimenter's gaze cues when the occluders were tubes or barriers that did not prevent the experimenter from seeing the location of the food after baiting, but not when the occluder was an overturned bowl. This suggests that chimpanzees do not understand that other individuals know that objects remain in their original place even when they are out of sight, akin to a lack of social "object-permanence". It remains to be tested whether other animals can use these types of behavioural cues or occluders to enhance their performance on object-choice tasks.

Of particular relevance here are an additional class of neurons in the macaque STS which respond to the sight of humans walking or reaching toward objects (Emery & Perrett, 2000) and such goal-directed actions combined with cues to another's attention (Chapter 4, this volume). These neurophysiological data are highly suggestive of a propensity for rhesus monkeys to solve the object-choice task with the aid of additional behavioural cues, such as those used by chimpanzees.

The domestication of social cognition

We have already seen that apes' abilities at gaze following and understanding seeing and object-choice tasks are somewhat limited. Indeed, recent studies have found that domestic dogs (*Canis familaris*) may be superior to apes in these tasks. Dogs can use human attention cues to locate hidden food (Hare & Tomasello, 1999; McKinley & Sambrook, 2000; Miklosi, Polgardi, Topal, & Csanyi, 1998); use novel cues, such as markers, to find food (Agnetta, Hare, & Tomasello, 2000); use conspecific cues (Hare & Tomasello, 1999); and use cues themselves to direct humans to food (Hare, Call, & Tomasello, 1998). Dogs have also demonstrated an understanding of seeing that is significantly better than chimpanzees (Young, 2003). Recently, Hare, Brown, Williamson, and Tomasello (2002) found that when compared directly on the same object-choice task, dogs outperform chimpanzees, 9/11 dogs choosing correctly compared to 2/11 chimpanzees. Hare and colleagues have suggested that it was the long domestication of dogs by humans that has selected for this skill in utilizing human social cues. Indeed, these paradigms depend on the reading of *cooperative* signals produced by humans. As such, animals that have been selected for their close relationship to humans should demonstrate a clear propensity to read such signals. This is in contrast to primates, which have not been selected for these skills. Although the data are scant, there is some suggestion that many working dogs which have been directly bred to understand human gestures or produce gestures comprehensive to humans, as during sheep herding and pointing toward a kill during a shoot perform better in social-cognition experiments than other dogs (Hare, Addessi, Call, Tomasello, & Visalberghi, 2002; McKinley & Sambrook, 2000; Miklosi, Kubinyl, Topal, Gacsi, Varanyi, & Csanyi, 2003).

To directly test the domestication of the social-cognition hypothesis, Hare et al. (2003b) compared domestic dogs and wolves on the same tasks. In the object-choice task, dogs located food correctly when provided with gaze plus point plus tap, gaze plus point, and point cues, whereas wolves were correct only when using the gaze plus point cue. On a nonsocial food-finding study that was not dependent on the use of human social cues, there was no difference in the performance of dogs and wolves. Finally, dog puppies at different ages (9–12 weeks, 13–16 weeks, and 17–26 weeks old) and with different rearing histories (litter-reared or human-reared) were tested on the object-choice task by gaze and gaze plus point cues. There was no difference between the litter-reared and the human-reared puppies, and no difference between the three age groups in their use of human social cues. This final result suggests that there was no effect of age or experience of humans in the use of human attention cues, therefore reinforcing the premise that the process of domestication was the key to the enhancement of sociocognitive abilities in domestic dogs.

There are some potential problems with this hypothesis. First, Miklosi et al. (2003) have performed similar experiments to Hare and colleagues (although focusing only on comprehension of human pointing) in dogs and socialized wolves. They found that four wolves could utilize touching cues to locate hidden food, two wolves could use proximal pointing (5–10 cm away from the object), and one wolf could use distal pointing (50 cm away from the object). Therefore, some socialized wolves could learn to use some human gestures. In two further, nonsocial tasks used to gain access to food, a rope-pulling task and a bin-opening task, there were no differences in the ability of wolves and dogs to perform this task. The tasks were then made impossible, that is, the bin was locked, so the food could not be reached or the rope was tied to a post, rather than to the food. When faced with insoluble problems, the dogs, but not the wolves, looked back at their owner and spent more time gazing at their owner than the wolves. Miklosi et al. (2003) suggested that the dogs were looking back at their owners either in an attempt to communicate with them that the food was not accessible or to derive information from their owners about how to perform the task (see also Gomez, 1991).

Second, general domesticity is often confounded with specific use as a working animal. Today, dogs are primarily kept as pets; however, throughout most of the period of domesticity, dogs were kept and trained as working animals. Interestingly, another domestic working animal, the horse (*Equus caballus*), has demonstrated some basic understanding of human-given social cues to locate food (McKinley & Sambrook, 2000). To remove the effects of domesticity and working, experiments should be performed on domestic animals which function only as pets, and thus should not have been selected to use human social cues. A good example would be the domestic cat. Relatives of domestic cats, such as lions, are successful pack hunters (Scheel & Packer, 1991), and so we would predict that if domestic cats have retained this trait, they should be able to utilize conspecific social cues (as would have been useful during a hunt), but they should fail to use human social cues because they have not been bred as working animals.

Visual perspective-taking: perceptual ToM 2

Distinguishing another individual's visual perspective from one's own is thought to be an important step in interpreting others' intentions and thoughts about the world (level-2 perspective-taking) (Flavell et al., 1981). It may also be a useful skill when used to manipulate another's behaviour and intentions, as in tactical deception (TD). The classic example of TD is the observation of a female hamadryas baboon grooming a subordinate male behind a rock out of view of the dominant male. In hamadryas society, dominant males mate and control a harem of females, and so have sole access to them, with subordinate males sneaking copulations out of the sight of the alpha male. It would therefore seem to be advantageous for the subordinate and his consort to hide their clandestine meetings from the alpha male. In this example, the female remains in view of the dominant, but the dominant cannot see what she is doing, or the recipient of what she is doing (Whiten & Byrne, 1988). One interpretation is that the female processed the dominant's line of sight, and positioned herself such that the rock was between the subordinate she was grooming and the dominant male, so that he was completely out of view. But this behaviour could have been learned by differential reinforcement without having any understanding of what looking means.

To test whether animals can understand another individual's visual perspective, long-tailed macaques were given a choice of where to drink a juice reward. One bottle of juice was hidden from the view of a threatening human experimenter, but a second bottle was in full view of the experimenter (Kummer, Anzenberger, & Hemelrijk, 1996). The macaques failed to discriminate between the two bottles, choosing randomly, and therefore failing to demonstrate an understanding of the human experimenter's visual perspective. Of course, there was little cost associated with taking the juice in the open as the monkey gained as much juice from that bottle as from the bottle which was hidden from view.

Many investigators have suggested that laboratory experiments based on an animal's natural history (high ecological validity) are likely to be more productive in eliciting mentalizing abilities than artificial paradigms. Examples of naturalistic laboratory studies include using conspecifics as protagonists, or basing studies on an animal's species-specific behavioural repertoire (Emery & Clayton, 2004; Hare, 2001; Matheson, Cooper, Weeks, Thompson, & Fragaszy, 1998; Purdy & Domjan, 1998). A more ecologically valid test for visual perspective taking in chimpanzees based on competition for food has recently been designed by Hare, Call, Agnetta, and Tomasello (2000). A subordinate and a dominant chimpanzee were allowed access to an arena where food had been previously hidden. The subordinate chimp could see both pieces of food, whereas the dominant chimp could see only one of them. The question was whether the subordinate chimp would make a decision about which food to approach based on the visual perspective of the dominant animal (that is, go for the food that the dominant could not see). When they were released into the arena together, the subordinate chimp did exactly this. To eliminate the possibility that the subordinate was not reasoning about the dominant's visual perspective, but only responding to simple behavioural cues (such as gaze direction and direction of movement), the subordinate was released a few seconds before the dominant. As before, the subordinate tended to retrieve the hidden food. Hare and colleagues have suggested that these positive results were due to implementation of a competitive rather than a cooperative paradigm, a more natural behavioural state for chimpanzees. The use of a conspecific as a protagonist rather than a human experimenter would also account for the positive results. The same paradigm has been used successfully in capuchins, in which the subordinates also preferred to choose food that was hidden from dominants. The subordinate capuchins, however, did not preferentially approach the hidden food first when given a head start (in contrast to the chimpanzees), suggesting that the capuchins were predicting the dominant's behaviour based on gaze and movement cues, but did not appreciate their perspective (Hare, et al., 2003a).

A recent alternative explanation of the understanding of another's visual perspective is that most animals prefer to feed at the periphery of a clearing to avoid potential predation, and so any preference for feeding behind a barrier may be due solely to fear of eating in the open rather than an appreciation of another's line of sight. This is termed the "peripheral feeding hypothesis" (PFH) (Karin-D'Arcy & Povinelli, 2002). A second argument is that dominants always go for the piece of food that is in view, and so the subordinate has no choice but to go for the food which only it can see. For the sake of the "visual perspective-taking" argument, only the food that is reached for first is important, as just reporting the total amount eaten or which food is eaten could be due to the subordinate's having no choice. This is exactly what Karin-D'Arcy and Povinelli (2002) found when attempting to replicate Hare et al.'s (2000) study, namely, that the subordinate chimpanzees tended to retrieve the hidden food rather than the food that could be seen by both chimpanzees, but that the subordinates did not selectively reach or move toward the hidden piece of food first. In all possible scenarios where only the subordinate was party to the location of the hidden food (and in a geometric position to retrieve it first), it gained the highest percentage of food. Even when the experimental design abolished all possibility of the dominant's injuring the subordinate, the subordinate did not selectively retrieve the hidden food. When the PFH was tested by barriers fully occluding or half-occluding food, transparent barriers in front of the food, or opaque barriers located beside the food (and so not removing the food from sight), Karin-D'Arcy and Povinelli (2002) found that the subordinate did not differentiate between the hidden or visible food in which they reached for, touched, or retained, thereby supporting the PFH. Of course, there are many possible reasons for the discrepancies between these two research groups. Povinelli and colleagues have begun to report a number of negative findings with respect to ToM in chimpanzees (also causal understanding of tool use) (Povinelli, 2000). This could be due to interference effects between the different types of cognitive experiments (using the same chimpanzees throughout), or detrimental effects in the lack of conspecific socialization during development.

An additional ecologically valid situation in which food is competed for, and which may also provide a good model for examining visual perspective taking in animals, is food caching and cache protection. Cachers that either live in a social group or have to defend territories may have to cache in front of conspecifics (and heterospecifics), some of which are potential cache pilferers. Many corvids, such as scrub-jays, magpies, and ravens, have demonstrated sophisticated cache protection strategies, such as delaying caching until a competitor has left the scene, making "false" caches, switching from larder hoarding (one large defendable cache site) to scatter hoarding (many smaller cache sites spread over a wide area) or vice versa, and reaching food items when competitors have left (Emery & Clayton, 2001; Emery, Dally, & Clayton, 2004; Heinrich & Pepper, 1998; Vander Wall, 1990) (see later section). Ravens have also been shown to cache selectively behind large obstacles, such as rocks and tree stumps, positioning the obstacle between themselves and the would-be thief (Bugnyar & Kotrschal, 2002). Ravens also tend to cache as far from competitors as possible (Bugnyar & Kotrschal, 2002) and possibly use distraction techniques (Heinrich, 1999).

An experimental investigation of scrub-jay caching revealed similar strategies to the ravens. If the jays were presented with caching locations near or far from an observing conspecific, they chose to cache in locations far from the conspecific, but they did not make this discrimination when they cached in private (Dally, Emery, & Clayton, in press). When presented with caching locations either behind barriers or in the open (removing distance as a factor), jays consistently chose to cache in locations out of sight of the observer (Dally et al., in press). This result did not appear to be because the jays were fearful of the presence of another jay, and so ceased caching or eating in the open, as the jays did not discriminate between caching locations when they were only given powdered (noncacheable) food. Future studies will examine whether jays can understand that the observer's view can either be completely or partially occluded depending on the position, and that different observers have different views of the same event. These studies should provide stronger tests of whether scrub-jays can appreciate what conspecifics can and cannot see.

Watve and colleagues (Smitha, Thakar, & Watve, 1999; Watve et al., 2002) suggested that another species of bird, the bee-eater, may also be a good candidate for ToM. Bee-eaters appear to respond to what a predator can see, as they do not tend to enter their nest (and so lead a predator to their offspring) if the nest is being watched. They therefore attempted to set up an experimental situation mimicking this in the wild, using human experimenters as "predators". They examined whether bee-eaters would be more likely to enter a nest if the view between the predator and the nest was blocked by a barrier, compared to a position in full view of the nest or in a position in view of the nest, but a great distance from it. A bee-eater was always positioned on a perch at an angle between the nest and the predator. Watve et al. (2002) found that the time taken before the subject made its first entry into the nest was greatest when the distance from the predator was small and the view was unimpeded. Distance appeared to have the least effect on the tendency to enter the nest. The bee-eaters also seemed to appreciate the gaze direction of the predator, entering the nest more frequently when the experimenter was looking away than when looking at the nest (Watve et al., 2002), and they may have understood something about the predator's knowledge (had it seen the nest before?) (Smitha et al., 1999). Although there are many methodological problems, this seminatural paradigm certainly warrants further investigation.

Intentional communication: the bridge between perceptual and motivational ToM

During intentional communication, "the behaviour of the sender must involve a goal and some flexibility in the means for attaining it" (Tomasello & Call, 1997, p. 243). As such, the sender may use different types of "gestures", vocalizations, or behavioural strategies in order to achieve the goal. These may include "attention-getting" behaviours which are used to capture the attention of the potential recipients so that they are ready to receive the communicative gesture, gaze alternation between the recipients and the object or event of interest, and the gesture itself, such as proto-imperative or proto-declarative pointing toward the goal. Based on these criteria, intentional communication may form a bridge between two forms of ToM; perceptual and motivational. In this section, I will deal only with intentional communication of visual signals; however, the reader is directed to Tomasello and Call (1997) for a discussion of intentional communication of vocalizations, such as alarm calls.

Attention-getting behaviours

The use of visually based gestures to communicate intentions to a second party is largely dependent on the recipient's being in an attentional state conducive to receiving the signal; that is, attending the signal sender. In their natural social interactions, chimpanzees will tailor the type of gesture directed to a conspecific according to whether they are facing the sender, or looking away. Tomasello, Call, Nagell, Olguin, & Carpenter (1994) found that the chimpanzees were more likely to use visual signals if the conspecific was looking at them, compared to using more auditory and tactile gestures when the conspecific was looking away. The issue of whether chimpanzees understand that their gestures should fit the attentional state of the recipient has been examined in three laboratory studies.

Gomez (1996) tested the attention-getting behaviours of a group of hand-reared and human-experienced chimpanzees. The chimpanzees were required to request food from an experimenter that was inattentive (eyes closed, back turned, head turned toward a corner, or gazing over the chimpanzee's head). The chimpanzees used attention-getting behaviours, such as touching the experimenter or attempting to make eye contact in 68% of the inattentive trials. The hand-reared chimpanzees used attention-getting behaviours more frequently than the human-experienced chimpanzees.

Theall and Povinelli (1999) performed a similar experiment in chimpanzees; however, the experimenter did not provide the food reward immediately after the chimpanzees made a begging gesture, but waited for 20 s. The experimenter's attentional state differed in four conditions: eyes open (EO) and following the movements of the subject, head movement (HM), attention above the subject (AC), and eyes closed (EC). Therefore, the subjects should have been more likely to use attention-getting behaviours (touching and vocalizations) during the AC and EC conditions, where the experimenter was inattentive. However, Theall and Povinelli (1999) did not find a difference between the conditions in the frequency of touching and vocalizations.

In a study of 49 captive chimpanzees, Hostetter, Cantero, & Hopkins (2001) examined a larger number of attention-getting behaviours than in previous studies (vocalizations, gestures, banging the cage, throwing objects, spitting, displaying, clapping, and pouting). Rather than examine the responses of chimpanzees to an inattentive human experimenter, based on the eyes, Hostetter et al. used only facing the subject and back turned to the subject as conditions (as Povinelli & Eddy, 1996, had reported that chimpanzees appear to understand that only a human facing away is inattentive, not when the eyes are covered). The chimpanzees emitted vocalizations faster, and made their first gesture more frequently when the experimenter was oriented away from the subject. These studies suggest that chimpanzees may understand something about the attentional state of a human experimenter; however, this ability develops only after prolonged interactions with humans during early development (see later section). As chimpanzees do not understand the special relationship between the eyes and seeing, it is important to provide the subjects with cues that they do comprehend, such as discriminating between a forward-facing experimenter and an experimenter whose back is turned.

Gaze alternation

The second criterion for the intentional communication of visually based gestures is that the sender continues to communicate with the recipient until its goal is achieved or the recipient leaves. Human infants, for example, do this by gaze alternation, that is, constantly looking between the recipient and the object of interest (Gomez, Sarrià, & Tamarit 1993). Gomez (1991) investigated whether a hand-reared young gorilla used similar gaze alternation when confronted with a series of problems that were outside its behavioural repertoire, such as opening a door to leave a room or obtaining an out-of-reach banana. Gomez found that, initially, the gorilla would physically attempt to move the experimenters toward the goal object, such as pulling them toward the door. Gomez reports that the gorilla would frequently touch the experimenter first, awaiting eye contact, and then lead the experimenter to the goal once eye contact had been made. Eventually, the gorilla would "signify its intentions" by alternating its gaze between the experimenter's eyes and the goal (door handle or banana).

Emery (2000) has discussed this issue in relation to the behaviour of some pet animals, which display behaviours which may be interpreted as gaze alternation (and attention getting):

> Many pet owners discuss the abilities of cats and dogs to look at the location of a food source or to the door to outside, then back to the pet

owner, then back to the food or the door ... This behaviour is usually associated with vocalizations. Although this behaviour is identical to that described above for gorillas, the domesticated pets would not be described as intentionally communicating with their owners. The pets are more likely to have been looking at the location of the food or outside at an earlier occasion and vocalizing because of the motivation to gain food or entry to outside. The pet owner happened to initiate the required action (get food or open the door) independent of the intentions of the cat or dog. The pet therefore learnt through association that looking and vocalizing at an object of interest leads to access to that resource by the actions of the owner. (p. 593)

Miklosi et al. (2000) have investigated whether pet dogs alternate their gaze with their owner's gaze and the location of a hidden piece of food or favourite toy. After controlling for baseline levels of gazing and attention-getting behaviours (by examining the levels of these behaviours when the dog was alone or when a second human familiar to the dog pets it), the subjects' gaze alternation behaviour was examined when food was hidden in their presence, but not in the presence of the owner. The dogs increased the frequency of vocalizations, sniffing the location of the food or toy, and increased the frequency of gazing at the owner and the food or toy compared to baseline conditions. These results suggest that dogs can communicate the location of hidden objects to their owners (see also Hare et al., 1998) by gaze alternation.

Pointing

Pointing has been proposed as a method by which human infants begin to communicate (nonverbally) with others (Baron-Cohen, 1991). There are two types of pointing described in the developmental psychology literature that may be present in animals: proto-imperative and proto-declarative (referential) pointing (Leavens & Hopkins, 1999). Proto-imperative pointing takes the form of reaching with the whole hand toward an out-of-reach object of interest which the agent wants or desires, whereas proto-declarative pointing typically takes the form of pointing with the index finger to show or notify others of the presence and location of objects and events (Povinelli & Davis, 1994). Leavens and Hopkins (1999) have suggested that pointing in apes (and probably other animals) resembles human pointing, as, although apes tend to point with their whole hand, they have been recorded pointing with the index finger, young children frequently point with the whole hand, chimpanzees point significantly more when others are present than when alone (Leavens, Hopkins, & Bard, 1996), chimpanzees vocalize less when pointing than young children (Leavens & Hopkins, 1998), and chimpanzees alternate their gaze between the object of interest and the human they are attempting to communicate with more frequently than children (Krause & Fouts, 1997; Leavens et al., 1996). Therefore, although ape pointing may be equivalent structurally and functionally to human pointing (but see arguments against this view by Povinelli and Davis, 1994), there is little evidence that apes use other body parts to point with, as humans readily do (Leavens & Hopkins, 1998) with the leg, shoulders, head, or chin).

Proto-imperative pointing has been reported for many captive species (Blaschke & Ettlinger, 1987; Hess, Novak, & Povinelli, 1993; Povinelli, Nelson, & Boysen, 1992; Povinelli, Parks, & Novak, 1991) and human infants, but not apes in the wild (Plooij, 1978). A similar gesture is holding out the hand, in the form of begging or solicitation (Bygott, 1979). By contrast, proto-declarative pointing has been described only for some enculturated apes (Call & Tomasello, 1994; Krause & Fouts, 1997), language-trained dolphins (Xitco, Gory, & Kuczaj, 2001), and normal human infants, but not infants with autism (Baron-Cohen, 1989). These examples may be party to alternative explanations; in particular, the dolphin case seems like over-interpretation, dolphin pointing described thus: "A dolphin would stop his forward progress, often less than 2 m from an object, and align the anterior–posterior axis of his body with the object for several seconds" (Xitco et al., 2001, p. 117).

Many species also appear able to comprehend other's pointing as a referential gesture, such as during the object-choice task (apes—Itakura & Tanaka, 1998; Peignot & Anderson, 1999; monkeys—Anderson et al., 1995, 1996; dogs—Hare & Tomasello, 1998; McKinley & Sambrook, 2000; Miklosi et al., 2003; Soproni, Miklosi, Topal, & Csanyi, 2001, 2002; dolphins—Herman, Abichandani, Elhajj, Herman, Sanchez, & Pack, 1999; Tschudin, Call, Dunbar, Harris, & van der Elst, 2001). The possibility arises that the response to pointing may be due to the distance between the hand and the object (local enhancement; Povinelli & O'Neill, 2000) rather than to understanding (e.g., Itakura & Tanaka, 1998). This has been controlled in experiments in dogs (Miklosi et al., 2003; Soproni et al., 2002) and gorillas (Peignot & Anderson, 1999), comparing responses to proximal and distal pointing cues.

Understanding intentional actions: motivational ToM

The term "ToM" first appeared in a paper by Premack and Woodruff in 1978. However, Premack and Woodruff were referring to understanding another's intentions or goals, or *motivational ToM*. They examined whether a language-trained chimpanzee, Sarah, could appreciate the correct solution to a problem given to a human demonstrator. Sarah was presented with a video sequence of either an actor locked in a cage, or shivering next to an unlighted heater, or unable to clean a dirty floor, or unable to listen to music on an unplugged stereo. After each sequence, the video was paused and Sarah was then provided with a number of alternative answers to the problems (as photographs), such as a key, a lighted paper wick, a connected hose, and a plugged-in cord, and she had to match the correct image with the appropriate video. Sarah was highly accurate in her selection of the photographs, and so it was argued that she understood the actor's intentions ("he wanted to get out of the cage", "he intended to listen to music", etc.). Needless to say, this interpretation has been criticized. Perhaps Sarah merely understood the relationship between objects (such as lock and key) that had been associated previously during her life in captivity. Savage-Rumbaugh et al. (1978), for example, presented their language-trained chimpanzees with different sets of cards, which included pairs of objects that were related, such as lock and key, and the chimpanzees correctly matched the two related cards far above chance. The fact that some of the solutions provided to Sarah were novel, however, suggests that this explanation cannot account for all Sarah's abilities.

A more explicit method for examining the ability to understand intentions was first developed by Povinelli (1991), and then tested more extensively by Povinelli, Perilloux, Reaux, and Bierschwale (1998) and Call and Tomasello (1998). Povinelli (1991) examined whether a language-trained chimpanzee, Sheba, could discriminate between a "bad" experimenter, who deliberately poured juice in front of her while simultaneously threatening her, and a "clumsy" experimenter, who dropped the juice on the floor accidentally. Sheba predominantly chose the clumsy experimenter; however, this may have been due to the fact that Sheba avoided choosing the nasty experimenter. Using a larger sample of laboratory-housed, but not enculturated chimpanzees, Povinelli et al. (1998) repeated these experiments. The subject had to beg or indicate toward one of the trainers to receive juice. One of the trainers then approached the subject and tripped over spilling the juice on the floor, a second trainer deliberately poured the juice on the floor in front of the subject, and a third aggressively poured the juice on the floor before the subject. Povinelli et al. (1998) found that their subjects did not discriminate between any of the trainers, suggesting that they did not understand the difference between intentional and accidental acts. By comparison, Call and Tomasello (1998) tested orang-utans, chimpanzees, and human children. The subjects were initially trained that a marker placed onto the top of a box denoted that food was hidden inside. The box containing food was baited in private, and then the subject was presented with three boxes (including the baited box). The experimenter then marked two boxes in turn; one intentionally (placing the marker carefully on top of the box) and one accidentally (dropping the marker onto the box). All three species chose the box that was intentionally marked. It should be noted that the older human children (over 3 years old) and an enculturated orang-utan (Chantek) were consistently better than the other apes.

Although the field of ToM began with the study of understanding intentions, very few studies have approached this subject experimentally. It is clear from these results that, at least, some apes can understand a human experimenter's intentions and that this ability is enhanced after extensive human contact during early development. It remains to be tested whether other species understand intentions, especially the intentions of conspecifics.

Certainly, neurophysiological evidence of neurons responding to goal-directed actions suggests that monkeys (and probably other animals) may appreciate another's purposive behaviour. What is perhaps the most difficult empirical problem is clearly differentiating between what are perceived as goal-directed actions (Dickinson & Balleine, 2000), and the mental state of intention. For example, Menzel (1974) described a series of studies based in a large enclosure, in which one chimpanzee had witnessed the hiding of food. When the entire group was released, Menzel recorded the group's accuracy in locating the hidden food using only the behavioural cues (direction and speed of travel, body orientation, and gaze direction) provided by the individual that was party to the location of the food. However, were the other group members responding to the knowledgeable chimpanzee's goal-directed movements or understanding their intentions?

Knowledge attribution: informational ToM 1

The third type of mentalizing that we will discuss is *informational ToM* or the mental state of *knowledge*, which is linked to perceptual ToM, in that knowledge states cannot exist without access to perception. This has been called the "seeing leads to knowing" relationship, but it is the same for all the senses. Cheney and Seyfarth (1990) were the first to examine whether nonhuman animals would attribute knowledge or ignorance to other individuals based on whether they had visual access to events or objects that would lead to knowledge. Female Japanese and rhesus macaques were shown food or a predator (a technician with a net), either in the presence of their offspring or when alone. Two questions were addressed: Did the females attempt to alert their offspring to the presence of either food or a predator (through the use of food or alarm calls), and did they differentiate between those offspring that had been present during exposure to these stimuli (knowledgeable) and those that were separated from their mothers (and so were ignorant)? The macaque mothers did not appear to differentiate knowledge from ignorance in their infants as they did not produce a higher frequency of alarm or food vocalizations toward the ignorant offspring.

Povinelli, Nelson, and Boysen (1990), adapting a paradigm designed by Premack (1988), examined the ability of chimpanzees to attribute different knowledge states to human experimenters, asking the question, "Do chimpanzees understand that seeing leads to knowing?" A chimpanzee was present while one of four containers was baited with food (although they could not see which container was baited). In the first condition, the "knower" baited the container while the "guesser" left the room. Once the container had been baited, the "guesser" re-entered the room, and both the "knower" and "guesser" pointed to a container. To receive the food reward, the chimp had to point to the container that the "knower" pointed to. The chimps pointed toward the "knower" in the majority of the trials; however, they did this greater than 70% correct only after 200–300 trials. During a transfer phase, a third experimenter baited a container, while the "knower" observed, and the "guesser" did not leave the room, but remained with a bag over the head. In this condition, the chimpanzees pointed significantly more toward the "knower". However, a re-analysis of the data found that the subjects did this consistently only after the first five trials (Povinelli, 1994). Importantly, the subjects in this study were 6 years old and above. Povinelli, Rulf, and Bierschwale (1994) replicated the study with 3–4-year-old chimpanzees, and all failed to distinguish between "knower" and "guesser".

One potential problem with this study is the fact that chimpanzees do not understand that humans with bags, buckets, or blindfolds on their heads cannot see (Povinelli & Eddy, 1996b). Therefore, the chimpanzees' inability to discriminate between "knower" and "guesser" during the first five trials of the transfer phase could be attributed to a lack of understanding at this level, rather than a failure to relate seeing to knowing. Call et al. (2000) attempted to control for this possibility by replicating Povinelli et al. (1990), but instead of the "guesser" leaving the room or remaining in the room with a bag over the head during baiting, both the "knower" and the "guesser" remained in the room, but the "guesser" turned their back to the subject, while the "knower" faced the subject. As an additional control, either the "knower" or a third experimenter baited the container with food. Only two enculturated chimpanzees chose the cue provided by the "knower" when the "knower" was the baiter, but not when the third experimenter baited the container.

An additional criticism of Povinelli et al. (1990) is the fact that the chimpanzee had to be taught to make begging gestures toward a human experimenter when they wanted food. Chimpanzees very rarely beg from others in the wild, and infants only from their parents; chimpanzees usually fight for access to food. Therefore, ToM may be more likely to have been selected for a role in competition rather than cooperation. In an extension of their earlier studies on visual perspective-taking, Hare, Call, and Tomasello (2001) examined knowledge attribution in chimpanzees with conspecifics. In this situation, a dominant and a subordinate chimp were present in cages to the side of an arena that contained two barriers, with food located behind one of the barriers on the subordinate's side. Compared to the earlier experiment, the dominant individuals either saw the food being hidden or moved (that is, were informed) or did not see the food being hidden or moved (that is, were uninformed). Subordinates, on the other hand, were always informed. If the subordinates were aware of what the dominants did or did not see during baiting, they should have preferred to go toward food that dominants did not know the location of, and that is what they did. In a second experiment, one dominant observed the food baiting, and then was switched with a second individual that had not seen the baiting. The subordinates tended to go for food that the switched animal had not seen being baited. Finally, however, when two pieces of food were baited, one that the dominant had seen and one that it had not, the subordinates did not have a preference for which one they went for.

Monkeys have not demonstrated any ability to attribute knowledge to others. Povinelli et al. (1992) tested rhesus monkeys by the same paradigm as used with the chimpanzees (Povinelli et al., 1990), and no subject reliably chose the "knower" over the "guesser" (Povinelli et al., 1992). Kuroshima, Fujita, Fuyuki, and Masuda (2002), by comparison, found that capuchin monkeys learned (over 330–470 trials) to choose one of three containers indicated by a "knower" compared to a "guesser". One difference in this study was that the "knower" looked into each container, whereas the "guesser" either did not look into the containers or only touched them. A second difference was that the subject had to choose the container hiding food rather than indicate the experimenter who would then give it the food if correct. This may have removed an additional level of complexity inherent in the Povinelli experiment.

There is some evidence that western scrub-jays may attribute knowledge to conspecifics. As I discussed earlier, many food-caching animals have to compete with conspecifics to protect their caches from theft. During caching, storers need to assess whether a conspecific can see them, and, if so, whether they possess information as to the location of their caches. Emery and Clayton (2001) examined whether scrub-jays would treat their caches differently, depending on whether they had cached in view of a conspecific or whether they had cached when the observer's view was occluded. To distinguish between responses based on to the observer's mental states, rather than learning a simple behavioural cue, the birds recovered their caches in private. When the birds had been observed by another bird during caching, they recovered and rehid their caches, all in new places unknown to the observer (see earlier). By contrast, they did little reaching when they had previously cached in private and certainly did not discriminate where they recached. The jays also recached in new sites when they were presented with interleaved trials; first, they were given a visuospatially unique caching tray in which to cache when observed, and then a second visuospatially unique tray in which to cache in private, again recovering the caches in private. These results suggest that the jays understood that the observer had knowledge of the location of their caches, and therefore they should protect them by moving them to new places, whereas the bird that did not witness caching (in private condition) would be ignorant of their location, and so recaching would not be required.

The only other species to have been examined for their understanding that seeing leads to knowing is the domestic pig (Held, Mendl, Devereux, & Byrne, 2001). Subjects were trained to locate food in one of four boxes baited by an experimenter, and given a reward if they chose the correct box. In nonrewarded probe tests, these subjects were then tested for their ability to follow one of two pigs that either did or did not have visual access to a baiting event (that is, were knowledgeable or ignorant). Almost all subjects failed to follow the knowledgeable conspecific; however, one subject did. This may have been due to previously learned associations prior to the experiment (although this seems unlikely from the design). Uninformed pigs could also locate hidden food by utilizing the behavioural cues of an informed pig that had previously witnessed the food being hidden by an experimenter (Held, Mendl, Devereux, & Byrne, 2000); however, the pigs did not have a choice between a knowledgeable and an ignorant pig.

Tactical deception (TD) and "false belief": informational ToM 2

TD refers to the intentional manipulation of another's beliefs, leading the other to believe something contrary to the truth. Unfortunately, most of the data on TD are based on anecdotes reported in response to a questionnaire sent to field primatologists. Byrne and Whiten (1988) accumulated all the anecdotes they were sent and sorted them into certain categories that would represent different forms of TD. One classic case of potential TD is as follows: "Subadult male ME attacks one of the young juveniles who screams. Adult male HL and several other adults run over the hill into view, giving aggressive pan grunt calls; ME, seeing them coming, stands on hind legs and stares into the distance across the valley. HL and the other newcomers stop and look in this direction; they do not threaten or attack ME" (Byrne & Whiten, 1988, p. 237). Byrne and Whiten have suggested that baboon ME may have been staring into the distance with the "intention" of forming the "false belief" in the "minds" of the other baboons that there was a predator close to them. Of course, this actual scenario could have happened previously when there *was* a predator present, or ME may actually have heard something in the bushes to divert his attention that could not be perceived by the researcher. Although Byrne has stated that he could not see anything, he may not have been in the appropriate position to see. While anecdotes are important for formulating testable hypotheses, direct evidence requires an interventionist approach.

Experimental studies of deception

There have been few experimental studies of tactical or intentional deception largely due to difficulties in designing a paradigm that can produce enough data from an infrequent behavioural strategy. (Such strategies are low-frequency events probably because their overuse would reduce their power as a competitive strategy.) The earliest experimental study which described deception within a competitive social framework was Menzel (1974) (see earlier). Although the informed chimpanzee tended to share food with the other members of its group, the dominant male chimp (Rock) increasingly monopolized the food bonanza, not sharing with others. The informed chimp (Belle) became less likely over time to move toward, or indicate the location of, food if Rock was present. Rock countered this by moving her off a patch if she was down for too long, and examined the locations where she had previously been or used her body orientation to determine where the food might be located. Belle finally learned to lead the group in completely the wrong direction to the food, and quickly tail back to retrieve it when the others' attention was elsewhere. This could be interpreted as TD or intentional deception (see also Hirata & Matsuzawa, 2001). Coussi-Korbel (1994) replicated this study in a more controlled manner with sooty mangabeys. She found that Rapide, a subordinate male, when informed of the location of food, was often attacked by the dominant male, Boss, who stole his food. Instead of moving directly toward the food, Rapide quickly changed strategies and followed an increasingly indirect route to the food when Boss was observing.

Bugnyar and Kotrschal (2002) have suggested that caching and raiding ravens may present an example of intentional deception through an attempt to manipulate another individual's attention, either to prevent opponents from gaining opportunities for stealing or to gain opportunities for learning socially from their opponents. They examined two forms in which another's attention may be manipulated: withholding information and directing another's attention away from caches (object of interest). During caching, ravens tended to withdraw from conspecifics, and were often found at a greater distance from conspecifics during caching than during other activities, such as feeding and resting. The storers also cached close to large objects, with 80% of the caches being placed between the storers and the observers, and outside the view of the observers. Cachers moved their caches if an observer moved toward them, and they also protected their cache sites. Cache raiders also employed a number of strategies to increase the potential for learning about cache sites, and for stealing caches. In 33% of cases, the observers changed their position relative to the structures that blocked their view of the cache sites, and in 32% of cases the observers changed their orientation and distance away from the cachers (see visual perspective-taking section). If a storer was close to a cache site, the observers delayed pilfering until the cacher had moved away from the caches, usually within 1 min of the cacher's leaving the cache site.

Such behaviours suggest that ravens not only appreciate the visual perspective of conspecifics, but also may use deceptive strategies and counter-strategies in an arms race to gain another's food caches or protect their own caches. Such strategies may be good candidates for intentional deception as they need to be applied flexibly, they are used in novel contexts, or they need to be newly created. Bugnyar and Kotrschal (2003) have recently described a novel strategy in ravens, not described within the context of protecting food caches: leading others away from cache sites.

A different paradigm, which was not based on the natural history of apes, was developed by Woodruff and Premack (1979), in which subjects had to first learn to "point" toward a container in which they had observed food being hidden by an experimenter to obtain that food. The subject was then presented with a condition in which a second trainer entered the room, and again the subject had to point to the food. One trainer was cooperative

(CoopT) and always shared the food with the subject, but the second trainer was competitive (CompT) and always kept food for himself. Woodruff and Premack (1979) were interested in whether the chimpanzee subjects would 1) point to the correct location of the food when presented with the CoopT; 2) refrain from indicating any container when presented with the CompT; 3) actively mislead the CompT by indicating the container which did not contain food. All four subjects learned to point to the baited container in the presence of the CoopT, and learned to withhold information as to the location of hidden food. Additionally, two subjects also began to point toward the empty container. Although Woodruff and Premack (1979) interpreted these results as evidence for intentional deception, the subjects had experienced hundreds of trials across 3 years, and so may have developed sophisticated social strategies to gain the food. Indeed, the subjects could have quickly learned a rule that producing an error with the CompT trainer, that is, indicating the location of the hidden food, resulted in loss of food, and so rapidly transferred to either withholding any response, or indicating any container except the one in which the food was actually hidden.

Mitchell and Anderson (1997) and Anderson, Kuroshima, Kuwahata, Fujita, and Vick (2001) have replicated this design with capuchin monkeys and squirrel monkeys, respectively. Mitchell and Anderson (1997) found that one capuchin monkey learned over many hundreds of trials to stop responding to the correct container in the presence of the CompT, whereas the second monkey pointed toward the empty container in the presence of the CompT. Similarly, a squirrel monkey learned over hundreds of trials to point to the incorrect container on CompT trials. However, once the containers were coloured to indicate the presence or absence of food (that is, green for food present, black for food absent), two subjects reached toward the positive container on CoopT trials, and decreased the frequency with which they reached for the positive container on CompT trials. Further control conditions indicated that these same monkeys could switch strategies appropriately and flexibly from trial to trial, depending on the type of trainer. Squirrel monkeys have not previously demonstrated sophisticated social strategies during interactions, so these results should be viewed with caution. Indeed, the monkeys received thousands of trials across the entire study, and so some learning process cannot be discounted. The high rate of "correct" responding by the subjects suggests that the use of deceptive strategies may have not been intentional, as deceptive acts lose their effectiveness when used frequently and predictably. Anderson et al. (2001) provided further evidence to suggest that the monkeys were not utilizing intentionally deceptive strategies, as the subjects did not appear to take the trainer's knowledge state into account when deciding to be deceptive. The CompT observed where the food was located before the subjects had to point to one of the containers, and they continued to point to the incorrect location or withhold pointing to the correct container. In a final study, the experimenter hid the food in the opposite container from the one expected (black instead of green). It was found that the subjects continued to reach for the green container, and refrained from reaching toward the black container, in the presence of the CoopT. These results all provide evidence that although squirrel monkeys can use deceptive strategies during competitive situations, they do not base these strategies on an understanding of the mental states of the protagonist.

A recent experiment examining whether capuchin monkeys would spontaneously deceive conspecifics has produced ambiguous results which are worthy of future study (Fujita, Kuroshima, & Masuda, 2002). Subordinate–dominant pairs were placed into a food-competition situation. Two feeder boxes were located between the two subjects, with the food visible and accessible to the subordinate, but invisible and not accessible to the dominant (until the subordinate had opened the box). Fujita et al. (2002) found that two out of four subordinate monkeys spontaneously started to open the unbaited box first; however, they did this on only 10% of the total trials.

Although the results of these various experimental studies (in seminatural environments and the laboratory, using humans or conspecifics as protagonists) provide strong evidence that ravens, monkeys, and apes use extremely sophisticated tactics to deceive opponents, they do not provide evidence that these species use such strategies within an intentional framework.

False-belief task: the reference standard for ToM?

Commentators on Premack and Woodruff's 1978 paper suggested that the most convincing evidence for ToM would be produced through an understanding of an agent's beliefs (Bennett, 1978; Dennett, 1978; Harman, 1978). However, as we discussed earlier, understanding that another individual may have *different* beliefs about the world from yourself, and that sensory information can be unreliable, may provide better evidence, the "false belief". This form of mental attribution has been examined extensively in children by the "Sally–Anne" task (or variants of this task). Language is a necessary feature of false-belief tasks used in children. This does not mean that creatures without access to language, such as animals and preverbal infants, do not possess understanding of false belief. However, it does make the creation of nonverbal false-belief tasks challenging. Premack (1988) was the first to develop a nonverbal false-belief task for apes and children, but failed to produce any positive results.

Gomez (1998) also developed a false-belief task, which has been used in a female orang-utan. During training, the subject was placed into a cage, with two boxes in front of the cage. The boxes were padlocked and the keys were kept in a container elsewhere. One experimenter (the caterer) entered the room, and used the keys to open one of the padlocks, and then returned the key to the container and left. A second experimenter (the giver) then entered the room and "asked" the subject where the food was. The subject was previously trained to point to the box containing food, and once she had pointed to one of the boxes, the giver retrieved the keys and opened the box indicated by the subject. The giver then gave the food to the subject if she made the correct choice of box, returned the keys, and left the room. In experimental probe trials, between the occasion when the caterer left the room and the giver entered the room, a third experimenter (the provider) entered the room and hid the keys in a new location. Therefore, when the giver entered the room, if the subject had attributed ignorance to the giver, she should have pointed to the keys as well as the food. To ensure that this was a test of ignorance, two control conditions were performed; the giver sees the keys being hidden or personally hides the keys. Gomez found that, although the orang-utan failed the first six probe trials, she was successful from then on (see also Gomez, 1996).

Although, at initial glance, this appears to be a well-controlled test for false belief, Heyes (1998) has suggested that the subject could solve this problem through associative learning. She states that the subject could have learned that pointing toward the keys in the training trials led to reward and so transferred this learning to the probe trials in which the provider hid the keys. However, Gomez stated that the subject was not required to point to anything except the food during training. Heyes also stated that an absence of pointing in the control trials, where the giver should not be ignorant of the keys' location, may reflect a generalization decrement, that is, that the subject failed to transfer learning from one context to another. These objections perhaps leave very little possibility of a mentalistic interpretation under any circumstances, and so are hard to reconcile without further experimental information. Whiten (2000) replicated this experiment with language-trained chimpanzees, and also found that they pointed to the keys before the food during the probe trials (provider present). The subjects' behaviour during control trials suggests that they were not attributing false beliefs. In control trials, the provider was present when the hider moved the keys to a new location, but was distracted. In this case, the subjects did not point to the new location of the keys, and so may have been basing their decisions on the presence versus absence of the provider.

The only other nonverbal test for false belief in nonhuman animals was adapted by Call and Tomasello (1999), and was used in chimpanzees, orang-utans, and children. One experimenter hid food out of the subject's view in one of two identical boxes. A second communicator (who had seen the baiting of the box) indicated which of the boxes contained food, and, in control trials, the subjects learned to choose the box that was marked by the communicator. In additional control trials, they also learned to choose the unmarked box if they saw the hider move the food from one box to another when the communicator was out of the room. Call and Tomasello suggested that if the subject knew where the food was (but the communicator did not), the subject should ignore the communicator's pointing, as he had a false belief that the food remained in the box he saw it placed into. Only 5-year-old children passed the "false-belief" component of this experiment, in which the hider swapped the boxes around, without showing the food, after the communicator had left the room, and the communicator returned and pointed at the wrong box. An understanding of false belief represents a case for third-order intentionality (I *know* that you *believe* that you *know* X), may therefore be beyond the cognitive capacities of animals, and may be completely dependent on a complex symbolic communication system, such as displayed by human language.

Role-taking and experience projection: simulation ToM

One aspect of mental attribution that has not been examined seriously in animals until recently is "simulation" theory (role taking and experience projection). Simulation "theory" has been proposed as an alternative to the "theory" ToM approach so far discussed in this chapter. "Theory" theory is a "cold" theory which posits that a mind-reader is a passive observer of the world, recognizing another's mental states in the same way as physical forces, such as gravity. One can predict the effects of gravity on objects, and it is proposed that the effects of mental states on another's behaviour are predicted in the same way (by constructing a theory). "Theory" ToM has no requirement for introspection. By contrast, "simulation" ToM posits that mind-readers use their own mind to simulate the mental processes of others (that is, "putting oneself in another's shoes"). As such, "simulation" ToM does require introspective processes, and so may be related to self-awareness (Gallup, 1982). At present, philosophers of mind and psychologists are divided as to the relative contributions of "theory" ToM and "simulation" ToM to human mental state attribution (Currie & Ravenscroft, 1997; Goldman, 1992; Gordon, 1986; see also papers in Carruthers & Smith, 1996). Recent proposals suggest that different aspects of "theory" ToM and "simulation" ToM contribute to mind-reading (Perner, 1996); indeed, different aspects of these two theories appear to be compromised in autism (Currie, 1996).

"Simulation" ToM has been examined in animals in two forms: role taking, or cognitive empathy (Povinelli, 1993, Povinelli et al., 1992), and experience projection (Emery & Clayton, 2001). Both Gallup (1982) and Whiten (1996, 2000) have suggested that demonstrating experience projection would provide good evidence for ToM in animals. However, in both cases, only a single experience or role is projected or transferred, whereas "simulation" theory attempts to cover the entire range of mental experience (Whiten, 2000). Projecting one's own experiences to another, however, may also be different from representing another's mental states; in fact, the specific experiences are not necessarily tied to a particular mental state, such as attention, desire, or belief. As such, experience projection may not be strictly dependent on language, and so individual behaviour may be used as an index to performance and, as such, may provide an unambiguous technique with which to investigate mentalizing in nonhuman animals.

Role taking has been examined in both chimpanzees and rhesus monkeys

(Povinelli, Nelson, & Boysen, 1992a; Povinelli, Parks, & Novak, 1992b). Subjects were presented with an apparatus first developed by Mason and Hollis (1962), in which an operator could control levers which moved food bowls from one side of the apparatus to the other. The "informant" could see whether one of the four food bowls was baited, but did not have access to the controls used to gain access to the food. The "operator", however, could not see which bowl was baited, but was able to control the apparatus. The informants therefore had to indicate, through pointing, which of the bowls contained food, so that the operator would use the controls to move the bowls toward the informant and the operator, so that they both received the food. The chimpanzees and rhesus monkeys were trained to perform one of the roles, and then they transferred to the opposing, new role. Three out of four chimpanzees transferred immediately to their new role, whereas the rhesus monkeys were never able to transfer to their new role. Unfortunately, the second task was not learned faster than the first task, thus providing an argument against role taking (Heyes, 1998). Heyes also suggested that experience projection may be ruled out, as the subjects' experiences outside the experiment cannot be ruled out, especially their comprehension and/or production of pointing, and the effects of pretraining.

Experience projection has been examined only once in an animal, a food-caching corvid, not a great ape (Emery & Clayton, 2001). As discussed earlier, western scrub-jays utilize different cache-protection strategies, depending on whether or not they had been watched during caching. Of particular relevance here to an understanding of the evolution of mental attribution is the fact that birds recached only when they themselves had previous experience of pilfering another bird's caches, again in new locations. Birds without this experience failed to recache, irrespective of whether they had previously cached in front of an observer or in private. This result raises the exciting possibility that birds with pilfering experience can project their own experience of being a thief onto the observing bird, and so counter what they would predict a thief would do in relation to their hidden food (Emery & Clayton, 2004).

Experience projection, cognitive empathy, and mirror-neurons

In the mid-1990s, a startling neurophysiological finding was published that has had a profound influence on social cognition research; namely, the finding of "mirror-neurons" in the macaque premotor cortex (area F5) (see Rizzolatti & Craighero, 2004, for review). Mirror-neurons are cells that respond selectively to the (visual) perception of another individual's motor action pattern (such as an experimenter reaching toward an object) *and* the action itself performed by the monkey in which the neurons are being recorded. Gallese and Goldman (1998) have made a connection between "simulation" theory and mirror-neurons, and Preston and de Waal (2002) have made the connection between empathy and mirror-neurons. However, I suggest that experience projection is the most neurobiologically plausible candidate for future investigations of the neural basis of social cognition, particularly in nonverbal creatures by single-cell neurophysiological techniques (see Chapter 4, this volume). Of course, this does not preclude the existence of complex neuronal circuits (or neural ensembles) representing different aspects of "simulation" theory. This is similar to the argument that mirror-neurons are unlikely to represent imitation per se, as imitation is the copying of a series of novel actions, not individual actions (as represented by mirror-neurons). As such, imitation may function through a circuit including area F5, but also such regions as the supplementary motor area (SMA), which contains neurons responsive to the physical motor performance of sequences of actions (Halsband, Matsuzaka, & Tanji, 1994; Tanji & Shima, 1994). As such, mirror-neurons in area F5 may also be one stage in a "social cognition pathway", which also includes the STS, amygdala, and medial prefrontal cortex, among others.

Arguments against ToM in animals

Some authors, in particular Heyes (1998), state that there is still no evidence that any animal has been unequivocally shown to possess ToM (although, to be fair, these statements were made before the recent competitive-paradigm studies of Emery and Clayton, 2001, and Hare et al., 2001). The basis for Heyes' position is that many of these experiments could be interpreted in both mentalistic (that is, understanding mental states) and nonmentalistic (that is, associative learning) terms. For example, in Povinelli's knowledge-attribution experiment (Povinelli et al., 1990), the chimps may have formed an association between the "knower" and the baited food, as the "knower" initially baited the food, while the "guesser" was out of the room. In the transfer condition, the "guesser" has a bag over the head; therefore, the chimps may have learned a new discrimination, or may have developed an aversive reaction to the bag, as we do not know whether the chimpanzees had experience of this stimulus prior to the experiment. In many respects, the Hare et al. (2001) study largely eliminated these simple, discrimination-based arguments either by using chimpanzees that have been misinformed about the location of food, or by using different individuals from the ones that had witnessed the baiting.

In another example, the role-taking experiment (Povinelli et al., 1992a, 1992b), there was no difference in the rate of learning between the preswitch and postswitch conditions; that is, the problem in the second condition was not learned any faster than the initial problem. A mentalistic explanation would predict the opposite of this, with a correct response on the first trial after the switch. Finally, in the visual perspective-taking experiment (Povinelli & Eddy, 1996a), the chimps did not selectively discriminate between trainers on the basis of various natural and artificial occluders to sight. In the one case where there was a successful discrimination (facing versus back turned), the chimpanzees may have been responding to a simple discrimination based on previous experience (the experimenters never had their backs turned when they gave food to the chimpanzees). The other discriminations (such as changes in eye gaze) may have been too difficult (or subtle) for the chimpanzees.

Heyes (1993, 1998) has also suggested that any attempt to assess ToM in animals must use *triangulation*, whereby an animal is trained on one set of conditions and is then tested in conditions that are conceptually, but not physically, similar, making it difficult for the animal to solve the new task by associative learning and stimulus generalization. Unfortunately, few tests for ToM have done this. Clearly, what is needed is a series of tests in which an animal that relied on associative learning would show the opposite result to that of an animal that used ToM. Only one study has attempted such a distinction, but this has been examined only with human subjects. Gagliardi, Kirkpatrick-Steger, Thomas, Allen, and Blumberg (1995) showed college students short videoclips of situations similar to the "knower–guesser" experiments, and the students were rewarded with money for each correct response. For one group, the "guesser" (whose back was turned while the container was baited) always pointed to the correct container, while the second group received the typical procedure in which the "knower" always pointed to the correct container. Thus, for one group, associative learning was inconsistent with ToM, and for the other group it was consistent. Interestingly, there was no difference between the two groups in speed of task acquisition, showing that subjects may use associative learning to perform the task even if they possess ToM. This might be a productive approach that could be developed for nonhuman species.

Heyes (1993) also suggested that the most convincing evidence for ToM in animals would be converging evidence from different experiments using the same animals; for example, experiments with visual perspective taking, knowledge attribution, and role taking. Interestingly, there is good evidence for these abilities in both chimpanzees and scrub-jays. This approach is certainly more powerful than positive results from a single experiment in a single, language-trained animal.

One argument against ToM in primates has been proposed by Povinelli, who now suggests that the evidence is thin or nonexistent (Povinelli et al., 2000; Povinelli & Vonk, 2003). Povinelli now takes the radical position that primate researchers are mistaken in their positive view of primate ToM and base their positive reasoning on the "argument by analogy", or the popular opinion that chimpanzees and the other great apes must have complex cognitive abilities, such as ToM, because they are our closest living relatives (Povinelli, Bering, & Giambrone, 2000). This view starkly contrasts with that of Tomasello and Call, who have changed their own position from "no evidence" (Tomasello & Call, 1997) to "positive evidence" (Tomasello, Call, & Hare, 2003a, 2003b). In both cases, the change in position seems to have been driven by the results of one critical experiment. Povinelli's position has changed after finding that chimpanzees cannot discriminate between a human that can see them and another that cannot (Povinelli & Eddy, 1996b). Tomasello and Call's position has changed after they found that chimpanzees know what conspecifics can and cannot see, and what they do and do not know (Hare et al., 2000, 2001). Although a prolonged discussion of these issues is outside the scope of this chapter, I would like to caution against restricting views of the evidence for and against ToM in animals to a subset of researchers. Research in species which are not closely related to humans, such as western scrub-jays, cannot be guilty of the "argument by analogy", and therefore may present the best evidence for ToM in nonhuman animals so far.

Summary and conclusions

In this chapter, I have reviewed and discussed all the evidence for and against the view that nonhuman animals possess the ability to represent other individual's mental states. Although I have attempted to cover all known studies of nonhuman mentalizing, I have particularly focused on those aspects of comparative social cognition which may be of interest to neuroscientists working with animals and humans alike. First, I discussed the prerequisites for complex social cognition—a large brain, complex social groups, and enhanced longevity—so that the correct species are targeted for future research. Second, I described a couple of theoretical tools which may be particularly useful in thinking about the neurobiology of social cognition: intentional stance and intervening variables. Third, I described the different types of social cognition that have been examined in animals: understanding attention, knowledge attribution, intentional communication, understanding beliefs and false beliefs, and simulation ToM (role taking and experience projection). Finally, I described some of the arguments against ToM in animals. In conclusion, the only positive evidence for ToM in nonhuman animals has been provided by recent experiments in chimpanzees and western scrub-jays. The available evidence supports multiple types of social cognition, and is presented as convergent evidence. The aspect of ToM which has yet to be demonstrated by any nonhuman animal is an understanding of false belief. This ability requires a third-order intentionality that may be beyond the capacity of the animal mind.

Finally, I would like to stress that we may never determine the neurocognitive mechanisms by which humans and other animals understand each other as social agents, and why these abilities fail, without collaboration between comparative and developmental psychologists, cognitive and behavioural neuroscientists, psychopathologists, psychiatrists, geneticists, and even philosophers.

Acknowledgements

I would like to thank Nicky Clayton for her insightful comments on an earlier draft of this chapter, and for extensive discussions of these issues. During the writing of this chapter, I was funded by a Royal Society University Research Fellowship.

References

Agnetta, B., Hare, B., & Tomasello, M. (2000). Cues to food location that domestic dogs (*Canis familiaris*) of different ages do and do not use. *Animal Cognition, 3*, 107–112.

Anderson, J. R., & Mitchell, R. W. (1999). Macaques, but not lemurs, co-orient visually with humans. *Folia Primatologica, 70*, 17–22.

Anderson, J. R., Kuroshima, H., Kuwahata, H., Fujita, K., & Vick, S.-J. (2001). Training squirrel monkeys (*Saimiri sciureus*) to deceive: Acquisition and analysis of behaviour toward cooperative and competitive trainers. *Journal of Comparative Psychology, 115*, 282–293.

Anderson, J. R., Montant, M., & Schmitt, D. (1996). Rhesus monkeys fail to use gaze direction as an experimenter-given cue in an object-choice task. *Behavioural Processes, 37*, 47–55.

Anderson, J. R., Sallaberry, P., & Barbier, H. (1995). Use of experimenter-given cues during object-choice tasks by capuchin monkeys. *Animal Behaviour, 49*, 201–208.

Baron-Cohen, S. (1989). Perceptual role-taking and protodeclarative pointing in autism. *British Journal of Developmental Psychology, 7*, 113–127.

Baron-Cohen, S. (1991). Precursors to a theory of mind: Understanding attention in others. In A. Whiten (Ed.), *Natural theories of mind: Evolution, development and simulation in everyday mindreading* (pp. 233–251). Oxford: Blackwell.

Baron-Cohen, S., Leslie, A. M., & Frith, U. (1985). Does the autistic child have a "theory of mind"? *Cognition, 21*, 37–46.

Barton, R., & Dunbar, R. I. M. (1997). Evolution of the social brain. In A. Whiten & R. W. Byrne (Eds.), *Machiavellian intelligence II: Evaluations and extensions* (pp. 240–263). Cambridge: Cambridge University Press.

Bennett, J. (1978). Some remarks about concepts. *Behavioral and Brain Sciences, 1*, 557–560.

Blaschke, M., & Ettlinger, G. (1987). Pointing by monkeys. *Animal Behaviour, 35*, 1520–1523.

Brothers, L. (1990). The social brain: A project for integrating primate behavior and neurophysiology in a new domain. *Concepts in Neuroscience, 1*, 27–51.

Bugnyar, T., & Kotrschal, K. (2002). Observational learning and the raiding of food caches in ravens, Corvus corax: Is it "tactical" deception? *Animal Behaviour, 64*, 185–195.

Bugnyar, T., & Kotrschal, K. (2003). Leading a conspecific away from food in ravens (*Corvus corax*)? *Animal Cognition, 7*, 69–79.

Burger, J., Gochfield, M., & Murray, B. G. (1992). Risk discrimination if eye contact and directness of approach in black iguanas (*Ctenosaurus similis*). *Journal of Comparative Psychology, 106*, 97–101.

Butterworth, G., & Jarrett, N. (1991). What minds have in common is space: Spatial mechanisms serving joint visual attention in infancy. *British Journal of Developmental Psychology, 9*, 55–72.

Byrne, R. W. (1999). Human cognitive evolution. In M. C. Corballis & S. E. G. Lea (Eds.), *Descent of mind: Psychological perspectives on hominid evolution* (pp. 71–87). Oxford: Oxford University Press.

Byrne, R. W., & Whiten, A. (1988). *Machiavellian intelligence: Social expertise and the evolution of intellect in monkeys, apes and humans*. Oxford: Clarendon Press.

Call, J., & Tomasello, M. (1994a). Production and comprehension of referential pointing by orangutans (*Pongo pygmaeus*). *Journal of Comparative Psychology, 108*, 307–317.

Call, J., & Tomasello, M. (1996). The effects of humans on the cognitive development of apes. In A. E. Russon, K. A. Bard, & S. T. Parker (Eds.), *Reaching into thought: The minds of the great apes* (pp. 371–403). New York: Cambridge University Press.

Call, J., & Tomasello, M. (1998). Distinguishing intentional from accidental actions in orangutans (*Pongo pygmaeus*), chimpanzees (*Pan troglodytes*) and human children (*Homo sapiens*). *Journal of Comparative Psychology, 112*, 192–206.

Call, J., & Tomasello, M. (1999). A nonverbal false belief task: The performance of children and great apes. *Child Development, 70*, 381–395.

Call, J., Agnetta, B., & Tomasello, M. (2000). Cues that chimpanzees do and do not use to find hidden objects. *Animal Cognition, 3*, 23–34.

Call, J., Hare, B., & Tomasello, M. (1998). Chimpanzee gaze following in an object-choice task. *Animal Cognition, 1*, 89–99.

Carruthers, P., & Smith, P. K. (Eds.) (1996). *Theories of theories of mind*. Cambridge: Cambridge University Press.

Cheney, D., & Seyfarth, R. (1990). Attending to behaviour versus attending to knowledge: Examining monkeys' attribution of mental states. *Animal Behaviour, 40*, 742–753.

Clements, W. A., & Perner, J. (1994). Implicit understanding of belief. *Cognitive Development, 9*, 377–397.

Connor, R. C., Heithaus, M. R., & Barre, L. M. (2001). Complex social structure, alliance stability and mating access in a bottlenose dolphin "super-alliance". *Proceedings of the Royal Society of London. Series B, 268*, 263–267.

Cooper, J. J., Ashton, C., Bishop, S., West, R., Mills, D. S., & Young, R. J. (2003). Clever hounds: Social cognition in the domestic dog (*Canis familiaris*). *Applied Animal Behaviour Science, 81*, 229–244.

Coss, R. G. (1978). Perceptual determinants of gaze aversion by the lesser mouse lemur (*Microcerbus murinus*): The role of two facing eyes. *Behaviour, 64*, 248–267.

Coussi-Korbel, S. (1994). Learning to outwit a competitor in mangabeys (*Cercocebus t. torquatus*). *Journal of Comparative Psychology, 108*, 164–171.

Currie, G. (1996). Simulation-theory, theory-theory and the evidence from autism. In P. Carruthers & P. K. Smith (Eds.), *Theories of theories of mind* (pp. 242–256). Cambridge: Cambridge University Press.

Currie, G., & Ravenscroft, I. (1997). Mental simulation and motor imagery. *Philosophy of Science, 64*, 161–180.

Dally, J. M., Emery, N. J., & Clayton, N. S. (in press). Cache protection strategies by western scrub-jays (*Aphelocoma californica*): Implications for social cognition. *Animal Behaviour*.

Dennett, D. C. (1978). Beliefs about beliefs. *Behavioral and Brain Sciences, 1*, 568–570.

Dennett, D. C. (1983). Intentional systems in cognitive ethology: The "Panglossian paradigm" defended. *Behavioral and Brain Sciences, 6*, 343–390.

de Waal, F. B. M. (1982). *Chimpanzee politics: Sex and power among apes*. Baltimore, MD: Johns Hopkins University Press.

de Waal, F. B. M., & Tyack, P. (2003). *Animal social complexity*. Cambridge, MA: Harvard University Press.

Dickinson, A., & Balleine, B. W. (2000). Causal cognition and goal directed action. In C. M. Heyes & L. Huber (Eds.), *Evolution of cognition* (pp. 185–204). Cambridge, MA: MIT Press.

Dunbar, R. I. M. (1992). Neocortex size as a constraint on group size in primates. *Journal of Human Evolution, 20*, 469–493.

Dunbar, R. I. M. (1998). The social brain hypothesis. *Evolutionary Anthropology, 6*, 178–190.

Emery, N. J. (2000). The eyes have it: The neuroethology, function and evolution of social gaze. *Neuroscience and Behavioural Reviews, 24*, 581–604.

Emery, N. J., & Clayton, N. S. (2001). Effects of experience and social context on prospective caching strategies by scrub jays. *Nature, 414*, 443–446.

Emery, N. J., & Clayton, N. S. (2004). Comparing the complex cognitive abilities of birds and primates. In L. J. Rogers & G. Kaplan (Eds.), *Comparative vertebrate cognition: Are primates superior to non-primates?* (pp. 3–55). New York: Kluwer.

Emery, N. J., Dally, J. M., & Clayton, N. S. (2004). Western scrub-jays (*Aphelocoma californica*) use cognitive strategies to protect their caches from thieving conspecifics. *Animal Cognition, 7*, 37–43.

Emery, N. J., Lorincz, E. N., Perrett, D. I., Oram, M. W., & Baker, C. I. (1997). Gaze following and joint attention in rhesus monkeys (*Macaca mulatta*). *Journal of Comparative Psychology, 111*, 286–293.

Feh, C. (1999). Alliances and reproductive success in Camargue stallions. *Animal Behaviour, 57*, 705–713.

Flavell, J. H., Everett, B. A., Croft, K., & Flavell, E. R. (1981). Young children's knowledge about visual perception: Further evidence for the level 1-level 2 distinction. *Developmental Psychology, 17*, 99–103.

Frith C. D., & Frith, U. (1999). Interacting minds—a biological basis. *Science, 286*, 1692–1695.

Fujita, K., Kuroshima, H., & Masuda, T. (2002). Do tufted capuchin monkeys (*Cebus apella*) spontaneously deceive opponents? A preliminary analysis of an experimental food-competition contest between monkeys. *Animal Cognition, 5*, 19–25.

Gagliardi, J. K., Kirkpatrick-Steger, K. K., Thomas, J., Allen, G. J., & Blumberg, M. S. (1995). Seeing and knowing: Knowledge attribution versus stimulus control in adult humans (*Homo sapiens*). *Journal of Comparative Psychology, 109*, 107–114.

Gallese, V., & Goldman, A. (1998). Mirror neurons and the simulation theory of mind-reading. *Trends in Cognitive Sciences, 2*, 493–501.

Goldman, A. (1992). In defence of the simulation theory. *Mind and Language, 7*, 104–119.

Gomez, J.-C. (1991). Visual behaviour as a window for reading the minds of others in primates. In A. Whiten (Ed.), *Natural theories of mind: Evolution, development and simulation of everyday mindreading* (pp. 195–207). Oxford: Blackwell.

Gomez, J.-C. (1996). Nonhuman primate theories of (nonhuman primate) minds: Some issues concerning the origins of mind-reading. In P. Carruthers & P. K. Smith (Eds.), *Theories of theories of mind* (pp. 330–343). Cambridge: Cambridge University Press.

Gomez, J.-C. (1998). Assessing theory of mind with non-verbal procedures: Problems with training methods and alternative "key" procedure. *Behavioral and Brain Sciences*, *21*, 119–120.

Gomez, J.-C., Sarriá, E., & Tamarit, J. (1993). The comparative study of early communication and theories of mind: Ontogeny, phylogeny and pathology. In S. Baron-Cohen, H. Tager-Flusberg, & D. Cohen (Eds.), *Understanding other minds: Perspectives from autism* (pp. 397–426). Oxford: Oxford University Press.

Gordon, R. M. (1986). Folk psychology as simulation. *Mind and Language*, *1*, 158–171.

Grinnell, J., Packer, C., & Pusey, A. E. (1995). Cooperation in male lions: Kinship, reciprocity or mutualism? *Animal Behaviour*, *49*, 95–105.

Halsband, V., Matsuzaka, Y., & Tanji, J. (1994). Neuronal activity in the primate supplementary, pre-supplementary, and pre-motor cortex during externally and internally instructed sequential movements. *Neuroscience Research*, *20*, 149–155.

Hampton, R. R. (1994). Sensitivity to information specifying the line of gaze of humans in sparrows (*Passer domesticus*). *Behaviour*, *130*, 41–51.

Hare, B. (2001). Can competitive paradigms increase the validity of experiments on primate social cognition? *Animal Cognition*, *4*, 269–280.

Hare, B., & Tomasello, M. (1999). Domestic dogs (*Canis familiaris*) use human and conspecific social cues to locate hidden food. *Journal of Comparative Psychology*, *113*, 173–177.

Hare, B., Addessi, E., Call, J., Tomasello, M., & Visalberghi, E. (2003). Do capuchin monkeys, *Cebus apella*, know what conspecifics do and do not see? *Animal Behaviour*, *65*, 131–142.

Hare, B., Brown, M., Williamson, C., & Tomasello, M. (2002). The domestication of social cognition in dogs. *Science*, *298*, 1634–1636.

Hare, B., Call, J., Agnetta, B., & Tomasello, M. (2000). Chimpanzees know what conspecifics do and do not see. *Animal Behaviour*, *59*, 771–785.

Hare, B., Call, J., & Tomasello, M. (1998). Communication of food location between human and dog (*Canis familiaris*). *Evolution of Communication*, *2*, 137–159.

Hare, B., Call, J., & Tomasello, M. (2001). Do chimpanzees know what conspecifics know? *Animal Behaviour*, *61*, 139–151.

Harman, G. (1978). Studying the chimpanzee's theory of mind. *Behavioral and Brain Sciences*, *1*, 576–577.

Hauser, M. D. (2000). *Wild minds*. London: Henry Holt.

Heinrich, B. (1999). *Mind of the raven*. London: Harper Collins.

Heinrich, B., & Pepper, J. W. (1998). Influence of competitors on caching behaviour in the common raven, *Corvus corax*. *Animal Behaviour*, *56*, 1083–1090.

Held, S., Mendl, M., Devereux, C., & Byrne, R. W. (2000). Social tactics of pigs in a competitive foraging task: The "informed forager" paradigm. *Animal Behaviour*, *59*, 569–576.

Held, S., Mendl, M., Devereux, C., & Byrne, R. W. (2001). Behaviour of domestic pigs in a visual perspective taking task. *Behaviour*, *138*, 1337–1354.

Herman, L. M., Abichandani, S. L., Elhajj, A. N., Herman, E. Y. K., Sanchez, J. L., & Pack, A. A. (1999). Dolphins (*Tursiops truncates*) comprehend the referential character of the human pointing gesture. *Journal of Comparative Psychology*, *113*, 347–364.

Hess, J., Novak, M. A., & Povinelli, D. J. (1993). "Natural pointing" in a rhesus monkey, but no evidence of empathy. *Animal Behaviour*, *46*, 1023–1025.

Heyes, C. M. (1993). Anecdotes, training, trapping and triangulating: Do animals attribute mental states? *Animal Behaviour, 46*, 177–188.

Heyes, C. M. (1998). Theory of mind in nonhuman primates. *Behavioral and Brain Sciences, 21*, 101–148.

Hirata, S., & Matsuzawa, T. (2001). Tactics to obtain a hidden food item in chimpanzee pairs (*Pan troglodytes*). *Animal Cognition, 4*, 285–295.

Hostetter, A. B., Cantero, M., & Hopkins, W. D. (2001). Differential use of vocal and gestural communication by chimpanzees (*Pan troglodytes*) in response to the attentional status of a human (*Homo sapiens*). *Journal of Comparative Psychology, 115*, 337–343.

Humphrey, N. K. (1976). The social function of intellect. In P. P. G. Bateson & R. A. Hinde (Eds.), *Growing points in ethology* (pp. 303–317). Cambridge: Cambridge University Press.

Humphrey, N. K. (1980). Nature's psychologists. In B. Josephson & V. Ramachandran (Eds.), *Consciousness and the physical world* (pp. 57–80). London: Pergamon.

Itakura, S. (1996). An exploratory study of gaze-monitoring in nonhuman primates. *Japanese Psychological Research, 38*, 174–180.

Itakura, S., & Anderson, J. R. (1996). Learning to use experimenter-given cues during an object-choice task by a capuchin monkey. *Current Psychology of Cognition, 15*, 103–112.

Itakura, S., & Tanaka, M. (1998). Use of experimenter-given cues during object-choice tasks by chimpanzees (*Pan troglodytes*), an orang-utan (*Pongo pygmaeus*), and human infants (*Homo sapiens*). *Journal of Comparative Psychology, 112*, 119–126.

Itakura, S., Agnetta, B., Hare, B., & Tomasello, M. (1999). Chimpanzee use of human and conspecific social cues to locate hidden food. *Developmental Science, 2*, 448–456.

Jolly, A. (1966). Lemur social behaviour and primate intelligence. *Science, 153*, 501–506.

Karin-D'Arcy, M. R., & Povinelli, D. J. (2002). Do chimpanzees know what each other see? A closer look. *International Journal of Comparative Psychology, 15*, 21–54.

Kummer, H., Anzenberger, G., & Hemelrijk, C. K. (1996). Hiding and perspective taking in long-tailed macaques (*Macaca fascicularis*). *Journal of Comparative Psychology, 110*, 97–102.

Kuroshima, H., Fujita, K., Fuyuki, A., & Masuda, T. (2002). Understanding of the relationship between seeing and knowing by tufted capuchin monkeys (*Cebus apella*). *Animal Cognition, 5*, 41–48.

Leavens, D. A., & Hopkins, W. D. (1998). Intentional communication by chimpanzees: A cross-sectional study of the use of referential gestures. *Developmental Psychology, 34*, 813–822.

Leavens, D. A., & Hopkins, W. D. (1999). The whole-hand point: The structure and function of pointing from a comparative perspective. *Journal of Comparative Psychology, 113*, 417–425.

Leavens, D. A., Hopkins, W. D. & Bard, K. A. (1996). Indexical and referential pointing in chimpanzees (*Pan troglodytes*). *Journal of Comparative Psychology, 110*, 346–353.

Lorincz, E. N., Baker, C. I., & Perrett, D. I. (1999). Visual cues for attention following in rhesus monkeys. *Current Psychology of Cognition, 18*, 973–1003.

Mason, W. A., & Hollis, J. H. (1962). Communication between young rhesus monkeys. *Animal Behaviour, 10*, 211–221.

Matheson, M., Cooper, M., Weeks, J., Thompson, R., & Fragaszy, D. (1998). Attribution is more likely demonstrated in more natural contexts. *Behavioural and Brain Sciences*, *21*, 124–126.
McKinley, J., & Sambrook, T. D. (2000). Use of human-given cues by domestic dogs (*Canis familiaris*) and horses (*Equus caballus*). *Animal Cognition*, *3*, 13–22.
Menzel, E. W. (1974). A group of young chimpanzees in a one-acre field. In A. M. Schrier & F. Stollnitz (Eds.), *Behavior of non-human primates* (Vol. 5, pp. 83–153). New York: Academic Press.
Miklosi, A., Kubinyl, E., Topal, J., Gacsi, M., Viranyi, Z., & Csanyi, V. (2003). A simple reason for a big difference: Wolves do not look back at humans, but dogs do. *Current Biology*, *13*, 763–766.
Miklosi, A., Polgardi, R., Topal, J., & Csanyi, V. (1998). Use of experimenter-given cues in dogs. *Animal Cognition*, *1*, 113–121.
Miklosi, A., Polgardi, R., Topal, J., & Csanyi, V. (2000). Intentional behaviour in dog–human communication: An experimental analysis of "showing" behaviour in the dog. *Animal Cognition*, *3*, 159–166.
Miller, N. E. (1959). Liberalization of basic S-R concepts. In S. Koch (Ed.), *Psychology: A study in science* (pp. 196–292). New York: McGraw-Hill.
Mitchell, R. W., & Anderson, J. R. (1997). Pointing, withholding information and deception in capuchin monkeys (*Cebus apella*). *Journal of Comparative Psychology*, *111*, 351–361.
Montague, P. R., Berns, G. S, Cohen, J. D., McClure, S. M., Pagnoni, G., Dhamala, M., et al. (2002). Hyperscanning: Simultaneous fMRI during linked social interaction. *NeuroImage*, *16*, 1159–1164.
Neiworth, J. J., Burman, M. A., Basile, B. M., & Licktig, M. T. (2002). Use of experimenter-given cues in visual co-orienting and in an object-choice task by a New World monkey species, cotton top tamarins (*Saguinus oedipus*). *Journal of Comparative Psychology*, *116*, 3–11.
Peignot, P., & Anderson, J. R. (1999). Use of experimenter-given manual and facial cues by gorillas (*Gorilla gorilla*) in an object choice task. *Journal of Comparative Psychology*, *113*, 253–260.
Perner, J. (1991). *Understanding the representational mind*. Cambridge, MA: MIT Press.
Perner, J. (1996). Simulation as explicitation of predication-implicit knowledge about the mind: Arguments for a simulation-theory mix. In P. Carruthers & P. K. Smith (Eds.), *Theories of theories of mind* (pp. 90–104). Cambridge: Cambridge University Press.
Plooij, F. X. (1978). Some basic traits of language in wild chimpanzees? In A. Lock (Ed.), *Action, gesture and symbol* (pp. 111–131). London: Academic Press.
Povinelli, D. J. (1991). Social intelligence in monkeys and apes. Unpublished doctoral dissertation, Yale University.
Povinelli, D. J. (1993). Reconstructing the evolution of mind. *American Psychologist*, *48*, 493–509.
Povinelli, D. J. (1994). Comparative studies of animal mental state attribution: a reply to Heyes. *Animal Behaviour*, *48*, 239–241.
Povinelli, D. J. (2000). *Folk physics for apes*. New York: Oxford University Press.
Povinelli, D. J., Bierschwale, D. T., & Cech, C. G. (1999). Comprehension of seeing as a referential act in young children, but not juvenile chimpanzees. *British Journal of Developmental Psychology*, *17*, 37–60.

Povinelli, D. J., & Davis, D. R. (1994). Differences between chimpanzees (*Pan troglodytes*) and humans (*Homo sapiens*) in the resting state of the index finger: Implications for pointing. *Journal of Comparative Psychology, 108,* 134–139.
Povinelli, D. J., & Eddy, T. J. (1996a). Chimpanzees: Joint visual attention. *Psychological Science, 7,* 129–135.
Povinelli, D. J., & Eddy, T. J. (1996b). *What young chimpanzees know about seeing.* Monographs of the Society for Research in Child Development, 61, Serial No. 247. Chicago: University of Chicago Press.
Povinelli, D. J., & Eddy, T. J. (1997). Specificity of gaze-following in young chimpanzees. *British Journal of Developmental Psychology, 15,* 213–222.
Povinelli, D. J., & O'Neill, D. K. (2000). Do chimpanzees use their gestures to instruct each other? In S. Baron-Cohen, H. Tager-Flusberg, & D. Cohen (Eds.), *Understanding other minds: Perspectives from developmental cognitive neuroscience* (2nd ed., pp. 459–487). Oxford: Oxford University Press.
Povinelli, D. J., & Vonk, J. (2003). Chimpanzee minds: Suspiciously human? *Trends in Cognitive Sciences, 7,* 157–160.
Povinelli, D. J., Bering, J. M., & Giambrone, S. (2000). Toward a science of other minds: Escaping the argument by analogy. *Cognitive Science, 24,* 509–541.
Povinelli, D. J., Nelson, K. E., & Boysen, S. T. (1990). Inferences about guessing and knowing by chimpanzees (*Pan troglodytes*). *Journal of Comparative Psychology, 104,* 203–210.
Povinelli, D. J., Nelson, K. E., & Boysen, S. T. (1992a). Comprehension of role reversal in chimpanzees: Evidence of empathy? *Animal Behaviour, 43,* 633–640.
Povinelli, D. J., Parks, K. A., & Novak, M. A. (1992b). Role reversal by rhesus monkeys, but no evidence of empathy. *Animal Behaviour, 44,* 269–281.
Povinelli, D. J., Parks, K. A., & Novak, M. A. (1991). Do rhesus monkeys (*Macaca mulatta*) attribute knowledge and ignorance to others? *Journal of Comparative Psychology, 105,* 318–325.
Povinelli, D. J., Perilloux, H. K., Reaux, J. E., & Bierschwale, D. T. (1998). Young and juvenile chimpanzees' (*Pan troglodytes*) reactions to intentional versus accidental and inadvertent actions. *Behavioural Processes, 42,* 205–218.
Povinelli, D. J., Rulf, A. B., & Bierschwale, D. T. (1994). Absence of knowledge attribution and self-recognition in young chimpanzees (*Pan troglodytes*). *Journal of Comparative Psychology, 108,* 74–80.
Premack, D. (1988). "Does the chimpanzee have a theory of mind?" revisited. In R. W. Byrne & A. Whiten (Eds.), *Machiavellian intelligence: Social expertise and the evolution of intellect in monkeys, apes and humans* (pp. 160–179). Oxford: Oxford University Press.
Premack, D., & Premack, A. J. (2002). *Original intelligence.* New York: McGraw-Hill.
Premack, D., & Woodruff, G. (1978). Does the chimpanzee have a theory of mind? *Behavioral and Brain Sciences, 1,* 515–526.
Purdy, J. E., & Domjan, M. (1998). Tactics in theory of mind research. *Behavioral and Brain Sciences,* 21, 129–130.
Reader, S. M., & Laland, K. N. (2002). Social intelligence, innovation, and enhanced brain size in primates. *Proceedings of the National Academy of Sciences of the USA, 99,* 4436–4441.
Reaux, J. E., Theall, L. A., & Povinelli, D. J. (1999). A longitudinal investigation of chimpanzees' understanding of visual perception. *Child Development, 70,* 275–290.

Rizzolatti, G., & Craighero, L. (2004). The mirror-neuron system. *Annual Review of Neuroscience, 27,* 169–192.

Savage-Rumbaugh, E. S., Rumbaugh, D. M., & Boysen, S. T. (1978). Sarah's problems in comprehension. *Behavioral and Brain Sciences, 1,* 555–557.

Scheel, D., & Packer, C. (1991). Group hunting behaviour of lions: A search for cooperation. *Animal Behaviour, 41,* 697–708.

Siegal, M., & Beattie, K. (1991). Where to look first for children's understanding of false beliefs. *Cognition, 38,* 1–12.

Smale, L., Holekamp, K. E., Weldele, M., Frank, L. G., & Glickman, S. E. (1995). Competition and cooperation between litter-mates in the spotted hyaena, *Crocuta crocuta. Animal Behaviour, 50,* 671–682.

Smitha, B., Thakar, J., & Watve, M. (1999). Do bee-eaters have a theory of mind? *Current Science, 76,* 574–577.

Soproni, K., Miklosi, A., Topal, J., & Csanyi, V. (2001). Comprehension of human communicative signs in pet dogs (*Canis familaris*). *Journal of Comparative Psychology, 115,* 122–126.

Soproni, K., Miklosi, A., Topal, J., & Csanyi, V. (2002). Dogs' (*Canis familiaris*) responsiveness to human pointing gestures. *Journal of Comparative Psychology, 116,* 27–34.

Tanji, J., & Shima, K. (1994). Role of supplementary motor cells in planning several movements ahead. *Nature, 371,* 413–416.

Theall, L. A., & Povinelli, D. J. (1999). Do chimpanzees tailor their gestural signals to fit the attentional state of others? *Animal Cognition, 2,* 207–214.

Tomasello, M., & Call, J. (1997). *Primate cognition.* New York: Oxford University Press.

Tomasello, M., Call, J., & Hare, B. (1998). Five primate species follow the visual gaze of conspecifics. *Animal Behaviour, 55,* 1063–1069.

Tomasello, M., Call, J., & Hare, B. (2003a). Chimpanzees understand psychological states—the question is which ones and to what extent. *Trends in Cognitive Sciences, 7,* 153–156.

Tomasello, M., Call, J., & Hare, B. (2003b). Chimpanzees versus humans: It's not that simple. *Trends in Cognitive Sciences, 7,* 239–240.

Tomasello, M., Call, J., Nagell, K., Olguin, K., & Carpenter, M. (1994). The learning and use of gestural signals by young chimpanzees: A trans-generational study. *Primates, 35,* 137–154.

Tomasello, M., Hare, B., & Agnetta, B. (1999). Chimpanzees follow gaze direction geometrically. *Animal Behaviour, 58,* 769–777.

Tschudin, A., Call, J., Dunbar, R. I. M., Harris, G., & van der Elst, C. (2001). Comprehension of signs by dolphins (*Tursiops truncates*). *Journal of Comparative Psychology, 115,* 100–115.

Vander Wall, S. B. (1990). *Food hoarding in animals.* Chicago: University of Chicago Press.

Watve, M., Thakar, J., Kale, A., Puntambekar, S., Shaikh, I., Vaze, K., et al. (2002). Bee-eaters (*Merops orientalis*) respond to what a predator can see. *Animal Cognition, 5,* 253–259.

Wellman, H. M., Cross, D., & Watson, J. (2001). Meta-analysis of theory of mind development: The truth about false belief. *Child Development, 72,* 655–684.

Whiten, A. (1996). When does smart behaviour-reading become mind-reading? In P. Carruthers & P. K. Smith (Eds.), *Theories of theories of mind* (pp. 277–292). Cambridge: Cambridge University Press.

Whiten, A. (2000). Theory of mind in non-verbal apes: Conceptual issues and the critical experiments. *Philosophy, S49*, 199–223.

Whiten, A., & Byrne, R. W. (1988). Tactical deception in primates. *Behavioral and Brain Sciences, 11*, 233–244.

Wimmer, H., & Perner, J. (1983). Beliefs about beliefs: Representation and constraining function of wrong beliefs in young children's understanding of deception. *Cognition, 13*, 103–128.

Woodruff, G., & Premack, D. (1979). Intentional communication in the chimpanzee: The development of deception. *Cognition, 7*, 333–362.

Xitco, M. J., Jr., Gory, J. D., & Kuczaj, S. A. (2001). Spontaneous pointing by bottlenosed dolphins (*Tursiops truncates*). *Animal Cognition, 4*, 115–123.

6 Functional anatomy of human social cognition

*Andrea S. Heberlein
and Ralph Adolphs*

Social cognitive processes

Humans and their ancestors have lived in social groups for millions of years. This history has provided selection pressures for the ability to predict conspecifics' actions (Cosmides & Tooby, 1992). Though it might be possible to predict people's behaviour directly by simple associative learning, doing so on the basis of inferred mental states and traits—including intentions and goals, emotions, personality traits, and beliefs—is more economical and may yield more accurate predictions, especially in complex social contexts (Dennett, 1987; Humphrey, 1984). Evidence from social and developmental psychology shows that humans are very sensitive, from an early age, to cues that can enable predictions about behaviour. In fact, our propensity to attribute mental states extends to inanimate objects, appearing as a tendency towards anthropomorphism (Boyer, 2003; Scholl & Tremoulet, 2000).

In the present chapter, we will focus on the neural circuitry subserving the attribution of animacy and intention (that an object is alive and that it is a mental object), emotional states, personality traits, and intentional or belief states ("theory of mind" [ToM]) to others. This focus is consistent with Brothers' (Brothers, 1990) definition of social cognition as "the processing of any information which culminates in the accurate perception of the dispositions and intentions of other individuals" (p. 28).

Some processes that fall under the rubric of social cognition appear to be *perceptual*, in that they are fast and apparently automatic, and seem to be relatively little influenced by top-down processes. Others appear to rely more on conceptual knowledge, and thus might more properly be called *attributional*. In this chapter, we will distinguish between these terms as follows. When processes appear to be primarily stimulus-driven, and to rely little or not at all on context or top-down contributions, we will refer to them as perception. When processes appear to be equal parts bottom-up and top-down, we will refer to them as recognition. Finally, when processes appear to be largely top-down, or when it is unclear how to categorize a given process or set of processes, we will refer to them as attribution.

A bit about organization: though this chapter is organized in terms of different social cognitive processes, it could have been organized in at least two other ways; that is, by anatomical structure (for example, a section reviewing all the social cognitive processes in which the amygdala is implicated) and by levels of processing (for example, structures which participate in the *perception* of socially relevant stimuli, structures which participate in the *emotional evaluation* of the perceived social stimuli, etc.). If a single region is implicated in multiple types of social cognitive processes, it does not necessarily follow that exactly the same region is active when a person is engaged in all of the different processes (see discussion of superior temporal sulcus (STS), below), or that it is engaged in the different processes at the same time. However, it is intriguing that some structures are implicated in multiple social cognitive tasks: For example, the amygdala has been linked to emotion recognition, racial in-group recognition/stereotyping, and ToM processes. There are at least three possible explanations: (1) the amygdalar nuclei perform the same processes in these apparently different social cognitive tasks; (2) different structures within the amygdala participate differently in different social tasks, but lack of resolution (at the level of either functional imaging or discussion) has made it difficult to detect these differences; (3) the same regions of the amygdalar nuclei are in fact involved in different processes, by virtue of their interactions within different anatomical circuits. Comparisons across studies, as well as future studies motivated by such comparisons, will help to distinguish between these possibilities. For the time being, we will discuss in turn animacy/intentionality perception, emotion recognition, personality/stereotype attribution, and belief attribution. Within each discussion, we will sequentially review findings relevant to individual brain regions, followed by a summary of how the different brain regions might participate in the process under discussion. The brain regions are all depicted in Figure 6.1.

Perception of animacy/socially salient cues

The processes by which we come to know that a given object is alive might come closest to appropriately being called "perceptual" (Scholl & Tremoulet, 2000): they appear to be fast, automatic, and stimulus-driven. For example, subjects watching a geometric shape portrayed on a computer screen moving in certain trajectories overwhelmingly perceive it as animate, despite their otherwise inescapable knowledge that it is a shape portrayed on a computer monitor. Two regions of extrastriate visual cortex appear to be relatively specialized to process specific types of signals that mark visual stimuli as potentially animate and intentional: a region in the occipitotemporal cortex known as the fusiform gyrus, and cortices along posterior sectors of the STS.

The fusiform gyrus

The fusiform gyrus (Figure 6.1) has been shown by lesion, functional imaging, magnetoencephalographic (MEG), and evoked potential (ERP) studies to

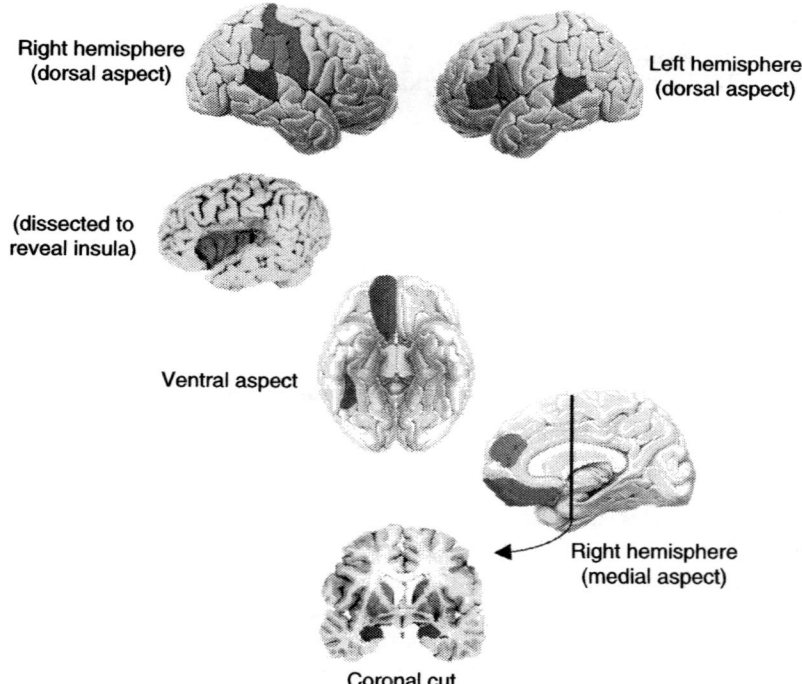

Figure 6.1 This figure highlights the cortical and subcortical regions which play critical roles in social cognitive processes (see text). Many of these regions are implicated in multiple different social cognitive processes. The **right somatosensory cortices** are highlighted in on the right hemisphere view (top left, with primary somatosensory cortex in a slightly darker shade). The **left frontal operculum** is highlighted on the left hemisphere view (upper right). Cortices around the **superior temporal sulcus** are highlighted in very dark gray on both the right and left hemispheres. The **insula** is visible only when overlying frontal and temporal cortices are cut away; here, it is highlighted in medium gray. The **orbitofrontal cortex** is highlighted on the ventral aspect, and is visible also on a medial view (shown here only on the right side). The **fusiform gyrus**, which includes the **fusiform face area**, is highlighted on the ventral view as well. The **medial prefrontal cortices**, specifically those regions implicated in ToM processes, are highlighted in lighter gray on the medial surface.

The **amygdala**, highlighted in dark gray, is visible in a coronal section at the bottom of the figure; the level of the cut is indicated on the right hemisphere medial view above it.

process the perceptual properties of faces. Activity in the fusiform gyrus in response to faces occurs shortly after stimulus onset (Allison, Puce, & McCarthy, 1999; McCarthy, Puce, Belger, & Allison, 1999; Pizzagalli, Lehmann, Hendrick, Regard, Pascual-Marqui, & Davidson, 2002; Puce, Allison, & McCarthy, 1999), and lesions in fusiform regions result in deficits in visual processing of faces (Farah, 1996; Farah, Wilson, Drain, & Tanaka, 1998). Particular attention has been focused on a region of the fusiform gyrus dubbed the fusiform face area (FFA) (Kanwisher, McDermott, & Chun, 1997), which is activated in functional imaging studies by faces (often bilaterally but more reliably on the right than on the left), as compared to other objects or scrambled images. Activation in this area can be modulated by attention (Haxby, Horwitz, Ungerleider, Maisog, Pietrini, & Grady, 1994). There has been some controversy over the extent to which the FFA is truly specialized for face processing, as opposed to subordinate-level processing of expertise objects. The fusiform gyrus is also activated by nonface objects when subjects are forced to engage in subordinate-level categorization (Gauthier, Anderson, Tarr, Skudlarski, & Gore, 1997) or automatically when subjects are experts at subordinate-level categorization of a particular kind of object (such as species of birds or makes of car; Gauthier, Skudlarski, Gore, & Anderson, 2000, or artificial objects; Gauthier, Tarr, Anderson, Skudlarski, & Gore, 1999). However, recent evidence suggests that even in such experts, there is greater FFA activation to faces than to the objects on which they are experts (McKone & Kanwisher, in press). It may be that the question of the "true role" of the FFA cannot be answered: almost all humans have vastly more expertise in face processing than any other type of visual object processing, at the subordinate level. Whether the existence of the FFA came about through an evolutionary pressure for face-processing ability, or instead was coopted for face processing because of its superb subordinate-categorization readiness, may have to remain an open question.

The FFA participates in constructing perceptually detailed representations of the structural, and primarily stable, properties of faces, which can then be linked to the retrieval of knowledge regarding that specific face; Haxby, Hoffman, & Gobbini (2002) posit that fusiform regions are critical for processing invariant aspects of faces, such as identity, whereas temporal regions process more variable aspects of faces, such as emotional expression. However, others suggest that one role of fusiform face-processing cortices may be to alert downstream social cognitive circuits to the presence of socially relevant stimuli (of which faces are a key, but not the sole, component) (Castelli, Frith, Happé, & Frith, 2002; Castelli, Happé, Frith, & Frith, 2000; Schultz et al., 2000).

Superior temporal sulcus (STS)

The involvement of cortex surrounding the STS in social processes was initially recognized from studies in nonhuman primates. Perrett, Rolls, & Caan (1982) characterized cells in macaque STS which responded selectively to faces, and later (Perrett et al., 1985) described cells responsive to specific body movements, such as particular head or body rotations, or movements of the whole body into view. In further studies, populations of cells in the anterior STS were found to be active when monkeys looked at specific views of head and/or gaze direction (Harries & Perrett, 1991), hand or mouth movements (Perrett, 1989), and body movements, even when those movements are depicted via point-light walkers (movies constructed by attaching small lights to a subject's major joints and filming movements in the dark) (Oram & Perrett, 1994). Comparison between monkey and human results is difficult both because homologies between human and nonhuman-primate STS are not fully characterized, and because of the difference in methodologies used to study response properties of these areas between species, that is, neurophysiological recordings in nonhuman primates and neuroimaging studies in humans (Allison et al., 2000). However, Logothetis, Guggenberger, Peled, & Pauls (1999) have shown that STS activation can be observed by blood oxygen level-dependent (BOLD) functional magnetic resonance imaging (fMRI) in anesthetized monkeys, in response to pictures of human and monkey faces. This study provides a connection between a method used to examine STS responses in humans and the cellular level responses previously obtained in monkeys to face stimuli.

Neuroimaging studies in humans have implicated areas of the STS in the visual perception of human bodies (Downing, Jiang, Shuman, & Kanwisher, 2001) and body movement (recently reviewed by Allison et al., 2000). Activations along the posterior STS have been noted when subjects viewed body movements, including eye gaze (Wicker, Michel, Henaff, & Decety, 1998) or eye movements (Hoffman & Haxby, 2000; Puce, Allison, Bentin, Gore, & McCarthy, 1998), mouth movements (Puce et al., 1998), static pictures implying movement (Kourtzi & Kanwisher, 2000), and point-light displays of hands or whole-body biological motion (Bonda, Petrides, Ostry, & Evans, 1996; Grezes & Decety, 2002; Grezes, Fonlupt, Bertenthal, Delon-Martin, Segebarth, & Decety, 2001; Grossman et al., 2000; Grossman & Blake, 2001; Howard, Brammer, Wright, Woodruff, Bullmore, & Zeki, 1996). The precise areas of activation differed between the studies, and were frequently unilateral in any given study, with side varying between studies. However, all of these activations occurred along the banks of the STS or closely adjoining cortex, either in the posterior part of the straight region, or along the ascending region (Allison et al., 2000).

The cortex surrounding the STS receives inputs from both dorsal stream areas and the inferior temporal regions critical for object recognition. Based on this convergence of inputs, Vaina, Solomon, Chowdhury, Sinha, & Belliveau (2001) have suggested that neurons in the STS cortex are able to integrate information from both dorsal and ventral streams. In support of this, they found that two tasks, one requiring subjects to discriminate biological motion from scrambled motion, and another which used the same stimuli, but required subjects to detect the overall direction of motion of a point-light walker, both activated areas in the dorsal pathway. In contrast, both the first task, discriminating biological motion, and a third task, judging the gender of faces, activated areas in the posterior STG and in the ventral pathway. Thus, cortices in the posterior STS may be uniquely situated to detect and process biological motion.

STS cortices appear to play a role not just in the representation of bodies and of body motion, but also in the processing of agency and goal-directedness from body movement stimuli (Bonda et al., 1996; Decety, et al., 1997; Decety, Chaminade, Grezes, & Meltzoff, 2002; Pelphrey, Mitchell, McKeown, Goldstein, Allison, & McCarthy, 2003) and from the movement of animated shapes (Castelli et al., 2000). In these studies, viewing or making judgements about goal-directed movements, as opposed to emotional movements (Bonda et al., 1996), non-goal-directed movements (Decety et al., 1997), or physically random movements (Castelli et al., 2000), activated posterior STS regions.

In addition to perception of body motion and recognition of agency, posterior STS regions are frequently found to be activated during tasks involving the attribution of mental states from a variety of different cues (Castelli et al., 2000; Fletcher et al., 1995; Gallagher, Happé, Brunswick, Fletcher, Frith, & Frith, 2000; Saxe & Kanwisher, 2003; Vogeley et al., 2001). These three component processes—recognition of body form and biological motion, recognition of goal-directedness, and mental state attribution—are all components of social cognition, and recent evidence indicates that distinct regions within posterior STS cortices subserve each of these three processes (Saxe, 2003; Saxe & Kanwisher, 2003). In a recent study by Saxe, Xiao, Kovacs, Perrett, & Kanwisher (2004), adjacent, but distinct, regions within individual subjects were activated in response to visual presentations of human bodies, to visual analysis of movement, especially with regard to goals and agency, and to attribution of intentional states. We will discuss this last process below; the relevant finding at this point is that nearby regions of cortex in the area of the posterior STS probably perform different tasks. This finding explains the recurrent reports of posterior STS activation both in ToM tasks and in response to body movement stimuli with no apparent ToM demands. Further, this result cautions us against anatomical vagueness when drawing conclusions about a given region's role in any process.

Summary: perception of agency and animacy

In summary, cortices in both the fusiform gyrus and the posterior STS respond relatively quickly to visual cues that signal the presence of a socially relevant entity, and thus are candidate structures for regions that participate in the perception of animacy and, in the case of the posterior STS, agency or intentionality. It has been suggested, in fact, that the perception of agency may precede or even be critical for the perception of animacy—that one of the features by which we recognize that something is alive is its goal-directed behavior (Johnson, 2000; Tremoulet & Feldman, 2000).

Recognition of emotion

Darwin noted that many facial and bodily expressions of emotions in humans seem to be similar to those which could be observed in other animals.

From this and other observations, he postulated that emotional expressions serve a function now and/or did so in some previous environment in which human ancestors lived (Darwin, 1872). Contemporary theorists following similar logic have posited that emotions facilitate interactions in recurring situations such as courtship, fighting, and fleeing predation (Panksepp, 1998; Tooby & Cosmides, 1990), and allow very fast, automatic appraisals of complex situations (Ekman, 1992). Emotional expressions can occur both as a part of an emotional response and as a communication device (Darwin, 1872; Fridlund, 1994). Depending on the context, both an involuntary expression and a voluntary modulation of that expression may play roles in the shaping of an expression. Though models differ as to which emotions can be considered "basic", six are commonly agreed upon: anger, disgust, fear, happiness, sadness, and surprise. These are considered basic primarily because facial expressions depicting these emotions seem to be produced, recognized, and categorized similarly across a wide range of cultures (Ekman, 1994). In addition, many theorists distinguish a second class of emotions, ones that are thought to occur later in development, and which are more determined by cultural context: the social, or complex emotions of shame or embarrassment, pride, jealousy, and guilt.

The process by which humans come to know, via various nonverbal cues, that a conspecific is experiencing one of the emotional states listed above is most commonly called "recognition". This word implies not only that there is some objective truth about the experience of the emoter, but also that the recognizer is matching the observed features of the expressed emotion to internal concepts regarding the emotion, and associated knowledge. One of the most compelling current theories about the processes of emotion recognition holds that humans map the expressions that they see or hear onto internal models of the associated body states in order to infer the feeling state that the observed person is in. This theory is known as *simulation theory*, and is considered further at the end of this chapter. In addition to simulation-based processes, it is likely that some socially relevant stimuli, especially those related to threat (such as angry or fearful faces), may be processed more quickly and via partially distinct pathways.

Neuroimaging and neuropsychological studies of emotion recognition implicate several structures in different aspects of these processes. Prominent among these are the amygdala, orbitofrontal cortices (OFC), right somatosensory cortices, and left frontal operculum (see Figure 6.1).

The amygdala in emotion recognition

The amygdala is involved in the processing of emotional faces, as well as of other emotional visual stimuli (such as body movements; also nonsocial emotional stimuli) and at least some emotional auditory cues. Lesion and functional imaging results both point to a role in the processing of threat and/or ambiguity-related stimuli (Adolphs, 2002; Whalen, 1998), consistent with the direction of attentional resources to potentially threatening stimuli. Results from these two methods appear to diverge, however, in the examination of a role for the amygdala in the processing of positive faces, such as prototypically happy faces, for which some imaging studies find amygdala activation (relative to neutral faces) (Breiter et al., 1996; Yang et al., 2002), but lesion studies fail to find recognition impairments (Adolphs, Russell, & Tranel, 1999b). This discrepancy may be at least partly resolved by a recent finding that individual differences in a personality trait, extraversion, are correlated with amygdala activity in response to happy faces (Canli, Sivers, Whitfield, Gotlib, & Gabrieli, 2002b); studies with a higher percentage of extraverted subjects may show a significant increase in amygdala activity overall in response to happy (compared with neutral) faces, but subject composition should not affect whether amygdala activity is observed in response to fearful faces, since this effect was observed across subjects.

Damage to the human amygdala impairs recognition of various negative facial expressions, including fear, in some experimental tasks (Adolphs et al., 1999b; Adolphs, Tranel, Damasio, & Damasio, 1995b; Broks et al., 1998; Calder, Young, Perrett, Hodges, & Etcoff, 1996; Schmolck & Squire, 2001; Sprengelmeyer et al., 1999; Young, Aggleton, Hellawell, Johnson, Broks, & Hanley, 1995). It is unclear how far this fear recognition deficit extends: some authors have also reported impairments in recognition of fear from vocal prosody cues (Scott, Young, Calder, Hellawell, Aggleton, & Johnson, 1997), but others have failed to find such an impairment (Adolphs & Tranel, 1999; Anderson & Phelps, 1998). However, it is certainly not the case that only facial expression processing is impaired after amygdala damage: such subjects are also impaired in recognizing emotions from body postures (Sprengelmeyer et al., 1999), body movements (Heberlein, 2002), and emotional sounds (Sprengelmeyer et al., 1999), and use fewer emotion words than matched normal controls when describing an ambiguous animated video (Heberlein & Adolphs, 2004).

In a series of studies, Adolphs and colleagues have characterized the deficits shown by a rare subject with selective bilateral amygdala damage, subject S.M. This subject consistently showed deficits in recognizing facial expressions of fear, but not of other emotions. When initially tested, she drew reasonably accurate facial expressions of other basic emotions, but had trouble drawing a fearful face (Adolphs et al., 1995b). However, she appeared to have substantial declarative knowledge about the concept of fear, as demonstrated by her appropriate use of words such as "fear", "afraid", and "frightened", and by her ability to describe what situations would evoke fear (ibid.). When rating the arousal (that is, level of excitation) and valence (that is, positivity or negativity) of facial expressions, words, and sentences depicting unpleasant emotions, S.M. showed normal recognition of the valence of these stimuli, but abnormal recognition of arousal (Adolphs et al., 1999a).

In contrast to the pattern of deficits observed in S.M., two other subjects with complete bilateral amygdala damage were initially reported to rate emotional facial expressions normally (Hamann et al., 1996). However, when these data were analyzed in more detail, these subjects were indeed found to be impaired; they were also impaired on a labelling task (Schmolck & Squire, 2001). Nevertheless, it is clear that amygdala damage results in different patterns of emotion-recognition impairment in different subjects: the two subjects reported by Hamann and colleagues (1996) were more impaired on labelling tasks than on rating tasks, whereas the opposite pattern was obtained with S.M. A possible explanation for this disparity is that S.M.'s damage was sustained in childhood: it is conceivable that the lack of amygdalar contribution to her social cognitive development led to a different pattern of emotion-recognition impairment than is observed after adult-onset amygdala damage.

To address the question of discrepancies in emotion-recognition impairments across subjects with bilateral amygdala damage, Adolphs et al. (1999b) compared nine subjects with bilateral amygdala damage on the same sensitive task of emotional facial expression recognition. None showed deficits in recognition of positive emotions (happiness), most showed deficits in recognition of one or more negative emotions, and a deficit in fear recognition was the most common across subjects (Adolphs et al., 1999b). This finding may be consistent with the aforementioned deficit observed in patient SM in recognizing the arousal level of unpleasant emotional stimuli (Adolphs et al., 1999b). The amygdala may serve as one component of a system which perceives threatening environmental stimuli (Adolphs et al., 1999a), an interpretation that accords well with aversive conditioning studies in humans and in nonhuman animals. It is also important to note, however, that the variance in performance on the same task shows that the amygdala is not critical for all aspects of emotion recognition.

Functional imaging studies in which subjects viewed emotional faces complement the findings of the lesion studies described above, and also extend them with regard to the processing of emotional expressions other than negative ones. Several studies have shown greater amygdala activation when subjects viewed fearful faces than neutral ones (Breiter et al., 1996; Morris, Öhman, & Dolan, 1998; Pessoa, McKenna, Gutierrez, & Ungerleider, 2002) or happy faces (Morris et al., 1996; Pessoa et al., 2002). In some reports, happy faces also resulted in greater amygdala activation than neutral faces (Breiter et al., 1996; Pessoa et al., 2002; Yang et al., 2002); as noted above, this may be due to individual differences among the subjects studied (Canli et al., 2002b). Interestingly, when neutral faces carry extra social significance, amygdala activity may be observed even in the absence of negative emotional expression: social phobics show greater activation in the amygdala to neutral faces than normal controls (Birbaumer et al., 1998), and younger children also show greater amygdala activation to neutral faces than happy faces (Thomas et al., 2001). This latter result may be due to a relative lack of experience with direct-gazing, unsmiling facial expressions in children; direct gaze yields amygdala activation in many primate species as well, and in the absence of experience with such faces in nonthreatening contexts, they may well be perceived as threatening.

Amygdala activation in response to fearful faces has also been observed when stimuli were presented subliminally (Whalen, Rauch, Etcoff, McInerney, Lee, & Jenike, 1998), and even in the absence of primary visual cortex (Morris, DeGelder, Weiskrantz, & Dolan, 2001), this latter most probably via projections to the amygdala more or less directly from the pulvinar nucleus of the thalamus, bypassing early visual cortices (Morris, Öhman, & Dolan, 1999). These latter findings from Morris and colleagues have led to further explorations regarding the necessity of attention, or even awareness, for amygdalar responses to negative facial expressions. Such studies have yielded mixed results to date: at least one group (Vuilleumier, Armony, Driver, & Dolan, 2001) reported amygdala activation to fearful faces during a simultaneous attention-demanding task, but a more recent study using an apparently more difficult and attention-demanding task found that attention was necessary for amygdala activation to face stimuli of any emotional valence (Pessoa et al., 2002).

In summary, the amygdala seems to be necessary for normal processing of negative emotional stimuli, and amygdala damage most often leads to impairments in recognizing threat and/or arousal-related information from visual stimuli. In neurologically intact subjects, these nuclei, or regions within them, are recruited for processing emotional faces, especially fearful faces, and it is possible that at least part of this recruitment occurs as the result of a direct, subcortical projection from the thalamus.

We hinted above at a fascinating new direction of research that will contribute to our understanding of amygdalar function in emotion recognition. Several recent studies have examined correlations between gender and individual differences, such as personality traits, and amygdala activation patterns during social judgement tasks (e.g., Cahill et al., 2001; Canli, Desmond, Zhao, & Gabrieli, 2002a; Canli et al., 2002b; Hariri et al., 2002). In one example of such a study, subjects' extraversion, a personality trait, correlated with amygdala activation in response to happy faces, but not fearful faces (all subjects showed amygdala activation to fearful faces, but only extraverted subjects showed amygdala activation to happy faces) (Canli et al., 2002b). In another study, a form of serotonin transporter promoter which results in reduced serotonin function was correlated with greater amygdala activity in response to fearful faces (Hariri et al., 2002). These studies indicate that variance in the amygdala activation reports across studies, as well as across subjects within a given study, is at least partially attributable to individual differences in subjects' personalities, some part of which can be further tied to genetic differences which affect subjects' sensitivities to social stimuli.

Orbitofrontal cortices (OFC) and emotion recognition

The amygdala and OFC are bidirectionally connected (Amaral, Price, Pitkanen, & Carmichael, 1992), and both receive projections from sensory cortices at several levels of processing, and project to hypothalamic and brainstem structures which coordinate physiological emotional responses. Thus, it is not surprising that OFC have also been implicated in emotion recognition, though not as broadly as the amygdala. Subjects with OFC damage, primarily on the right, were found to be impaired in emotion recognition from faces in one study (Hornak, Rolls, & Wade, 1996), and in a case study, a subject showed a sharp decrease in recognition of fearful faces after resection of the right prefrontal cortex (PFC) for the treatment of epilepsy (Marinkovic, Trebon, Chauvel, & Halgren, 2000).

Imaging studies have observed activation in the OFC or more lateral regions of the ventral PFC when subjects viewed or held in memory emotional faces (Dolan, Fletcher, Morris, Kapur, Deakin, & Frith, 1996; Vuilleumier et al., 2001). A single-unit recording study in humans also supports a role for the OFC in emotion recognition: the activity of single units in the right ventral PFC has also been shown to distinguish happy from fearful facial expressions (Kawasaki et al., 2001). Finally, the OFC appears to be more responsive to angry faces than sad faces, as observed in a PET study in which subjects made gender judgements while observing sad and angry faces (Blair, Morris, Frith, Perrett, & Dolan, 1999). These findings suggest that the ventral prefrontal cortices, and especially OFC, play an important role in emotion recognition.

Right-hemisphere cortices in emotion recognition

Cortices in the right hemisphere appear to be critical for recognizing the emotion expressed by another person, though it is likely that they play a somewhat different role from the amygdala and OFC. Suggestions of a disproportionate involvement of right-hemisphere cortices came from neuropsychological studies in which subjects with right-hemisphere damage were significantly worse than left hemisphere-damaged patients or normal controls at recognizing emotion from faces and other visual cues (Benowitz, Bear, Rosenthal, Mesulam, Zaidel, & Sperry, 1983; Borod et al., 1998; Bowers, Bauer, Coslett, & Heilman, 1985; Kucharska-Pietura, Phillips, Gernand, & David, 2003), as well as in the production and reception of vocal prosody (Adolphs, Damasio, & Tranel, 2002; Kucharska-Pietura et al., 2003; Ross, 1993; Ross, Thompson, & Yenkosky, 1997) and in the processing of emotional words (Borod, Andelman, Obler, Tweedy, & Welkowitz, 1992). Consistent with such a specialization of right-hemisphere cortices for emotion-recognition processes, subjects rely more on the left side of the face (which is processed largely by right-side visual cortices) when judging expression, as well as gender, attractiveness, and age, from chimeric faces

(Burt & Perrett, 1997). In addition, subjects rely more extensively on information from the left hemispace when making fine-grained judgements about negative emotional expressions (Jansari, Tranel, & Adolphs, 2000).

Recently, focus on the right hemisphere's role in emotion recognition was narrowed somewhat to the frontoparietal regions: Adolphs, Damasio, Tranel, Cooper, & Damasio (2000) compared the lesion locations of 108 people who had been tested with tasks involving recognition of six basic emotions from facial expressions (Ekman & Friesen, 1976), comparing the overlap of damage of those subjects who performed poorly on tasks of emotion recognition from facial expression to the overlap of damage of those subjects who performed normally. This analysis identified two critical regions wherein damage was systematically associated with impaired emotion recognition: right somatosensory-related areas including S1 (BA 1–3), insula, and underlying white matter, and the left frontal operculum (Broca's area/BA 44–45). In a similar analysis comparing the lesion locations of 66 subjects with regard to their performance on tasks of recognition of emotional prosody, Adolphs et al. (2002) again found that damage to either right somatosensory areas or the left frontal operculum disproportionately impaired subjects' performance. A recent lesion overlap study using emotional point-light body movement stimuli also found maximal overlap in right postcentral and supramarginal gyri in impaired subjects (Heberlein et al., 2004).

In summary, cortices in the right hemisphere, and especially somatosensory cortices, play an important role in emotion recognition. In contrast to the amygdala and right OFC, which appear to be specifically involved in recognizing negative emotions, the right somatosensory cortices appear to be important for recognizing emotions across the board. These regions may participate in a modeling of what it *feels like* to be in a given emotional state; this idea is discussed in more detail below. Finally, right-hemisphere structures may also be important in recognizing other kinds of social information (see below).

Left frontal operculum in emotion recognition

The finding that subjects with left frontal operculum damage are impaired in recognition of emotion from facial expressions (Adolphs et al., 2000) and from prosody (Adolphs et al., 2002) is interesting in light of findings from humans and nonhuman primates which imply that this area is critical for mapping observed actions onto one's internal representations of the same actions. First described in monkey single-unit experiments (Gallese, Fadiga, Fogassi, & Rizzolatti, 1996; Rizzolati, Fadiga, Gallese, & Fogassi, 1996), "mirror-neurons" found in the frontal operculum are active both when subjects perform an action and when they observe another individual performing the same action.

Though homology between monkey and human premotor cortical areas is not clear, a PET study in humans noted activity in the frontal operculum, especially on the left, when subjects imitated finger movements that they observed another person performing (Iacoboni et al., 1999); activity in the frontal operculum is also evident when subjects observe an action with instructions to remember it in order to imitate it later (Decety et al., 1997). These findings imply that neurons in the human premotor cortex may also serve a mirror-neuron-like function. Interestingly, when subjects watched actions performed by different body parts, Buccino et al. (2001) observed activation of premotor cortical areas that was somatotopic with respect to the body parts involved in the action. In sum, the premotor cortex, including the frontal operculum, seems to be critically involved in internally simulating observed actions, and may constitute an "observation/execution matching system" (Gallese & Goldman, 1998).

Though the role of "mirror-neurons" and premotor cortices in such perception-action matching (Preston & de Waal, 2002) has primarily been described for attribution of goals or intentions based on observed movements, in what has been called a simulation theory of intention recognition (Blakemore & Decety, 2001; Gallese & Goldman, 1998), several findings suggest that similar systems underlie emotion recognition. Recent studies have reported premotor cortex activity when subjects process emotional stimuli, including both emotional facial expressions (Kesler-West et al., 2001) and emotional prosody (George et al., 1996; Imaizumi et al., 1997). These findings converge nicely with Adolphs et al.'s (2000, 2002) findings of deficits in emotion recognition consequent to frontal operculum damage. Left premotor cortices may be important for recognizing not only intentions from another's actions, but also emotions from observed behaviour.

Summary: emotion recognition

A general scheme of the roles of the neural regions briefly reviewed here might work as follows. Amygdalar structures receive early visual input via the pulvinar (Jones & Burton, 1976), and also receive input from visual and other sensory cortices at multiple levels of processing, including face-specific regions of the ventral visual stream. Both the amygdala and OFC may respond quickly to emotionally salient stimuli, including emotional faces and auditory cues, based on input from extrastriate pathways, and may also coordinate an emotional response in the subject observing another person's emotional expressions. STS cortices, through a convergence of dorsal- and ventral-stream visual information, are able to recognize certain types of body movement. These regions project to both amygdala (Amaral et al., 1992) and OFC (Barbas, 1993). Thus, particular body-movement patterns may be linked to emotional reactions to these movements. Indirect projections from the STS to premotor regions, including the frontal operculum, may allow the construction of internal models of the perceived movements (Gallese & Goldman, 1998). These premotor representations may allow feed-forward processing, including representations in the right somatosensory cortices of what it would *feel like* to have moved in the manner observed; connections between somatosensory cortices and the OFC (Barbas, 1993, 2000) could facilitate this internal representation of the feelings associated with emotions.

Attribution of personality traits and stereotyping

We quickly recognize emotional states in others, using multiple cues that enable quick and accurate assessments of others' feelings, including as little as 10 s of nonverbal behaviour (Ambady & Rosenthal, 1992, 1993; Bernieri & Gillis, 1995). In contrast to emotions, which exist for shorter periods of time, personality traits (such as warmth, reliability, and neuroticism) are generally considered to be stable over time. There is some debate as to the existence of stable behavioral dispositions (Gilbert, 1998; Mischel, 1968; Mischel & Shoda, 1995). In part because of this uncertainty about the existence of dispositional personality traits, the term "attribution" is commonly used to describe the process by which people decide that a given person is, for example, untrustworthy: untrustworthiness may not actually exist in the behaving person, except in a certain context. However, there appears to be a consensus among researchers that people make attributional judgements quickly and with little effort, and only more slowly and with effort take into account contextual information (or other factors that might argue against a dispositional explanation for behaviour) (Fiske, 1993; Gilbert, 1998).

The amygdala and personality trait attribution; stereotyping

The evidence reviewed above with regard to the role of the amygdala in emotion recognition is consistent with the hypothesis that the amygdala is important for drawing attention to potential social threat. Further evidence in support of this hypothesis comes from two studies, a lesion study and a functional imaging study, in which subjects were presented with faces normally rated on a continuum from trustworthy to untrustworthy. In the lesion study, three subjects with bilateral amygdala damage were more likely to rate unfamiliar faces as more trustworthy and more approachable than subjects with unilateral amygdala damage, or normal controls (Adolphs, Tranel, & Damasio, 1998). An fMRI study found complementary results: both left and right amygdalae were more active when subjects viewed faces rated as untrustworthy, even when the subjects were engaged in rating the age, and not the trustworthiness, of the faces (Winston, Strange, O'Doherty, & Dolan, 2002).

Interestingly, Hart, Whalen, Shin, McInerney, Fischer, & Rauch (2000) found amygdala activation in response to neutral faces that habituated more slowly for racial out-group faces than for racial in-group faces, and Phelps et al. (2000) found a correlation between amygdala activation in white subjects viewing black faces and those subjects' scores on a test of implicit negative racial attitudes. These same subjects, notably, did not show similar amygdala activation patterns when presented with familiar, well-regarded black individuals, as compared to similarly prominent white individuals; this implies that amygdala activity reflects implicit, cultural categorization of members of certain social groups as threatening, but that this attributional tendency can be modified by experience (Phelps et al., 2000). More recently, Cunningham, Johnson, Raye, Gatenby, Gore, & Banaji (2004) have shown that subliminal presentation of black faces to white subjects yielded significantly greater amygdala activity than subliminal presentation of white faces. This effect disappeared when the faces were presented supraliminally. In addition, with supraliminal presentation, regions in the right dorsolateral and ventrolateral PFC as well as the anterior cingulate cortex, were more active when subjects were presented with black, as compared to white, faces. Similar prefrontal regions have been implicated in modulation of amygdala activity in emotion-regulation paradigms (Beauregard et al., 2001; Ochsner et al., 2002; Schaefer et al., 2002). These data support a model in which amygdala activity automatically (and unconsciously) classifies faces by racial in-group versus racial out-group, but is modulated by prefrontal activity as subjects attempt to suppress or temper their reactions (Cunningham et al., 2004).

Frontal lobe regions and person-related judgements: medial PFC, left frontal operculum, and OFC

Three recent studies have implicated PFC in judgements about personality traits or stereotypes. The first study presented subjects with adjective–noun pairings in which some of the nouns were person names, and asked subjects to assess whether the pairing could be appropriate. Person-related judgements resulted in smaller deactivations in the medial PFC (Figure 6.1), as well as other areas (Mitchell, Heatherton, & Macrae, 2002). Though it is difficult to draw conclusions based on deactivations from baseline, the authors of this study interpret their results in light of Gusnard and Raichle's (Gusnard & Raichle, 2001; Raichle, MacLeod, Snyder, Powers, Gusnard, & Shulman, 2001) model of "default" modes of function: activity in regions of the medial PFC is frequently observed during baseline scans, in which subjects are presumably lying at rest. Mitchell et al. (2002) posit that the function of regions which are tonically active and frequently deactivate during specific cognitive tasks can be understood by observing what tasks result in less or no deactivation from baseline. By this logic, the medial PFC, which is tonically active during resting baselines, but frequently deactivates during other cognitive tasks, and deactivates less during person-judgement tasks, is likely to be engaged in person-judgement processes when subjects are at "rest". Given the other tasks which yield similar results (see below), this may be a bit strong: It is unlikely, for example, that subjects are engaging in person judgements (Mitchell et al., 2002), ToM processes (Gallagher & Frith, 2003), and moral judgements (Greene, Sommerville, Nystrom, Darley, & Cohen, 2001), all during "rest". However, it is certainly possible that subjects in "resting baseline" scans are frequently engaged in some mental process related to person judgements (more so than to object judgements).

In a second recent study, a large group of subjects with brain damage was asked to attribute personality traits to point-light body movement stimuli, and the lesion locations of those whose attributions were greater than two standard deviations away from those of normal subjects were mapped. Subjects who were abnormal on this task showed maximal lesion overlap in left inferior frontal gyrus—the same frontal opercular area implicated in some emotion studies (see above) (Heberlein et al., 2004). Interestingly, most of these subjects identified emotions from the same stimuli normally, implying that judging personality and judging emotion, at least from body movements, rely on partially dissociable neural circuits. It is unclear, however, why damage to this region leads to emotion-recognition deficits from faces and from prosodic cues (see above), but not from body movement stimuli.

In a third recent study, subjects with damage to the OFC showed less evidence of implicit gender stereotyping (Milne & Grafman, 2001). Though it may appear strange to call decreases in stereotyping a "deficit" in social cognition, recall that our ability to use categorical thinking with regard to socially relevant traits appears to play an important role in social cognition (Adolphs, 2002; Macrae & Bodenhausen, 2000), and thus that decreases in gender stereotyping may be part of a more global deficit in categorical social cognition. However, this study was limited in that it did not include a control task that measured over learned nonsocial associations. Thus, though it is consistent with other studies showing social impairments consequent to OFC, or, more generally, ventromedial PFC damage (Anderson, Bechara, Damasio, Tranel, & Damasio, 1999; Damasio, 1994; Damasio, Grabowski, Frank, Galaburda, & Damasio, 1994; Stone, Baron-Cohen, & Knight, 1998a; Stone, Baron-Cohen, Young, Calder, & Keane, 1998b), this study constitutes only a preliminary indication that OFC damage specifically impairs access to stereotype knowledge.

Summary: personality attribution and/or stereotyping

The amygdala appears not just to be important for recognizing threat or potential threat from emotional faces and other stimuli, but also to be critical for recognizing a somewhat more subtle threat-related feature, "trustworthiness". Though, as noted above, it is debatable to what extent such a feature is present as a disposition in a given individual, lesion and imaging data implicate amygdalar nuclei in detecting or responding to features that reliably lead to this attribution. In addition, amygdalar responses correlate with the assignment of faces to racial in-groups as compared with out-groups, though such responses are modulated by prefrontal regions.

To summarize the handful of studies implicating PFC regions in personality trait attribution or stereotyping: ventrolateral and dorsolateral prefrontal regions, possibly more so on the right, modulate amygdala responses to racial out-group faces (Cunningham et al., 2004). Left prefrontal regions similar to those identified in studies of imitation and "mirror-neuron" activity appear to be important for personality trait attribution in at least certain contexts (Adolphs, 2002; Heberlein et al., 2004). Medial prefrontal areas are more involved in assigning trait words to people than in assigning descriptive adjectives to objects (Mitchell et al., 2002). Finally, orbitofrontal areas may be important for at least one type of social categorization (Milne & Grafman, 2001).

Belief attribution: intentions and theory of mind (ToM)

Premack and Woodruff (1978), studying the ability of chimpanzees to reason about psychological states in order to predict the actions of others, coined the term "theory of mind" (ToM) to describe the model of other minds that would be necessary to engage in such reasoning. This term has come to refer generally to internal representations of the psychological states of others, and the ability to form such representations is frequently called "mentalizing".

Though ToM can in principle apply to representations of goals, desires, or emotions, probably the best-known test of an individual's ability to model another's mind focuses on belief attribution: the false-belief test. The ability to recognize another's beliefs when those beliefs are at odds with the actual "state of the world" has been called an "acid test" of the ability to attribute mental states to others, because tasks which involve veridical beliefs could presumably be solved without imputing belief states (Dennett, 1978). In a common false-belief task, the Sally–Anne task, the subject is introduced to two characters, Sally and Anne. Sally has a toy, and places it in location A. She then leaves the room, and Anne moves the toy to location B while she is gone. When Sally returns, the subject is asked, where will she look for the toy? If the subject can independently represent Sally's knowledge, she will be able to understand that Sally *thinks* the toy is still in location A, and therefore will look there. Sally's belief, of course, is false; children younger than about 3 years (Wimmer & Perner, 1983), as well as many individuals with autism at significantly higher ages (Baron-Cohen, Leslie, & Frith, 1985), fail to represent Sally's knowledge as different from their own, omniscient view. Second-order ToM tasks have also been used to test subjects' ability to represent mental states (Perner & Wimmer, 1985). For example, in the above scenario, subjects could be asked where Anne thinks Sally would look. This task is thought to be somewhat more difficult than a first-order ToM task because of the complexity of representation required.

Normally developing children pass false-belief tasks by around age 4. Before this, however, it is hardly the case that they are unable to represent other minds at all: infants have some understanding of other people's emotions and goals by about 12 months (Saarni, Mumme, & Campos, 1997), and by around 18 months, reliably act as though they understand that another person can have a desire or preference different from their own (Repacholi,

1998). Thus, understanding of intentions and emotions precedes, and may be critical for, development of other aspects of ToM, such as the attribution of belief states to others (reviewed in Saarni et al., 1997).

Functional neuroimaging and neuropsychological studies of intention attribution have included both studies of attribution of intentionality, or agency (as discussed in a previous section of this chapter), and studies of specific mental state attribution processes, such as false-belief tasks (for recent reviews, see Gallagher & Frith, 2003; Siegal & Varley, 2002). Often, it has appeared that the same or similar regions are implicated in both the attribution of intentionality and the attribution of specific intentions or mental states; thus, we discuss both types of tasks here. Though the OFC and amygdala have been implicated in false-belief tasks, as have right-hemisphere cortices in general, the two regions most commonly implicated in functional imaging studies of ToM are the posterior STC and a region in the mPFC just anterior to the anterior cingulate cortex. We discuss results implicating the OFC, amygdala, and right-hemisphere cortices briefly before concentrating on the latter two regions.

OFC, amygdala, and attribution of mental states

Subjects with OFC damage show normal performance on tests of certain types of moral reasoning, listing possible response options to social situations, and other forms of abstract social cognition (Saver & Damasio, 1991). In addition, these subjects often pass false-belief tests normally (Stone et al., 1998a) and, as discussed above, only infrequently have been reported to have emotion-recognition impairments. However, these subjects often appear to be unable to use social and emotional cues to guide their behaviour normally. Damasio and colleagues have characterized the deficits in social cognition and decision making following damage to OFC as "acquired sociopathy"; "acquired", because the patients were normal until the brain damage, and "sociopathy", because many of the features of sociopathic behaviour, including insensitivity to future consequences and relatively antisocial behaviour, are found in these individuals (Damasio, 1994; Damasio, Tranel, & Damasio, 1990). Damasio and colleagues posit that the structures in ventromedial PFC, and especially OFC, are critical for associating certain types of situations with emotional states previously experienced in similar situations. Neurologically intact people develop *somatic markers*, representations of body states, which are then used to guide future behaviour, often without conscious awareness of the contingencies involved (akin to gut feelings, or hunches). When this association process is compromised, as a result of damage to critical neural substrates, people fail to use prior experience to appropriately guide their behavior (Damasio, 1994, 1996). Notably, two recently described subjects with OFC damage sustained in infancy were similar to subjects with adult-onset damage in striking deficits in social behaviour, as well as insensitivity to future consequences of decisions. However, these subjects were different from adult OFC-lesioned subjects in that they also failed to reason normally about social situations in the abstract (Anderson et al., 1999). Anderson and colleagues hypothesized that these two patients failed to learn social rules because they grew up without critical substrates for using somatic markers.

Eslinger (1998) characterizes the social cognitive deficits which occur after damage to the PFC as a failure of empathy: subjects with OFC damage show deficits in emotional sensitivity to others and in the cognitive ability to model independent mental states in others. However, despite their impairments in real-life social interactions, subjects with damage to the ventromedial PFC frequently perform normally on false-belief tasks, including those that test second-order false belief (Stone et al., 1998a). In an attempt to better characterize the deficits in social cognition shown by such patients, Stone et al. (1998a) designed a clever task that requires the detection of "faux pas" in stories. In this task, subjects have to recognize that "someone said something they shouldn't have". In order to perform this task normally, subjects must represent the emotional state of the characters in the story and be aware of which character knows or is aware of what information; however, they must also relate the two forms of information. Subjects with OFC damage performed poorly on this task. Although their answers to questions regarding the emotional states of the characters, as well as their performance on false-belief tasks, were normal, indicating that they can represent the emotional states and the belief states of others, OFC-lesioned subjects were less likely than both normal controls and dorsolateral frontal-lesioned subjects to recognize that "someone said something they shouldn't have" (Stone et al., 1998a). Stone interprets this not as a failure of the metarepresentational ability to have beliefs about beliefs, which is probably mediated by more dorsal regions (see below), but rather as a failure to use empathic understanding of other people's emotional states (Valerie Stone, personal communication). In contrast, another study described deficits in detecting deception, a task requiring mental state attribution but probably not empathy, in subjects with frontal lobe damage that was either on the right or bilateral (although each group, bilaterally damaged or right-frontal damaged, was not significantly worse than controls when compared individually, suggesting that the effect size was not large) (Stuss, Gallup & Alexander, 2001). Most of the subjects in the combined right/bilateral group had ventromedial PFC damage, supporting a role for ventromedial/PFC and OFC in mental state attribution processes other than empathy. Such a role for the right OFC was in fact suggested by a single-photon emission computed tomography (SPECT) study, which found increased right OFC activity during a task requiring the recognition of mental state terms (Baron-Cohen, Ring, Moriarty, Schmitz, Costa, & Ell, 1994).

Recently, Stone, Baron-Cohen, Calder, Keane, & Young (2003) reported that two subjects with bilateral amygdala damage also performed poorly on the faux pas task. In addition, a subject with selective bilateral amygdala damage described a video depicting the movements of geometric shapes, which is normally described in social terms (Heider & Simmel, 1944), using many fewer anthropomorphic and social words than matched normal controls (Heberlein & Adolphs, 2004). These results imply that amygdalar nuclei are involved not just in the recognition of emotion, or in the representation of emotional valence or threat, but also in processing nonemotional mental states. Further examination of the role of the amygdala and OFC in belief attribution is necessary to clarify when, and how, these structures participate in ToM processes.

Right-hemisphere cortices and attribution of mental states

In addition to their role in emotion recognition, right-hemisphere structures may also be involved in ToM processes. Subjects with right-hemisphere damage show disturbances in discourse, including deficits in interpreting nonliteral statements (Kaplan, Brownell, Jacobs, & Gardner, 1990) and in distinguishing lies from jokes (Wimmer & Perner, 1983). Both of these latter groups of authors suggested that deficits in recognizing speakers' intent may underlie right-hemisphere-damaged subjects' discourse-comprehension deficits, and this conjecture is supported by the finding of Winner, Brownell, Happé, Blum, & Pincus (1998) that the same subjects who had problems distinguishing lies from jokes were impaired on second-order ToM tasks. Other authors have reported deficits in mental state attribution consequent to right-hemisphere damage (Happé, Brownell, & Winner, 1999; Schlottmann & Surian, 1999). Happé et al. (1999) found that subjects with right-hemisphere damage were impaired on three tests of ToM, in which subjects had to interpret stories or cartoons by attributing mental states to the characters. A control group with left-hemisphere damage did not show the same pattern of impairment, though since many of these subjects had aphasia, a modified forced-choice version of the task was used. It is difficult to interpret these latter findings because of the difference in task between the groups, and because of the poor localization of lesions within each hemisphere. Relatively small differences in tasks have been shown to have an effect on subjects' performance on ToM tasks: subjects with right-hemisphere damage performed as well as subjects with left-hemisphere damage on a very simple ToM task if they were given visual aids illustrating the premises of each scenario, but these same subjects performed less well on the same task without visual aids (Surian & Siegal, 2001).

In summary, while there is some evidence that right-hemisphere regions, broadly defined, participate in ToM reasoning, further research is necessary to determine which structures within the right hemisphere participate in these processes, and what their more specific roles are.

Left-hemisphere cortices and attribution of mental states; mirror-neurons

In contrast to the findings with right-hemisphere damage, at least one lesion study supports the role of left-anterior cortices in attributing mental states to others. Subjects with left anterior lesions, but not left-posterior or right-hemisphere lesions, showed deficits in comprehension of stories requiring ToM (Channon & Crawford, 2000); these subjects, for the most part, did not have damage which included mesial regions, which have been implicated in mentalizing by many functional imaging studies (see below). Furthermore, it is not clear why these authors found deficits consequent to left-anterior damage when Happé et al. (1999) (see above) found similar deficits consequent to right-hemisphere damage.

Left-hemisphere cortices are also implicated in tasks that are very different from story or cartoon comprehension, but that are relevant here because of a goal-attribution component. In the above section on emotion recognition, we described mirror-neurons first identified in monkeys (Rizzolati et al., 1996), which respond both when subjects observe an action and when they perform the same action. Regions in left (or bilateral; see Koski, Iacoboni, Dubeau, Woods, & Mazziotta, 2003) premotor cortices in human subjects appear to have mirror-neuron-like response properties (Buccino et al., 2001; Gallese & Goldman, 1998; Iacoboni et al., 2001). Further monkey studies suggest that the presence of a goal or target for the action—that is, that it is not an undirected movement—is critical for the response properties of this area (Umilta et al., 2001); it is noteworthy that the goal need not be visible, but that the subject must know it is there, for mirror-neurons to respond to views of actions.

These findings have been used to support a model of mental state attribution which requires internal simulation of observed actions (Blakemore & Decety, 2001; Gallese & Goldman, 1998), and they certainly imply that perceptual and motor representations are linked. Other authors have used evidence of links between perceptual and motor systems to construct theories of empathy (Preston & de Waal, 2002), and there is evidence consistent with a simulation basis for emotion recognition as well, as discussed above and elsewhere (Adolphs, 2002). However, that premotor cortices, primarily on the left side, are responsive to goal-directed actions and are also implicated in imitation of such actions does not mean that these regions are involved in the attribution, per se, of goals. Future work examining the response properties of mirror-neuron-like regions (and, ideally, cells) in humans, and the roles of these regions in attributing intentions and other mental states, is needed to draw firmer conclusions about the relationship between recognition that an action is goal-directed, and attribution of a specific goal or intention.

Medial PFC structures and ToM

Several neuroimaging studies have observed activations in left medial frontal areas, principally the medial superior frontal gyrus (Brodmann's areas 8/9; Figure 6.1), when subjects performed tasks requiring them to attribute mental states, relative to tasks which were designed to be comparable except in this mentalizing component. For example, Fletcher et al. (1995) asked subjects to read stories which required mental state attribution and stories which did not. They found that the mental state task elicited greater activation of both posterior cingulate cortex and left medial frontal cortex. Goel, Grafman, Sadato, & Hallett (1995) found similar left medial frontal activation in a fairly different task in which subjects had to attribute knowledge about the form and function of novel objects to other people. In an fMRI study using both Fletcher et al.'s (1995) story task and a similar task with caption-less cartoons requiring either a mentalistic or a nonmentalistic interpretation, subjects showed greater activation in the medial frontal gyrus and anterior cingulate gyrus when performing the tasks requiring mental state attribution (Gallagher et al., 2000). Other studies have observed similar differences in medial PFC activation during a wide range of mental state attribution tasks: interpreting cartoons requiring intention attribution, as compared to cartoons without this requirement (Brunet, Sarfati, Hardy-Bayle, & Decety 2000); reading stories requiring attributing mental states to self or to others, as compared to stories without such requirements (Vogeley et al., 2001); and viewing animated shapes moving in patterns which suggest intentional actions, as compared to patterns which suggest less mentalistic interpretations (Castelli et al., 2000).

Interpretation of these imaging results is made more complicated by the finding, recently garnering considerable discussion, that several brain regions are more active than others in a subject "at rest", and are found to show decreases in activation (or "deactivations") when subjects focus on a wide range of cognitive tasks (Gusnard, Akbudak, Shulman, & Raichle, 2001; Gusnard & Raichle, 2001; Raichle et al., 2001). The regions thus described include the medial PFC, cortices at the posterior end of the lateral fissure and STS, and posterior cingulate and medial parietal regions. The relatively higher activation levels of these regions have been hypothesized to be due to cognitive processes engaged in by subjects not otherwise focusing on a task, and further investigations of the roles of these regions may in fact illuminate the processes occurring at "rest". In the meantime, however, it is important to use care in interpreting deactivations: if an area putatively involved in ToM processes is less engaged by a ToM task than by whatever ruminations are occurring during rest, it seems premature to call such an area a "ToM area". Many authors do not report per cent signal change from a baseline, but instead report differences between task conditions, such as reading ToM stories compared with reading non-ToM stories. This practice allows us to conclude which regions are more critical for one task than for another (that is ideally identical except for the process of interest), but makes it difficult to generalize across studies. When authors do report per cent signal change from baseline, it is often the case that the target task results in a smaller deactivation than the comparison task, and not a greater increase over baseline (e.g. Mitchell et al., 2002, described above; but see Greene et al., 2001, described below). As authors increasingly report activations relative to appropriate baseline conditions, and become increasingly sophisticated in the use of carefully matched control tasks, we will gain both a better understanding of the role of medial PFC regions in mental state attribution processes, and a better understanding of what these regions might be doing when subjects are not engaged in a specific cognitive task.

Lesion results have so far not contributed greatly to our understanding of the role of dorsal medial PFC in ToM or other social cognitive behaviours, in part because lesions affecting only this region (and not large portions of other PFC) are rare. However, causes of damage to OFC or ventromedial PFC, such as trauma and surgery, often also affect medial prefrontal regions immediately above orbital regions. Though in some cases, patients' damage was confined to more ventral regions (e.g. Stone et al., 1998a), many subjects reported as having ventromedial prefrontal cases also have more dorsal medial damage, and it is possible that the damage in these regions at least contributed to the social cognitive impairments shown in these cases (Greene & Haidt, 2002).

STS and attribution of intentionality and of specific mental states

As noted in an earlier section of this chapter, activation in the posterior STS has been observed both when subjects view biological motion, and when they attribute intentional states to others. Castelli et al. (2000) asked subjects to judge the level of intentionality in three types of Heider-and-Simmel-like animations: random movements (such as bouncing), goal-directed movements (such as chasing), and movements implying higher-level mental content, which they termed "theory of mind movements" (coaxing, mocking, and seducing). Temporoparietal areas corresponding to the posterior STS (as well as the medial prefrontal/superior frontal gyrus, as described just above, and the fusiform gyrus) showed greater activity when subjects viewed the ToM movements than when they viewed the other two types of animations. In addition, activity in these areas correlated with subjects' ratings of intentionality in the movies, regardless of the movie type. Using somewhat different animated shape stimuli, Blakemore et al. (2001) observed bilateral STS activations when subjects observed Michotte-like "causal" animations, as compared to when they observed movements which did not appear to contain a physical causation event. This finding implies that movements that imply just physical causation, and not psychological causation, activate posterior STS cortices. However, similar posterior STS activations during mind-attribution tasks were observed in two studies which used stimuli with no visual motion component.

Gallagher et al. (2000) observed increased BOLD activity in both the temporoparietal cortex (in the region of the posterior STS) and the medial PFC bilaterally when subjects read stories requiring a mental explanation, as compared with a nonmental explanation. These authors suggest that rather than simply (!) perceiving biological motion, this area may be critical for perceiving intentions in others. Two recent studies by Saxe and colleagues help to clarify these findings. In the first (Saxe & Kanwisher, 2003), a region in the temporoparietal junction (TPJ) outside the extrastriate body area (EBA) (Downing et al., 2001) was identified. This region, which the authors dubbed the TPJ-m (for mentalizing), responds more to stories requiring mental state attribution than to stories which do not, but which contain descriptions of the physical characteristics of people, thus confirming for the first time that it is mental content, and not merely person-related content, to which this region preferentially responds. In a second paper (Saxe et al., 2004), these authors identify three distinct regions within individual subjects' TPJ region: the EBA, the TPJ-m, and an area which is active during visual analysis of goal-directed movements. Notably, these changes were all increases from baseline, and thus not subject to the difficulties of explaining relative deactivations. Saxe and Kanwisher's findings clarified previous reports implicating posterior STS or TPJ activity in observation both of human bodies and of biological motion (reviewed above) and in tasks requiring mental state attribution. Though neighbouring regions are implicated in different social cognitive processes (motivating theories that biological motion perception may be critically linked to social cognition (Frith & Frith, 1999)), the cortical regions subserving these different processes appear to be distinct.

Summary: attribution of intentionality and of mental states

The two regions most often identified as active in mental state attribution are the medial PFC and posterior STS. Though it is not clear from many of the reports which have implicated these regions whether relatively smaller decreases or actual increases from baseline yielded this activation difference, it is not implausible that at least some of the spontaneous thoughts of subjects lying "at rest" are related to mental state attribution. In addition, these regions have been implicated in at least a few functional imaging studies observing greater-than-baseline activity during ToM tasks (e.g. Saxe et al., submitted). Finally, in addition to the medial PFC and posterior STS or TPJ, the amygdala and OFC may play a role in mental state attribution.

Other social cognitive tasks

Three other social cognitive tasks are included here. They are relevant to the interpretation of the sections above because they seem to rely upon similar cortical regions (the OFC in the first case, and the amygdala, medial PFC, and posterior STS in the other two), and they can also be described as cognition directly relevant to social behaviour. However, they do not involve directly attribution of animacy or agency, emotion, personality traits, or mental states.

The first of these tasks is a variation on the Wason card selection task, which is used to examine reasoning abilities (Wason, 1966). Subjects given a conditional rule in the form "if p, then q" are given four cards, with the information "p", "not-p", "q", and "not-q" presented. Each card has the corresponding condition or outcome on the reverse, and subjects are permitted to turn over two cards to verify the rule. Subjects have a great deal of difficulty with this task, even given fairly familiar rules in conditional format, but, interestingly, appear to show less difficulty when the rule given them is a social one, such as, for example, regarding taboo violation or social contract (Cosmides, 1989). Two groups have shown that subjects with ventromedial PFC or OFC damage do not show the normal advantage for social forms of this problem. In the first report, subjects with ventromedial frontal (VMF) damage chose the logically correct cards more often than matched normal controls for nonsocial rules, but chose the logically correct cards less frequently than controls for social rules (and about as frequently as they did for nonsocial rules [Adolphs, Bechara, Tranet, Damasio, & Damasio, 1995a; see also Adolphs, 1999]). All subjects in this group had bilateral VMF cortex lesions. A recent paper found a similar pattern in a single subject with a large lesion including both ventromedial frontal cortices and temporal poles (and thereby indirectly affecting bilateral amygdalae, though these were technically spared) (Stone, Cosmides, Tooby, Kroll, & Knight, 2002). This subject was more impaired on social contract Wason tasks (for example, if you collect retirement, you must have worked for the company for 5 years) than on closely difficulty-matched hazard precaution Wason tasks (for example, if you enter the construction site, you must wear a hard hat). In contrast, two other patients, one with bilateral VMF damage and the other with bilateral temporal pole damage, did not show differential performance on the two tasks. Stone et al. (2002) conclude from this that both the VMF cortex and amygdala must be damaged for subjects to be impaired on this form of reasoning. However, this conclusion does not explain Adolphs et al.'s (1995a) findings of deficits in subjects with VMF damage and spared amygdalae. It is difficult to relate this task to emotion recognition, or even to mental state attribution: subjects need not attribute beliefs, it seems, to understand many forms of social contracts. Both groups of authors interpret their results as support for a system more or less devoted to social cognition, in which ventromedial PFC and the amygdala play critical roles.

Two other tasks with social cognitive components address moral judgements. Moll, Eslinger, & Oliveira-Souza (2001) compared activations when subjects judged sentences with moral content (for example, "We break the law when necessary"; "They hanged an innocent") or without ("Stones are made of water"). Comparing moral judgements to nonmoral ones, they found greater activations in frontal pole, medial frontal regions, right temporal pole, left OFC, right cerebellum, STC, left precuneus, and posterior globus pallidus. In subsequent studies, Moll and colleagues compared judgements of similar moral content sentences to judgements with emotional and social content (for example, "He licked the dirty toilet"), and found more left medial OFC activity for the moral judgements and left lateral OFC and amygdala for the nonmoral social judgements (Moll et al., 2002). While these authors attempted to factor out the emotional component of subjects' responses (Moll et al., 2001), thus isolating the moral but nonemotional component of moral reasoning, another group has taken a different approach. Greene and colleagues (2001) distinguish two types of moral judgements, those with a personal component (that is, that involve directly harming another individual), and those that lack this personal component. When subjects make judgements as to the appropriateness of an action in dilemmas of the latter type, they engage cortical regions similar to those engaged during nonmoral reasoning, including the dorsolateral PFC. This was the case even though the impersonal dilemmas could have serious consequences (for example, is it appropriate to throw a switch that will redirect a runaway trolley so that it spares the lives of five people on one track, but will then kill the one person on the other track?). In contrast, when subjects make judgements as to the appropriateness of personal moral dilemmas (for example, is it appropriate to push a large person in front of a runaway trolley so that it will stop, saving the lives of five people on the track, but killing the large person?), they engage regions implicated in emotional and social processing: the medial PFC, posterior cingulate gyrus, posterior STS, and inferior parietal lobule (Greene et al., 2001). Interestingly, this medial PFC activation during evaluation of personal moral dilemmas was greater than baseline, suggesting that, unlike most ToM tasks, consideration of these dilemmas engages the medial PFC more than the thoughts normally engaged in while lying in a scanner at "rest". Greene and colleagues conclude that logically similar moral dilemmas may differ in the degree to which they engage emotional processes, and thus the kinds of cognition used to answer them (see also Greene & Haidt, 2002).

Conclusions

Many different processes fall under the rubric of social cognition, and a number of these have been investigated in neuroscience. In this chapter, we have reviewed the evidence from functional neuroimaging and the study of focally damaged patients on the following key components of social cognition: perceiving that something is animate or has agency; recognizing emotion in another person; attributing personality traits, stereotypes, or social group membership; attributing intentionality and theory of mind; performing socially relevant logical reasoning; and making moral judgements. It is hardly surprising that many different brain areas are implicated in lesion and functional imaging studies of these processes, because the processes themselves seem intuitively to be very different from each other. On the other hand, the intuitive differences between different social cognitive processes make the convergence in brain regions implicated across processes that much more striking.

Because similar neural regions are implicated in more than one social process, it is tempting to think of these regions as somehow specialized for social cognition, perhaps as part of a relatively specialized social cognitive circuit (Brothers, 1990). Regions repeatedly identified as important include the OFC (in emotion recognition and in several types of complex social reasoning); more dorsal medial PFC (primarily in ToM and other higher-level social reasoning); the amygdalar nuclei (in emotion recognition, stereotyping/group recognition, and social reasoning); and the cortices around the posterior STC (in perception of animacy/agency, body representation, and ToM). Strikingly, all of these regions, except for dorsal medial PFC, were identified as potential candidates in a social cognitive circuit, in a seminal paper which motivated a great deal of research on the neurobiology of social cognition (Brothers, 1990). Considering regions as components in a circuit is critical: though any given study may identify one region that is significantly more active for a given social process, that region's inputs and downstream targets obviously also participate. We outlined a model for emotion recognition, the process for which the neural circuitry seems best understood among social cognitive processes. In this model, the amygdala, OFC, left frontal operculum, and right somatosensory regions play critical, and probably fairly specific roles. As our understanding of both the components of social cognitive processes and the connectivity and responsivity of these neural regions continues to expand, we will be able to expand this model, and also to relate it to similar models for other types of social cognitive processes.

The nature of the relationships among different processes, which appear to rely upon so many of the same (or closely neighbouring) regions of cortex and subcortical nuclei, promises to be a fruitful area of research. Greene and colleagues (Greene et al., 2001; Greene & Haidt, 2002) have related neural regions implicated in emotional experience, including the posterior cingulate cortex (Maddock, 1999), and those involved in social cognitive processes, including the medial PFC, to moral decision making. However, these results do not show that moral decision making and emotional experience/social reasoning are separate processes, but rather that moral reasoning engages these structures *because* (in some cases at least) it relies on emotional or social processing. This interpretation echoes that of Damasio and colleagues (Damasio, 1994, 1996): the implication of VMF cortices in multiple types of tasks, including social cognition and certain types of on-line decision making, suggests an underlying role for VMF cortices in utilizing emotional body-state information to guide behaviour.

In a rough model for hierarchies of social information processing, some degree of perceptual processing would occur first. Some rapid, coarse, and possibly subliminal processing may form a bias that influences more fine-grained perceptual processing—for example, how we perceive facial features might be influenced by expectations, some of them potentially activated by rapid, subcortical inputs to the amygdala. Early perceptual processing may function to alert higher social cognitive regions to the presence of an animate or intentional entity. Multiple tracks of information processing would enable further elaboration of initial perceptions (see Adolphs, 2003). As discussed just above, a critical question regards the extent to which later processes, such as belief attribution, rely on earlier processes, or are independent of them.

Acknowledgements

We thank Martha Farah and Josh Greene for providing extensive comments on earlier versions of this chapter. Portions of the chapter were taken from a doctoral dissertation completed by the first author in fulfillment of the PhD requirements in the Neuroscience Program at the University of Iowa, USA. A.S.H. was supported by National Institutes of Health (NIH) T32-NS07413, at the Children's Hospital of Philadelphia, during preparation of the final manuscript.

References

Adolphs, R. (1999). Social cognition and the human brain. *Trends in Cognitive Sciences*, *3*, 469–479.

Adolphs, R. (2002). Recognizing emotion from facial expressions: Psychological and neurological mechanisms. *Behavioural and Cognitive Neuroscience Reviews*, *1*, 21–61.

Adolphs, R., Bechara, A., Tranel, D., Damasio, H., & Damasio, A. (1995a). Neuropsychological approaches to reasoning and decision making. In Y. Christen, A. R. Damasio, & H. Damasio (Eds.), *Neurobiology of decision making* (pp. 157–179). New York: Springer-Verlag.

Adolphs, R., Damasio, H., & Tranel, D. (2002). Neural systems for recognition of emotional prosody: A 3-D lesion study. *Emotion*, *2*, 23–51.

Adolphs, R., Damasio, H., Tranel, D., Cooper, G., & Damasio, A. R. (2000). A role for somatosensory cortices in the visual recognition of emotion as revealed by three-dimensional lesion mapping. *Journal of Neuroscience*, *20*, 2683–2690.

Adolphs, R., Russell, J., & Tranel, D. (1999a). A role for the human amygdala in recognizing emotional arousal from unpleasant stimuli. *Psychological Science*, *10*, 167–171.

Adolphs, R., & Tranel, D. (1999). Intact recognition of emotional prosody following amygdala damage. *Neuropsychologia*, *37*, 1285–1292.

Adolphs, R., Tranel, D., & Damasio, A. R. (1998). The human amygdala in social judgement. *Nature, 393*, 470–474.

Adolphs, R., Tranel, D., Damasio, H., & Damasio, A. R. (1995b). Fear and the human amygdala. *Journal of Neuroscience, 15*, 5879–5891.

Adolphs, R., Tranel, D., Hamann, S., Young, A. W., Calder, A. J., Phelps, E. A., et al. (1999b). Recognition of facial emotion in nine individuals with bilateral amygdala damage. *Neuropsychologia, 37*, 1111–1117.

Allison, T., Puce, A., & McCarthy, G. (2000). Social perception from visual cues: Role of the STS region. *Trends in Cognitive Sciences, 4*, 267–278.

Allison, T., Puce, A., Spencer, D. D., & McCarthy, G. (1999). Electrophysiological studies of human face perception. I. Potentials generated in occipitotemporal cortex by face and non-face stimuli. *Cerebral Cortex, 9*, 415–430.

Amaral, D. G., Price, J. L., Pitkanen, A., & Carmichael, S. T. (1992). Anatomical organization of the primate amygdaloid complex. In J. P. Aggleton (Ed.), *The amygdala: Neurobiological aspects of emotion, memory, and mental dysfunction* (pp. 1–66). New York: Wiley-Liss.

Ambady, N., & Rosenthal, R. (1992). Thin slices of expressive behaviour as predictors of interpersonal consequences: A meta-analysis. *Psychological Bulletin, 111*, 256–274.

Ambady, N., & Rosenthal, R. (1993). Half a minute: Predicting teacher evaluations from thin slices of nonverbal behaviour and physical attractiveness. *Journal of Personality and Social Psychology, 64*, 431–441.

Anderson, A. K., & Phelps, E. A. (1998). Intact recognition of vocal expressions of fear following bilateral lesions of the amygdala. *Neuroreport, 9*, 3607–3613.

Anderson, S. W., Bechara, A., Damasio, H., Tranel, D., & Damasio, A. R. (1999). Impairment of social and moral behaviour related to early damage in human prefrontal cortex. *Nature Neuroscience, 2*, 1032–1037.

Barbas, H. (1993). Organization of cortical afferent input to orbitofrontal areas in the rhesus monkey. *Neuroscience, 56*, 841–864.

Barbas, H. (2000). Connections underlying the synthesis of cognition, memory, and emotion in primate prefrontal cortices. *Brain Research Bulletin, 52*, 319–330.

Baron-Cohen, S., Leslie, A., & Frith, U. (1985). Does the autistic child have a "theory of mind"? *Cognition, 1*, 37–46.

Baron-Cohen, S., Ring, H., Moriarty, J., Schmitz, B., Costa, D., & Ell, P. (1994). Recognition of mental state terms. Clinical findings in children with autism and a functional neuroimaging study of normal adults. *British Journal of Psychiatry, 165*, 640–649.

Beauregard, M., Levesque, L., & Bourgouin, P. (2001). Neural correlates of conscious self-regulation of emotion. *Journal of Neuroscience, 21*, RC165.

Benowitz, L. I., Bear, D. M., Rosenthal, R., Mesulam, M. M., Zaidel, E., & Sperry, R. W. (1983). Hemispheric specialization in nonverbal communication. *Cortex, 19*, 5–11.

Bernieri, F. J., & Gillis, J. S. (1995). Personality correlates of accuracy in a social perception task. *Perceptual and Motor Skills, 81*, 168–170.

Birbaumer, N., Grodd, W., Diedrich, O., Klose, U., Erb, M., Lotze, M., et al. (1998). fMRI reveals amygdala activation to human faces in social phobics. *Neuroreport, 9*, 1223–1226.

Blair, R. J., Morris, J. S., Frith, C. D., Perrett, D. I., & Dolan, R. J. (1999). Dissociable neural responses to facial expressions of sadness and anger. *Brain, 122*, 883–893.

Blakemore, S.-J., & Decety, J. (2001). From the perception of action to the understanding of intention. *Nature Reviews Neuroscience, 2,* 561–567.

Blakemore, S.-J., Fonlupt, P., Pachot-Clouard, M., Darmon, C., Boyer, P., Meltzoff, A. N., et al. (2001). How the brain perceives causality: An event-related fMRI study. *Neuroreport, 12,* 3741–3746.

Bonda, E., Petrides, M., Ostry, D., & Evans, A. (1996). Specific involvement of human parietal systems and the amygdala in the perception of biological motion. *Journal of Neuroscience, 16,* 3737–3744.

Borod, J. C., Andelman, F., Obler, L. K., Tweedy, J. R., & Welkowitz, J. (1992). Right hemisphere specialization for the identification of emotional words and sentences: Evidence from stroke patients. *Neuropsychologia, 30,* 827–844.

Borod, J. C., Obler, L. K., Erhan, H. M., Grunwald, I. S., Cicero, B. A., Welkowitz, J., et al. (1998). Right hemisphere emotional perception: Evidence across multiple channels. *Neuropsychology, 12,* 446–458.

Bowers, D., Bauer, R. M., Coslett, H. B., & Heilman, K. M. (1985). Processing of faces by patients with unilateral hemisphere lesions. I. Dissociation between judgements of facial affect and facial identity. *Brain and Cognition, 4,* 258–272.

Boyer, P. (2003). Religious thought and behaviour as by-products of brain function. *Trends in Cognitive Science, 7,* 119–124.

Breiter, H. C., Etcoff, N. L., Whalen, P. J., Kennedy, W. A., Rauch, S. L., Buckner, R. L., et al. (1996). Response and habituation of the human amygdala during visual processing of facial expression. *Neuron, 17,* 875–887.

Broks, P., Young, A. W., Maratos, E. J., Coffey, P. J., Calder, A. J., Isaac, C. L., et al. (1998). Face processing impairments after encephalitis: Amygdala damage and recognition of fear. *Neuropsychologia, 36,* 59–70.

Brothers, L. (1990). The social brain: A project for integrating primate behaviour and neurophysiology in a new domain. *Concepts in Neuroscience, 1,* 27–51.

Brunet, E., Sarfati, Y., Hardy-Bayle, M. C., & Decety, J. (2000). A PET investigation of the attribution of intentions with a nonverbal task. *NeuroImage, 11,* 157–166.

Buccino, G., Binkofski, F., Fink, G. R., Fadiga, L., Fogassi, L., Gallese, V., et al. (2001). Action observation activates premotor and parietal areas in a somatotopic manner: An fMRI study. *European Journal of Neuroscience, 13,* 400–404.

Burt, D. M., & Perrett, D. I. (1997). Perceptual asymmetries in judgements of facial attractiveness, age, gender, speech and expression. *Neuropsychologia, 35,* 685–693.

Cahill, L., Haier R. J., White, N. S., Fallon, J., Kilpatrick, L., Lawrence, C., et al. (2001). Sex-related difference in amygdala activity during emotionally influenced memory storage. *Neurobiology of Learning and Memory, 75,* 1–9.

Calder, A. J., Young, A. W., Perrett, D. I., Hodges, J. R., & Etcoff, N. L. (1996). Facial emotion recognition after bilateral amygdala damage: Differentially severe impairment of fear. *Cognitive Neuropsychology, 13,* 699–745.

Canli, T., Desmond, J. E., Zhao, Z., & Gabrieli, J. D. (2002a). Sex differences in the neural basis of emotional memories. *Proceedings of the National Academy of Sciences of the USA, 99,* 10789–10794.

Canli, T., Sivers, H., Whitfield, S. L., Gotlib, I. H., & Gabrieli, J. D. (2002b). Amygdala response to happy faces as a function of extraversion. *Science, 296,* 2191.

Castelli, F., Frith, C. D., Happé, F., & Frith, U. (2002). Autism, Asperger syndrome and brain mechanisms for the attribution of mental states to animated shapes. *Brain, 125,* 1839–1849.

Castelli, F., Happé, F., Frith, U., & Frith, C. D. (2000). Movement and mind: A functional imaging study of perception and interpretation of complex intentional movement patterns. *NeuroImage, 12,* 314–325.

Channon, S., & Crawford, S. (2000). The effects of anterior lesions on performance on a story comprehension test: Left anterior impairment on a theory of mind-type task. *Neuropsychologia, 38,* 1006–1017.

Cosmides, L. (1989). The logic of social exchange: Has natural selection shaped how humans reason? Studies with the Wason selection task. *Cognition, 31,* 187–276.

Cosmides, L., & Tooby, J. (1992). Cognitive adaptations for social exchange. In J. H. Barkow, L. Cosmides, & J. Tooby (Eds.), *The adapted mind: Evolutionary psychology and the generation of culture* (pp. 163–228). Oxford: Oxford University Press.

Cunningham, W. A., Johnson, M. K., Raye, C. L., Gatenby, J. C., Gore, J. C., & Banaji (2004). Separable neural components in the processing of black and white faces. *Psychological Science, 15,* 806–813.

Damasio, A. R. (1994). *Descartes' error: Emotion, reason, and the human brain.* New York: Grosset/Putnam.

Damasio, A. R. (1996). The somatic marker hypothesis and the possible functions of the prefrontal cortex. *Philosophical Transactions of the Royal Society of London: Series B, 351,* 1413–1420.

Damasio, A. R., Tranel, D., & Damasio, H. (1990). Individuals with sociopathic behaviour caused by frontal damage fail to respond autonomically to social stimuli. *Behavioural Brain Research, 41,* 81–94.

Damasio, H., Grabowski, T., Frank, R., Galaburda, A. M., & Damasio, A. R. (1994). The return of Phineas Gage: Clues about the brain from the skull of a famous patient. *Science, 264,* 1102–1105.

Darwin, C. (1872; 1998). *The expression of the emotions in man and animals.* P. Ekman (Ed.). Oxford: Oxford University Press.

Decety, J., Chaminade, T., Grezes, J., & Meltzoff, A. N. (2002). A PET exploration of the neural mechanisms involved in reciprocal imitation. *NeuroImage, 15,* 265–272.

Decety, J., Grezes, J., Costes N., Perani, D., Jeannerod, M., Procyk, E., et al. (1997). Brain activity during observation of actions: Influence of action content and subject's strategy. *Brain, 120,* 1763–1777.

Dennett, D. (1978). Beliefs about beliefs. *Behavioural and Brain Sciences, 4,* 568–570.

Dennett, D. (1987). *The intentional stance.* Cambridge, MA: MIT Press.

Dolan, R. J., Fletcher, P. C., Morris, J. S., Kapur, N. N., Deakin, J. F. W., & Frith, C. D. (1996). Neural activation during covert processing of positive emotional facial expressions. *NeuroImage, 4,* 194–200.

Downing, P. E., Jiang, Y., Shuman, M., & Kanwisher, N. (2001). A cortical area selective for visual processing of the human body. *Science, 293,* 2470–2473.

Ekman, P. (1992). An argument for basic emotions. *Cognition and Emotion, 6,* 169–200.

Ekman, P. (1994). Strong evidence for universals in facial expressions: A reply to Russell's mistaken critique. *Psychological Bulletin, 115,* 268–287.

Ekman, P., & Friesen, W. (1976). *Pictures of facial affect.* Palo Alto, CA: Consulting Psychologists.

Eslinger, P. (1998). Neurological and neuropsychological bases of empathy. *European Neurology, 39*, 193–199.
Farah, M. J. (1996). Is face recognition "special"? Evidence from neuropsychology. *Behavioural Brain Research, 76*, 181–189.
Farah, M. J., Wilson, K. D., Drain, M., & Tanaka, J. N. (1998). What is "special" about face perception? *Psychological Review, 105*, 482–498.
Fiske, S. T. (1993). Social cognition and social perception. *Annual Reviews in Psychology, 44*, 155–194.
Fletcher, P., Happe, F., Frith, U., Baker, S., Dolan, R., Frackowiak, R., et al. (1995). Other minds in the brain: A functional imaging study of "theory of mind" in story comprehension. *Cognition, 57*, 109–128.
Fridlund, A. J. (1994). *Human facial expression*. New York: Academic Press.
Frith, C. D., & Frith, U. (1999). Interacting minds—a biological basis. *Science, 286*, 1692–1695.
Gallagher, H. L., & Frith, C. D. (2003). Functional imaging of "theory of mind". *Trends in Cognitive Sciences, 7*, 77–83.
Gallagher, H. L., Happé, F., Brunswick, N., Fletcher, P. C., Frith, U., & Frith, C. D. (2000). Reading the mind in cartoons and stories: An fMRI study of "theory of mind" in verbal and nonverbal tasks. *Neuropsychologia, 38*, 11–21.
Gallese, V., Fadiga, L., Fogassi, L., & Rizzolatti, G. (1996). Action recognition in the premotor cortex. *Brain, 119*, 593–609.
Gallese, V., & Goldman, A. (1998). Mirror neurons and the simulation theory of mind-reading. *Trends in Cognitive Sciences, 2*, 493–501.
Gauthier, I., Anderson, A. W., Tarr, M. J., Skudlarski, P., & Gore, C. (1997). Levels of categorization in visual recognition studied using functional magnetic resonance imaging. *Current Biology, 7*, 645–651.
Gauthier, I., Skudlarski, P., Gore, J. C., & Anderson, A. W. (2000). Expertise for cars and birds recruits brain areas involved in face recognition. *Nature Neuroscience, 3*, 191–197.
Gauthier, I., Tarr, M. J., Anderson, A. W., Skudlarski, P., & Gore, J. C. (1999). Activation of the middle fusiform "face area" increases with expertise in recognizing novel objects. *Nature Neuroscience, 2*, 568–573.
George, M. S., Parekh, P. I., Rosinsky, N., Ketter, T. A., Kimbrell, T. A., Heilman, K. M., et al. (1996). Understanding emotional prosody activates right hemisphere regions. *Archives of Neurology, 53*, 665–670.
Gilbert, D. T. (1998). Ordinary personology. In S. T. Fiske, D. T. Gilbert, & G. Lindzey (Eds.) (pp. 89–150). *The handbook of social psychology* New York: McGraw-Hill.
Goel, V., Grafman, J., Sadato, N., & Hallett, M. (1995). Modeling other minds. *Neuroreport, 6*, 1741–1746.
Greene, J. D., & Haidt, J. (2002). How (and where) does moral judgement work? *Trends in Cognitive Sciences, 16*, 517–523.
Greene, J. D., Sommerville, J. B., Nystrom, L. E., Darley, J. M., & Cohen, J. D. (2001). An fMRI investigation of emotional engagement in moral judgement. *Science, 293*, 2105–2108.
Grezes, J., & Decety, J. (2002). Does visual perception of object afford action? Evidence from a neuroimaging study. *Neuropsychologia, 40*, 212–222.
Grezes, J., Fonlupt, P., Bertenthal, B., Delon-Martin, C., Segebarth, C., & Decety, J. (2001). Does perception of biological motion rely on specific brain regions? *NeuroImage, 13*, 775–785.

Grossman, E., Donnelly, M., Price, R., Pickens, D., Morgan, V., Neighbor, G., et al. (2000). Brain areas involved in perception of biological motion. *Journal of Cognitive Neuroscience, 12*, 711–720.

Grossman, E. D., & Blake, R. (2001). Brain activity evoked by inverted and imagined biological motion. *Vision Research, 41*, 1475–1482.

Gusnard, D. A., Akbudak, E., Shulman, G. L., & Raichle, M. E. (2001). Medial prefrontal cortex and self-referential mental activity: Relation to a default mode of brain function. *Proceedings of the National Academy of Sciences of the USA, 98*, 4259–4264.

Gusnard, D. A., & Raichle, M. E. (2001). Searching for a baseline: functional imaging and the resting human brain. *Nature Reviews Neuroscience, 2*, 685–694.

Hamann, S. B., Stefanacci, L., Squire, L. R., Adolphs, R., Tranel, D., Damasio, H., et al. (1996). Recognizing facial emotion. *Nature, 379*, 497.

Happé, F., Brownell, H., & Winner, E. (1999). Acquired "theory of mind" impairments following stroke. *Cognition, 70*, 211–240.

Hariri, A. R., Mattay, V. S., Tessitore, A., Kolachana, B., Fera, F., Goldman, D., et al. (2002). Serotonin transporter genetic variation and the response of the human amygdala. *Science, 297*, 400–403.

Harries, M. H., & Perrett, D. I. (1991). Visual processing of faces in temporal cortex: Physiological evidence for a modular organization and possible anatomical correlates. *Journal of Cognitive Neuroscience, 3*, 9–24.

Hart, A. J., Whalen, P. J., Shin, L. M., McInerney, S. C., Fischer, H., & Rauch, S. L. (2000). Differential response in the human amygdala to racial out-group vs. in-group face stimuli. *Neuroreport, 11*, 2351–2355.

Haxby, J. V., Hoffman, E. A., & Gobbini, M. I. (2002). Human neural systems for face recognition and social communication. *Biological Psychiatry, 51*, 59–67.

Haxby, J. V., Horwitz, B., Ungerleider, L. G., Maisog, J. M., Pietrini, P., & Grady, C. L. (1994). The functional organization of human extrastriate cortex: A PET-rCBF study of selective attention to faces and locations. *Journal of Neuroscience, 14*, 6336–6353.

Heberlein, A. S. (2002). Neural substrates for social cognition from motion cues: Lesion studies in humans. Iowa City, IA, University of Iowa (unpublished dissertation).

Heberlein, A. S. & Adolphs, R. (2004) Impaired spontaneous anthropomorphizing despite intact perception and social knowledge. *Proceedings of the National Academy of Sciences of the USA, 101*, 7487–7491.

Heberlein, A. S., Adolphs, R., Tranel, D., & Damasio, H. (2004). Cortical regions for judgments of emotions and personality traits from pointlight walkers. *Journal of Cognitive Neuroscience, 16*, 1143–1158.

Heider, F., & Simmel, M. (1944). An experimental study of apparent behaviour. *American Journal of Psychology, 57*, 243–259.

Hoffman, E. A., & Haxby, J. V. (2000). Distinct representations of eye gaze and identity in the distributed human neural system for face perception. *Nature Neuroscience, 3*, 80–84.

Hornak, J., Rolls, E. T., & Wade, D. (1996). Face and voice expression identification in patients with emotional and behavioural changes following ventral frontal lobe damage. *Neuropsychologia, 34*, 247–261.

Howard, R. J., Brammer, M., Wright, I., Woodruff, P. W., Bullmore, E. T., & Zeki, S. (1996). A direct demonstration of functional specialization within motion-related visual and auditory cortex of the human brain. *Current Biology, 6*, 1015–1019.

Humphrey, N. (1984). *Consciousness regained*. Oxford: Oxford University Press.
Iacoboni, M., Koski, L. M., Brass, M., Bekkering, H., Woods, R. P., Dubeau, M-C., et al. (2001). Reafferent copies of imitated actions in the right superior temporal cortex. *Proceedings of the National Academy of Sciences of the USA, 98*, 13995–13999.
Iacoboni, M., Woods, R., Brass, M., Bekkering, H., Mazziotta, J., & Rizzolati, G. (1999). Cortical mechanisms of human imitation. *Science, 286*, 2526–2528.
Imaizumi, S., Mori, K., Kiritani, S., Kawashima, R., Sugiura, M., Fukuda, H., et al. (1997). Vocal identification of speaker and emotion activates different brain regions. *Neuroreport, 8*, 2809–2812.
Jansari, A., Tranel, D., & Adolphs, R. (2000). A valence-specific lateral bias for discriminating emotional facial expressions in free field. *Cognition and Emotion, 14*, 341–353.
Johnson, S. C. (2000). The recognition of mentalistic agents in infancy. *Trends in Cognitive Sciences, 4*, 22–28.
Jones, E. G., & Burton, H. (1976). A projection from the medial pulvinar to the amygdala in primates. *Brain Research, 104*, 142–147.
Kanwisher, N., McDermott, J., & Chun, M. M. (1997). The fusiform face area: A module in human extrastriate cortex specialized for face perception. *Journal of Neuroscience, 17*, 4302–4311.
Kaplan, J. A., Brownell, H. H., Jacobs, J. R., & Gardner, H. (1990). The effects of right hemisphere damage on the pragmatic interpretation of conversational remarks. *Brain and Language, 38*, 315–333.
Kawasaki, H., Adolphs, R., Kaufman, O., Damasio, H., Damasio, A. R., Granner, M., et al. (2001). Single-unit responses to emotional visual stimuli recorded in human ventral prefrontal cortex. *Nature Neuroscience, 4*, 15–16.
Kesler-West, M. L., Andersen, A. H., Smith, C. D., Avison, M. J., Davis, C. E., Kryscio, R. J., et al. (2001). Neural substrates of facial emotion processing using fMRI. *Cognitive Brain Research, 11*, 213–226.
Koski, L., Iacoboni, M., Dubeau, M. C., Woods, R. P., & Mazziotta, J. C. (2003). Modulation of cortical activity during different imitative behaviours. *Journal of Neurophysiology, 89*, 460–471.
Kourtzi, Z., & Kanwisher, N. (2000). Activation in human MT/MST by static images with implied motion. *Journal of Cognitive Neuroscience, 12*, 48–55.
Kucharska-Pietura, K., Phillips, M. L., Gernand, W., & David, A. S. (2003). Perception of emotions from faces and voices following unilateral brain damage. *Neuropsychologia, 41*, 1082–1090.
Logothetis, N. K., Guggenberger, H., Peled, S., & Pauls, J. (1999). Functional imaging of the monkey brain. *Nature Neuroscience, 2*, 555–562.
Macrae, C. N., & Bodenhausen, G. V. (2000). Social cognition: Thinking categorically about others. *Annual Review of Psychology, 51*, 93–120.
Maddock, R. J. (1999). The retrosplenial cortex and emotion: New insights from functional neuroimaging of the human brain. *Trends in Neuroscience, 22*, 310–316.
Marinkovic, K., Trebon P., Chauvel, P., & Halgren, E. (2000). Localized face processing by the human prefrontal cortex: Face-selective intracerebral potentials and post-lesion deficits. *Cognitive Neuropsychology, 17*, 187–199.
McCarthy, G., Puce, A., Belger, A., & Allison, T. (1999). Electrophysiological studies of human face perception. II. Response properties of face-specific potentials generated in occipitotemporal cortex. *Cerebral Cortex, 9*, 431–444.

McKone, E., & Kanwisher, N. (in press). Does the human brain process objects of expertise like faces? A review of the evidence. In G. Rizzolatti (Ed.), *From monkey brain to human brain*. Cambridge, MA: MIT Press.

Milne, E., & Grafman, J. (2001). Ventromedial prefrontal cortex lesions in humans eliminate implicit gender stereotyping. *Journal of Neuroscience, 21*, RC150.

Mischel, W. (1968). *Personality and assessment*. New York: Wiley.

Mischel, W., & Shoda, Y. (1995). A cognitive-affective system theory of personality: Reconceptualizing situations, dispositions, dynamics, and invariance in personality structure. *Psychological Review, 102*, 246–268.

Mitchell, J. P., Heatherton, T. F., & Macrae, C. N. (2002). Distinct neural systems subserve person and object knowledge. *Proceedings of the National Academy of Sciences of the USA, 99*, 15238–15243.

Moll, J., de Oliveira-Souza, R., Bramati, I. E., & Grafman, J. (2002). Functional networks in emotional moral and nonmoral social judgements. *NeuroImage, 16*, 696–703.

Moll, J., Eslinger, P. J., & Oliveira-Souza, R. (2001). Frontopolar and anterior temporal cortex activation in a moral judgement task: Preliminary functional MRI results in normal subjects. *Arquivos de Neuro Psiquiatria, 59*, 657–664.

Morris, J. S., DeGelder, B., Weiskrantz, L., & Dolan, R. J. (2001). Differential extrageniculostriate and amygdala responses to presentation of emotional faces in a cortically blind field. *Brain, 124*, 1241–1252.

Morris, J. S., Frith, C. D., Perrett, D. I., Rowland, D., Young, A. W., Calder, A. J., et al. (1996). A differential neural response in the human amygdala to fearful and happy facial expressions. *Nature, 383*, 812–815.

Morris, J. S., Öhman, A., & Dolan, R. J. (1999). A subcortical pathway to the right amygdala mediating "unseen" fear. *Proceedings of the National Academy of Sciences of the USA, 96*, 1680–1685.

Morris, J. S., Öhman, A., & Dolan, R. J. (1998). Conscious and unconscious emotional learning in the human amygdala. *Nature, 393*, 467–470.

Ochsner, K. N., Bunge S. A., Gross, J. J., & Gabrieli, J. D. (2002). Rethinking feelings: An fMRI study of the cognitive regulation of emotion. *Journal of Cognitive Neuroscience, 14*, 1215–1229.

Oram, M. W., & Perrett, D. I. (1994). Responses of anterior superior temporal polysensory (STPa) neurons to "biological motion" stimuli. *Journal of Cognitive Neuroscience, 6*, 99–116.

Panksepp, J. (1998). *Affective neuroscience*. New York: Oxford University Press.

Pelphrey, K. A., Mitchell, T. V., McKeown, M. J., Goldstein, J., Allison, T., & McCarthy, G. (2003). Brain activity evoked by the perception of human walking: Controlling for meaningful coherent motion. *Journal of Neuroscience, 23*, 6819–6825.

Perner, J., & Wimmer, H. (1985). "John thinks that Mary thinks that . . .": Attribution of second-order beliefs by 5–10-year-old children. *Journal of Experimental Child Psychology, 39*, 437–471.

Perrett, D. I. (1989). Frameworks of analysis for the neural representation of animate objects and actions. *Journal of Experimental Biology, 146*, 87–113.

Perrett, D. I., Rolls, E. T., & Caan, W. (1982). Visual neurones responsive to faces in the monkey temporal cortex. *Experimental Brain Research, 47*, 329–342.

Perrett, D. I., Smith, P. A. J., Mistlin, A. J., Chitty, A. J., Head, A. S., Potter D. D., et al. (1985). Visual analysis of body movements by neurones in the temporal cortex of the macaque monkey: A preliminary report. *Behavioural Brain Research*, *16*, 153–170.

Pessoa, L., McKenna, M., Gutierrez, E., & Ungerleider, L. G. (2002). Neural processing of emotional faces requires attention. *Proceedings of the National Academy of Sciences of the USA*, *99*, 11458–11463.

Phelps, E. A., O'Connor, K. L., Cunningham, W. A., Funayama, E. S., Gatenby, J. C., Gore, J. C., et al. (2000). Performance on indirect measures of race evaluation predicts amygdala activation. *Journal of Cognitive Neuroscience*, *12*, 729–738.

Pizzagalli, D. A., Lehmann, D., Hendrick, A. M., Regard, M., Pascual-Marqui, R. D., & Davidson, R. J. (2002). Affective judgements of faces modulate early activity (approximately 160 ms) within the fusiform gyri. *NeuroImage*, *16*, 663–677.

Premack, D., & Woodruff, G. (1978). Chimpanzee problem solving: A test for comprehension. *Science*, *202*, 532–535.

Preston, S. D., & de Waal, F. B. M. (2002). Empathy: Its ultimate and proximate bases. *Behavioural and Brain Sciences*, *25*, 1–72.

Puce, A., Allison, T., Bentin, S., Gore, J. C., & McCarthy, G. (1998). Temporal cortex activation in humans viewing eye and mouth movements. *Journal of Neuroscience*, *18*, 2188–2199.

Puce, A., Allison, T., & McCarthy, G. (1999). Electrophysiological studies of human face perception. III. Effects of top-down processing on face-specific potentials. *Cerebral Cortex*, *9*, 445–458.

Raichle, M. E., MacLeod, A. M., Snyder, A, Z., Powers, W. J., Gusnard, D. A., & Shulman, G. L. (2001). A default mode of brain function. *Proceedings of the National Academy of Sciences of the USA*, *98*, 676–682.

Repacholi, B. M. (1998). Infants' use of attentional cues to identify the referent of another person's emotional expression. *Developmental Psychology*, *34*, 1017–1025.

Rizzolati, G., Fadiga, L., Gallese, L., & Fogassi, L. (1996). Premotor cortex and the recognition of motor actions. *Cognitive Brain Research*, *3*, 131–141.

Ross, E. D. (1993). Nonverbal aspects of language. *Neurologic Clinics*, *11*, 9–23.

Ross, E. D., Thompson, R. D., & Yenkosky, J. (1997). Lateralization of affective prosody in brain and the callosal integration of hemispheric language functions. *Brain and Language*, *56*, 27–54.

Saarni, C., Mumme, D., & Campos, J. J. (1997). Social, emotional, and personality development. In W. Damon (Ed.), *Handbook of child psychology* (pp. 237–309). New York: Wiley.

Saver, J. L., & Damasio, A. R. (1991). Preserved access and processing of social knowledge in a patient with acquired sociopathy due to ventromedial frontal damage. *Neuropsychologia*, *29*, 1241–1249.

Saxe, R. (2003). *What fMRI can tell us about theory of mind*. Ph.D. Thesis, Brain and Cognitive Sciences Division, Massachusetts Institute of Technology, Cambridge, MA.

Saxe, R., & Kanwisher, N. (2003). People thinking about thinking people: The role of the temporoparietal junction in "theory of mind". *NeuroImage*, *19*, 1835–1842.

Saxe, R., Xiao, D. K., Kovacs, G., Perrett, D. I., & Kanwisher, N. (2004). A region of right posterior superior temporal sulcus responds to observed intentional actions. *Neuropsychologia*, *42*, 1435–1446.

Schaefer, S. M., Jackson, D. C., Davidson, R. J., Aguirre, G. K., Kimberg, D. Y., & Thompson-Schill, S. L. (2002). Modulation of amygdalar activity by the conscious regulation of negative emotion. *Journal of Cognitive Neuroscience*, *14*, 913–921.

Schlottmann, A., & Surian, L. (1999). Do 9-month-olds perceive causation-at-a-distance? *Perception, 28*, 1105–1113.
Schmolck, H., & Squire, L. R. (2001). Impaired perception of facial emotions following bilateral damage to the anterior temporal lobe. *Neuropsychology, 15*, 30–38.
Scholl, B. J., & Tremoulet, P. D. (2000). Perceptual causality and animacy. *Trends in Cognitive Sciences, 4*, 299–309.
Schultz, R. T., Gauthier, I., Klin, A., Fulbright, R. K., Anderson, A. W., Volkmar, F., Skudlarski, P., et al. (2000). Abnormal ventral temporal cortical activity during face discrimination among individuals with autism and Asperger syndrome. *Archives of General Psychiatry, 57*, 331–340.
Scott, S. K., Young, A. W., Calder, A. J., Hellawell, D. J., Aggleton, J. P., & Johnson, M. (1997). Impaired auditory recognition of fear and anger following bilateral amygdala lesions. *Nature, 385*, 254–257.
Siegal, M., & Varley, R. (2002). Neural systems involved in "theory of mind". *Nature Reviews Neuroscience, 3*, 463–471.
Sprengelmeyer, R., Young, A., Schroeder, U., Grossenbacher, P. G., Federlein, J., Buettner, T., et al. (1999). Knowing no fear. *Proceedings of the Royal Society of London: Series B, 266*, 2451–2456.
Stone, V. E., Baron-Cohen, S., Calder, A., Keane, J., & Young, A. (2003). Acquired theory of mind impairments in individuals with bilateral amygdala lesions. *Neuropsychologia, 41*, 209–220.
Stone, V. E., Baron-Cohen, S., & Knight, R. T. (1998a). Frontal lobe contributions to theory of mind. *Journal of Cognitive Neuroscience, 10*, 640–656.
Stone, V. E., Baron-Cohen, S., Young A. W., Calder, A., & Keane, J. (1998b). Impairments in social cognition following orbitofrontal or amygdala damage. *Society for Neuroscience Abstracts, 463*, 4.
Stone, V. E., Cosmides, L., Tooby, J., Kroll, N., & Knight, R. T. (2002). Selective impairment of reasoning about social exchange in a patient with bilateral limbic system damage. *Proceedings of the National Academy of Sciences of the USA, 99*, 11531–11536.
Stuss, D. T., Gallup, G. G., Jr., & Alexander, M. P. (2001). The frontal lobes are necessary for "theory of mind". *Brain, 124*, 279–286.
Surian, L., & Siegal, M. (2001). Sources of performance on theory of mind tasks in right hemisphere-damaged patients. *Brain and Language, 78*, 224–232.
Thomas, K. M., Drevets, W. C., Whalen, P. J., Eccard, C. H., Dahl, R. E., Ryan, R. D., et al. (2001). Amygdala response to facial expressions in children and adults. *Biological Psychiatry, 49*, 309–316.
Tooby, J., and Cosmides, L. (1990). The past explains the present: Emotional adaptations and the structure of ancestral environments. *Ethology and Sociobiology, 11*, 375–421.
Tremoulet, P. D., & Feldman, J. (2000). Perception of animacy from the motion of a single object. *Perception, 29*, 943–951.
Umilta, M. A., Kohler, E., Gallese, V., Fogassi, L., Fadiga, L., Keysers, C., et al. (2001). I know what you are doing: A neurophysiological study. *Neuron, 31*, 155–165.
Vaina, L. M., Solomon, J., Chowdhury, S., Sinha, P., & Belliveau, J. W. (2001). Functional neuroanatomy of biological motion perception in humans. *Proceedings of the National Academy of Sciences of the USA, 98*, 11656–11661.

Vogeley, K., Bussfeld, P., Newen, A., Herrmann, S., Happe, F., Falkai, P., et al. (2001). Mind-reading: Neural mechanisms of theory of mind and self-perspective. *NeuroImage, 14*, 170–181.

Vuilleumier, P., Armony, J. L., Driver, J., & Dolan, R. J. (2001). Effects of attention and emotion on face processing in the human brain: An event-related fMRI study. *Neuron, 30*, 829–841.

Wason, P. (1966). *Reasoning. New horizons in psychology*. Harmondsworth, UK: B. M. Foss.

Whalen, P. J. (1998). Fear, vigilance, and ambiguity: Initial neuroimaging studies of the human amygdala. *Current Directions in Psychological Science, 7*, 177–188.

Whalen, P. J., Rauch, S. L., Etcoff, N. L., McInerney, S. C., Lee, M. B., & Jenike, M. A. (1998). Masked presentations of emotional facial expressions modulate amygdala activity without explicit knowledge. *Journal of Neuroscience, 18*, 411–418.

Wicker, B., Michel, F., Henaff, M. A., & Decety, J. (1998). Brain regions involved in the perception of gaze: A PET study. *NeuroImage, 8*, 221–227.

Wimmer, H., & Perner, J. (1983). Beliefs about beliefs: Representation and constraining function of wrong beliefs in young children's understanding of deception. *Cognition, 13*, 103–128.

Winner, E., Brownell, H. H., Happé, F., Blum, A., & Pincus, D. (1998). Distinguishing lies from jokes: Theory of mind deficits and discourse interpretation in right hemisphere brain-damaged patients. *Brain and Language, 62*, 89–106.

Winston, J. S., Strange, B. A., O'Doherty, J., & Dolan, R. J. (2002). Automatic and intentional brain responses during evaluation of trustworthiness of faces. *Nature Neuroscience, 5*, 277–283.

Yang, T. T., Menon, V., Eliez, S., Blasey, C., White, C. D., Reid, A. J., et al. (2002). Amygdalar activation associated with positive and negative facial expressions. *Neuroreport, 13*, 1737–1741.

Young, A. W., Aggleton, J. P., Hellawell, D. J., Johnson, M., Broks, P., & Hanley, J. R. (1995). Face processing impairments after amygdalotomy. *Brain, 118*, 15–24.

7 The self and social perception: Three kinds of questions in social cognitive neuroscience

*Matthew D. Lieberman
and Jennifer H. Pfeifer*

"A man has as many social selves as there are individuals who recognize him."
William James (1890), *Principles of Psychology* (Vol. I, p. 294)

"The world is twofold for man in accordance with his twofold nature."
Martin Buber (1937), *I and Thou* (p. 82)

A great deal of research in social psychology is motivated by one of two broad goals: (1) to understand the mental processes involved in how people make sense of the social world; (2) to understand how self-processes are shaped by the social world. In other words, social psychologists are deeply interested in the interplay between intrapersonal and interpersonal processes. In the final analysis, most social psychologists agree that neither can be understood in isolation. Though many naively take for granted a sovereign self that is inaccessible to others and independent of their influence, the opening quotation from William James, as well as the theoretical and empirical history of social psychology, suggests that the development and maintenance of the self is shaped by one's situational context. Alternatively, many believe that perceiving the social world is a relatively objective process akin to, albeit more complicated than, perceiving the nonsocial world. Endless evidence suggests that this, too, is a naive view, an issue addressed in the philosophy of Martin Buber. Perceiving the social world is a subjective process shaped by an individual's current motivation, emotion, and cognition, as well as his or her more long-standing traits such as personalities, self-schemas, and chronically accessible constructs. An even more extreme position was taken by the philosopher Nietzsche, who suggested that social perception is nothing but the projection of our own idiosyncratic representations onto the world in his claim, "Whoever thought that he had understood something of me had merely construed something out of me, after his own image" (Nietzsche, 1908/1969, p. 261).

Now that the methods of cognitive neuroscience are being applied to social psychological questions, it is to be expected that early research efforts turn to social perception and self-processes as appropriate starting points. In this chapter, we review the work that has been done with human subject populations in the growing area of social cognitive neuroscience (Adolphs, 1999; Klein & Kihlstrom, 1998; Ochsner & Lieberman, 2001; for a review of the broader field of social neuroscience, see Cacioppo et al., 2002). This chapter is organized around three types of questions that can be addressed with a social cognitive neuroscience approach: (1) where is the process in the brain? (2) what kinds of computations or cognitions are involved in the process? (3) how does the process of interest change as a function of contextual factors, other ongoing mental activity, and learning history? To foreshadow one of our main conclusions, although it is natural to first study these topics separately, social cognitive neuroscientists must ultimately reconcile these initial accounts with the ways in which self-processes and social perception are bound up with one another. The separate study of each is merely a convenience carved out by our research methods, rather than an indication that either can be understood alone.

Three questions

We begin by laying out three questions that can be asked with a social cognitive neuroscience approach and what is gained from each type of question. The questions are presented in the order they are typically asked. Though questions 2 and 3 may be of greater intrinsic significance than question 1, typically, they cannot be empirically addressed until question 1 has been answered.

Question 1: Where is the process in the brain?

The best cognitive neuroscience research always informs psychological theories, and social cognitive neuroscience should aspire to no less. Yet, discovering the neural correlates of a social psychological process appears thoroughly irrelevant to theory at first blush. Indeed, if research began and ended with brain-mapping studies of this sort, psychologists would have little reason for enthusiasm. Straightforward brain-mapping studies serve an important purpose when considered from a broader context. Psychologists frequently generate novel hypotheses based upon the anecdotal experience of everyday life. Icheiser (1943) and Heider (1958) noticed that people tend to attribute observed behaviour to the enduring dispositions of the actor without sufficiently considering the impact of the situation on the actor's behaviour. These insights have guided over three decades of empirical work on attributional inference (Gilbert & Malone, 1995; Jones & Davis, 1965). In a similar manner, brain mapping provides us with anecdotes previously unavailable to the senses, as each study connects a group of brain regions to a particular macrolevel process or experience. The activation of region x while performing task y is not sufficient to identify region x with the performance of task y; however, each study provides a clue. For instance, region x may make some minor contribution that is a necessary but nonobvious component of performing task *y*. Intuitions about the function(s) of region *x* will be built up as it is activated by a number of superficially different tasks. The payoff of brain-mapping studies is that we can begin to hypothesize about the computations common to the range of tasks and ultimately conduct targeted tests of this hypothesis. However, this requires us to know which candidate regions are potentially involved in a process of interest before we can begin more precise hypothesis testing. Determining these candidate regions is largely the result of brain-mapping studies.

Question 2: What kind of computations/cognitions are involved in the process?

From the extensive brain mapping done over the past decade, cognitive neuroscientists now have a catalogue of associations between cognition and brain regions. To name just a few, we know of specific regions of the brain associated with various forms of sensory processing, episodic memory, semantic memory, working memory, implicit learning, face processing, automatic affect, and conflict monitoring. Though this index of neurocognitive correlations is constantly being refined and updated, it allows us to test hypotheses regarding the different mental processes involved in performing any task. One might hypothesize that some task involves subprocesses *P1, P2*, and *P3* which are known to be associated with neural regions *N1, N2*, and *N3*, respectively. While it is often difficult to assess the simultaneous contributions of multiple cognitive processes to a task in behavioural studies, neuroimaging methods are well suited for it. Looking for the presence or absence of five neural regions in the performance of a task is often no more difficult than looking for three or one. The presence or absence of *N1, N2*, and *N3* thus allows us to infer the involvement of psychological processes *P1, P2*, and *P3*. Social psychologists often want to examine the extent to which their process of interest relies on automatic or controlled processing, "hot" affect or "cold" cognition, visual or linguistic processing, and episodic or semantic memory. Neuroimaging provides data bearing on each of these processes without having to interrupt a participant's mental activity to assess dependent variables.

Question 3: How does the process of interest change as a function of contextual factors, other ongoing mental activity, and learning history?

The benefit of cognitive neuroscience cataloguing correlations between brain regions and cognitive operations is that we can now address question 2 and assess the common computations underlying different social psychological processes. The downside to this cataloguing process is that this enterprise leads to the compartmentalization of mental processing, such that it is easy to believe that these brain regions function independently of one another.

Compartmentalization of mental processes has an empirical legacy extending back to Wundt and the introspectionists (Kohler, 1947). For example, Ebbinghaus (1885/1964) examined memory processes by studying nonsense syllables. He believed that by avoiding content with affective and semantic meaning one could study the true roots of episodic memory. However, research from the past two decades has shown that affective processing is not an independent process added on top of, and therefore linearly separable from, episodic memory. Quite the contrary, episodic memory encoding in the medial temporal lobe is critically modulated by the affective significance of the stimulus by way of beta noradrenergic outputs from the amygdala (Cahill & McGaugh, 1998). Social psychological theory has a long tradition, inspired by Gestalt psychology, of emphasizing the interdependence of different social cognitive processes. For example, part of what makes the self an object of study for social psychology is its multifaceted nature, with different facets presenting themselves, depending on the social context. There is little reason to believe that the neural underpinnings of the self would be any less flexible in the face of social pressures than are the self's behavioural and cognitive expressions.

One of the advantages of current fMRI data-analysis techniques is our ability to examine how and to what extent the interplay between different brain regions changes as a function of context, motivation, priming, and so on. Recall the above example involving neural processes *N1*, *N2*, and *N3*. It might be the case that these areas are always activated in a particular process, and yet the coordination of activity between the three regions may change as a function of current motivational and contextual conditions. The extent to which the regions operate together in lock step is termed *functional connectivity*, the analysis of which will prove critical to the social cognitive neuroscience approach. To elaborate, rather than merely showing whether two brain regions are activated by a task, functional connectivity analyses assess the extent to which the regions respond in concert to the task. The assessment of functional connectivity as motivation, cognition, or context changes allows us to determine how different aspects of social cognition affect one another.

The remainder of this review is divided into sections on the self and on social perception, including the following specific topics: self-knowledge, self-awareness, self-control, recognizing others, attribution, and stereotyping. We discuss how each of these topics has been investigated according to the three questions described above. Naturally, given the short history of neuroscientific research on these topics, there is a good deal more work addressing the first question (brain mapping) than the second (function) and third (mediator/moderator processes), as each tends to build on the answers to the previous questions.

The self

Until the advent of neuroimaging in recent years, most insights into the neural bases of the self came from neuropsychological cases, the most famous of which is the case of Phineas Gage, which has been described at length elsewhere (Damasio, 1994; Macmillan, 2000). After a tamping iron was literally shot through Gage's skull, his cognitive, perceptual, and motor skills were left surprisingly unimpaired. However, Gage underwent a radical personality shift and, from all accounts, was no longer the same person. The damage also appeared to alter his social judgement, and Gage went on to make a string of poor social decisions that left him alone and penniless at the end of his life. The accident caused damage to his ventromedial prefrontal cortex, suggesting that this region of the brain might be critical for both social perception and self-processes.

Before proceeding with our discussion of a social cognitive neuroscience approach to the self, we must define and outline how modern social psychologists organize their study of the self. Rather than examine the self in its monolithic entirety, three aspects of self-processing are typically focused upon: self-knowledge, self-awareness, and self-control (Baumeister, 1998). Self-knowledge includes both the capacity to recognize oneself and the storehouse of information that one keeps regarding one's own personality, preferences, and autobiographical history. Self-awareness refers to the capacity to reflect upon and identify with one's own ongoing experience and actions. Self-control is the regulatory capacity to strategically overcome one's own impulses and habits.

Self-knowledge and self-recognition

Neural correlates

Because self-recognition depends on identification with an external aspect of the self that is intersubjectively available, it is perhaps the most empirically tractable of self-processes and thus has already been the subject of a number of cognitive neuroscience studies in recent years. Two neuropsychological investigations suggest that self-recognition is lateralized to one hemisphere but draw opposite conclusions as to which hemisphere is dominant. While undergoing a Wada test, which anaesthetizes the two hemispheres one at a time, patients were shown a picture that was created by morphing their own face with that of a famous person (Keenan, Nelson, O'Connor, & Pascual-Leone, 2001; see also Keenan, McCutcheon, Freund, Gallup, Sanders, & Pascual-Leone, 1999). Participants were then asked to choose which of the two unmorphed faces they had been shown. When only the right hemisphere was functioning, patients uniformly believed the face shown was their own, whereas the face was construed more often as the other famous individual when only the left hemisphere was functioning. Alternatively, a split-brain patient demonstrated a distinct left hemisphere advantage for self-recognition (Turk, Heatherton, Kelley, Funnell, Gazzaniga, & Macrae, 2002). Two fMRI studies revealed a complex pattern of left and right hemisphere structures participating in self-recognition (Kircher et al., 2000). Both studies found right hemisphere activations in the hippocampus, anterior cingulate, precuneus, and cerebellum and left hemisphere activations in the lateral prefrontal cortex and inferior parietal lobe.

Self-knowledge, in terms of knowing one's own personality, preferences, and autobiography, is a more complicated topic of study, as these are conspicuously subjective features of the self. Everyone can agree that a photograph of a person taken yesterday is really of that person, but not everyone agrees on the personality traits of an individual—often, friends and loved ones can see a person quite differently than does the individual him- or herself. Despite this obstacle, self-knowledge has been the most frequently studied aspect of the self in cognitive neuroscience studies. Klein and colleagues (Klein, Cosmides, Costabile, & Mei, 2002; Klein, Loftus, & Kihlstrom, 1996) have examined patients with compromised declarative memory systems to determine whether these are critical to self-knowledge. Amazingly, they have found complete sparing of self-knowledge despite massive impairments to explicit memory for other phenomena. In one case (Klein, Loftus, & Kihlstrom, 1996), a woman with head trauma reported a given personality while unable to recall most of her life history, and still reported the same personality when her memory later returned. This would appear to fly in the face of Kant's theory of indirect self-knowledge, subsequently embodied in Bem's (1972) self-perception theory. Bem argued that people come to know themselves by observing their own behaviour, in the same way that people learn about the preferences and personality of others, rather than through introspection. Bem's theory suggests that knowing one's self is dependent on remembering one's own behaviour. One could argue that in the case of the head trauma patient, the woman had been able to reflect on her behaviour for many years before the injury and may have developed semantic self-knowledge that would have been unaffected by her temporary amnesia (McClelland, McNaughton, & O'Reilly, 1995). However, Klein et al. (2002) have shown that an autistic patient with compromised semantic memory still maintained accurate self-knowledge, suggesting that not all self-knowledge is developed explicitly.

Additionally, a neuropsychological study of 12 permanently amnesic patients (Lieberman, Ochsner, Gilbert, & Schacter, 2001) demonstrated that new behaviours led to updated self-knowledge even though the patients never had explicit memory of their behaviour. Social psychological research has shown that engaging in freely chosen counter-attitudinal behaviour is sufficient to change the attitudes and preferences of the actor, a process referred to as cognitive dissonance reduction. Noticing the conflict between one's behaviour and beliefs is thought to cause cognitive dissonance, a state of psychological distress that typically leads people to change their beliefs to fit their behaviour. In other words, people engage in rationalization to keep up the appearance of self-consistency, both in their own eyes and those of others around them. Lieberman et al., however, found that amnesic patients incapable of forming new memories demonstrated as much attitude change after engaging in freely chosen counter-attitudinal behaviour as did healthy controls. Just seconds after performing it, these patients could not remember engaging in the counter-attitudinal behaviour—yet, their self was modified to take account of this behaviour. This suggests that if self-perception is truly a source of self-knowledge it cannot require elaborate, time-consuming, conscious consideration of one's behaviours; it must instead be a more automatic consequence of observing the self, at least some of the time (Shultz & Lepper, 1995).

Contrary to the neuropsychological findings, imaging studies of self-knowledge processes typically find activations associated with episodic retrieval and explicit thought. Three positron emission tomography (PET) studies (Craik et al., 1999; Fink, Markowitsch, Reinkemeier, Bruckbauer, Kessler, & Heiss, 1996; Kjaer, Nowak, & Lou, 2002), along with four fMRI studies (Johnson, Baxter, Wilder, Pipe, Heiserman, & Prigatano, 2002; Kelley, Macrae, Wyland, Caglar, Inati, & Heatheron, 2002; Kircher et al., 2000; Lieberman, Jarcho, & Satpute, 2004c), have each used similar paradigms in which participants had to judge whether words were self-descriptive. As seen in Table 7.1, six of the seven studies found activation in the region of the precuneus and posterior cingulate. The medial prefrontal cortex (BA 9/10), extending into the ventromedial prefrontal cortex (BA 11), was active in four of the seven studies. Right inferotemporal cortex (BA 21/38) and inferior parietal (BA 40) activations were reported in three of the six studies. The ventrolateral prefrontal cortex (BA 44/45/47), basal ganglia, and insula were each reported in two of the studies.

Neurocognitive processes

Knowing which regions of the brain support self-knowledge can only be of theoretical value to the extent that the functions of these regions can be specified. The most frequently activated regions (precuneus, medial prefrontal cortex, and lateral temporal cortex) are far from completely understood, but do seem to perform functions consistent with explicit knowledge processes. The medial prefrontal cortex is just now beginning to be understood. As described later in the section on attribution, the medial prefrontal cortex is involved in making explicit attributions about the mental states of others (Castelli et al., 2002; Gallagher & Frith, 2003) and thus may be similarly involved in making attributions about the self (Bem, 1972). Mounting evidence suggests that the precuneus in the parietal lobe plays a role in perspective taking, differentiating self and other, and retrieval of episodic memories. The precuneus will be discussed at greater length below in the section on self-awareness. Finally, the right inferotemporal

Table 7.1 Neural correlates of self-knowledge retrieval from seven studies

Brain region	Brodmann area(s)	Side	Kircher et al. (2000)	Johnson et al. (2002)	Craik et al. (1999)	Kelley et al. (2002)	Fink et al. (1996)	Lieberman et al. (in press)	Kjaer et al. (2002)	Total
Precuneus and posterior cingulate	7/31	Both	•	•		•	•	•	•	6/7
Medial and ventromedial prefrontal	9/10/11	Both		•	•	•		•		4/7
Inferotemporal	21/38	Right		•			•	•		3/7
Inferior parietal	40	Both	•		•			•		3/7
Ventrolateral prefrontal	44/45/47	Right						•	•	2/7
Basal ganglia		Left	•					•		2/7
Insula		Both	•				•			2/7

cortex and temporal pole may play a role in the storage of declarative self-knowledge.

The putative functions of the areas most active when making self-knowledge judgements present a picture that is consistent with seventeenth-century philosopher John Locke's claim about the role of explicit thought and memory processes in the maintenance of self-knowledge. Locke (1690/1975) claimed that "as far as this consciousness can be extended backwards to any past action or thought, so far reaches the identity of that person" (Bk. II, Ch. 27–29). In other words, without being able to recall what one has done in the past, how can one answer questions about what kind of person one is in general? In this model of self-knowledge, we judge our own trait characteristics (such as "generous") by explicitly retrieving and considering exemplars of past behaviour in which we exhibited behaviour consistent or inconsistent with that trait. The activations in the precuneus, the medial prefrontal cortex, and the temporal lobe during self-knowledge judgements fit this model of *evidence-based* self-knowledge processing.

A reconciliation between Klein's work and the neuroimaging findings is possible if it is assumed that (1) there are multiple self-knowledge systems and (2) individuals access evidence-based self-knowledge when required to make self-judgements, even though they could use other sources of self-knowledge if they suffered from impairments to the neural systems involved in evidence-based self-knowledge.

Contextual factors

To this point, there is good evidence to suggest that evidence-based self-knowledge is not the only self-knowledge system that operates in humans. Other than the presumed existence of at least one other self-knowledge system, virtually nothing is known about the nature of this second system. Some have claimed that its representations are prototypes or schemas, but cognitive psychologists continue to debate whether these representations are truly distinct from exemplar models (Allen & Brooks, 1991; Nosofsky & Palmieri, 1997).

Lieberman, Jarcho, and Satpute (2004c) recently conducted an fMRI study to identify the neural correlates of *intuition-based* self-knowledge, a possible second self-knowledge system. From previous behavioural work (Klein, Loftus, Trafton, & Fuhrman, 1992; Markus, 1977), it was assumed that the amount of experience in a domain would moderate a shift in reliance from evidence-based to intuition-based self-knowledge. More specifically, Klein et al. (1992) found support for evidence-based self-knowledge use when participants made self-judgements in a domain with which they had little experience, but no indication of evidence-based self-knowledge use in domains of high experience. Lieberman et al. (2004c) hypothesized that the neural correlates of the two kinds of self-knowledge would be differentially activated as a function of domain experience.

Eleven professional actors and 11 college athletes were scanned while judging the self-descriptiveness of acting and athletic trait words. It was hypothesized that neural correlates of intuition-based self-knowledge would be more activated when participants made high-experience domain judgements, and the neural correlates of evidence-based self-knowledge would be more activated when participants made low-experience domain judgements. From previous research (Lieberman, 2003; Lieberman, Gaunt, Gilbert, & Trope, 2002), it was hypothesized that evidence-based self-processes would be associated with the medial temporal lobe, precuneus, and lateral prefrontal cortex, whereas intuition-based self-knowledge would be associated with the ventromedial prefrontal cortex, basal ganglia, and amygdala. Initial group analyses of self-judgements in a domain of high experience produced activations in the ventromedial prefrontal cortex, nucleus accumbens in the basal ganglia, amygdala, and posterior parietal cortex largely consistent with the hypotheses. No regions were more active in this group analysis of low-experience self-judgements. By the magnitude of each participant's reaction time advantage for high-experience domain judgements over low-experience domain judgements, participants were divided into two post hoc groups (*schematics* and *nonschematics*) for further analysis. Schematics, when analysed alone, produced high-experience self-judgement activations in the ventromedial prefrontal cortex, nucleus accumbens, amygdala, and precuneus along with a relative *deactivation* in hippocampus. Alternatively, nonschematics produced high-experience self-judgement activations in the hippocampus, precuneus, and lateral prefrontal cortex along with a relative *deactivation* in the ventromedial prefrontal cortex. In a between-groups analysis, schematics produced more activation in the ventromedial prefrontal cortex, whereas nonschematics produced more activation in the hippocampus (Figure 7.1).

This study demonstrates both that self-knowledge is instantiated in multiple networks in the brain that support different components of self-knowledge, and that these networks have qualitatively different operating characteristics. Future studies will be able to examine how various contextual factors, including the presence of other people, goals, emotion, motivation, and cognitive resources, determine when each of these networks is dominant in guiding our use of self-knowledge.

Self-awareness and introspection

William James (1890) described the self as composed of the "I" and the "me" (see also Mead, 1934; Sartre, 1936), and Allport (1955) similarly described the self dichotomously, as the knower and the known. The "me" or known self corresponds roughly to self-knowledge, as discussed in the previous section. It refers to relatively static information that one possesses regarding one's own personality, preferences, abilities, and the like. The composite "me" from all of these representations is relatively stable, such that people typically believe their "me" of last year and next year will be similar to their me of

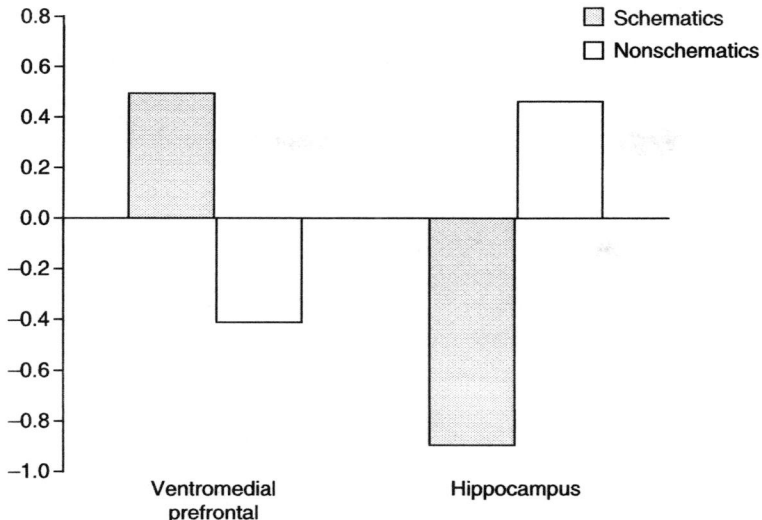

Figure 7.1 Relative activation in the ventromedial prefrontal cortex and hippocampus for schematics and nonschematics.

today (cf. Dweck, 1999). The knower or "I" refers to the feelings of spontaneous and active experience of the self in the moment. Inspired by cybernetic models of human cognition (Carver & Scheier, 1981; Miller, Galanter, & Pribram, 1960; Weiner, 1948), social psychologists have often divided the study of the "I" into two parts: self-awareness and self-control.

The simplest cybernetic models explain the activity of self-regulatory mechanisms such as thermostats. Thermostats computationally consist of two operations: *test* and *operate* (Miller et al., 1960). Thus, they test whether the ambient temperature is below some preset threshold; if so, the thermostat operates on the environment by turning on the heat until a new test comes back indicating the desirable temperature has been reached. Self-awareness, introspection, or self-focused attention seem to be the phenomenological analogues of the test function, whereas exerting self-control seems to be the phenomenological analogue to the operate function. In this section, we assess what is known about the neurocognitive underpinnings of self-awareness.

Neural correlates

There are few if any better examples of punctate self-awareness than the experience of pain. People do not feel pain and then wonder whose pain it is. Instead, the onset of pain leads to the immediate conclusion that the pain is one's own and that something must be done to rectify the situation as quickly as possible. The subjective response to pain and the subsequent behaviour initiated by this experience nicely demonstrate the test–operate aspects of cybernetic models. Though less dramatic, a plethora of other conflicts also produce momentary self-awareness. For instance, struggling with a Stroop task leads to awareness of one's own compulsion to say the colour named by the word rather than the colour of the ink that the word is written in as an answer. Realizing too late that one has just put the wrong answer on a test leads to self-awareness, and staring at a Necker cube may lead to self-focused attention on one's inability to hold the percept constant. Each of these conflict-ridden events prompting self-awareness activates the anterior cingulate cortex on the medial surface of the brain (Botvinick, Braver, Barch, Carter, & Cohen, 2001; Eisenberger, Satpute, & Lieberman, 2003; Rainville et al., 1997). Most anterior cingulate activations appear to simultaneously produce an experience of self-awareness and set in motion cognitive, behavioural, and physiological responses to remove the conflict if possible. Furthermore, Lane et al. (1997) have found that the magnitude of anterior cingulate reactivity to emotional stimuli presentation is highly correlated with self-reported levels of chronic self-awareness.

Whereas the anterior cingulate has been implicated in bottom-up induced self-awareness, the posterior parietal cortex may be involved in the kind of indirect self-awareness proposed by Kant, Mead, and Bem. Patients with damage to the posterior parietal cortex, occurring frequently as a result of a stroke, have difficulty appreciating their own cognitive and behavioural impairments, a condition referred to as *anosognosia*. For example, Ramachandran (1995) described patients with right parietal damage who denied the paralysis of their left arm. When asked if her left arm was paralysed, one patient indicated that her left arm was fine—just as strong as the right one. When asked to point with her left hand, instead of admitting that she could not move it, the patient claimed she had decided she did not *want* to move her hand. Patients with anosognosia are known for generating contorted rationalizations for their deficits rather than acknowledging the deficit itself. Given that there are certain treatments that can temporarily remove the anosognosia, it appears that the patients are not using the rationalization as an explicit defence mechanism. Rather, it appears that damage to the parietal lobe truly prevents patients from experiencing and identifying with the deficit at all.

Neurocognitive processes

Self-awareness of a conflict and self-control exerted to overcome the conflict are naturally co-occurring events, as one typically leads to the other. Not surprisingly, it has been difficult to tease apart the neural contributors to these two processes. Most studies of tasks requiring self-control have shown activation of both the anterior cingulate and prefrontal cortex. Cohen and colleagues (Carter et al., 2000) have performed a series of elegant neuroimaging studies that suggest the anterior cingulate performs computations critical to self-awareness of conflict, without being directly involved in the exertion of self-control. They used a modified Stroop-like task that allowed analysis of brain region activity covarying with the detection of the need for self-control separate from brain region activity covarying with the actual exertion of control (Carter et al., 1998, 2000). They found a double dissociation such that the anterior cingulate responded during the detection of the need for control, but not the exertion of control, whereas the lateral prefrontal cortex responded during the exertion of control, but not the detection of the need for control.

The neurocognitive properties of the posterior parietal cortex (including the wedge of cortex consisting of precuneus, intraparietal sulcus, and inferior parietal lobe) are just beginning to emerge with respect to self-awareness. The posterior parietal cortex has typically been assigned two functions, one as a nonexecutive maintenance component of working memory (Cabeza & Nyberg, 2000) and one as a spatial processing area (Goldman-Rakic, 1988). A variety of studies that have heretofore been unconnected suggest that the posterior parietal cortex may be the location where nonsymbolic, parallel, distributed representations are translated into symbolic, serial, local representations. It is these symbolic representations which we are aware of as distinct "figures" emerging from the tacit, unattended-to background that makes up the stream of consciousness. This claim is made plausible given the strong innervation of the posterior parietal cortex from ventral temporal and occipital areas, where visual information is analysed into objects and categories without necessarily reaching consciousness. A number of studies have shown that for stimuli presented near the subliminal/supraliminal border, the posterior parietal activation predicts when the stimuli will be perceived as a meaningful entity (Beck, Rees, Frith, & Lavie, 2001; Kjaer, Nowak, Kjaer, Lou, & Lou, 2001; Portas, Strange, Friston, Dolan, & Frith, 2000).

The capacity for true symbolic processing may be critical for perspective-taking capacity. Whereas distributed associative representations compute similarity functions, symbols can be used in propositions that explicitly represent asymmetric relations between entities (Holyoak & Hummel, 2000; Lieberman et al., 2002; Sloman, 1996). Perspective taking depends on representing asymmetric relationships, as the perspective taker must be able to differentiate his perspective from that of his target. A handful of recent studies have found that perspective-taking efforts are associated with posterior parietal activations (Chaminade & Decety, 2002; Farrer & Frith, 2002; Farrow et al., 2001; Ruby & Decety, 2001). Moreover, the precuneus in the posterior parietal cortex is consistently activated in episodic retrieval effort (Cabeza & Nyberg, 2000; Fletcher et al., 1995) and must be intact for successful episodic retrieval in rodents (Izquierdo et al., 1997). Combining these findings, some have suggested that during episodic retrieval one is attempting to take one's own perspective from a previous point in time, indicating a form of self-perspective taking. This prospect highlights an interesting paradox about the self. For the current active self to retrieve information about its own past, it must suspend its current perspective. One might think that the currently active self would, introspectively, be automatically in touch with the past self, but this may turn out not to be the case. Indeed, this complicated process of taking a former perspective is not always successful, especially in the case of memory for prior beliefs and feelings (Bem & McConnell, 1970; Fredrickson, 2000; Hawkins & Hastie, 1990; Kahneman, Fredrickson, Schreiber, & Redelmeier, 1993; Ross, 1989).

Prominent social psychological theories have suggested that just as we must engage in perspective taking to retrieve our past selves, we must also engage in perspective taking to be aware of and understand our current self. Mead (1934) suggested that we come to know ourselves by seeing ourselves through the eyes of others around us. It is hard to directly size up our own abilities ("How can I figure out how smart I am on my own?"), but humans have an uncanny knack for automatically casting judgement on others (see section on attribution below). Even though people might not be able to know themselves directly, they can count on those around them to have already made these judgements. Learning about one's self can then be as simple as learning what others have already learned about one's self. To the extent that this process characterizes the acquisition of self-knowledge, it suggests: (1) self-knowledge generation is a fundamentally social process in contrast to the naive "introspective access" theory that most people hold; (2) the neural correlates of perspective taking should be central to the self-awareness that helps us to generate and retrieve self-knowledge.

Contextual factors

Recall that in the earlier section on self-knowledge, the precuneus was the most commonly activated area associated with self-judgements. We can now hypothesize that this activation reflects some combination of self-perspective taking to retrieve information about the self of the past and taking the views of important others on the self. To the extent that these perspective-taking processes are entangled, it may become increasingly difficult to dissociate self-processing from social processing. Future studies could benefit from independently manipulating these two processes, through priming and direct instruction, in order to get a clearer picture of the neurocognitive contributions of each to self-processing.

Self-control

Neural correlates

A variety of neuropsychological disorders suggest that self-control, the paradoxical ability to exert oneself in the service of overcoming one's own impulses (Lakoff & Johnson, 1999; Turner, 1976), is associated with the lateral prefrontal cortex and the basal ganglia. Disorders of self-control including Parkinson's disease, Huntington's disease, obsessive-compulsive disorder, and Tourette's syndrome each highlight the delicate neural balance that is necessary for healthy individuals to control their own thoughts and behaviour. All of these disorders have been found to affect the prefrontal cortex, basal ganglia, and anterior cingulate. We have already reviewed the test–operate cybernetic model of self-regulation, and the anterior cingulate's role is clearly relegated to the *test* function. The prefrontal cortex and basal ganglia are thus involved in the remaining operate function. The basal ganglia have been hypothesized to be involved in more automatic forms of self-control built up from habit (Lieberman, 2000), leaving the prefrontal cortex as the major brain region associated with effortful self-control.

Neurocognitive processes

There are at least three neurocognitive functions of the lateral prefrontal cortex that contribute to its role in effortful self-control. The lateral prefrontal cortex has consistently been associated with working memory and language processes, which together produce the ability to compose novel propositions from a series of symbolic representations and then hold these in mind. This planning capacity, which differentiates us from all other animals excepting a few primates who may have immature prototypes of these processes (Deacon, 1997), allows humans to imagine a variety of futures which have not yet come to pass and consider the consequences of following their impulses. Although we can choose alternative courses of action from those suggested by our impulses, this flexibility clearly comes at a cost. Exciting new data suggest that these prefrontal capacities have many of the properties of a muscle. Whereas self-control capacities may strengthen with use over time, they become "tired" and depleted in the short term with overuse such that rapid-fire bouts of self-control tend to produce increasingly poor results (Vohs & Heatherton, 2000).

There are three different computational mechanisms by which the propositional activation of the prefrontal cortex can lead to self-control. First, the products of prefrontal activity—in the form of conclusions and behavioural intentions—can activate the motor system directly, taking control away from more automatic neural processes. The downside to this mechanism is evident in the example of learning to touch-type. The individual must form an intention to type each letter, one at a time, a slow and fragile process that interferes with the ability to think about the content of what one would like to communicate. This direct guidance of behaviour is incredibly flexible and useful in novel circumstances, but it operates serially on behaviours and requires effort and attention. Moreover, the conclusions formed from the judgements and logic of the prefrontal cortex are far from perfect, often making the problem at hand worse (Wegener & Petty, 1995, Wegner, 1994). Indeed, decision making research suggests that explicit attempts at decision making tend to systematically leave out critical pieces of information even when they are available (Gilbert & Wilson, 2000; Tversky & Kahneman, 1972).

A second way the prefrontal cortex can exert self-control is by facilitating the activation of weaker processes and representations so that they can compete with more automatic ones (Shallice, 1988). Cohen and colleagues (Botvinick et al., 2001; Miller & Cohen, 2002; O'Reilly, Braver, & Cohen, 1999) suggest that this facilitation is the route to successful performance during the Stroop task; the prefrontal cortex promotes the less automatic process of colour naming in order to overcome the more automatic process of word reading. Note that neither colour naming nor word reading is presumed to be carried out by the prefrontal cortex; rather, the prefrontal cortex directs what phenomenologically corresponds to attention to the weaker process. Similarly, the prefrontal cortex may help resolve the identity of an object shown from a noncanonical viewpoint by activating mental imagery associated with the object's hypothesized identity (Kosslyn, Thomson, & Alpert, 1997). During attempts at memory retrieval, the prefrontal cortex has been shown to activate neurons in the temporal lobe corresponding to the appropriate representations in the temporal cortex to help boost these to a higher level than competing representations (Tomita et al., 1999).

The last way that the prefrontal cortex may exert control is by inhibiting the problematic impulses and representations. A number of rodent studies have suggested that the capacity to override pre-existing associative impulses is dependent on the lateral orbital frontal cortex (Baxter, Parker, Lindner, Izquierdo, & Murray, 2000; Elliott, Dolan, & Frith, 2000; Schoenbaum, Chiba, & Gallagher, 1999, 2000). This area of the rodent brain overlaps with what in human imaging research is often called the ventrolateral or inferior prefrontal cortex (Ongur & Price, 2000).

Neuropsychological and imaging studies have shown that attempts to inhibit prepotent behavioural responses produced ventrolateral prefrontal activations (Cools, Clark, Owen, & Robbins, 2002; Garavan, Ross, & Stein, 1999; Iversen & Mishkin, 1970; Jonides, Smith, Marshuetz, Koeppe, & Reuter-Lorenz, 1998; Konishi et al., 1999; Leung et al., 2000; Levine, Freedman, Dawson, Black, & Stuff, 1999; Monchi, Petrides, Petre, Worsley, & Dagher, 2001). Three recent studies have extended this research into the domain of explicit attempts at emotional self-regulation (Beauregard, Levesque, & Bourgouin, 2001; Ochsner, Bunge, Gross, & Gabrieli, 2002; Small, Zatorre, Dagher, Evans, & Jones-Gotman, 2001), and each study found that the attempt to override a prepotent affective response was associated with ventrolateral prefrontal activations. For instance, Ochsner et al. presented participants with images pretested to produce negative affect. In one condition, participants merely attended to the images, whereas in a second condition, participants were asked to actively reframe or "reappraise" the meaning of the images so as to diminish the negative affect associated with them. This method of reappraisal has long been the subject of study in social psychological theories of emotion (Gross, 1999; Lazarus, 1992; Schachter & Singer, 1962), and evidence suggests that as the meaning of an event changes for an individual, so the affect changes. Whereas fear-related activations in the amygdala were prominent during the "attend" condition, these activations disappeared during the reappraisal trials. Moreover, in the reappraise condition, a strong negative correlation emerged between the amygdala and ventrolateral prefrontal cortex, suggesting that the latter was inhibiting the former. Also suggestive are two PET studies of bipolar patients during their manic phase. These studies revealed decreased ventrolateral prefrontal activity during decision making, suggesting that one reason these patients become increasingly impulsive during their manic phase is that the ventrolateral prefrontal cortex is temporarily unable to inhibit these impulses (Blumberg et al., 1999; Rubinsztein et al., 2001).

Self-regulation by way of placebos and hypnotic suggestion also implicates the ventrolateral prefrontal cortex. In a recent PET study of placebic analgesia (Lieberman et al., 2004b), patients with irritable bowel syndrome evidenced symptom-related decreases in anterior cingulate responses to painful stimulation. Anterior cingulate activity in response to pain is a remarkably good index of the affective distress given in self-reports (Rainville et al., 1997), and thus placebo analgesia would be expected to reduce anterior cingulate activity. It remains unclear how suggestion and expectation associated with placebos bring about this change. Lieberman et al. ran functional connectivity analyses and found the magnitude of anterior cingulate attenuation after taking placebo was well predicted by the magnitude of right ventrolateral prefrontal activations ($r = -.52$).

Whereas the preceding review of self-control relates effortful attempts at self-regulation with the ventrolateral prefrontal cortex, we have been led to hypothesize that there might also be automatic self-regulatory consequences of engaging the parts of the brain that typically promote self-control. In other words, in most of the previous studies, people were quite intentionally engaging in self-control, the success of which appears to be mediated by the ventrolateral prefrontal cortex. If the ventrolateral prefrontal cortex is capable of inhibiting unwanted impulses in the amygdala and elsewhere, perhaps the mere activation of the ventrolateral prefrontal cortex is sufficient to inhibit automatic affective impulses *even when the activating thoughts are not self-regulatory* (Hariri, Bookheimer, & Mazziotta, 2000; Lieberman, 2003; Lieberman, Hariri, Jarcho, & Bookheimer, 2002).

Contextual factors

Though social psychologists have long been interested in the effects of social and motivational factors on the deployment and efficacy of self-control resources (Baumeister, 1984; Fiske & Neuberg, 1990; Kruglanski & Freund, 1983; Tetlock, 1983), no work has been done within a social cognitive neuroscience framework assessing these interactions. Hopefully, work along these lines will be conducted in the near future.

Social perception

At times, social cognition has been almost synonymous with social perception. Understanding the personality, intentions, beliefs, and identity of others may be the most important form of perception humans engage in. Rhesus monkeys who are unable to appreciate where they stand in the dominance hierarchy, relative to others they interact with, are expelled from the group before they are old enough to fend for themselves (Suomi, in press). Decades of research in social cognition has detailed the processes by which these inferences are made, most often highlighting the common errors that result from these processes. Attribution and stereotyping processes both involve making inferences about the personality, attitudes, intentions, and moral status of others, with attribution focused on behaviour and stereotyping focused on group membership. Both of these areas have begun to be examined from a social cognitive neuroscience approach. In addition, this section will also review work on recognizing others that has emerged primarily from the cognitive neuroscience literature on face processing, as the identity of others is relevant to our production of attributions or access to stereotypes. Though the decoding of emotional expressions is another important domain of social perception, this area has received enough attention to warrant reviews of its own, and thus we direct the reader to them (Lane & Nadel, 2000).

Recognizing others

Neural correlates

Recognizing familiar others seems so basic that social psychologists have rarely ever considered how humans perform this task. Neuropsychological damage impairing face-recognition abilities provides us with dramatic examples of how complex and delicate this recognition process really is. Perhaps the strangest of social perception impairments is Capgras syndrome (also known as reduplicative amnesia). Capgras patients suffer from the delusion that emotionally close, familiar others have been replaced with exact duplicates. These patients admit that the impostors look and act in the same way as the people they replaced, yet despite this evidence, the belief persists. An extraordinary example of the beliefs of a Capgras patient can be found in a client–patient dialogue reprinted in Stuss (1991, pp. 71–73). Though the neural basis of Capgras syndrome has yet to be precisely characterized, research suggests that right hemisphere dysfunction (right orbitofrontal, cingulate, parietal, basal ganglia, and amygdala) is indicative of Capgras and other delusions of misidentification (Breen, Caine, Coltheart, Hendy, & Roberts, 2000; Edelstyn & Oyebode, 1998; Malloy et al., 1992; Papageorgiou et al., 2002).

Another striking disorder of face recognition is prosopagnosia. Prosopagnosics are impaired in their ability to interpret the elements of faces (eyes, ears, nose, and mouth) coherently, and as such are often incapable of recognizing familiar others by sight alone. However, prosopagnosics are not often impaired in their ability to recognize objects other than faces, which distinguishes them from individuals with other visual agnosias (Farah, 1996). Prosopagnosia results from damage to the occipitotemporal cortex, a fact which led some to speculate that this region may be selective for recognizing faces (Damasio et al., 1982, 1990; Farah, 1994; Meadows, 1974). Face recognition has now been extensively studied in normal populations, and is strongly associated with activity in the mid-fusiform gyrus, on the ventral surface of the brain near the juncture of the temporal and occipital lobes (fusiform face area [FFA]) (Kanwisher, McDermott, & Chun, 1997; see also McCarthy, Puce, Gore, & Allison, 1997; Puce et al., 1995). Recent research also suggests areas of the superior temporal sulcus may be face selective, attending to details of facial structure (e.g. Allison et al., 2000; Andrews et al., 2002; Haxby et al., 2000).

Neurocognitive processes

Although it has been traditionally accounted for by psychodynamic explanations, the discovery of Capgras syndrome resulting from neurological conditions has had implications for our understanding of normal face-recognition processes (Ellis & Lewis, 2001). This greater understanding has arisen from comparisons between Capgras patients and prosopagnosics. Ellis and Young (1990) suggested that prosopagnosia and the Capgras delusion are mirror images of each other. Proposagnosics, while unable to overtly recognize familiar others, often show signs of covert face-recognition abilities which Capgras patients lack, such as differential skin conductance responses (SCRs) to familiar faces (Ellis, Burton, Young, & Flude, 1997; Ellis, Lewis, Moselhy & Young, 2000; Hirstein & Ramachandran, 1997). Clearly, however, Capgras patients must still possess some overt face-recognition abilities: while denying its authenticity, they report that a familiar other's face *looks exactly like* their loved one's.

This differentiation led researchers to suggest that normal face-recognition processes include both overt and covert components. Processes of overt face recognition, as described above, are thought to take place in the fusiform gyrus. Covert face recognition includes both affective responses to familiar faces and behavioural or cognitive recognition as reflected in visual or semantic priming (Ellis et al., 2000). The affective response to familiar faces is associated with amygdala activity, particularly in the right hemisphere (Breen, Caine, & Coltheart, 2000; Ellis et al., 2000; Seeck et al., 1993). It may be this affective response to familiar faces that Capgras patients are missing, and that many prosopagnosics retain. Ellis and Lewis (2001) speculate that the delusion is thus driven by a lack of affective "glow", which James (1890) postulated was the basis of our sense of familiarity when encountering someone we know well.

Capgras patients, unlike prosopagnosics, are able to recognize faces by their intact ability to interpret the face as a whole, a process some deem critical to face recognition. Proponents of face recognition via holistic processing note that recognition of facial features is much more successful when encoded in the context of the whole face, rather than alone (Tanaka & Farah, 1993). Configural, or view-dependent, processing is often named either concurrently with or as an alternative to holistic processing (Diamond & Carey, 1986). Both were proposed to account for the inversion effect in face recognition first discovered by Yin (1969), wherein recognition of faces is disproportionately impaired when they are presented inverted (upside-down), in comparison to recognition impairments caused when other categories of objects are inverted (Farah, Tanaka, & Drain, 1995).

Evidence supporting the configural or holistic processing function of the FFA includes findings that experts with some category of nonface objects (such as birds or dogs) demonstrate both inversion effects for recognition of these objects and neural activation comparable to that seen in normal humans viewing faces (Diamond & Carey, 1986; Gauthier, Skudlarski, Gore, & Anderson, 2000; Tanaka & Curran, 2001). Although researchers have found, relative to upright faces, only a slight reduction of activity in the FFA for viewing inverted faces compared to objects, these results do not necessarily disconfirm this proposed functional explanation (Tong, Nakayama, Moscovitch, Weinrib, & Kanwisher, 2000; see also Kanwisher, Tong, & Nakayama, 1998). For example, Haxby et al. (Haxby, Ungerleider, Clark, Schouten, Hoffman, & Martin, 1999) suggest that, first, nearby regions involved in parts-based processing of objects are activated by inverted faces; after determining the object is indeed a face, information is shunted to the FFA for further analysis. This proposal was supported by greater activation of object-processing regions when viewing inverted faces relative to upright faces, and relatively later activation of the FFA when viewing inverted faces relative to upright faces.

Gauthier and her colleagues (Gauthier, Anderson, Tarr, Skudlarski, & Gore, 1997; Gauthier, Tarr, Anderson, Skudlarski, & Gore, 1999; Gauthier, Tarr, Moylan, Anderson, Skudlarski, & Gore, 2000) have proposed a counterargument to the domain-specific distinction between parts-based and configural or holistic processing. Her studies have suggested that the unique processes performed in the fusiform gyrus and surrounding regions may be better described as subordinate-level identification. The criticism of previous work supporting a mechanism—and region—selectively engaged in face recognition is that control stimuli in these experiments were not best suited to make such a determination (Gauthier & Tarr, 1997). Specifically, control stimuli in previous behavioural and fMRI studies were members of categories typically recognized at the *basic level* ("That's a radio"), whereas faces are typically recognized at the *subordinate level* ("That's John"). Compared to the basic level, participants recognizing objects at the subordinate level were shown to activate the same region of fusiform and inferotemporal cortex used for face recognition (defined independently for each subject) (Gauthier et al., 2000).

Face detection is yet another functional explanation for the activity seen in the FFA, whether construed broadly as responsiveness to a variety of face-like stimuli or strictly as conscious awareness of faces. Tong et al. (2000) suggested the former role on the basis of research showing FFA activation for a variety of face-like stimuli including human faces, schematic faces, cat faces, and caricatures. The latter functional explanation is suggested by recent research utilizing Rubin's face/vase illusion (Andrews, Schluppeck, Homfray, Matthews, & Blakemore, 2002; Hasson, Hendler, Bashat, & Malach, 2001). Rubin's face/vase illusion is an ambiguous stimulus, which viewers perceive as alternating between a face and a vase. Using an event-related design, Andrews et al. (2002) found that activity in the fusiform gyrus predicted participants' self-reported conscious awareness of perceiving a face in the illusion. They argue that this cortical area explicitly interprets the stimulus as a face, bringing it to conscious awareness, and this process is associated with fusiform activity.

Contextual factors

Although contextual factors have been only recently explored in this realm of research, there are several examples of their application to our understanding of face recognition. One such example is the contrast between the race or ethnicity of the viewer and that of the individual whose face is being recognized. A well-studied and robust phenomenon in the face-recognition literature, the own-race bias (ORB), is that same-race faces are recognized more accurately than other-race faces (also known as other-race effect or cross-race effect) (Malpass & Kravitz, 1969). Golby, Gabrieli, Chiao, & Eberhardt (2000) recently demonstrated that when regions of interest preferentially responsive to faces were individually defined, these regions (left fusiform, right parahippocampus, and hippocampus) were shown to be more reactive to same-race faces. Greater activation in these regions during encoding predicted more accurate recognition outside the scanner.

ORB is a concern in the legal system, as it has implications for eyewitness identification (Meissner & Brigham, 2001). Interestingly, the context of many eyewitness identification scenarios illuminates other factors for future study. For example, face-recognition accuracy is also diminished when weapons are present, because the weapon diverts the observer's attention from the face of the perpetrator ("weapons focus effect") (Kramer, Buckhout, & Eugenio, 1990; Loftus, Loftus, & Messo, 1987). Wojciulik, Kanwisher, & Driver (1998) found that attention (whether internally generated or elicited by factors such as stimulus quality and location) modulated activity in the FFA. Other related contextual factors, which remain to be studied, are the effects of extreme arousal, stress, and motivation on the neural processes of face recognition.

Although we may be suspicious of identifications of familiar others when the eyewitness is motivated to lie, the accuracy of eyewitness testimony is probably most extensively questioned when the perpetrator is unfamiliar to the eyewitness. The differing neural systems involved in recognition of familiar and unfamiliar faces is another prime illustration of the role contextual factors play in the process of face recognition (Leveroni, Seidenberg, Mayer, Mead, Binder, & Rao, 2000). Leveroni et al. found that recognition of famous faces activated additional temporofrontal regions including the superior, middle, and inferior prefrontal areas and the lateral surface of the middle temporal gyrus. They speculate that this reflects the retrieval of additional semantic information associated with the familiar individual's personal identity (the person-identity system; see also Haxby, Hoffman, & Gobbini, 2002; Reinkemeier, Markowitsch, Rausch, & Kessler, 1997).

Attribution

Attributions are a hallmark of the unique human capacity for appreciating the intentions, beliefs, desires, and enduring psychological traits of others. When students raise their hand in class, the teacher easily infers the students' desire to speak. When a student continuously speaks loudly in a library, the librarian has no trouble inferring that this person has a loud disposition, is disrespectful, or both. Social psychological theories have delineated the appropriate rules for inferring mental states and traits from observed behaviours (Jones & Davis, 1965; Kelley, 1967). For instance, it is more appropriate to infer that an enduring disposition was guiding a person's behaviour when the behaviour is counternormative (such as a loud student in the library). To the extent that a behaviour was provoked by situational norms, it is impossible to disentangle the contributions of the norm and a potential internal disposition (for example, a quiet student in the library).

We have introduced most of the previous sections with a neuropsychological condition that produces impaired functioning in the relevant area of social cognition. In the case of attribution, both normals and neurologically affected patients have difficulty, but in very different ways. Autism is a developmental disorder associated with a reduced capacity to infer the mental states of others and is reviewed at length elsewhere in this volume (Chapters 6 and 8). Healthy adults, on the other hand, make the error of too often assuming that the behaviour of others is the product of corresponding dispositions (Gilbert & Malone, 1995; Jones & Davis, 1965). Icheiser (1943) first observed that "Instead of saying, for instance, that individual X acted in a certain way because he was in a certain situation, we are prone to believe that he behaved in a certain way because he possessed certain personal qualities" (p. 152). Jones and Davis (1965) first provided evidence for this phenomenon when subjects indicated that a target's essay indicated the target's true beliefs even when subjects were informed that the target had been forced to espouse certain beliefs in the essay. This phenomenon, the *correspondence bias* (also called the *fundamental attribution error*; Ross, 1977), occurs when the disposition corresponding to a behaviour is inferred from the behaviour even when a clear situational explanation for the behaviour is present.

It is fair to say, then, that if autistics have an *under*developed capacity for inferring the mental states of others as causing behaviour, healthy adults have an *over*developed capacity for inferring these mental states. Though the bias is obvious in autistics, it may be less immediately debilitating in adults (Funder, 1987; Swann, 1984). Nevertheless, social psychologists have argued that the correspondence bias leads us to hold others personally responsible when they are mere victims of circumstance. The scale of this problem is global, as nations in long-standing disputes see themselves as reacting to the provocations of the other country while assuming the other nations's actions are driven by the immoral character of its leaders (Griffin & Ross, 1991). Because of the treatment given to attributional difficulties in autistics in other parts of this volume, we will focus primarily on the neural bases of normal attributional processes and why these "normal" processes produce systematically biased attributions.

Neural correlates

The tendency for normal individuals to overattribute behaviour to the internal dispositions of the actor was clearly demonstrated by Heider and Simmel (1944). They showed subjects short videoclips of "fighting triangles" and circles moving around in a coordinated fashion. Though it is immediately obvious upon a moment's reflection that these shapes have no minds at all, it is irresistible to see and describe the movement of the shapes in terms of goals, beliefs, and personality. It is appropriate then, that, modern versions of these clips have been used in many studies to identify a common set of neural regions associated with social perception. Two laboratories (Castelli, Frith, Happe, & Frith, 2002; Schultz et al., 2003) have each found activations in the bilateral superior temporal sulcus, right temporal pole and amygdala, fusiform gyrus, and medial prefrontal cortex in conjunction with watching these videoclips. Iacoboni et al. (2004) also found activation in each of these areas when participants watched videoclips of actual people having different kinds of social interactions.

Neurocognitive processes

Gilbert's sequential operations model (1989; see also Trope, 1986) suggests that the attribution process can be decomposed into three stages that occur in sequence: behavioural categorization, dispositional characterization, and correction. According to this model, observed behaviour is initially identified as some specific kind of behaviour ("He is talking in a loud voice in the library"), followed by an inference that this behaviour was caused by an internal disposition ("He is a loud person in general"). In some cases, the dispositional inference will be subsequently corrected to take account of situational factors that could have provoked the behaviour. ("He is talking to someone who is hard of hearing. Maybe he is not as dispositionally loud as I first thought.") Critical to this model, the correction stage is presumed to require greater cognitive and motivational resources than the first two stages and will fail if those resources are not available. In other words, it takes mental effort and a desire for accuracy before mitigating situational factors are taken into account. Gilbert suggested that because these resources are often absent in daily life, people would be expected to show the correspondence bias. In a series of studies, Gilbert, Pelham, and Krull (1988) found that when individuals are placed under cognitive load the correspondence bias is enhanced, suggesting: (1) the first two stages of the attribution process are automatic enough to occur while still under cognitive load; (2) the correction stage that incorporates situational factors does not occur under cognitive load.

In a social cognitive neuroscience model of the attribution process (Lieberman, Gaunt, Gilbert, & Trope, 2002), we have suggested that this correction stage depends on the lateral prefrontal cortex, as it is associated with effortful mental processing and the use of propositional logic (Bunge, Hazeltine, Scanlon, Rosen, & Gabrieli, 2002) that mental correction would require. Recent fMRI evidence also suggests that frontal poles may be involved in the correction process (Christoff & Gabrieli, 2000; Kroger et al., 2002). It is not surprising that fMRI studies of attribution have not observed lateral prefrontal activations, because in these studies there was no need for attributional correction and no situational factors relevant to the attributions being made. Presumably, future studies will examine this correction process more directly.

Lieberman et al. (2002) theorized that the lateral and ventral temporal cortex, whose representations are bidirectionally linked in an associative network (Rolls, 1999; Suzuki, Saleem, & Tanaka, 2000), contributes directly to the tendency to conflate behaviours with the corresponding dispositions. These regions of the temporal lobe, from the fusiform gyrus posteriorly to the temporal pole anteriorly, are involved in object identity, categorization, and linking semantic attributes to an object. As described in the previous section, prosopagnosics with fusiform gyrus damage have difficulty linking facial perceptual information to a person's identity. Alternatively, patients with the temporal variant of frontotemporal dementia (FTD_T; also called semantic dementia) have difficulty retrieving semantic facts about people (Hodges & Graham, 1998). FTD_T is thought to begin by damaging the temporal poles and then slowly work back through the lateral sections of the temporal lobe (Garrard & Hodges, 2000; Mummery, Patterson, Hodges, & Wise, 2000).

The superior temporal sulcus (and gyrus) across numerous studies has been associated with behavioural identification (Alison, Puce, & McCarthy, 2000; Haxby, Hoffman, & Gobbini, 2000), particularly for behaviours that *could* be described as intentional. For instance, Perrett, Jellema, Frigerio, and Burt

(2001) have shown that viewing the same intention enacted different ways activates the same neurons in the primate superior temporal sulcus. However, behaviours that are not seen as intentional (such as falling down) do not activate this region. Some have suggested that this area is central to extracting the possible intentions from perceived biological motion (Gallagher & Frith, 2003); however, the activation of this area in the studies with Heider and Simmel's (1944) "fighting triangles" suggests a more general role in identifying intentions from behaviour. When the triangles in these videos appear to be fighting, there is little in common visually with the biological motion one might observe in an actual fight. It is, however, possible that individuals imagine actual human behaviour while watching these clips and activate the superior temporal sulcus in a top-down, rather than bottom-up, manner.

Because the lateral temporal cortex contains more distributed representations than regions such as the medial temporal cortex and prefrontal cortex (O'Reilly, Braver, & Cohen, 1999), its representations are more like statistical generalizations than distinct symbolic entities (McClelland, McNaughton, & O'Reilly, 1995; O'Reilly & Norman, 2003) and consequently are associatively, rather than propositionally, linked (Holyoak & Hummel, 2000; Sloman, 1996; Smith & DeCoster, 2000). This arrangement may promote the blurring between an actor's current behaviour and the actor's dispositional propensity to that kind of behaviour. In essence, this blurring between action and actor is a neural account of the correspondence bias.

Contextual factors

Social psychologists have long known that various contextual factors can change the attribution process. For instance, people are far more likely to consider the situational antecedents of their own negative behaviour than those of the negative behaviour of others (Dunning, 2003; Ross & Sicoly, 1979). This *self-serving bias* is so named because the self is given the benefit of the doubt, but others are not. The self-serving bias may promote *positive illusions* (Taylor & Brown, 1988) in which views of the self in various domains are aggrandized. Recently, Blackwood et al. (2003) used a vignette-based attribution methodology in an fMRI study to assess the neural correlates of the self-serving bias in attribution. In their study, bilateral basal ganglia activations were associated with this bias. This finding fits well with previous work suggesting the basal ganglia's involvement in automatic positive affect (Depue & Collins, 1999; Knutson, Adams, Hong, & Hommer, 2001; Lieberman, 2000) and automatic self-knowledge processes (Lieberman, Jarcho, & Satpute, 2004c).

People show evidence of a positive motivational bias in drawing inferences about others if those others are part of the observers' in-group. In one study (Pettigrew, 1979), Pakistani and Indian subjects observed either a Pakistani or an Indian target engage in positive or negative behaviour. Participants inferred that the negative behaviour of a racial out-group member was more indicative of their internal dispositions than the same behaviour enacted by a member of their racial in-group. This study suggests that the self-serving bias extends beyond the corporeal self to others that the self shares group membership with or empathizes with.

Empathy may then be considered a key contextual factor moderating attribution processes. As reported above, Iacoboni et al. (2004) found similar activations as the studies that have adapted Heider and Simmel's (1944) "fighting triangles" paradigm. In addition to these shared activations, Iacoboni et al. also found substantial activation in the precuneus. Recall that the main difference between Iacoboni et al. and the other studies was that Iacoboni et al. had participants watch videoclips of real people interacting. Perhaps these videoclips allowed people to identify or empathize with the actors, whereas identification with triangles is unlikely despite the ability of participants to draw inferences about those triangles.

Empathy has just begun to be studied within cognitive neuroscience, but it has a long history within philosophy and social psychology as a critical factor in producing prosocial behaviour and cognition (Batson, 1991; Buber, 1937). Farrow et al. (2001) recently found that both an empathy task and forgiveness judgements, which would seem to require empathy, activated the precuneus whereas other social judgements did not. Earlier, in the section on self-awareness, we described social psychological theories (Mead, 1934) that proposed that each self comes into existence as one takes the perspective of others on oneself. From this view, the self is ontologically dependent on other people treating us as if we have a self and our ability to appreciate that they have this view. The precuneus, associated with perspective taking, a prerequisite for empathy, has been found to be activated in the majority of self-knowledge studies. Here, in this section, work by Iacoboni et al. (2004) and Farrow et al. suggests that this same process may work in reverse such that empathy projects the self onto others, allowing more benevolent attributions about the intentions behind their behaviour.

While self and social perception are not the same thing, they are deeply intertwined. Ultimately, neither can be understood in the absence of the other. Social cognitive neuroscience research has not yet produced a programme of research in which the two are systematically manipulated with respect to each other. Social psychologists, following the tradition of Mead, have created numerous experimental paradigms that activate different social reference points while subjects are making self-judgements. For instance, Baldwin and Holmes (1987) found that subjects produced different self-judgements after being prompted to think about their friends or a family member. Duval and Wicklund (1973) found that participants made different self-judgements while sitting in front of a mirror, as this served as a reminder of the self that is seen by others. Seen from this vantage point, participants tended to evaluate their own behaviour the way a typical observer would (see also Storms, 1973). It is as yet unknown how the neural processes of self-judgement might differ as a result of these activated social referents.

Similarly, it is unknown how the attributions made about others might differ neurally as a function of relationship between the target and the participant.

Before leaving the section on attribution, it is important to briefly mention neuroimaging research on moral attributions (for reviews, see Greene & Haidt, 2002; Moll, Oliveira-Souza, & Eslinger, 2003), which provides another example of how contextual factors can modify the neural structures recruited in a task. For many years, attribution theorists assumed that the rules of logical inference applied to all domains of dispositional inference. Reeder (1993) has demonstrated that there are domain-specific changes in the rules that are applied. For instance, in a skill domain, only successes are construed as diagnostic of ability because ability is considered to be a necessary condition for successful performances, whereas failure might be the result of numerous situational factors. On the other hand, in moral domains, only failures are diagnostic—knowing that someone has lied once tells us more about their moral character than knowing that they told the truth once. The moral domain also differs from other dispositional domains in the corrections made for situational provocations (Reeder et al., 2002). Knowing that Jack tripped Jill, but only did it because he was paid $100, will lead people to infer that Jack is not as dispositionally aggressive as someone who enacted the same behaviour without financial inducement. However, Jack will be seen as equally immoral in both cases.

As with the behavioural work differentiating moral attributions from other kinds of dispositional attributions, fMRI studies by Moll and colleagues suggest that moral attributions are neurally distinct from other dispositional attributions. In their work, moral attributions activate much of the same network described above, including the superior temporal sulcus, medial prefrontal cortex, and amygdala (Moll, Oliveira-Souza, & Eslinger, 2003), but in several studies moral attributions also activated regions in orbitofrontal cortex (de Oliveira & Moll, 2000; Moll, Oliveira-Souza, Bramati, & Grafman, 2002a; Moll et al., 2002b). Additionally, in these studies, the orbitofrontal cortex exhibited strong functional connectivity with other attributional regions, suggesting a possible modulation of activity in these other regions by the orbitofrontal cortex.

Stereotyping

Humans use category membership to guide behaviour in almost every aspect of life. Learning to use a rental car takes little effort because the assumptions we make about cars in general largely hold true for any rental car. Stereotypes about people in groups are similar to other forms of categorization in many ways; for instance, they increase the efficiency with which we process information about members of those groups (Macrae, Milne, & Bodenhausen, 1994). Social group-based stereotyping is, however, different from object categorization in important ways. Stereotypes often involve negative generalizations about the intelligence, ability, and moral character of group members. That is to say, stereotypes of race, gender, age, and sexual orientation typically involve an affective component that is absent in our stereotypes of paper clips and light bulbs. Moreover, unlike light bulbs, humans can react to being stereotyped. Stigmatized groups often fight publicly against the stereotypes applied to them. Unfortunately, the self-awareness that stigmatized group members have of their group's stereotype can actually lead to self-fulfilling prophecies in which the individuals end up confirming stereotypes that were not originally true (Davies, Spencer, Quinn, & Gerhardstein, 2002; Steele & Aronson, 1995). Additionally, in a liberal society, people are aware that most disapprove of these negative social generalizations, and thus people often will not admit their prejudices publicly, even though, cognitively and behaviourally, there is ample evidence of their continued existence. Thus, a great deal of effort may go into self-regulating behaviour that could be perceived as prejudiced. Finally, some stereotypes appear to be so pervasive that people with otherwise egalitarian views may still show evidence of implicit stereotyping even though these beliefs are not held consciously. Implicit stereotyping can be just as pernicious as explicit stereotyping (Word, Zanna, & Cooper, 1974), even more so in some ways, as it may go unchecked.

Though stereotyping processes have begun to be studied with the techniques of cognitive neuroscience, the work thus far has been primarily at the level of brain mapping, in determining the regions of interest that will be probed in later experiments. Here we briefly summarize the results of these studies. A number of studies have shown that visual presentations of black faces activate the amygdala to a greater degree than the presentation of white faces (Cunningham, 2001; Hart et al., 2000; Lieberman, Hariri, Jarcho, Eisenberger, & Bookheimer, 2004a; Phelps et al., 2000). Phelps et al. found that the magnitude and extent of amygdala activity correlated with a behavioural measure of implicit stereotypes obtained outside the scanner. Given that implicit stereotypes are thought to be largely the product of repetitious negative presentations of stigmatized groups in schools, media, and elsewhere (Banaji & Greenwald, 1994), it has been suggested that both blacks and whites have negative implicit stereotypes of blacks. Lieberman et al. ran both white ($n=11$) and black ($n=8$) participants to examine this hypothesis and found that both whites and blacks produced more amygdala activity to black faces than to white faces. Milne and Grafman (1999) tested patients with lesions in the ventromedial prefrontal cortex and found no evidence of implicit gender stereotypes. This finding parallels the self-schema work (Lieberman et al., 2004c) described above, in which the ventromedial prefrontal cortex was also activated, especially given that self-schemas could easily be described as implicit self-stereotypes. Amodio, Harmon-Jones, Devine, Curtin, Hartley, & Covert (2004) found increased anterior cingulate activation when subjects performed a task designed to make participants feel self-conscious about using their stereotypes. Lastly, Richeson & Shelton (in press) have found that interracial interactions deplete controlled processing resources, leading to poorer performance on a subsequent controlled processing task. They have followed this study up (Richeson et al., 2003) with an fMRI study suggesting that prefrontal activity involved in self-regulating one's own prejudicial responses may mediate the later controlled processing depletion. This fits with the work by Lieberman et al. (2004a) that found that the degree of amygdala suppression is highly correlated with prefrontal activity.

Conclusion

The purpose of this chapter was twofold. First, we wanted to review human research in the social cognitive neuroscience of self-processing and social perception. In just the past few years, there has been a rapid increase in research in these areas, and we suspect that in a few years it will be no more possible to review the two topics together comprehensively than it is to review vision and memory together. We reviewed them together here in the hope of raising awareness of some of the ways that the two areas are linked. Without social perception, it is possible there might not be self-processing. Social perception and the ability to take the perspective of others are potentially critical not only to the inception of the self, but also to the way the self is constructed and maintained at different moments in time. There is a temptation to think of the self as an object with stable attributes—indeed, this is a temptation not just for scientists but for all people who are attached to their sense of self and independence. However, the self appears to be at least partly constructed and reconstructed over time as a function of situational and interpersonal constraints. A complete understanding of the neural bases of self-processes must necessarily take account of these social factors. Similarly, social perception is quite different depending on whether perceivers put themselves in the shoes of the perceived. Unlike some types of perception, social perception is largely motivational. Social stimuli are often ambiguous and are often interpreted in accordance with our self-serving biases. Consequently, neither the study of the self nor the study of social perception can proceed for too long without consideration of the other.

The second purpose of this chapter was to describe three different kinds of questions that social psychologists can ask by the methods of cognitive neuroscience. The first question, that of brain mapping, is one for which social psychologists might possess some scepticism. What is the value of knowing where in the brain a social psychological process lives? We have suggested that this answer has value, but that its value is as a means rather than an end. Knowing where a phenomenon is allows us to ask the other questions about cognitive operations, mediators, and moderators. Social psychologists are deeply interested in the questions of how social psychological processes work (that is, the cognitive and affective characteristics) and how these processes interact with other processes and contextual factors (that is, mediators and moderators). To the extent that cognitive and behavioural testing can answer these questions, neuroscience is unneeded. It would be foolish to think that lots of money needs to be spent on expensive technology just to confirm what we already know is true from behavioural work that has greater statistical power and is frequently more tightly controlled. But there are questions that remain despite our best efforts with cognitive and behavioural measures. Here the methods of cognitive neuroscience may add an important piece to the puzzle. We cannot imagine that the three types of questions we have put forward here are the only kinds that social cognitive neuroscientists will ask in the coming years. Rather, we hope they are a good starting point for thinking broadly about why social psychologists should care about the brain.

Acknowledgements

This work was supported in part by a National Science Foundation grant (BCS-0074562) and a McDonnell-Pew grant (JSMF 99-25 CN-QUA.05) to Matthew Lieberman, and a National Science Foundation graduate fellowship to Jennifer Pfeifer.

References

Adolphs, R. (1999). Social cognition and the human brain. *Trends in Cognitive Sciences, 3*, 469–479.

Allen, S. W., & Brooks, L. R. (1991). Specializing the operation of an explicit rule. *Journal of Experimental Psychology: General, 120*, 3–19.

Allison, T., Puce, A., & McCarthy, G. (2000). Social perception from visual cues: Role of the STS region. *Trends in Cognitive Sciences, 4*, 267–278.

Allport, G. W. (1955). *Becoming: Basic considerations for a psychology of personality.* New Haven, CT: Yale University Press.

Amodio, D. M., Harmon-Jones, E., Devine, P. G., Curtin, J. J., Hartley, S. L., & Covert, A. E. (2004). Neural signals for the detection of unintentional race bias. *Psychological Science, 15*, 88–93.

Baldwin, M. W., & Holmes, J. G. (1987). Salient private audiences and awareness of the self. *Journal of Personality and Social Psychology, 52*, 1087–1098.

Banaji, M. R., & Greenwald, A. G. (1994). Implicit stereotyping and prejudice. In M. P. Zanna & J. M. Olson (Eds.), *The psychology of prejudice: The Ontario symposium* (Vol. 7, pp. 55–76). Hillsdale, NJ: Lawrence Erlbaum Associates, Inc.

Batson, C. D. (1991). *The altruism question: Toward a social-psychological answer.* Hillsdale, NJ: Lawrence Erlbaum Associates, Inc.

Baumeister, R. F. (1984). Choking under pressure: Self-consciousness and paradoxical effects of incentives on skillful performance. *Journal of Personality and Social Psychology, 46*, 610–620.

Baumeister, R. F. (1998). The self. In D. T. Gilbert, S. T. Fiske & G. Lindzey (Eds.), *The handbook of social psychology* (pp. 680–740). Boston: McGraw-Hill.

Baxter, M. G., Parker, A., Lindner, C. C., Izquierdo, A. D., & Murray, E. A. (2000). Control of response selection by reinforcer value requires interaction of amygdala and orbital prefrontal cortex. *Journal of Neuroscience, 20*, 4311–4319.

Beauregard, M., Levesque, J., & Bourgouin, P. (2001). Neural correlates of conscious self-regulation of emotion. *Journal of Neuroscience, 21,* 6993–7000.
Beck, D. M., Rees, D. M., Frith, C. D., & Lavie, N. (2001). Neural correlates of change detection and change blindness. *Nature Neuroscience, 4,* 645–650.
Bem, D. J. (1972). Self-perception theory. In L. Berkowitz (Ed.), *Advances in experimental social psychology* (pp. 1–62). New York: Academic Press.
Bem, D. J., & McConnell, H. K. (1970). Testing the self-perception explanation of dissonance phenomena: On the salience of premanipulated attitudes. *Journal of Personality and Social Psychology, 14,* 23–31.
Blackwood, N. J., Bentall, R. P., Ffytche, D. H., Simmons, A., & Murray, R. M. (2003). Self-responsibility and the self-serving bias: An fMRI investigation of causal attributions. *NeuroImage, 20,* 1076–1085.
Blumberg, H. P., Stern, E., Ricketts, S., Martinez, D., de Asis, J., White, T., et al. (1999). Rostral and orbital prefrontal cortex dysfunction in the manic state of bipolar disorder. *American Journal of Psychiatry, 156,* 1986–1988.
Botvinick, M. M., Braver, T. D., Barch, D. M., Carter, C. S., & Cohen, J. D. (2001). Conflict monitoring and cognitive control. *Psychological Review, 108,* 624–652.
Breen, N., Caine, D., & Coltheart, M. (2000). Models of face recognition and delusional misidentification: A critical review. *Cognitive Neuropsychology.* Special Issue: *The cognitive neuroscience of face processing, 17,* 55–71.
Breen, N., Caine, D., Coltheart, M., Hendy, J., & Roberts, C. (2000). Towards an understanding of delusions of misidentification: Four case studies. *Mind and Language.* Special Issue: *Pathologies of belief, 15,* 74–110.
Buber, M. (1937). *I and thou.* New York: Scribners & Sons.
Bunge, S. A., Hazeltine, E., Scanlon, M. D., Rosen, A. C., & Gabrieli, D. E. (2002). Dissociable contributions of prefrontal and parietal cortices to response selection. *NeuroImage, 17,* 1562–1571.
Cabeza, R., & Nyberg, L. (2000). Imaging cognition. II. An empirical review of 275 PET and fMRI studies. *Journal of Cognitive Neuroscience, 12,* 1–47.
Cacioppo, J. T., Berntson, G. G., Adolphs, R., Carter, C. S., Davidson, R. J., McClinton, M., et al. (2002). *Foundations in social neuroscience.* Cambridge, MA: MIT Press.
Cahill, L., & McGaugh, L. (1998). Mechanisms of emotional arousal and lasting declarative memory. *Trends in Neuroscience, 21,* 294–299.
Carter, C. S., Braver, T. S., Barch, D. M., Botvinick, M. M., Noll, D., & Cohen, J. D. (1998). Anterior cingulate cortex, error detection, and the online monitoring of performance. *Science, 280,* 747–749.
Carter, C. S., MacDonald, A. W., Botvinick, M. M., Ross, L. L., Stenger, V. A., Noll, D., et al. (2000). Parsing executive processes: Strategic vs. evaluative functions of the anterior cingulate cortex. *Proceedings of the National Academy of Sciences of the USA, 97,* 1944–1948.
Carver, C. S., & Scheier, M. F. (1981). *Attention and self-regulation: A control theory approach to human behavior.* New York: Springer-Verlag.
Castelli, F., Frith, C. D., Happe, F., & Frith, U. (2002). Autism, Asperger syndrome and brain mechanisms for the attribution of mental states to animated shapes. *Brain, 125,* 1839–1849.
Chaminade, T., & Decety, J. (2002). Leader or follower? Involvement of the inferior parietal lobule in agency. *Neuroreport, 13,* 1975–1978.
Christoff, K., & Gabrieli, D. E. (2000). The frontopolar cortex and human cognition:

Evidence for a rostrocaudal hierarchical organization within the human prefrontal cortex. *Psychobiology, 28*, 168–186.

Cools, R., Clark, L., Owen, A. M., & Robbins, T. W. (2002). Defining the neural mechanisms of probabilistic reversal learning using event-related functional magnetic resonance imaging. *Journal of Neuroscience, 22*, 4563–4567.

Craik, F. I. M., Moroz, T. M., Moscovitch, M., Stuss, D. T., Winocur, G., Tulving, E., et al. (1999). In search of the self: A positron emission tomography study. *Psychological Science, 10*, 26–34.

Cunningham, W. A., Johnson, M. K., Gatenby, J. C., Gore, J. C., & Banaji, M. R. (2001). *An fMRI study on the conscious and unconscious evaluations of social groups.* Paper presented at the UCLA Conference on Social Cognitive Neuroscience, Los Angeles, CA.

Damasio, A. R. (1994). *Descartes' error: Emotion, reason, and the human brain.* New York: Putnam.

Damasio, A. R., Tranel, D., & Damasio, H. (1990). Face agnosia and the neural substrates of memory. *Annual Review of Neuroscience, 13*, 89–109.

Davies, P. G., Spencer, S. J., Quinn, D. M., & Gerhardstein, R. (2002). Consuming images: How television commercials that elicit stereotype threat can restrain women academically and professionally. *Personality and Social Psychology Bulletin, 28*, 1615–1628.

Deacon, T. W. (1997). *The symbolic species: The co-evolution of language and the brain.* New York: Norton.

de Oliveira-Souza, R., & Moll, J. (2000). The moral brain: A functional MRI study of moral judgement. *Neurology, 54* (7 Suppl 3), A104.

Depue, R. A., & Collins, P. F. (1999). Neurobiology of the structure of personality: Dopamine, facilitation of incentive motivation, and extraversion. *Behavioral and Brain Sciences, 22*, 491–569.

Dewey, J. (1910). *How we think.* Boston: D. C. Heath.

Diamond, R., & Carey, S. (1986). Why faces are and are not special: An effect of expertise. *Journal of Experimental Psychology: General, 115*, 107–117.

Dunning, D. (2003). The zealous self-affirmer: How and why the self lurks so pervasively behind social judgement. In S. Spencer & S. Fein (Eds.), *Motivated social cognition: The 9th Ontario symposium on social cognition* (pp. 45–72). Hillsdale, NJ: Lawrence Erlbaum Associates, Inc.

Duval, S., & Wicklund, R. A. (1973). Effects of objective self-awareness on attribution of causality. *Journal of Experimental Social Psychology, 9*, 17–31.

Dweck, C. S. (1999). *Self-theories: Their role in motivation, personality, and development.* Bristol, PA: Taylor & Francis.

Ebbinghaus, H. (1885/1964). *Memory: A contribution to experimental psychology.* New York: Dover.

Edelstyn, N. M. J., & Oyebode, F. (1999). A review of the phenomenology and cognitive neuropsychological origins of the Capgras syndrome. *International Journal of Geriatric Psychiatry, 14*, 48–59.

Eisenberger, N. I., Satpute, A. B., & Lieberman, M. D. (2003). Self-awareness of arousal states and the anterior cingulate cortex: An fMRI study of personality. *Journal of Cognitive Neuroscience, 15*, s64.

Elliott, R., Dolan, R. J., & Frith, C. D. (2000). Dissociable functions in the medial and lateral orbitofrontal cortex: Evidence from human neuroimaging studies. *Cerebral Cortex, 10*, 308–317.

Ellis, A. W., Burton, A. M., Young, A., & Flude, B. M. (1997). Repetition priming between parts and wholes: Tests of a computational model of familiar face recognition. *British Journal of Psychology, 88*, 579–608.
Ellis, H. D., & Lewis, M. B. (2001). Capgras delusion: A window on face recognition. *Trends in Cognitive Sciences, 5*, 149–156.
Ellis, H. D., Lewis, M. B., Moselhy, H. F., & Young, A. W. (2000). Automatic without autonomic responses to familiar faces: Differential components of covert face recognition in a case of Capgras delusion. *Cognitive Neuropsychiatry, 5*, 255–269.
Ellis, H. D., & Young, A. W. (1990). Accounting for delusional misidentifications. *British Journal of Psychiatry, 157*, 239–248.
Farah, M. J. (1993). Dissociated overt and covert recognition as an emergent property of a lesioned neural network. *Psychological Review, 100*, 571–588.
Farah, M. J. (1994). Neuropsychological inference with an interactive brain: A critique of the "locality" assumption. *Behavioral and Brain Sciences, 17*, 43–104.
Farah, M. J. (1996). Is face recognition "special"? Evidence from neuropsychology. *Behavioural Brain Research, 76*(1–2), 181–189.
Farah, M. J., Wilson, K. D., Drain, H. M., & Tanaka, J. R. (1995). The inverted face inversion effect in prosopagnosia: Evidence for mandatory, face-specific perceptual mechanisms. *Vision Research, 35*, 2089–2093.
Farrer, C., & Frith, C. D. (2002). Experiencing oneself vs another person as being the cause of an action: The neural correlates of the experience of agency. *NeuroImage, 15*, 596–603.
Farrow, T. F., Zheng, Y., Wilkinson, I. D., Spence, S. A., Deakin, J. F., Tarrier, N., et al. (2001). Investigating the functional anatomy of empathy and forgiveness. *Neuroreport, 12*, 2433–2438.
Fink, G. R., Markowitsch, H. J., Reinkemeier, M., Bruckbauer, T., Kessler, J., & Heiss, W. (1996). Cerebral representation of one's own past: Neural networks involved in autobiographical memory. *Journal of Neuroscience, 16*, 4275–4282.
Fiske, S. T., & Neuberg, S. L. (1990). A continuum of impression formation, from category-based to individuating processes: Influences of information and motivation on attention and interpretation. In M. P. Zanna (Ed.), *Advances in experimental social psychology* (Vol. 23, pp. 1–74). New York: Academic Press.
Fletcher, P. C., Frith, C. D., Baker, S. C., Shallice, T., Frackowiak, R. S., & Dolan, R. J. (1995). The mind's eye—precuneus activation in memory-related imagery. *NeuroImage, 2*, 195–200.
Fredrickson, B. L. (2000). Extracting meaning from past affective experiences: The importance of peaks, ends, and specific emotions. *Cognition and Emotion, 14*, 577–606.
Funder, D. C. (1987). Errors and mistakes: Evaluating the accuracy of social judgement. *Psychological Bulletin, 101*, 75–90.
Gallagher, H. L., & Frith, C. D. (2003). Functional imaging of "theory of mind". *Trends in Cognitive Sciences, 7*, 77–83.
Garavan, H., Ross, T. J., & Stein, E. A. (1999). Right hemispheric dominance of inhibitory control: An event-related functional MRI study. *Proceedings of the National Academy of Sciences of the USA, 96*, 8301–8306.
Garrard, P., & Hodges, J. R. (2000). Semantic dementia: Clinical, radiological and pathological perspectives. *Journal of Neurology, 247*, 409–422.
Gauthier, I., Skudlarski, P., Gore, J. C., & Anderson, A. (2000). Expertise for cars

and birds recruit brain areas involved in face recognition. *Nature Neuroscience, 3*, 191–197.

Gauthier, I., & Tarr, M. J. (1997). Becoming a "greeble" expert: Exploring mechanisms for face recognition. *Vision Research, 37*, 1673–1682.

Gauthier, I., Tarr, M. J., Anderson, A. W., Skudlarski, P., & Gore, J. C. (1999). Activation of the middle fusiform "face area" increases with expertise in recognizing novel objects. *Nature Neuroscience, 2*, 568–573.

Gauthier, I., Tarr, M. J., Moylan, J., Anderson, A. W., Skudlarski, P., & Gore, J. C. (2000). Does visual subordinate-level categorisation engage the functionally defined fusiform face area? *Cognitive Neuropsychology.* Special Issue: *The cognitive neuroscience of face processing, 17*, 143–163.

Gilbert, D. T. (1989). Thinking lightly about others: Automatic components of the social inference process. In J. S. Uleman & J. A. Bargh (Eds.), *Unintended thought* (pp. 189–211). New York: Guilford Press.

Gilbert, D. T., & Malone, P. S. (1995). The correspondence bias. *Psychological Bulletin, 117*, 21–38.

Gilbert, D. T., Pelham, B. W., & Krull, D. S. (1988). On cognitive busyness: When person perceivers meet persons perceived. *Journal of Personality and Social Psychology, 54*, 733–740.

Gilbert, D. T., & Wilson, T. D. (2000). Miswanting: Some problems in the forecasting of future affective states. In J. Forgas (Ed.), *Feeling and thinking: The role of affect in social cognition* (pp. 178–197). Cambridge: Cambridge University Press.

Golby, A. J., Gabrieli, J. D. E., Chiao, J. Y., & Eberhardt, J. L. (2001). Differential responses in the fusiform region to same-race and other-race faces. *Nature Neuroscience, 4*, 845–850.

Goldman-Rakic, P. S. (1988). Topography of cognition: Parallel distributed networks in primate association cortex. *Annual Review of Neuroscience, 11*, 137–156.

Greene, J., & Haidt, J. (2002). How (and where) does moral judgement work? *Trends in Cognitive Sciences, 6*, 517–523.

Griffin, D. W., & Ross, L. (1991). Subject construal, social inference, and human misunderstanding. In M. P. Zanna (Ed.), *Advances in experimental social psychology* (Vol. 24, pp. 319–359). San Diego, CA: Academic Press.

Gross, J. J. (1999). Emotion regulation: Past, present, and future. *Cognition and Emotion, 13*, 551–573.

Hariri, A. R., Bookheimer, S. Y., & Mazziotta, J. C. (2000). Modulating emotional response: Effects of a neocortical network on the limbic system. *Neuroreport, 11*, 43–48.

Hart, A. J., Whalen, P. J., Shin, L. M., McInerney, S. C., Fischer, H., & Rauch, S. L. (2000). Differential response in the human amygdala to racial out-group vs in-group face stimuli. *Neuroreport, 11*, 2351–2355.

Hasson, U., Hendler, T., Bashat, D. B., & Malach, R. (2001). Vase or face? A neural correlates of shape-selective grouping processes in the human brain. *Journal of Cognitive Neuroscience, 13*, 744–753.

Hawkins, S. A., & Hastie, R. (1990). Hindsight: Biased judgements of past events after the outcomes are known. *Psychological Bulletin, 107*, 311–327.

Haxby, J. V., Hoffman, E. A., & Gobbini, M. I. (2000). The distributed human neural system for face perception. *Trends in Cognitive Sciences, 4*, 223–233.

Haxby, J. V., Hoffman, E. A., & Gobbini, M. I. (2002). Human neural systems for face recognition and social communication. *Biological Psychiatry, 51*, 59–67.

Haxby, J. V., Ungerleider, L. G., Clark, V. P., Schouten, J. L., Hoffman, E. A., & Martin, A. (1999). The effect of face inversion on activity in human neural systems for face and object perception. *Neuron, 22*, 189–199.

Heider, F. (1958). *The psychology of interpersonal relations.* New York: Wiley.

Heider, F., & Simmel, M. (1944). An experimental study of apparent behavior. *American Journal of Psychology, 57*, 243–259.

Hirstein, W., & Ramachandran, V. S. (1997). Capgras syndrome: A novel probe for understanding the neural representation of the identity and familiarity of persons. *Proceedings of the Royal Society of London: Series B, 264*, 437–444.

Hodges, J. R., & Graham, K. S. (1998). A reversal of the temporal gradient for famous person knowledge in semantic dementia: Implications for the neural organisation of long-term memory. *Neuropsychologia, 36*, 803–825.

Holyoak, K. J., & Hummel, J. E. (2000). The proper treatment of symbols in a connectionist architecture. In E. Dietrich & A. B. Markman (Eds.), *Cognitive dynamics: Conceptual and representational change in humans and machines* (pp. 229–263). Mahwah, NJ: Lawrence Erlbaum Associates, Inc.

Iacoboni, M., Lieberman, M. D., Knowlton, B. J., Molnar-Szakacs, I., Moritz, M., Throop, C. J., et al. (2004). Watching social interactions produces dorsomedial prefrontal cortex and medial parietal BOLD fMRI signal increases compared to a resting baseline. *NeuroImage, 21*, 1167–1173.

Ichheiser, G. (1943). Misinterpretations of personality in everyday life and the psychologist's frame of reference. *Character and Personality, 12*, 145–160.

Iversen, S. D., & Mishkin, M. (1970). Perseverative interference in monkeys following selective lesions of the inferior prefrontal convexity. *Experimental Brain Research, 11*, 376–386.

Izquierda, I., Quillfield, J. A., Zanatta, M. S., Quevedo, J., Schaeffer, E., Schmitz, P. K., et al. (1997). Sequential role of hippocampus and amygdala, entorhinal cortex and parietal cortex in formation and retrieval of memory for inhibitory avoidance in rats. *European Journal of Neuroscience, 9*, 786–793.

James, W. (1890/1950). *The principles of psychology.* New York: Dover.

Johnson, S. C., Baxter, L. C., Wilder, L. S., Pipe, J. G., Heiserman, J. E., & Prigatano, G. P. (2002). Neural correlates of self-reflection. *Brain, 125*, 1808–1814.

Jones, E. E., & Davis, K. E. (1965). From acts to dispositions: The attribution process in person perception. In L. Berkowitz (Ed.), *Advances in experimental social psychology* (Vol. 2, pp. 220–266). New York: Academic Press.

Jonides, J., Smith, E. E., Marshuetz, C., Koeppe, R. A., & Reuter-Lorenz, P. A. (1998). Inhibition in verbal working memory revealed by brain activation. *Proceedings of the National Academy of Sciences of the USA, 95*, 8410–8413.

Kahneman, D., Fredrickson, B. L., Schreiber, C. A., & Redelmeier, D. A. (1993). When more pain is preferred to less: Adding a better ending. *Psychological Science, 4*, 401–405.

Kanwisher, N., McDermott, J., & Chun, M. M. (1997). The fusiform face area: A module in human extrastriate cortex specialized for face perception. *Journal of Neuroscience, 17*, 4302–4311.

Kanwisher, N., Tong, F., & Nakayama, K. (1998). The effect of face inversion on the human fusiform face area. *Cognition, 68*, B1–B11.

Keenan, J. P., McCutcheon, B., Freund, S., Gallup, G. G., Jr., Sanders, G., & Pascual-Leone, A. (1999). Left hand advantage in a self-face recognition task. *Neuropsychologia, 37*, 1421–1425.

Keenan, J. P., Nelson, A., O'Connor, M., & Pascual-Leone, A. (2001). Self-recognition and the right hemisphere. *Nature, 409*, 305.

Kelley, H. H. (1967). Attribution theory in social psychology. In D. Levine (Ed.), *Nebraska Symposium on Motivation* (Vol. 15, pp. 192–240). Lincoln: University of Nebraska Press.

Kelley, W. M., Macrae, C. N., Wyland, C. L., Caglar, S., Inati, S., & Heatherton, T. F. (2002). Finding the self?: An event-related fMRI study. *Journal of Cognitive Neuroscience, 14*, 785–794.

Kircher, T. T. J., Senior, C., Phillips, M. L., Benson, P. J., Bullmore, E. T., Brammer, M., et al. (2000). Towards a functional neuroanatomy of self-processing: Effects of faces and words. *Cognitive Brain Research, 10*, 133–144.

Kjaer, K. W., Nowak, M., & Lou, H. C. (2002). Reflective self-awareness and conscious states: PET evidence for a common midline parieto-frontal core. *NeuroImage, 17*, 1080–1086.

Kjaer, T. W., Nowak, M., Kjaer, K. W., Lou, A. R., & Lou, H. C. (2001). Precuneus-prefrontal activity during awareness of visual verbal stimuli. *Consciousness and Cognition, 10*, 356–365.

Klein, S. B., Cosmides, L., Costabile, K. A., & Mei, L. (2002). Is there something special about the self? A neuropsychological case study. *Journal of Research in Personality, 36*, 490–506.

Klein, S. B., & Kihlstrom, J. F. (1998). On bridging the gap between social-personality psychology and neuropsychology. *Personality and Social Psychology Review, 2*, 228–242.

Klein, S. B., Loftus, J., & Kihlstrom, J. F. (1996). Self-knowledge of an amnesic patient: Toward a neuropsychology of personality and social psychology. *Journal of Experimental Psychology: General, 125*, 250–260.

Klein, S. B., Loftus, J., Trafton, J. G., & Fuhrman, R. W. (1992). Use of exemplars and abstractions in trait judgements: A model of trait knowledge about the self and others. *Journal of Personality and Social Psychology, 63*, 739–753.

Knutson, B., Adams, C. M., Hong, G. W., & Hommer, D. (2001). Anticipation of increasing monetary reward selectively recruits nucleus accumbens. *Journal of Neuroscience, 21*, 1–5.

Kohler, W. (1947). *Gestalt psychology*. New York: Liveright.

Konishi, S., Nakajima, K., Uchida, I., Kikyo, H., Kameyama, M., & Miyashita, Y. (1999). Common inhibitory mechanism in human inferior prefrontal cortex revealed by event-related functional MRI. *Brain, 122*, 981–999.

Kosslyn, S. M., Thompson, W. L., & Alpert, N. M. (1997). Neural systems shared by visual imagery and visual perception: A positron emission tomography study. *NeuroImage, 6*, 320–334.

Kramer, T. H., Buckhout, R., & Eugenio, P. (1990). Weapon focus, arousal, and eyewitness memory: Attention must be paid. *Law and Human Behavior, 14*, 167–184.

Kroger, J. K., Sabb, F. W., Fales, C. L., Bookheimer, S. Y., Cohen, M. S., & Holyoak, K. J. (2002). Recruitment of anterior dorsolateral prefrontal cortex in human reasoning: A parametric study of relational complexity. *Cerebral Cortex, 12*, 477–485.

Kruglanski, A. W., & Freund, T. (1983). The freezing and unfreezing of lay inferences: Effects on impressional primacy, ethnic stereotyping, and numerical anchoring. *Journal of Experimental Social Psychology, 19*, 448–468.

Lakoff, G., & Johnson, M. (1999). *Philosophy in the flesh: The embodied mind and its challenge to Western thought*. New York: Basic Books.
Lane, R. D., Fink, G. R., Chau, P. M.-L., & Dolan, R. J. (1997). Neural activation during selective attention to subjective emotional responses. *Neuroreport, 8*, 3969–3972.
Lane, R. D., & Nadel, L. (2000). *Cognitive neuroscience of emotion*. New York: Oxford University Press.
Lazarus, R. S. (1991). *Emotion and adaptation*. New York: Oxford University Press.
Leung, H. C., Skudlarski, P., Gatenby, J. C., Peterson, B. S., & Gore, J. E. (2000). An event-related functional MRI study of the Stroop color word interference task. *Cerebral Cortex, 10*, 552–560.
Leveroni, C. L., Seidenberg, M., Mayer, A. R., Mead, L. A., Binder, J. R., & Rao, S. M. (2000). Neural systems underlying the recognition of familiar and newly learned faces. *Journal of Neuroscience, 20*, 878–886.
Levine, B., Freedman, M., Dawson, D., Black, S., & Stuss, D. T. (1999). Ventral frontal contribution to self-regulation: Convergence of episodic memory and inhibition. *Neurocase, 5*, 263–275.
Lieberman, M. D. (2000). Intuition: A social cognitive neuroscience approach. *Psychological Bulletin, 126*, 109–137.
Lieberman, M. D. (2003). Reflective and reflexive judgement processes: A social cognitive neuroscience approach. In J. P. Forgas, K. R. Williams, & W. von Hippel (Eds.), *Social judgements: Explicit and implicit processes* (pp. 44–67). New York: Cambridge University Press.
Lieberman, M. D., Gaunt, R., Gilbert, D. T., & Trope, Y. (2002). Reflection and reflexion: A social cognitive neuroscience approach to attributional inference. In M. P. Zanna (Ed.), *Advances in experimental social psychology* (Vol. 34, pp. 199–249). New York: Academic Press.
Lieberman, M. D., Hariri, A., Jarcho, J. J., Eisenberger, N. I., & Bookheimer, S. Y. (2004a). *An fMRI investigation of the associative and perceptual nature of race-related amygdala activity*. Unpublished manuscript.
Lieberman, M. D., Jarcho, J. M., Berman, S., Naliboff, B., Suyenobu, B. Y., Mandelkern, M. & Mayer, E. (2004b). The neural correlates of placebo effects: A disruption account. *NeuroImage, 22*, 447–455.
Lieberman, M. D., Jarcho, J. M., & Satpute, A. B. (2004c). Evidence-based and intuition-based self-knowledge: An fMRI study. *Journal of Personality and Social Psychology, 87*, 421–435.
Lieberman, M. D., Ochsner, K. N., Gilbert, D. T., & Schacter, D. L. (2001). Do amnesics exhibit cognitive dissonance reduction? The role of explicit memory and attention in attitude change. *Psychological Science, 121*, 135–140.
Locke, J. (1975). *An essay concerning human understanding*. Oxford: Oxford University Press.
Loftus, E. F., Loftus, G. R., & Messo, J. (1987). Some facts about "weapon focus". *Law and Human Behavior, 11*, 55–62.
Macmillan, M. (2000). *An odd kind of fame*. Cambridge, MA: MIT Press.
Macrae, C. N., Milne, A. B., & Bodenhausen, G. V. (1994). Stereotypes as energy-saving devices: A peek inside the cognitive toolbox. *Journal of Personality and Social Psychology, 66*, 37–47.
Malloy, P., Cimino, C., & Westlake, R. (1992). Differential diagnosis of primary and

secondary Capgras delusions. *Neuropsychiatry, Neuropsychology, and Behavioral Neurology, 5*, 83–96.

Malpass, R. S., & Kravitz, J. (1969). Recognition for faces of own and other race. *Journal of Personality and Social Psychology, 13*, 330–334.

Markus, H. R. (1977). Self-schemata and processing information about the self. *Journal of Personalty and Social Psychology, 35*, 63–78.

McCarthy, G., Puce, A., Gore, J. C., & Allison, T. (1997). Face-specific processing in the human fusiform gyrus. *Journal of Cognitive Neuroscience, 9*, 605–610.

McClelland, J. L., McNaughton, B. L., & O'Reilly, R. C. (1995). Why there are complementary learning systems in the hippocampus and neocortex: Insights from the successes and failures of connectionist models of learning and memory. *Psychological Review, 102*, 419–457.

Mead, G. H. (1934). *Mind, self, and society*. Chicago: University of Chicago Press.

Meadows, J. C. (1974). The anatomical basis of prosopagnosia. *Journal of Neurology, Neurosurgery and Psychiatry, 37*, 489–501.

Meissner, C. A., & Brigham, J. C. (2001). Thirty years of investigating the own-race bias in memory for faces: A meta-analytic review. *Psychology, Public Policy, and Law, 7*, 3–35.

Miller, E. K., & Cohen, J. D. (2001). An integrative theory of prefrontal cortex function. *Annual Review of Neuroscience, 24*, 167–202.

Miller, G. A., Galanter, E., & Pribram, K. (1960). *Plans and the structure of behavior*. New York: Holt, Rinehart & Winston.

Milne, E., & Grafman, J. (2001). Ventromedial prefrontal cortex lesions in humans eliminate implicit gender stereotyping. *Journal of Neuroscience, 21*, 151–156.

Moll, J., de Oliveira-Souza, R., Bramati, I. E., & Grafman, J. (2002a). Functional networks in emotional moral and nonmoral social judgements. *NeuroImage, 16*, 696–703.

Moll, J., de Oliveira-Souza, R., & Eslinger, P. J. (2003). Morals and the human brain: A working model. *Neuroreport, 14*, 299–305.

Moll, J., de Oliveira-Souza, R., Eslinger, P. J., Bramati, I. E., Muourao-Miranda, J., Andreiuolo, P. A., et al. (2002b). The neural correlates of moral sensitivity: A functional magnetic resonance imaging investigation of basic and moral emotions. *Journal of Neuroscience, 22*, 2730–2736.

Monchi, O., Petrides, M., Petre, V., Worsley, K., & Dagher, A. (2001). Wisconsin card sorting revisited: Distinct neural circuits participating in different stages of the task identified by event-related functional magnetic resonance imaging. *Journal of Neuroscience, 21*, 7733–7741.

Mummery, C. J., Patterson, K., Hodges, J. R., & Wise, R. J. S. (2000). A voxel based morphometry study of semantic dementia: Relationship between temporal lobe atrophy and semantic memory. *Annals of Neurology, 47*, 36–45.

Nietzsche, F. (1909/1969). *Ecce homo*. New York: Vintage Books.

Nosofsky, R. M., & Palmeri, T. J. (1997). An exemplar-based random walk model of speeded classification. *Psychological Review, 104*, 266–300.

Ochsner, K. N., Bunge, S. A., Gross, J. J., & Gabrieli, J. D. (2002). Rethinking feelings: An fMRI study of the cognitive regulation of emotion. *Journal of Cognitive Neuroscience, 14*, 1215–1229.

Ochsner, K. N., & Lieberman, M. D. (2001). The emergence of social cognitive neuroscience. *American Psychologist, 56*, 717–734.

Ongur, D., & Price, J. L. (2000). The organization of networks within the orbital and medial prefrontal cortex of rats, monkeys and humans. *Cerebral Cortex, 10*, 206–219.

O'Reilly, R. C., Braver, T. S., & Cohen, J. D. (1999). A biologically based computational model of working memory. In A. Miyake & P. Shah (Eds.), *Models of working memory: Mechanisms of active maintenance and executive control* (pp. 375–411). New York: Cambridge University Press.

O'Reilly, R. C., & Norman, K. A. (2003). Hippocampal and neocortical contributions to memory: Advances in the complementary learning systems framework. *Trends in Cognitive Sciences, 6*, 505–510.

Papageorgiou, C., Lykouras, L., Ventouras, E., Uzunoglu, N., & Christodoulou, G. N. (2002). Abnormal P300 in a case of delusional misidentification with coinciding Capgras and Fregoli symptoms. *Progress in Neuro-Psychopharmacology and Biological Psychiatry, 26*, 805–810.

Perrett, D. I., Jellema, T., Frigerio, E., & Burt, M. (2001). *Using "social attention" cues (where others are attending) to interpret actions, intentions and emotions of others.* Paper presented at the UCLA Conference on Social Cognitive Neuroscience, Los Angeles, CA.

Pettigrew, T. F. (1979). The ultimate attribution error: Extending Allport's cognitive analysis of prejudice. *Personality and Social Psychology Bulletin, 5*, 461–476.

Phelps, E. A., O'Connor, K. J., Cunningham, W. A., Funayama, E. S., Gatenby, J. C., Gore, J. C., et al. (2000). Performance on indirect measures of race evaluation predicts amygdala activation. *Journal of Cognitive Neuroscience, 12*, 729–738.

Portas, C. M., Strange, B. A., Friston, K. J., Dolan, R. J., & Frith, C. D. (2000). How does the brain sustain a visual percept? *Proceedings of the Royal Society of London: Series B, 267*, 845–850.

Puce, A., Allison, T., Gore, J. C., & McCarthy, G. (1995). Face-sensitive regions in human extrastriate cortex studied by functional MRI. *Journal of Neurophysiology, 74*, 1192–1199.

Rainville, P., Duncan, G. H., Price, D. D., Carrier, B., & Bushnell, M. C. (1997). Pain affect encoded in human anterior cingulate but not somatosensory cortex. *Science, 277*, 968–971.

Ramachandran, V. S. (1995). Anosognosia in parietal lobe syndrome. *Consciousness and Cognition, 4*, 22–51.

Reeder, G. D. (1993). Trait–behavior relations and dispositional inference. *Personality and Social Psychology Bulletin, 19*, 586–593.

Reeder, G. D., Kumar, S., Hesson-McInnis, M. S., & Trafimow, D. (2002). Inferences about the morality of an aggressor: The role of perceived motive. *Journal of Personality and Social Psychology, 83*, 789–803.

Reinkemeier, M., Markowitsch, H. J., Rauch, M., & Kessler, J. (1997). Differential impairments in recalling people's names: A case study in search of neuroanatomical correlates. *Neuropsychologia, 35*, 677–684.

Richeson, J. A., Baird, A. A., Gordon, H. L., Heatherton, T. F., Wyland, C. L., Trawalter, S., et al. (2003). An fMRI investigation of the impact of interracial contact on executive function. *Nature Neuroscience, 6*, 1323–1328.

Richeson, J. A., & Shelton, J. N. (2003). When prejudice does not pay: Effects of interracial contact on executive function. *Psychological Science, 14*, 287–290.

Rolls, E. T. (1999). *The brain and emotion*. New York: Oxford University Press.

Ross, L. (1977). The intuitive psychologist and his shortcomings. In L. Berkowitz

(Ed.), *Advances in Experimental Social Psychology* (Vol. 10, pp. 173–220). New York: Academic Press.
Ross, M. (1989). The relation of implicit theories to the construction of personal histories. *Psychological Review, 96,* 341–357.
Ross, M., & Sicoly, F. (1979). Egocentric biases in availability and attribution. *Journal of Personality and Social Psychology, 37,* 322–336.
Rubinsztein, J. S., Fletcher, P. C., Rogers, R. D., Ho, L. W., Aigbirhio, F. I., Paykel, E. S., et al. (2001). Decision making in mania: A PET study. *Brain, 124,* 2550–2563.
Ruby, P., & Decety, J. (2001). Effect of subjective perspective taking during simulation of action: A PET investigation of agency. *Nature Neuroscience, 4,* 546–550.
Sartre, J. P. (1937). *Transcendence of the ego.* New York: Hill & Wang.
Schachter, S., & Singer, J. E. (1962). Cognitive, social, and physiological determinants of emotional state. *Psychological Review, 69,* 379–399.
Schoenbaum, G., Chiba, A. A., & Gallagher, M. (1999). Neural encoding in orbitofrontal cortex and basolateral amygdala during olfactory discrimination learning. *Journal of Neuroscience, 19,* 1876–1884.
Schoenbaum, G., Chiba, A. A., & Gallagher, M. (2000). Changes in functional connectivity in orbitofrontal cortex and basolateral amygdala during learning and reversal training. *Journal of Neuroscience, 20,* 5179–5189.
Schultz, R. T., Grelotti, D. J., Klin, A., Kleinman, J., Van der Gaag, C., Marois, R., et al. (2003). The role of the fusiform face area in social cognition: Implications for the pathobiology of autism. *Philosophical Transactions of the Royal Society of London: Series B, 358,* 415–427.
Seeck, M., Mainwaring, N., Ives, J., Blume, H., Dubuisson, D., Cosgrove, R., et al. (1993). Differential neural activity in the human temporal lobe evoked by faces of family members and friends. *Annals of Neurology, 34,* 369–372.
Shallice, T. (1988). *From neuropsychology to mental structure.* Cambridge: Cambridge University Press.
Shultz, T. R., & Lepper, M. R. (1995). Cognitive dissonance reduction as constraint satisfaction. *Psychological Review, 103,* 219–240.
Sloman, S. A. (1996). The empirical case for two systems of reasoning. *Psychological Bulletin, 119,* 3–22.
Small, D. M., Zatorre, R. J., Dagher, A., Evans, A. C., & Jones-Gotman, M. (2001). Changes in brain activity related to eating chocolate: From pleasure to aversion. *Brain, 124,* 1720–1733.
Smith, E. R., & DeCoster, J. (2000). Dual-process models in social and cognitive psychology: Conceptual integration and links to underlying memory systems. *Personality and Social Psychology Review, 4,* 108–131.
Steele, C. M., & Aronson, J. (1995). Stereotype threat and the intellectual test performance of African Americans. *Journal of Personality and Social Psychology, 69,* 797–811.
Storms, M. D. (1973). Videotape and the attribution process: Reversing actors' and observers' points of view. *Journal of Personality and Social Psychology, 27,* 165–175.
Stuss, D. T. (1991). Self, awareness, and the frontal lobes: A neuropsychological perspective. In J. Strauss & G. R. Goethals (Eds.), *The self: Interdisciplinary approaches* (pp. 255–277). New York: Springer-Verlag.
Suomi, S. J. (2003). Gene–environment interactions and the neurobiology of social conflict. *Annals of the New York Academy of Sciences, 1008,* 132–139.

Suzuki, W., Saleem, K. S., & Tanaka, K. (2000). Divergent backward projections from the anterior part of the inferotemporal cortex (area TE) in the macaque. *Journal of Comparative Neurology, 422*, 206–228.
Swann, W. B. (1984). Quest for accuracy in person perception: A matter of pragmatics. *Psychological Review, 91*, 457–477.
Tanaka, J. R., & Curran, T. (2001). A neural basis for expert object recognition. *Psychological Science, 12*, 43–47.
Tanaka, J. W., & Farah, M. J. (1993). Parts and wholes in face recognition. *Quarterly Journal of Experimental Psychology: Human Experimental Psychology, 46A*, 225–245.
Taylor, S. E., & Brown, J. D. (1988). Illusion and well-being: A social psychological perspective on mental health. *Psychological Bulletin, 103*, 193–210.
Tetlock, P. E. (1983). Accountability and complexity of thought. *Journal of Personality and Social Psychology, 45*, 74–83.
Tomita, H., Ohbayashi, M., Nakahara, K., Hasegawa, I., & Miyashita, Y. (1999). Top-down signal from prefrontal cortex in executive control of memory retrieval. *Nature, 401*, 699–701.
Tong, F., Nakayama, K., Moscovitch, M., Weinrib, O., & Kanwisher, N. (2000). Response properties of the human fusiform face area. *Cognitive Neuropsychology. Special Issue: The cognitive neuroscience of face processing, 17*, 257–279.
Trope, Y. (1986). Identification and inferential processes in dispositional attribution. *Psychological Review, 93*, 239–257.
Turk, D. J., Heatherton, T. F., Kelley, W. M., Funnell, M. G., Gazzaniga, M. S., & Macrae, C. N. (2002). Mike or me? Self-recognition in a split-brain patient. *Nature Neuroscience, 5*, 841–842.
Turner, R. H. (1976). The real self: From institution to impulse. *American Journal of Sociology, 81*, 989–1016.
Tversky, A., & Kahneman, D. (1974). Judgement under uncertainty: Heuristics and biases. *Science, 185*, 1124–1131.
Vohs, K. D., & Heatherton, T. F. (2000). Self-regulatory failure: A resource-depletion approach. *Psychological Science, 11*, 249–254.
Wegener, D. T., & Petty, R. E. (1995). Flexible correction processes in social judgement: The role of naive theories in corrections for perceived bias. *Journal of Personality and Social Psychology, 68*, 36–51.
Wegner, D. M. (1994). Ironic processes of mental control. *Psychological Review, 101*, 34–52.
Whitehead, A. N. (1911). *An introduction to mathematics*. London: Williams and Norgate.
Wiener, N. (1948). *Cybernetics: Control and communication in the animal and the machine*. Cambridge, MA: MIT Press.
Wojciulik, E., Kanwisher, N., & Driver, J. (1998). Covert visual attention modulates face-specific activity in the human fusiform gyrus: fMRI study. *Journal of Neurophysiology, 79*, 1574–1578.
Word, C. O., Zanna, M. P., & Cooper, J. (1974). The nonverbal mediation of self-fulfilling prophecies in interracial interaction. *Journal of Experimental Social Psychology, 10*, 109–120.
Yin, R. K. (1969). Looking at upside-down faces. *Journal of Experimental Psychology, 81*, 141–145.

Part III
Human disorders of social behaviour and cognition

8 Autism and the origins of social neuroscience

Simon Baron-Cohen

"Social neuroscience" is something of a new phrase, and the editors of this volume are to be congratulated for collecting together the fragmented work, and thereby helping the creation of a new field. In their introduction to this book, they cover the history of this idea; but for me there are some themes—even lessons—worth highlighting.

Lessons from history

Nonsocial neuroscience

When I started in psychology some 20 years ago, there was almost no hint of social neuroscience. Cognitive neuroscience was alive and well, so this was not a reflection of a lack of activity in the wider field. Rather, it reflects that studies of the brain were for the most part *non*social. We had, for example, Blakemore's and Weiskrantz's classic studies of the visual system in kittens, monkeys, and humans to tell us which (nonsocial) features of the environment were perceived and how. We had Luria's and Shallice's classic studies of the (nonsocial) control of action to reveal not just a "central executive" for planning in the brain, but a syndrome of executive dysfunction. We had a wealth of other studies investigating conditions such as amnesia and agnosia to tell us how memory and knowledge of information *in general* worked in the brain. Even Wernicke's and Broca's classic studies of the language system in brain-damaged patients focused for the most part on the production and comprehension of words *in general* by the normal brain. But such aphasias were lexical or syntactic or semantic, and ignored the social aspects of communication: pragmatics.

Why was this? After all, cognitive neuroscientists then were not fools. They knew then, just as we know now, that the human brain, and indeed most primate brains, exists *first and foremost* in a social world. Primates do not sit in solitary, solipsistic universes. So why did they treat the brain as if it had no special interest in the social world?

My guess is that there are (at least) two explanations for this. First, cognitive neuroscience followed a parsimonious approach of assuming that the brain is a *general* information processor. Whether tacitly or explicitly, the assumption has been that the visual system, or the auditory system, or the memory systems, or the planning system, work on input of a general kind, where content plays little role. Of course, distinctions have been drawn, such as visual versus auditory memory, but, within a given system, it was held to not matter whether the visual input is a tree or a car: the search was to identify the general operating principles of the visual system. The same applies to memory. It matters little if we are studying memory of cars or of animals. We should still be able to identify the general operating principles of the memory system.

Such a content-free approach was laudable in its parsimony, as the danger otherwise was that neuroscience could have ended up positing a very large number of specialized circuits for different classes of information, and then the whole enterprise of understanding the basic laws of the brain would have been thrown off course. However, throughout this enterprise, there were always cracks appearing in this "brain-as-a-general-processor" theory. Just one example was the case of prosopagnosia, where some clinicians claimed that some patients could recognize any kind of object *except* faces. And the publication of Fodor's landmark book (1983) on *modularity* still stands as a major challenge to such a general theory.

The second possible explanation relates to cognitive neuroscientists as natural scientists. The nature of natural science is to try to isolate variables in a system under controlled conditions. The ultimate model for natural scientists is physics, and it is no surprise that even in the study of the human brain, the dominant approach has been to study how the brain responds to the manipulation of elementary features of the input. Is a vertical edge detected by the same assembly of neurons as a horizontal edge? Is a regular verb processed in the same way as an irregular verb? Again, such a focus on controllable, simple stimuli or features is laudable, since in this way one can make inferences about how the system works. If one were dealing with the complexity of the social world, how on earth could one begin to isolate what was causing what?

This is not intended as a criticism of cognitive neuroscience in adopting a general or a nonsocial approach. The natural science methodology has reaped great benefits and has reappropriated the study of the mind from the hands of psychoanalysts and social scientists, who ignored the brain and biology for decades. We have much to be grateful for. But there may be a set of parallels that emerge from a range of fields within psychology that show a similar disregard of the special nature of the social world. The lessons have been learned late.

Nonsocial psychology

The study of child development began with a disproportionate focus on the nonsocial aspects of cognition. Piaget's classic studies of object permanence and what is really "folk physics" predominated until the 1980s, when Bruner (in Oxford) and his students reminded the field that children have minds that are trying to make sense of a social world, and not just a physical world. Indeed, the shift of focus to the pragmatics of communication (and away from traditional, Chomskian approaches to language acquisition), and the "discovery" of the developing child's "theory of mind" (Astington, Harris, & Olson, 1988; Wellman, 1990), owes a lot to Bruner's repeated concern that we were treating the child-as-scientist and ignoring the child-in-relationships (Bruner, 1983).

The same history unfolded in the field of intelligence. Almost all the early and classical IQ tests sought to assess the person's nonsocial IQ: David Wechsler's nonverbal subtests of object assembly or block design, or his verbal subtests of vocabulary or digit span, or Raven's matrices taught us an enormous amount about the predictive power of IQ (Raven, 1956; Wechsler, 1939), but virtually ignored what today is called "social intelligence" or "emotional intelligence" (Goleman, 1995). Equally, cognitive psychology focused in large part on the nonsocial aspects of cognition, with the new field of "social cognition" only coming in quite late in the twentieth century (Shantz, 1983).

If we look at the field of primatology, we can see a similar pattern. The attempt to understand the evolution of intelligence and the evolution of the brain focused on humans-as-tool-users and general problem solvers (or early hominids as "folk physicists") as the driving force behind the evolution of a larger, more powerful brain. It was rather late in the twentieth century when it was asked, "Does the chimpanzee have a theory of mind?" (Premack & Woodruff, 1978), and when it was proposed that the driving force behind the evolution of intelligence and the brain may have been the need to socially outwit competitors (the "Machiavellian intelligence hypothesis" [Whiten, 1997]).

I lay out this brief and partial history because I think there may be lessons to be learnt. Naturally, there is a risk of painting the history as too black and white; too nonsocial when all along there was a streak of social neuroscience running through it. We know that Piaget's concept of "egocentrism" applied not only to the child's folk physics (to explain the child's errors in understanding conservation of mass, for example) but also to the child's folk psychology (to explain the child's errors in communication). And we know that Charles Gross's classic single-cell recording studies were identifying cell assemblies that fired not only in response to nonsocial aspects of the visual environment, but also in response to specifically social features such as hands and faces (Gross, Rocha-Miranda, & Bender, 1972). We know that Harry Harlow's, Robert Hinde's, and John Bowlby's classic studies of the attachment system in monkeys and humans progressed despite this history, and indeed ethology never lost sight of its social context (Bowlby, 1969). But these exceptions to the rule do not, I think, invalidate the broad picture I have painted. Rather, they were the seeds for the new field of social neuroscience.

From nonsocial to social accounts of autism

The study of autism has followed a similar history. The psychological theories of autism before the 1980s were for the most part nonsocial. The child's social difficulties were attributed to a failure to generalize (Rimland, 1964) or were seen as secondary to a language disorder (Rutter, 1978), or thought to reflect a failure to process meaning (or semantics) (Hermelin & O'Connor, 1970), for example. For this reason, the proposal (by my colleagues and me in the 1980s) that the social and communication difficulties that are the hallmark of autism might reflect a *specific* deficit in an aspect of *social cognition* was treated as quite novel. Our idea was that there might be specific brain regions or neural circuits that underpinned social understanding, and ultimately social behaviour. We opened this area of investigation by asking, "Does the autistic child have a theory of mind?" (Baron-Cohen, Leslie, & Frith, 1985). A related investigation into emotion recognition in autism (Hobson, 1986) was also regarded as new and important. Later in this chapter, I summarize how this work has unfolded in the subsequent 20 years.

The social brain

My own theoretical and empirical work was greatly enriched by Leslie Brothers' important proposal of a network of neural regions that comprise the "social brain" (Brothers, 1990). She suggested that this included areas of the prefrontal cortex (orbital and medial areas particularly), the superior temporal sulcus, and the amygdala. Since the neurodevelopmental condition of autism involves deficits in what today I refer to as "empathizing" (Baron-Cohen, 2002), it is plausible that autism may be caused by an abnormality in one or more of these brain areas.

The idea that social understanding might be independent of general intelligence comes from three sources:

(1) There are individuals who are capable of considerable understanding of the nonsocial world (as in physics, maths, and engineering) but who readily admit to finding the social world confusing (Baron-Cohen, Wheelwright, Stone, & Rutherford, 1999; Sacks, 1994).
(2) The opposite type of individual also exists: people who have no difficulty interacting with the social world but who find nonsocial problem solving confusing (Karmiloff-Smith, Grant, Bellugi, & Baron-Cohen, 1995).
(3) Certain kinds of brain damage (as to the amygdala) can cause selective impairment in social judgement (Damasio, Tranel, & Damasio, 1990) without any necessary loss to general problem solving ability. Loss of social judgement can, of course, coexist with memory and executive dysfunction (Tranel & Hyman, 1990), but the functional double dissociation between empathizing and nonsocial aspects of intelligence suggests their neural independence.

In the remainder of this chapter, I review the evidence for the normal development of empathizing. I then review the literature suggesting autism involves an empathizing deficit. Finally, I end with a summary of the evidence for the role of the amygdala in empathy. The evidence for the social function of the orbito- and medial prefrontal cortex, and the superior temporal sulcus, is reviewed elsewhere (Baron-Cohen & Ring, 1994; Baron-Cohen, Ring, Moriarty, Shmitz, Costa, & Ell, 1994).

The empathizing theory of autism

Autism is diagnosed when a child or adult has abnormalities in a "triad" of behavioural domains: social development, communication, and repetitive behaviour/obsessive interests (American Psychiatric Association, 1994; ICD-10, 1994). Asperger syndrome (AS) was first described by Asperger (1944). The descriptions of the children he documented overlapped considerably with the accounts of childhood autism (Kanner, 1943). Little was published on AS in English until relatively recently (Frith, 1991; Wing, 1981). Current diagnostic practice recognizes people with AS as meeting the same criteria as for high-functioning autism (HFA), but with no history of language delay, and with no cognitive delay.

The mind-blindness theory of autism (Baron-Cohen, 1995), and its extension into empathizing theory (Baron-Cohen, 2002) proposes that in autism spectrum conditions there are deficits in the normal process of empathizing, relative to mental age. These deficits can occur by degrees. The term "empathizing" encompasses the following earlier terms: "theory of mind", "mind-reading", and taking the "intentional stance" (Dennett, 1987).

Empathizing involves two major elements: (1) the ability to attribute mental states to oneself and others, as a natural way to understand agents (Baron-Cohen, 1994; Leslie, 1995; Premack, 1990); (2) having an emotional reaction that is appropriate to the other person's mental state. In this sense, it includes what is normally meant by the term "theory of mind" (the attributional component), but it goes beyond this, to also include having some affective reaction (such as sympathy).

The first of these, the mental state attribution component, has been widely discussed in terms of being an evolved ability, the response of a cognitive system to a universe that can be broadly divided into two kinds of entities: those that do and those that do not possess intentionality (Brentano, 1970). The mental state attribution component is effectively judging whether this is the sort of entity that might possess intentionality. Intentionality is defined as the capacity of something to refer or point to things other than itself. A chair cannot point to anything. It just is. In contrast, a rabbit can "look" at a carrot, it can "want" the carrot, it can "think" that this is a carrot, etc. Essentially, agents have intentionality, but nonagents do not. This means that when we observe agents and nonagents move, we construe their motion as having different causes (Csibra, Gergely, Biro, Koos, & Brockbanck, 1999;

Gelman & Hirschfield, 1994). Agents can move by self-propulsion, which we naturally interpret as driven by their goals and desires, but nonagents cannot.

The second of these, the affective reaction component, is closer to what we ordinarily refer to by the word "empathy". Thus, we not only attribute a mental state to the agent in front of us (for example, the man is in pain), but we also react to his emotional state with an appropriate emotion ourselves (we feel sorry for him). Empathizing thus essentially allows us to make sense of the behaviour of other agents we are observing, predict what they might do next, and imagine how they might feel. And it allows us to feel connected to another agent's experience, and respond appropriately to them.

The normal development of empathizing

Empathizing develops from human infancy (Johnson, 2000). In the infancy period, it includes

- being able to judge whether something is an agent or not (Premack, 1990)
- being able to judge whether another agent is looking at you or not (Baron-Cohen & Goodhart, 1994b)
- being able to judge whether an agent is expressing a basic emotion (Ekman, 1992), and, if so, what type
- engaging in shared attention, as by following gaze or pointing gestures (Mundy & Crowson, 1997; Scaife & Bruner, 1975; Tomasello, 1988)
- showing concern or basic empathy at another's distress, or responding appropriately to another's basic emotional state (Yirmiya, Sigman, Kasari, & Mundy, 1992)
- being able to judge an agent's goal or basic intention (Premack, 1990).

Empathizing can be identified and studied from at least 12 months of age (Baron-Cohen, 1994; Premack, 1990). Thus, infants dishabituate to actions of "agents" who appear to violate goal-directedness (Gergely, Nadasdy, Gergely, & Biro, 1995; Rochat, Morgan, & Carpenter, 1997). They also expect agents to "emote" (express emotion), and expect this to be consistent across modalities (between face and voice) (Walker, 1982). They are also highly sensitive to where another person is looking, and by 14 months will strive to establish joint attention (Butterworth, 1991; Hood, Willen, & Driver, 1997; Scaife & Bruner, 1975). By 14 months, they also start to produce and understand pretence (Bates, Benigni, Bretherton, Camaioni, & Volterra, 1979; Leslie, 1987). By 18 months, they begin to show concern at the distress of others (Yirmiya et al., 1992). By 2 years old, they begin to use mental state words in their speech (Wellman & Bartsch, 1988).

Empathizing of course develops beyond early childhood, and continues to develop throughout the lifespan. These later developments include:

- attribution of the range of mental states to oneself and others, including pretence, deception, and belief (Leslie & Keeble, 1987)
- recognizing and responding appropriately to complex emotions, not just basic ones (Harris, Johnson, Hutton, Andrews, & Cooke, 1989)
- linking mental states to action, including language, and therefore understanding and producing pragmatically appropriate language (Tager-Flusberg, 1993)
- making sense of others' behaviour, predicting it, and even manipulating it (Whiten, 1991)
- judging what is appropriate in different social contexts, based on what others will think of our own behaviour
- communicating an empathic understanding of another mind.

Thus, by 3 years of age, children can understand relationships between mental states, such as that seeing leads to knowing (Pratt & Bryant, 1990). By 4 years, they can understand that people can hold false beliefs (Wimmer & Perner, 1983). By 5-6 years, they can understand that people can hold beliefs about beliefs (Perner & Wimmer, 1985). By 7 years, they begin to understand what not to say in order to avoid offending others (Baron-Cohen, O'Riordan, Jones, Stone, & Plaisted, 1999). With age, mental state attribution becomes increasingly more complex (Baron-Cohen, Joliffe, Mortimore, & Robertson, 1997; Happe, 1993). The little cross-cultural evidence that exists suggests a similar picture in very different cultures (Avis & Harris, 1991).

These developmental data have been interpreted in terms of an innate module being part of the infant cognitive architecture. This has been dubbed a theory of mind mechanism (ToMM) (Leslie, 1995). But, as we have suggested, empathizing also encompasses the skills that are involved in normal reciprocal social relationships (including intimate ones) and in sensitive communication. Empathizing is a narrowly defined domain, namely, *understanding and responding to people's minds*. Deficits in empathizing are referred to as degrees of mind-blindness.

Empathizing in autism spectrum conditions

Since the first test of mind-blindness in children with autism (Baron-Cohen et al., 1985), there have been more than 30 experimental tests. The vast majority of these have revealed profound impairments in the development of their empathizing ability. These are reviewed elsewhere (Baron-Cohen, 1995; Baron-Cohen, Tager-Flusberg, & Cohen, 1993) but include deficits in the following:

- joint attention (Baron-Cohen, 1989b)
- use of mental state terms in language (Tager-Flusberg, 1993)
- production and comprehension of pretence (Baron-Cohen, 1987; Wing & Gould, 1979)

- understanding that "seeing-leads-to-knowing" (Baron-Cohen & Goodhart, 1994b; Leslie & Frith, 1988)
- distinguishing mental from physical entities (Baron-Cohen, 1989b; Ozonoff, Pennington, & Rogers, 1990)
- making the appearance–reality distinction (Baron-Cohen, 1989a)
- understanding false belief (Baron-Cohen et al., 1985)
- understanding beliefs about beliefs (Baron-Cohen, 1989c)
- understanding complex emotions (Baron-Cohen, 1991)
- showing concern at another's pain (Yirmiya et al., 1992).

Some children and adults with AS show their empathizing deficits only on age-appropriate adult tests (Baron-Cohen, Jolliffe, Mortimore, & Robertson, 1997; Baron-Cohen, Wheelwright, Hill, Raste, & Plumb, 1997; Baron-Cohen, Wheelwright, & Jolliffe, 2001), or on age-appropriate screening instruments such as the empathy quotient (EQ) (Baron-Cohen, Richler, Bisarya, Gurunathan, & Wheelwright, 2003).

Evidence for the contribution of the amygdala in the social brain and in autism

There are several important lines of evidence implicating the amygdala in primate social behaviour. Extensive reviews exist elsewhere (Kling & Brothers, 1992). We also know that the human amygdala is activated in humans when decoding signals of social importance, such as gaze, expression-recognition (especially of fearful faces), and body movements (Baron-Cohen, Ring et al., 1999; Bonda, Petrides, Ostry, & Evans, 1996; Kawashima et al., 1999; Morris et al., 1996; Whalen et al., 1998; Wicker, Michel, Henaff, & Decety, 1998). But there are six lines of evidence for an amygdala deficit in autism.

Post-mortem evidence

A neuroanatomical study of autism at post-mortem found microscopic pathology (in the form of increased cell density) in the amygdala, in the presence of normal amygdala volume (Bauman & Kemper, 1994; Rapin & Katzman, 1998).

An animal model of autism

The only animal model of autism involves ablation of the amygdala (in rhesus monkeys) (Bachevalier, 1991). There are obviously limits to any animal model of autism, given that the syndrome involves deficits in higher-order cognition, but Bachevalier makes the case that the effects of amygdala lesions in monkeys resemble some of the symptoms of autism. In particular, the Klüver–Bucy syndrome seems a fairly good animal model of autism (Hetzler & Griffin, 1981).

Similarities between autism and patients following amygdalotomy

Patients with amygdala lesions show impairments in social judgement (Adolphs, Tranel, Damasio, & Damasio, 1994; Young, Hellawell, De Wal, & Johnson, 1996) that have been likened to "acquired autism" (Stone, 2000). The age of onset of deficits in acquired versus idiopathic cases is likely to mean that the two syndromes also differ in many ways, too. Similarly, patients with autism tend to show a similar pattern of deficits to those seen in patients with amygdala lesions (Adolphs, Sears, & Piven, 2001).

The effects of temporal lobe tubers

In cases of tuberous sclerosis, autistic comorbidity is determined by hamartomata in the temporal lobe (Bolton & Griffiths, 1997)[1].

Structural neuroimaging

A structural magnetic resonance imaging study of autism reported reduced amygdala volume (Abell et al., 1999).

Functional neuroimaging

In single photon emission computed tomography (SPECT), patients with autism spectrum conditions show significant reductions in temporal lobe blood flow. This is not simply an effect of temporal lobe epilepsy (Gillberg, Bjure, Uvebrant, Vestergren, & Gillberg, 1993). In our earlier functional magnetic resonance imaging (fMRI) study, we found that adults with high functioning autism (HFA) or AS showed significantly less amygdala activation during an empathizing task (the "reading the mind in the eyes" task), than normal controls (Baron-Cohen et al., 1999). Adults with HFA or AS, with intelligence in the normal range, show deficits on this task (Baron-Cohen et al., 1997; Baron-Cohen et al., 2001), as do parents of children with autism/AS (Baron-Cohen & Hammer, 1997). Children with Williams syndrome are not impaired on this test, despite their general retardation (Tager-Flusberg, Boshart, & Baron-Cohen, 1998).

Other brain areas that might be abnormal in autism

While this chapter highlights the role that amygdala abnormality plays in autism, we do not suggest that this is the only abnormal neural region. For

---

1 We emphasize the amygdala theory of autism, though some of the lines of evidence cited here implicate temporal lobe structures, which include the amygdala but also other adjacent mesiotemporal areas. It remains for future work to establish the specificity of an amygdala deficit in autism.

example, the case has been made for anomalous functioning in the cerebellum (Courchesne et al., 1994), hippocampal formation (De Long, 1992), medial frontal cortex (Happe et al., 1996), and frontolimbic connections (Bishop, 1993) in autism. Reduced neuron size and increased cell-packing density have also been found in the limbic system, specifically the hippocampus, subiculum, entorhinal cortex, amygdala, mamillary bodies, anterior cingulate, and septum in autism (Bauman & Kemper, 1985, 1986, 1988, 1994b; Raymond, Bauman, & Kemper, 1996). A full review of neuroimaging of autism may be found elsewhere (Filipek, 1999). Here, we instead follow a line of argument begun by other authors emphasizing an amygdala theory of autism (Bachevalier, 1994; Baron-Cohen et al., 2000; Bauman & Kemper, 1988; Hetzler & Griffin, 1981). In the closing section of this chapter, we briefly turn from brain regions to the neurochemistry, and particularly the neuroendocrinology, of social development.

Foetal testosterone (FT) and brain development

Foetal testosterone (FT) acts on the developing brain to influence cerebral lateralization (Kimura, 1999; Wilson, Foster, Kronenberg, & Larsen, 1998). Evidence for this derives from both animal studies (Harris & Levine, 1962; Arnold & Gorski, 1984; Williams, Barnett, & Meck, 1990), and the effects of abnormal hormonal environments during human pregnancy, such as congenital adrenal hyperplasia or synthetic hormone injections (Collaer & Hines, 1995; Hines & Shipley, 1984).

There is reason to believe that sex hormones are inversely related to social and language development (Geschwind & Galaburda, 1985a, 1985b, 1985c, 1985). Sex differences (female superiority) have been found in studies of normal language and social development (Baron-Cohen, 2002; Connellan, Baron-Cohen, Wheelwright, Ba'tki, & Ahluwalia, 2001; Hyde & Linn, 1988; Maccoby & Jacklin, 1974), and recent studies suggest an inverse correlation between levels of FT as measured in amniotic fluid, and both amount of eye contact measured at 12 months old (Lutchmaya, Baron-Cohen, & Raggatt, 2002a) and vocabulary size at 18 and 24 months old (Lutchmaya et al., 2002b). Geschwind's theory was that FT might accelerate the growth of the right hemisphere at the expense of the left, which is usually dominant in language functions and which may also be of some significance for empathy.

Summary and future work

Social neuroscience is now an important part of cognitive neuroscience. Studies of autism have contributed to this new field, and the literature reviewed earlier hints at the validity of an amygdala theory of autism. Future studies will be needed to test this more extensively. Secondly, future research will need to specify in greater detail which of the 13 nuclei in the amygdala are intact in autism, and which are impaired. Finally, the intriguing possibility that FT mediates empathy through testosterone receptors in the amygdala and other parts of the "social brain" will be an important hypothesis to test, when methods become available.

Acknowledgements

The Medical Research Council, the National Alliance for Autism Research, Cure Autism Now, and the James S. McDonnell Foundation provided valuable support during the period of this work. Portions of this chapter appeared in Baron-Cohen et al. (2000).

References

Abell, F., Krams, M., Ashburner, J., Passingham, R., Friston, K., Frackowiak, R., et al. (1999). The neuranatomy of autism: A voxel-based whole brain analysis of structural scans. *Cognitive Neuroscience, 10*, 1647–1651.

Adolphs, R., Sears, L., & Piven, J. (2001). Abnormal processing of social information from faces in autism. *Journal of Cognitive Neuroscience, 13*, 232–240.

Adolphs, R., Tranel, D., Damasio, H., & Damasio, A. (1994). Impaired recognition of emotion in facial expressions following bilateral damage to the human amygdala. *Nature, 372*, 669–672.

American Psychiatric Association (1994). *DSM-IV. Diagnostic and statistical manual of mental disorders, 4th Edn.* Washington, DC: American Psychiatric Association.

Arnold, A. P., & Gorski, R. A. (1984). Gonadal steroid induction of structural sex differences in the CNS. *Annual Review of Neurosciences, 7*, 413–442.

Asperger, H. (1944). Die "Autistischen Psychopathen" im Kindesalter. *Archiv für Psychiatrie und Nervenkrankheiten, 117*, 76–136.

Astington, J., Harris, P., & Olson, D. (1988). *Developing theories of mind.* New York: Cambridge University Press.

Avis, J., & Harris, P. (1991). Belief-desire reasoning among Baka children: Evidence for a universal conception of mind. *Child Development, 62*, 460–467.

Bachevalier, J. (1991). An animal model for childhood autism: Memory loss and socioemotional disturbances following neonatal damage to the limbic system in monkeys. In C. Tamminga & S. Schulz (Eds.), *Advances in neuropsychiatry and psychopharmacology: Volume 1. Schizophrenia research.* New York: Raven Press.

Bachevalier, J. (1994). Medial temporal lobe structures and autism: A review of clinical and experimental findings. *Neuropsychologia, 32*, 627–648.

Baron-Cohen, S., Joliffe, T., Mortimore, C., & Robertson, M. (1997). Another advanced test of theory of mind: Evidence from very high functioning adults with autism or Asperger syndrome. *Journal of Child Psychology and Psychiatry, 38*, 813–822.

Baron-Cohen, S. (1987). Perception in autistic children. In D. Cohen (Ed.), *Handbook of autism and pervasive developmental disorders.* New York: Wiley.

Baron-Cohen, S. (1989a). Are autistic children behaviourists? An examination of their mental-physical and appearance-reality distinctions. *Journal of Autism and Developmental Disorders, 19*, 579–600.

Baron-Cohen, S. (1989b). Joint attention deficits in autism: Towards a cognitive analysis. *Development and Psychopathology, 1*, 185–189.

Baron-Cohen, S. (1989c). The autistic child's theory of mind: A case of specific developmental delay. *Journal of Child Psychology and Psychiatry, 30,* 285–298.

Baron-Cohen, S. (1991). Do people with autism understand what causes emotion? *Child Development, 62,* 385–395.

Baron-Cohen, S. (1994). How to build a baby that can read minds: Cognitive mechanisms in mind-reading. *Cahiers de Psychologie Cognitive/Current Psychology of Cognition, 13,* 513–552.

Baron-Cohen, S. (1995). *Mindblindness: An essay on autism and theory of mind.* Boston, MA: MIT Press/Bradford Books.

Baron-Cohen, S. (2002). The extreme male brain theory of autism. *Trends in Cognitive Sciences, 6,* 248–254.

Baron-Cohen, S., & Goodhart, F. (1994a). The mind-reading system: New directions for research. *Current Psychology of Cognition, 13,* 724–750.

Baron-Cohen, S., & Goodhart, F. (1994b). The "seeing leads to knowing" deficit in autism: The Pratt and Bryant probe. *British Journal of Developmental Psychology, 12,* 397–402.

Baron-Cohen, S., & Hammer, J. (1997). Is autism an extreme form of the male brain? *Advances in Infancy Research, 11,* 193–217.

Baron-Cohen, S., Leslie, A. M., & Frith, U. (1985). Does the autistic child have a "theory of mind"? *Cognition, 21,* 37–46.

Baron-Cohen, S., O'Riordan, M., Jones, R., Stone, V., & Plaisted, K. (1999). A new test of social sensitivity: Detection of faux pas in normal children and children with Asperger syndrome. *Journal of Autism and Developmental Disorders, 29,* 407–418.

Baron-Cohen, S., Richler, J., Bisarya, D., Gurunathan, N., & Wheelwright, S. (2003). The Systemising Quotient (SQ): An investigation of adults with Asperger syndrome or high functioning autism and normal sex differences. *Philosophical Transactions of the Royal Society, Series B, Special issue on "Autism: Mind and brain", 358,* 361–374.

Baron-Cohen, S., & Ring, H. (1994). A model of the mind-reading system: Neuropsychological and neurobiological perspectives. In P. Mitchell & C. Lewis (Eds.), *Origins of an understanding of mind.* Hove, UK: Lawrence Erlbaum Associates Ltd.

Baron-Cohen, S., Ring, H., Bullmore, E., Wheelwright, S., Ashwin, C., & Williams, S. (2000). The amygdala theory of autism. *Neuroscience and Behavioural Reviews, 24,* 355–364.

Baron-Cohen, S., Ring, H., Moriarty, J., Shmitz, P., Costa, D., & Ell, P. (1994). Recognition of mental state terms: A clinical study of autism, and a functional neuroimaging study of normal adults. *British Journal of Psychiatry, 165,* 640–649.

Baron-Cohen, S., Ring, H., Wheelwright, S., Bullmore, E. T., Brammer, M. J., Simmons, A., et al. (1999). Social intelligence in the normal and autistic brain: An fMRI study. *European Journal of Neuroscience, 11,* 1891–1898.

Baron-Cohen, S., Tager-Flusberg, H., & Cohen, D (Eds.) (1993). *Understanding other minds: Perspectives from autism.* Oxford: Oxford University Press.

Baron-Cohen, S., & Wheelwright, S. (2004). The empathy quotient (EQ). An investigation of adults with Asperger syndrome or high functioning autism, and normal sex differences. *Journal of Autism and Developmental Disorders, 34,* 163–175.

Baron-Cohen, S., Wheelwright, S., Hill, J., Raste, Y., & Plumb, I. (2001). The "Reading the Mind in the Eyes" test revised version: A study with normal adults, and adults with Asperger syndrome or high-functioning autism. *Journal of Child Psychiatry and Psychiatry, 42,* 241–252.

Baron-Cohen, S., Wheelwright, S., & Jolliffe, T. (1997). Is there a "language of the eyes"? Evidence from normal adults and adults with autism or Asperger syndrome. *Visual Cognition, 4*, 311–331.

Baron-Cohen, S., Wheelwright, S., Stone, V., & Rutherford, M. (1999). A mathematician, a physicist, and a computer scientist with Asperger syndrome: Performance on folk psychology and folk physics test. *Neurocase, 5*, 475–483.

Bates, E., Benigni, L., Bretherton, I., Camaioni, L., & Volterra, V. (1979). Cognition and communication from 9–13 months: Correlational findings. In E. Bates (Ed.), *The emergence of symbols: Cognition and communication in infancy*. New York: Academic Press.

Bauman, M., & Kemper, T. (1985). Histoanatomic observation of the brain in early infantile autism. *Neurology, 35*, 866–874.

Bauman, M. L., & Kemper, T. L. (1986). Developmental cerebellar abnormalities: A consistent finding in early infantile autism. *Neurology, 36*, 190.

Bauman, M., & Kemper, T. (1988). Limbic and cerebellar abnormalities: Consistent findings in infantile autism. *Journal of Neuropathology and Experimental Neurology, 47*, 369.

Bauman, M., & Kemper, T. (1994a). *The neurobiology of autism*. Baltimore, MD: Johns Hopkins University Press.

Bauman, M. L., & Kemper, T. L. (1994b). Neuroanatomic observations of the brain in autism. In M. L. Bauman & T. L. Kemper (Eds.), *The neurobiology of autism* (pp. 119–145). Baltimore, MD: Johns Hopkins University Press.

Bishop, D. V. M. (1993). Annotation: Autism, executive functions, and theory of mind: A neuropsychological perspective. *Journal of Child Psychology and Psychiatry, 54*, 279–293.

Bolton, P., & Griffiths, P. (1997). Association of tuberous sclerosis of temporal lobes with autism and atypical autism. *Lancet, 349*, 392–395.

Bonda, E., Petrides, M., Ostry, D., & Evans, A. (1996). Specific involvement of human parietal systems and the amygdala in the perception of biological motion. *Journal of Neuroscience, 15*, 3737–3744.

Bowlby, J. (1969). *Attachment*. London: Hogarth Press.

Brentano, F. (1970). *Psychology from an empirical standpoint*. London: Routledge, and Kegan Paul.

Brothers, L. (1990). The social brain: A project for integrating primate behaviour and neurophysiology in a new domain. *Concepts in Neuroscience, 1*, 27–51.

Bruner, J. (1983). *Child's talk: Learning to use language*. Oxford: Oxford University Press.

Butterworth, G. (1991). The ontogeny and phylogeny of joint visual attention. In Whiten, A. (Ed.), *Natural theories of mind*. Oxford: Blackwell.

Collaer, M., & Hines, M. (1995). Human behavioural sex differences: A role for gonadal hormones during early development? *Psychological Bulletin, 118*, 55–107.

Connellan, J., Baron-Cohen, S., Wheelwright, S., Ba'tki, A., & Ahluwalia, J. (2001). Sex differences in human neonatal social perception. *Infant Behavior and Development, 23*, 113–118.

Courchesne, E., Townsend, J., Akshoomoff, N. A., Yeung-Courchesne, R., Lincoln, A. J., Press, G., et al. (1994). A new finding: Impairment in shifting attention in autistic and cerebellar patients. In S. H. Broman & J. Grafman (Eds.), *Atypical cognitive deficits in developmental disorders: Implications for brain function*. Hillsdale, NJ: Lawrence Erlbaum Associates, Inc.

Csibra, G., Gergely, G., Biro, S., Koos, O., & Brockbanck, M. (1999). Goal attribution without agency cues: The perception of "pure reason" in infancy. *Cognition, 72*, 253–284.

Damasio, A., Tranel, D., & Damasio, H. (1990). Individuals with sociopathic behaviour caused by frontal lobe damage fail to respond autonomically to socially charged stimuli. *Behavioural Brain Research, 14*, 81–94.

De Long, G. R. (1992). Autism, amnesia, hippocampus, and learning. *Neuroscience Behaviour Review, 16*, 63–70.

Dennett, D. (1987). *The intentional stance.* Cambridge, MA: MIT Press/Bradford Books.

Ekman, P. (1992). Facial expressions of emotion: An old controversy and new findings. *Philosophical Transactions of the Royal Society of London. Series B: Biological Sciences, 335*, 63–69.

Filipek, P. A. (1999). Neuroimaging in the developmental disorders: The state of the science. *Journal of Child Psychology and Psychiatry, 40*, 113–128.

Fodor, J. (1983). *The modularity of mind.* Cambridge, MA: Bradford Books.

Frith, U. (1991). *Autism and Asperger's syndrome.* Cambridge: Cambridge University Press.

Gelman, S., & Hirschfield, L. (1994). *Mapping the mind.* Cambridge: Press Syndicate, University of Cambridge.

Gergely, G., Nadasdy, Z., Gergely, C., & Biro, S. (1995). Taking the intentional stance at 12 months of age. *Cognition, 56*, 165–193.

Geschwind, N., & Galaburda, A. (1987). *Cerebral lateralization.* Cambridge, MA: MIT Press.

Geschwind, N., & Galaburda, A. M. (1985a). Cerebral lateralization. Biological mechanisms, associations, and pathology. I. A hypothesis and a program for research. *Archives of Neurology, 42*, 428–459.

Geschwind, N., & Galaburda, A. M. (1985b). Cerebral lateralization: Biological mechanisms, associations and pathology. II. A hypothesis and a program for research. *Archives of Neurology, 42*, 521–552.

Geschwind, N., & Galaburda, A. M. (1985c). Cerebral lateralization: Biological mechanisms, associations and pathology. III. A hypothesis and a program for research. *Archives of Neurology, 42*, 634–654.

Gillberg, I., Bjure, J., Uvebrant, P., Vestergren, E., & Gillberg, C. (1993). SPECT in 31 children and adolescents with autism and autistic like syndromes. *European Child and Adolescent Psychiatry, 2*, 50–59.

Goleman, D. (1995). *Emotional intelligence.* New York: Bantam Books.

Gross, C., Rocha-Miranda, C., & Bender, D. (1972). Visual properties of neurons in the inferotemporal cortex of the macaque. *Journal of Neurophysiology, 35*, 96–111.

Happe, F. (1993). Communicative competence and theory of mind in autism: A test of relevance theory. *Cognition, 48*, 101–119.

Happe, F., Ehlers, S., Fletcher, P., Frith, U., Johansson, M., Gillberg, C., et al. (1996). Theory of mind in the brain. Evidence from a PET scan study of Asperger syndrome. *Neuroreport, 8*, 197–201.

Harris, G. W., & Levine, S. (1962). Sexual differentiation of the brain and its experimental control. *Journal of Physiology, 181*, 379–400.

Harris, P., Johnson, C. N., Hutton, D., Andrews, G., & Cooke, T. (1989). Young children's theory of mind and emotion. *Cognition and Emotion, 3*, 379–400.

Hermelin, B., & O'Connor, N. (1970). *Psychological experiments with autistic children.* London: Pergamon Press.

Hetzler, B., & Griffin, J. (1981). Infantile autism and the temporal lobe of the brain. *Journal of Autism and Developmental Disorders, 9,* 153–157.

Hines, M., & Shipley, C. (1984). Prenatal exposure to diethylstilbestrol (DES) and the development of sexually dimorphic cognitive abilities and cerebral lateralisation. *Developmental Psychology, 20,* 81–94.

Hobson, R. P. (1986). The autistic child's appraisal of expressions of emotion. *Journal of Child Psychology and Psychiatry, 27,* 321–342.

Hood, B., Willen, J., & Driver, J. (1997). *An eye-direction detector triggers shifts of visual attention in human infants.* Unpublished manuscript, Harvard University.

Hyde, J. S., & Linn, M. C. (1988). Gender differences in verbal ability: A meta-analysis. *Psychological Bulletin, 104,* 53–69.

ICD-10 (1994). *International classification of diseases* (10th edn). Geneva, Switzerland: World Health Organization.

Johnson, S. (2000). The recognition of mentalistic agents in infancy. *Trends in Cognitive Sciences, 4,* 22–28.

Kanner, L. (1943). Autistic disturbance of affective contact. *Nervous Child, 2,* 217–250.

Karmiloff-Smith, A., Grant, J., Bellugi, U., & Baron-Cohen, S. (1995). Is there a social module? Language, face-processing and theory of mind in Williams syndrome and autism. *Journal of Cognitive Neuroscience, 7,* 196–208.

Kawashima, R., Sugiura, M., Kato, T., Nakamura, A., Hatano, K., Ito, K., et al. (1999). The human amygdala plays an important role in gaze monitoring. *Brain, 122,* 779–783.

Kimura, D. (1999). *Sex and cognition.* Cambridge, MA: MIT Press.

Kling, A., & Brothers, L. (1992). The amygdala and social behavior. In J. Aggleton (Ed.), *Neurobiological aspects of emotion, memory, and mental dysfunction.* New York: Wiley-Liss.

Leslie, A. M. (1987). Pretence and representation: The origins of "theory of mind". *Psychological Review, 94,* 412–426.

Leslie, A. (1995). ToMM, ToBy, and agency: Core architecture and domain specificity. In L. Hirschfeld & S. Gelman (Eds.), *Domain specificity in cognition and culture.* New York: Cambridge University Press.

Leslie, A., & Keeble, S. (1987). Do six-month old infants perceive causality? *Cognition, 25,* 265–288.

Leslie, A. M., & Frith, U. (1988). Autistic children's understanding of seeing, knowing, and believing. *British Journal of Developmental Psychology, 6,* 315–324.

Lutchmaya, S., Baron-Cohen, S., & Raggatt, P. (2002a). Foetal testosterone and eye contact in 12 month old infants. *Infant Behavior and Development, 25,* 327–335.

Lutchmaya, S., Baron-Cohen, S., & Raggatt, P. (2002b). Foetal testosterone and vocabulary size in 18- and 24-month-old infants. *Infant Behavior and Development, 24,* 418–424.

Maccoby, E., & Jacklin, N. (1974). *The psychology of sex differences.* Stanford, CA: Stanford University Press.

Morris, J., Frith, C., Perrett, D., Rowland, D., Young, A., Calder, A., et al. (1996). A differential neural response in the human amygdala to fearful and happy facial expressions. *Nature, 383,* 812–815.

Mundy, P., & Crowson, M. (1997). Joint attention and early social communication. *Journal of Autism and Developmental Disorders, 27,* 653–676.

Ozonoff, S., Pennington, B., & Rogers, S. J. (1990). Are there emotion perception deficits in young autistic children? *Journal of Child Psychology and Psychiatry, 31,* 343–363.

Perner, J., & Wimmer, H. (1985). "John thinks that Mary thinks that . . ." Attribution of second-order beliefs by 5–10 year old children. *Journal of Experimental Child Psychology, 39,* 437–471.

Pratt, C., & Bryant, P. (1990). Young children understand that looking leads to knowing (so long as they are looking into a single barrel). *Child Development, 61,* 973–983.

Premack, D. (1990). The infant's theory of self-propelled objects. *Cognition, 36,* 1–16.

Premack, D., & Woodruff, G. (1978). Does the chimpanzee have a "theory of mind"? *Behaviour and Brain Sciences, 4,* 515–526.

Rapin, I., & Katzman, R. (1998). Neurobiology of autism. *Annals of Neurology, 43,* 7–14.

Raven, J. C. (1956). *Coloured progressive matrices.* London: H. K. Lewis.

Raymond, G., Bauman, M., & Kemper, T. (1996). Hippocampus in autism: A Golgi analysis. *Acta Neuropathologica, 91,* 117–119.

Rimland, B. (1964). *Infantile autism: The syndrome and its implications for a neural theory of behaviour.* New York: Appleton-Century-Crofts.

Rochat, P., Morgan, R., & Carpenter, M. (1997). Young infants' sensitivity to movement information specifying social causality. *Cognitive Development, 12,* 537–561.

Rutter, M. (1978). Language disorder and infantile autism. In M. Rutter & E. Schopler (Eds.), *Autism: A reappraisal of concepts and treatment.* New York: Plenum.

Sacks, O. (1994). *An anthropologist on Mars.* New York: Knopf.

Scaife, M., & Bruner, J. (1975). The capacity for joint visual attention in the infant. *Nature, 253,* 265–266.

Shantz, C. (1983). Social cognition. In P. Mussen (Ed.), *Handbook of child psychology. Volume 3: Cognitive development* (pp. 495–555). New York: Wiley.

Tager-Flusberg, H. (1993). What language reveals about the understanding of minds in children with autism. In S. Baron-Cohen, H. Tager-Flusberg, & D. Cohen (Eds.), *Understanding other minds: Perspectives from autism.* Oxford: Oxford University Press.

Tager-Flusberg, H., Boshart, J., & Baron-Cohen, S. (1998). Reading the windows of the soul: Evidence of domain specificity sparing in Williams syndrome. *Journal of Cognitive Neuroscience, 10,* 631–639.

Tomasello, M. (1988). The role of joint-attentional processes in early language acquisition. *Language Sciences, 10,* 69–88.

Tranel, D., & Hyman, B. T. (1990). Neuropsychological correlates of bilateral amygdala damage. *Archives of Neurology, 47,* 349–355.

Walker, A. S. (1982). Intermodal perception of expressive behaviours by human infants. *Journal of Experimental Child Psychology, 33,* 514–535.

Wechsler, D. (1939). *The measurement of adult intelligence.* Baltimore, MD: Williams and Wilkins.

Wellman, H. (1990). *Children's theories of mind.* Cambridge, MA: MIT Press.

Wellman, H., & Bartsch, K. (1988). Young children's reasoning about beliefs. *Cognition, 30,* 239–277.

Whalen, P. J., Rauch, S. L., Etcoff, N. L., McInerney, S. C., Lee, M. B., & Jenike, M. A. (1998). Masked presentations of emotional facial expressions modulate amygdala activity without explicit knowledge. *Journal of Neuroscience, 18,* 411–418.

Whiten, A. (1991). *Natural theories of mind*. Oxford: Basil Blackwell.
Whiten, A. (1997). The Machiavellian mindreader. In A. Whiten & R. W. Byrne (Eds.), *Machiavellian intelligence II: Evaluations and extensions*. Cambridge: Cambridge University Press.
Wicker, B., Michel, F., Henaff, M., & Decety, J. (1998). Brain regions involved in the perception of gaze: A PET study. *NeuroImage, 8*, 221–227.
Williams, C., Barnett, A., & Meck, W. (1990). Organisational effects of early gonadal secretions on sexual differentiation in spatial memory. *Behavioural Neuroscience, 104*, 84–97.
Wilson, J. D., Foster, D. W., Kronenberg, H. M., & Larsen, P. R. (Eds.). (1998). *Williams Textbook of Endocrinology*. Philadelphia: W. B. Saunders.
Wimmer, H., & Perner, J. (1983). Beliefs about beliefs: Representation and constraining function of wrong beliefs in young children's understanding of deception. *Cognition, 13*, 103–128.
Wing, L. (1981). Asperger syndrome: A clinical account. *Psychological Medicine, 11*, 115–130.
Wing, L., & Gould, J. (1979). Severe impairments of social interaction and associated abnormalities in children: Epidemiology and classification. *Journal of Autism and Developmental Disorders, 9*, 11–29.
Yirmiya, N., Sigman, M., Kasari, C., & Mundy, P. (1992). Empathy and cognition in high functioning children with autism. *Child Development, 63*, 150–160.
Young, A., Hellawell, D., De Wal, C., & Johnson, M. (1996). Facial expression processing after amygdalectomy. *Neuropsychologia, 34*, 31–39.

9 The neurobiology of social cognition and its relationship to unipolar depression

Zoë Kyte and Ian Goodyer

The aim of this chapter is to provide a review of current knowledge regarding the development of social cognitive neuroscience as a discipline and its relevance to the study of depression. The work discussed focuses on the idea that unipolar depression is now seen as a disorder not only of emotion regulation, but also of alterations in the neuropsychological, and hence social cognition, of affected individuals. In this sense, a relationship exists not only as a result of commonalities between the neurobiology of the emotional and social brain, but also as a result of the relationship between deficits in social cognition (executive functions such as decision making, and more obviously disruptions in emotion) and the presence and persistence of unipolar depression.

Introduction

Depressive syndromes constitute a group of serious mental disorders with considerable risk of recurrence and subsequent psychosocial impairment with, in some cases, onset in childhood and adolescence and continuity into adult life (American Psychiatric Association, 1994; Harrington & Dubicka, 2001). Use of the DSM-IV clinical criteria (American Psychiatric Association, 1994) successfully identifies the same clinical syndromes in school age children, adolescents, and adults. Phenomenological psychopathology remains the core construct guiding the identification of criteria for diagnosis with no dependency on putative causation. This system has proven highly successful in generating a common language for the diagnosis of depressive disorders that makes research findings comparable between investigations despite marked differences in the nature of the populations studied. This categorical approach to classification of depression is not without its detractors, however. For example, it is widely recognized that meeting inclusion criteria still allows for considerable variation in clinical presentation, including high levels of nondepressive symptoms, giving rise to marked individual differences in the descriptive psychopathology of depression. With the main research emphasis on the quantity of depressive symptoms as predictors of subsequent onset of depression, little attention has been paid as yet to the relative importance of different types of symptoms, or their salience to the subject, for evolving a depressive disorder. In addition, many individuals present with a range of symptoms that fall below inclusion threshold for a diagnosis (too few or insufficient duration) but are of sufficient severity to cause personal impairment (Costello et al., 1996).

An essential feature is that of a change in mood from pleasant (euphoric) to unpleasant (dysphoric) or even painful. This mood shift is experienced as relatively pervasive, persisting over time and place and sufficiently severe to interrupt everyday functioning. This negative mood state is accompanied by other sets of features in varying combinations, including negative and distorted cognitions about the self, impaired concentration and attention, and an adverse alteration in a range of physical characteristics including eating, sleeping, energy, and activity.

Unipolar major depression

Most research into affective disorders over the past four decades has been focused on unipolar major depression (from here on referred to as unipolar depression). According to DSM-IV (American Psychiatric Association, 1994), a diagnosis of unipolar depression requires the establishment, firstly, of the mandatory presence of lowered mood (dysphoria, or irritability in children) or loss of interest/pleasure (anhedonia) together with four of seven other possible nonmandatory symptoms from the two broad domains of disordered cognitions and physical changes. These are shown in Table 9.1.

It is essential that the five symptoms occur concurrently over a minimum 2-week period. In children and adolescents, but not in adults, the entry criteria of lowered mood can be irritability. It is important to establish that these symptoms are not accounted for by the direct effects of substance misuse or a general medical condition, particularly one that involves known brain changes, as this reduces the likelihood of reliable and valid mental state assessments. In addition, the symptoms should not be accounted for by recent bereavement. It is worth noting, however, that these caveats do not

Table 9.1 Symptoms of unipolar depression in childhood and adolescence

Mood*	Cognitive	Physical
Dysphoria or irritability in children	Anhedonia* Feelings of worthlessness Inappropriate guilt Diminished ability to think/concentrate Recurrent thoughts of death/suicide	Weight change (includes failure to make expected weight gains) Fatigue or loss of energy Psychomotor agitation or retardation

* The diagnosis can be made only when five or more symptoms are present over a 2-week period. Dysphoric mood (or irritability in children) or anhedonia must be present.

imply that such subjects cannot be subsequently clinically depressed as a consequence of these experiences, but rather that symptoms essential to the diagnosis may be acute or transient and therefore increase the liability of a false-positive diagnosis at the time of presentation.

There are no requirements for a particular pattern of cognition and/or physical symptoms. No distinction is made regarding the duration of this disorder, which, providing symptoms have been present for at least 2 weeks, may vary in length for any period of time, up to a number of years. The disorder may also differ in its severity or degree of personal psychosocial impairment, ranging from mild, indicating only a modest deviation from normal behavioural functioning, to patients being unable to care for themselves and requiring 24-h intensive psychiatric care. Finally, in both community and clinical studies, 50–80% of unipolar depressions present with concurrent nondepressive comorbid disorders involving symptoms of antisocial behaviour, obsessionality, general anxiety, or substance misuse. The precise temporal relationship between depressive and nondepressive symptoms remains an important component of developmental research. It is likely that a proportion of unipolar depressions are preceded by nondepressive difficulties, whereas for others the emergence of unipolar depression increases the liability to other comorbid disorders.

There is now general agreement that unipolar (and other) depression is heterogeneous in aetiology and clinical presentation. Genetic and environmental (physiological, psychological, and social) processes combine in as yet undetermined ways to increase the liability to these complex and common mental disorders. For some, episodes are sporadic and relatively short-lived (weeks), whereas, for others, a first episode heralds the emergence of a protracted and disabling condition with a high risk of recurrence and persistence for many months and years (Goodyer, 2003). The purpose of the rest of this chapter is to consider our current understanding of how affective-cognitive processes may be involved in the aetiology and course of this mental disorder.

Unipolar depression and development

Depressive disorders occur throughout the lifespan, although the nature, characteristics, and outcomes of the condition may vary with age (Goodyer, 2003; Kovacs, 1996). Critical to a complete understanding is to establish whether children, adolescents, adults, and the elderly all suffer from the same disorder, sharing a common aetiology and a similar response to treatment.

Research to date supports the view that specific developmental differences are observed, despite concurrent reports of similarities in the clinical picture and longitudinal course of unipolar depression in children, adolescents, and adults (Kovacs, 1996). One of the most notable differences has been in the response of patients at different ages to treatment, with depressed children failing to respond to tricyclic antidepressants in the same manner seen in older age groups (Hazell, O'Connell, Heathcote, Robertson, & Henry, 1995;

Keller et al., 2001), and the elderly perhaps being more responsive to interpersonal therapies than previously supposed (Reynolds, Frank, & Perel, 1999). Similarly, differences have also been reported in the neurobiological correlates of the disorder across development, with depressed children failing to show evidence of hypercortisolaemia as frequently as seen in adolescent and adult populations (Kaufman & Ryan, 1999; Lupien et al., 1999).

A number of these discrepancies may be explained by the fact that many of the neurobiological systems implicated in the pathophysiology of unipolar depression, and many of the neuronal circuits thought to correspond to specific behaviours, are not fully developed until adulthood. There is also increasing evidence that, in the prepubertal child, environmental effects, such as maltreatment, social, and/or nutritional deprivation, may have significant effects on brain circuits involved in affect regulation (Lupien, King, Meaney, & McEwen, 2001). Of particular significance are the toxic effects of persistently or intermittently elevated cortisol levels in the amygdala and hippocampus in some such individuals, making glucocorticoid receptors vulnerable to other toxins and leading to atrophy and loss of function (Sapolsky, 2000). Thus, some children may develop vulnerable brain systems that subserve affective-cognitive processes involved in depressions. This may result in these systems being unable to adapt at times of subsequent stress, and rather than a sporadic recovery following subsequent negative life events, persistent dysfunction at the neural level with persisting adverse effects on the affective and cognitive processing is more likely to accrue. As yet, we have no longitudinal data to determine whether children showing cortisol hypersecretion in prepubertal childhood are significantly more at risk in later life of cognitive dysfunction and/or elevated levels of unipolar depression. During adolescence, however, morning elevations of cortisol are associated with the subsequent onset of unipolar depression (Goodyer, Herbert, Tamplin, & Altham, 2000). Experimentally inducing high cortisol levels is associated with impairments in cognitive functions (Newcomer et al., 1999). The issue is complex, however, as cortisol in the normal range is essential for efficient information processing, suggesting an inverted U-shaped curve for its role in cognitive function with persistent high and low levels leading to impairments (Lupien, Wilkinson, Briere, Menard, Ng Ying Kin, & Nair, 2002a; Lupien, Wilkinson, Briere, Ng Ying Kin, Meaney, & Nair 2002b).

There are several factors, other than glucocorticoid effects, that may also be important in explaining discrepancies between younger and older populations. For example, the extent to which genetic and environmental factors and processes contribute to the onset of unipolar depression may vary according to the developmental components of ageing. In particular, the liability to serotonin depletion on the onset and course of depression may vary with the genetic characteristics of the serotonin-transporter gene, whose influence may change with age; the liability to neural vulnerability may increase following activation of the hypothalamic-pituitary-gonadal axis, leading to marked increase in circulating sex hormones in the periphery and the brain;

and the rise and fall of dehydroepiandrosterone (DHEA) levels in the brain may alter the neurovascular sensitivity of brain circuits to events such as infections, adverse social experiences and medical illness. Detailed discussion of these and other related issues concerning the biology of unipolar depressions across the lifespan is beyond the scope of this chapter. However, the interested reader may wish to consult *Unipolar Depression: A Lifespan Perspective* (Goodyer, 2003), as a preliminary guide to the field of developmental and clinical affective neuroscience.

Collectively, the evidence suggests that there are both developmental differences and similarities between child, adolescent, adult, and late life depressions (Kaufman, Martin, King, & Charney, 2001). These include maturation of the hypothalamic-pituitary and hypothalamic-gonadal axes through the second decade of life, menopausal factors in mid-life, and vascular and neural changes in late life. To what extent these changes correlate with affective-cognitive processes related to the liability for and outcomes of affective disorders remains to be established.

Cognitive theories of depression

One of the most common characteristics of unipolar depression is a predominantly negative view of the self and the individual's experiences. This is reflected in one of the most influential of the cognitive theories, proposed by Aaron Beck (1967, 1976). Beck's theory of depression is based on clinical observations leading to the assumption that people who experience depression are vulnerable as a result of possessing negative cognitive schemas. These schemas are defined as underlying cognitive structures that are implemented for screening, coding, and evaluating stimuli to ultimately allow an individual to categorize and interpret experiences in a meaningful manner. They are thought to form in childhood and remain relatively stable throughout the lifespan. However, they persist in a latent state, becoming activated only when the individual is exposed to negative circumstances. Once activated, these schemas are thought to bias information processing so as to select and encode negative at the expense of positive stimuli, even if this involves distorting the balance of information being perceived or altering the perception of a situation so as to match the affective tone of the bias. The result is a "negative cognitive triad" in which patterns of negative thinking are concerned with three critical aspects of life: the self (a view of oneself as inadequate or worthless), the world (drawing the most negative possible interpretation), and the future (the belief that current difficulties and suffering will continue indefinitely). In addition, more specific distortions (or "errors in logic") may serve as a second mechanism of depression in which the individual overgeneralizes (draws global conclusions about worth, ability, or performance on the basis of a single fact), makes arbitrary inferences (jumps to unsupported negative conclusions), and magnifies or minimizes specific events (makes gross errors of evaluation in which small negative events are magnified and large positive events are minimized). The consequence is a vicious cycle in which an increase in negative thinking lowers mood, which in turn increases activation of schemas and hence increases negative thinking. This cycle is hypothesized to be important in both the aetiology and maintenance of unipolar depression as part of a pattern of interacting mechanisms that includes biological, psychological, and social factors (Teasdale & Barnard, 1993).

A second influential cognitive theory that reflects upon vulnerability to depression is that of the "learned helplessness theory" put forward by Seligman (1975). In this theory, depression is viewed as a result of the expectation of future helplessness (that is, expecting bad events to occur and believing there is nothing that can be done to prevent them). This theory is based on the finding that when dogs are exposed to unavoidable and unescapable electric shocks, they experience three consequences which do not occur in dogs that experience the same amount of shock but are able to control it: motivational deficits (not initiating subsequent escape responses in the presence of stress), cognitive deficits (slower to learn that responses could control future stress as a result of acquiring a cognitive set in which responses are irrelevant to outcome), and emotional deficits (transient emotional effects as a result of inescapable trauma).

Although helplessness is viewed as arising from the perception of uncontrollability within the boundaries of learned helplessness theory, an important determinant was later thought to be both the type and the importance of the event experienced in conjunction with the explanation that the individual attributes to the cause of the event. Based on this assumption, the original learned helplessness theory was reformulated (Abramson, Seligman, & Teasdale, 1978) to include three attributional dimensions that were proposed to govern when and where future helplessness deficits would be displayed: internal–external (that is, whether the cause is seen to be due to something about the individual [internal] or due to something about other people or circumstances [external]), stable–unstable (that is, whether the cause is something permanent or transient), and global–specific (that is, whether the cause will produce failure in a wide variety of circumstances or only in similar circumstances). Consequently, the emotional, motivational, and cognitive deficits seen in unipolar depression are proposed to be accounted for by a particular set of attributions following the occurrence of a negative event, with the crucial attribution type being internal–stable–global for the causes of negative events, and external–unstable–specific for positive events.

In contrast to more clinically derived cognitive theories of depression, alternative theories have also been developed out of experimental investigations into aspects of information processing in both depressed patients and well individuals induced into a state of sadness. The findings of such studies provided the challenge to develop an exploratory theoretical account, which was attempted by Gordon Bower through his associative network theory of mood and memory (Bower, 1981). This theory proposes that concepts, events, and meaning are all represented in memory by nodes within a network. Activation within this network depends on a number of factors, including the proximity of nodes to each other, the strength of the initial activation, and the time lapse since activation. The theory makes the broad prediction that each emotion has a specific node within the network, which then becomes associated with a range of perceptual, attentional, and mnemonic biases via the interaction of the emotion node with other nodes.

Application of this network theory to clinical depression suggests that there is a reciprocal relationship between negative thinking and the depressed mood activated when social adversities cause dysphoria in vulnerable individuals. This interdependence results in the individual experiencing a recursive and potentiating cycle in which depressed mood increases access to negative thoughts, leading to an increase in a negative bias toward the interpretation of current events and difficulties. This negative affective-cognitive cycle is postulated as responsible for the emergence of clinically impairing depression (Teasdale & Barnard, 1993).

The "differential activation hypothesis" (Teasdale, 1983, 1988) takes the associative network theory a step further by suggesting that vulnerability to intense and persistent depression may be determined by individual differences in the patterns of negative thinking that become activated during a state of mild depression or dysphoria. During such a state, vulnerable individuals are hypothesized to access qualitatively different types of negative cognitions than nonvulnerable individuals, thereby determining why it is that not all individuals who experience mild depression enter into the vicious cycle in which negative self-cognitions and dysphoric mood act upon each other, thus intensifying and maintaining depression.

The diversity of unipolar depression

Despite existing accounts of vulnerability to depression and attempts to elucidate mechanisms of predisposition or precipitation, the heterogeneous nature of the disorder means that it remains unclear what combination of genetic, physiological, psychological, and social factors are required to activate the onset of a depressive episode. Furthermore, it also remains unclear whether repeatedly observed specific profiles of cognition and behaviour occur as a consequence or a cause of the disorder, and whether such patterns remain stable with recurrent episodes of unipolar depression.

Although the answers to these questions may vary according to the stage of development within which an episode occurs, there are several other factors that may alter the experience and manifestation of disorder. Primarily, distinctions between individual subtypes of affective disorder are likely to yield different patterns of performance both experimentally and behaviourally. The most obvious of these is between unipolar and bipolar depression, where reports include differences not only in clinical presentation and symptoms, but also in profiles of neuropsychological function (Borkowska & Rybakowski, 2001) and information biasing (Murphy et al., 1999). For the purposes of the current chapter, attention will be focused on a discussion of social cognition within the context of unipolar depression only.

A second notable distinction is between first and recurrent-episode unipolar depression. Not only may differences be identified in relation to the predictors of first onset versus recurrence, but also in terms of how risk processes may differ (Goodyer, Herbert, Secher, & Pearson, 1997; Lewinsohn, Allen, Seeley, & Gotlib, 1999). For example, Post (Post, 1992; Post, Weiss, Leverich, George, Frye, & Ketter, 1996) proposed a "stress sensitization" model in which higher levels of stress are required to trigger an initial episode of depression than subsequent episodes, to the extent that eventually episodes may occur in the complete absence of stress. This notion of recurrent episodes being triggered without a social precipitant has received support from an investigation of a large sample of twins, which showed an inverse association between negative life events and number of episodes of depression over many years (Kendler, Thornton, & Gardner, 2000). It appears that there may be two distinct pathways of the liability to this kindling effect (that is, onset of a depressive episode as a consequence of evolving internal sensitivities in brain processes without further external precipitants), one through multiple social adversities, and another through genetic effects on recurrence (Kendler, Thornton, & Gardner, 2001). The implications of these changes in mind–brain relationships as a consequence of recurrent disorder, for psychological theories of depression, have yet to be determined.

Teasdale's (1983, 1988) differential activation hypothesis recognizes the putative importance of distinguishing between first onset and recurrent episodes in that the links between "depressogenic" information-processing patterns and dysphoria are hypothesized to be stronger in individuals with previous experience of an episode anticipating a possible kindling effect (Teasdale & Dent, 1987).

A final issue is that of comorbidity. It is now well known that unipolar depression in adolescence and adulthood is often comorbid with numerous other diagnoses, including anxiety disorders, obsessive-compulsive disorder, conduct disorder, and substance abuse (Angold, Costello, & Erkanli, 1999; Costello, Angold, & Keeler, 1999). The presence of link comorbidity is thought to be more common in younger than older patients (Cassidy, Ahearn, & Carroll, 2001), with reports indicating a poorer short-term outcome and the potential for a greater degree of impairment (Harrington, Fudge, Rutter, Pickles, & Hill, 1991) in those patients with one or more comorbid diagnoses.

Social cognition, unipolar depression, and the brain

Social cognition refers to the cognitive processes that subserve the diverse and flexible social behaviours seen in humans and other primates alike. Studies of these processes have long been conducted within developmental, comparative, and social psychology. However, more recent advances have focused on elucidating the underlying neural mechanisms of processes collectively involved in social cognition, including decision making, attention, memory, and emotion (Adolphs, 2001). This offers a possible reconciliation of biological and psychological approaches to social behaviour through "the realisation that neural regulation reflects both innate, automatic and cognitively impenetrable mechanisms, as well as acquired, contextual and volitional aspects" (Adolphs, 2003, p. 165).

As will be discussed, unipolar depression is characterized by a number of deficits in functions that come under the umbrella of social cognition (including decision making and, more obviously, emotion). As a result of recent applications of neuroimaging and the development of cognitive neuroscience as a discipline, unipolar depression is now becoming recognized as a disorder not only of emotion regulation, but also of alterations in the neuropsychological functioning of affected individuals. The result is the potential for more detailed accounts of the neural mechanisms underlying features of depression, including lack of motivation and interest; inability to initiate, organize, and concentrate; and suboptimal decision making, which ultimately compromise behaviour within a range of social contexts, from relationships to careers.

The emotional and social brain

Grady and Keightley (2002) outline 10 regions of the brain believed to be associated with various critical components within the domain of social cognition. These include regions of the anterior cingulate, that is, the subgenual cingulate (autonomic responses and reward mechanisms; Damasio, Tranel & Damasio, 1990; Price, 1999, respectively), the rostral cingulate (processing of emotional stimuli; Taylor, Liberson, Fig, Decker, Minoshima, & Koeppe, 1998; Whalen, Rauch, Etcoff, McInerney, Lee, & Jenike, 1998), and the dorsal cingulate (error monitoring and selecting among competing responses; Bush, Whalen, Rosen, McInerney, & Jenike, 1998; Pardo, Pardo, Janer, & Raichle, 1990; Paus, Petrides, Evans, & Meyer, 1993); regions thought to be involved in face perception, that is, the fusiform gyrus (face discrimination; Haxby, Haxby, Horwitz, Ungerleider, Maisog, Pietrini, & Grady, 1994), the superior temporal sulcus (gaze direction and motion of body parts; Puce, Allison, Bentin, Gore, & Pantelis, 1998; Decety & Grezes, 1999; Hoffman & Haxby, 2000), and the amygdala (emotional processing; Le Doux, 2000); and regions within the prefrontal cortex (PFC), that is, the orbitofrontal cortex (OFC; decision making in the context of emotional situations; Bechara, Tranel, & Damasio, 2000a; Rogers et al., 1999b), the ventrolateral PFC (VLPFC; responding to reward contingencies; Rogers et al., 1999b), the dorsolateral PFC (DLPFC; executive functions and working memory; D'Esposito, Postle, Ballard, & Lease, 1999), and the dorsomedial PFC (DMPFC; self-reference and internal versus external focus; Craik, Moroz,

Moscovitch, Stuss, Winocur, & Tulving, 1999; Gusnard, Akbudak, Shulman, & Raichle, 2001).

Thus, social cognition arises from a coordinated neural network which gives rise to a pattern of processes that modulate action responses. The psychological output of these processes includes memory, decision making, attention, and motivation. Interestingly, the majority of brain structures subserving social cognition also process emotions. This demonstrates a putatively critical set of relations between feeling and thought and, perhaps not surprisingly, suggests that the basis of disorders of emotion is in the same neural systems (Grady & Keightley, 2002).

Social cognition, the brain, and unipolar depression

PET studies conducted on adults with unipolar depression have demonstrated changes in regional cerebral blood flow (rCBF) and glucose metabolism in areas including the amygdala, the anterior cingulate, the OFC, and the DLPFC (Bench, Friston, Brown, & Scott, 1992; Dolan, Bench, Brown, Scott, & Frackowiak, 1994; Drevets, 2001; Elliott et al., 1997; Mayberg et al., 1999). Specifically, areas that are reportedly involved in higher cognitive function, such as the DLPFC, appear deactivated, while structures mediating emotional and stress responses are increasingly activated. Reports of increased activity in the amygdala, in particular, have been interpreted as possibly reflecting stimulation of cortical structures involved in declarative memory, thus accounting for the tendency of individuals with depression to ruminate about memories that are emotionally negative (Drevets, 2000). In addition, increased metabolic activity in the ventromedial PFC (VMPFC) has been associated with severity of depression (Drevets, Price, Simpson, Todd, Reich, & Vannier, 1997), and there is existing evidence that greater activity in the rostral cingulate may be critical in the recovery from depression (Mayberg, Brannan, Mahurin, Jerabek, Brickman, & Tekell, 1997).

Of these abnormalities, those that are located in regions where CBF increases during normal and other pathological emotional states appear to be mood-state dependent, increasing or decreasing in response to the emotional and cognitive manifestations of the disorder. On the other hand, abnormalities found in orbital and medial PFC areas appear to persist following remission of symptoms, and in this case have been linked more often to the presence of anatomic differences between depressed and nondepressed individuals, and are therefore suggested to be involved in the pathogenesis of depressive symptoms (Drevets, 2000). More specifically, postmortem studies of patients with unipolar depression have reported reductions in cortical thickness, neuronal sizes, and neuronal and glial densities (Rajkowska et al., 1999), raising the possibility that these neuropathological changes bring about impairment in orbital function which then predispose an individual to disorder.

Both mood-state-dependent and anatomically based abnormalities are consistent with abnormalities shown during not only a state of clinical depression, but also experimentally induced sad mood. For instance, Mayberg et al. (1999) demonstrated that provoked sadness was associated with increases in rCBF in the ventral limbic and paralimbic regions (including the subgenual cingulate and insula), but also with decreases in rCBF in dorsal cortical regions (namely, right dorsal prefrontal, inferior parietal, dorsal anterior cingulate, and posterior cingulate). In comparison to depressed individuals in remission, changes were reported in the same brain regions as in healthy individuals experiencing transient sadness, but in the reversed direction (namely, increases in dorsal cortical regions and decreases in ventral limbic and paralimbic regions). They concluded that sad mood appears to be associated with a specific pattern of change in the limbic and cortical regions—areas that are altered in depression—and that resolution of negative mood symptoms in depressive illness results in normalization of this pattern. Similarly, an earlier study conducted by Mayberg, Liotti, Brannan, McGinnis, Mahurin, & Jerabek (1998) reported results from a mood-induction procedure comparing individuals in remission from depression with acutely depressed individuals and controls, whereby mood-related changes were reported to be similar with the exception of the rostral cingulate. Decreased activity in this region within the remitted group, increased activity in the acutely ill patients, and no change in the control group suggest that this region may play a unique role in regulating emotional health.

Given that unipolar depression appears to be associated with abnormal functioning in both higher cognitive *and* limbic domains, a consensus is now emerging to explain the phenomenology of depression on the basis of a malfunction in the regulation of an entire network of brain regions involved in both emotional behaviour and social cognition (Mayberg et al., 1997). Supported by comparative anatomical studies, reciprocal pathways linking limbic structures (amygdala, cingulate, hypothalamus, and hippocampus) with widely distributed brainstem, striatal, paralimbic, and neocortical sites have been defined in rhesus monkeys (Pandya & Yeterian, 1996) and associated with specific motivational and emotional behaviours in marmosets (Dias, Roberts, & Robbins, 1996). Extrapolating from nonhuman primates to humans, we can perhaps assume that these same neural structures are also responsible for the culmination of sensory, cognitive, and autonomic processing that exists at the core of both normal and abnormal emotional experience (Mayberg et al., 1999). These neural structures are now considered within two critical circuits: a limbic-thalamic-cortical (LTC) circuit, involving the amygdala, medial thalamus, and orbital and medial PFC; and a limbic-cortical-striatal-pallidal-thalamic (LCSPT) circuit, involving components of the previous circuit with the addition of related parts of the striatum and pallidum (Drevets, Videen, Price, Preskorn, Carmichael, & Raichle, 1992). The presence of these circuits supports a neural model of unipolar depression in which dysfunction involving regions that modulate or inhibit emotional behaviour may, either directly or indirectly, result in the emotional, motivation, cognitive, and behavioural manifestations of mood disorders.

Cognitive and social manifestations of unipolar depression

Recent advances in neuroscience have opened up possibilities for characterizing the neural mechanisms underlying mood disorders, and this, in turn, has contributed to a more advanced understanding of the cognitive and social manifestations of unipolar depression. There is now considerable acceptance that there are substantial deficits in cognitive, motor, perceptual, and communication tasks, noted by Miller (1975), in patients with unipolar depression. These observations have been further detailed in recent years. For instance, Brown, Scott, Bench, & Dolan (1994) proposed that cognitive dysfunction is *intrinsic* to unipolar depression and directly related to the neurobiology of the disorder. Veiel (1997) and Goodwin (1997) also propose that although deficits in depressed patients have been reported in many cognitive domains, it may be *executive* deficits (that is, deficits in the cognitive processes that are required during social interactions for optimal performance) that are particularly prominent. Current debate now centres on the exact nature of these deficits, within the context of what this can add to our existing knowledge about the neuroanatomical profile of unipolar depression.

What are executive functions?

Executive functions are inherent in all purposeful behaviour, including arousal of interest, intentional action, and the attainment of reward. They are cognitive processes that are required in many instances of human social interaction due to their ability to allow an individual to perform and interact within a variety of challenging contexts efficiently and optimally (Baddeley, 1986). Although distinct from the cognitive domains of perception, memory, and language, they are thought to overlap with capacities of attention, reasoning, and problem solving.

Within the domain of human social interaction, performance of any task generally requires a sequence of operations, including both mental processes and overt actions (Duncan, 1986). Among others, these consist of developing an awareness of the desired goal or outcome of the event, developing a strategic plan of action in order to achieve this goal, and inhibiting or deferring inappropriate behavioural responses so that the most appropriate response option can be initiated. Each of these individual processes, or "context-specific action selections" (Pennington & Ozonoff, 1996), is thought to be dependent upon the integration of information from a range of abilities, including attention, planning, decision making, inhibition, and memory (Tamminga, 2000), and it is these abilities that are referred to as executive functions. Any social interaction or circumstance that demands optimal responding is therefore likely to recruit and be reliant upon, at least in part, the expression of these abilities.

The role of executive functions in unipolar depression

Since the early reports of cognitive dysfunction (Miller, 1975), studies have been unsuccessful in accumulating evidence to suggest a profile of deficits that is specific to unipolar depression compared to other psychopathologies (Veiel, 1997). Instead, it seems there is an extensive range of neuropsychological deficits that are associated with a global-diffuse impairment in brain function, consistent with the neural model of unipolar depression. As assessed by standard neuropsychological testing, deficits have been typically dominated by difficulties in the areas of attention (Franke, Maier, Hardt, Frieboes, Lichtermann, & Hain, 1993; Purcell, Maruff, Kyrios, & Pantelis, 1997), behavioural inhibition (Murphy et al., 1999), memory (Abas, Sahakian, & Teasdale, 1990; Ilsley, Moffoot, & O'Carroll, 1995), decision making (Murphy et al., 2001; Rahman, Sahakian, Cardinal, Rogers, & Robbins, 2001), and planning (Beats, Sahakian, & Levy, 1996).

Studies examining how the presence of unipolar depression interferes with executive skills have generally focused on currently ill adult and often elderly populations, resulting in a lack of clarity as to the issue of cause or consequence of disorder. Studies are also lacking in clarity as to whether similar deficits in cognitive function also occur in younger, first-episode depressed populations, and, if so, what the nature of these deficits is (Purcell et al., 1997), although studies are beginning to emerge that document executive skills in child and adolescent populations (Kyte, Goodyer, & Sahakian, 2004; Luciana, Lindeke, Georgieff, Mills, & Nelson, 1999; Luciana & Nelson, 1998). Of the studies on adult populations, many are conflicting in their accounts of deficits, possibly as a result of the diversity in clinical and demographic profiles of patients, with some profiles having a more direct effect on performance than others. Alternatively, features such as stage of development, lack of motivation (Miller, 1975), diminished cognitive capacity and processing resources (Hasher & Zacks, 1979), narrowing of attentional focus to mood-congruent thoughts (Ellis & Ashbrook, 1988) or abnormal response to performance feedback (Elliott et al., 1997; Elliott, Sahakian, McKay, Herrod, Robbins, & Paykel, 1996) may also account for many of the differential reports of neuropsychological impairments in unipolar depression across studies.

Decision making in unipolar depression

One cognitive process which not only guides social cognition, but is also an example of an executive function which has been reported as disrupted in unipolar depression, is that of decision making (Murphy et al., 2001). The role of decision making in social cognition is clearly represented by the need for individuals to choose between alternative courses of action in order to keep their behaviour coherent and efficient during everyday social interactions. Making such decisions is likely to involve considering and anticipating desired future outcomes, in addition to weighing up the probability of that outcome within the context of the resources that are both available and necessary to achieve that outcome. Central components of the decision making process are therefore likely to rely upon attentional and working-memory resources, as well as being composed of a highly emotional content as a consequence of the influence that mood and affect are proposed to have on decision making (Le Doux, 1996; Zajonc, 1984).

The role of emotions in effective decision making was demonstrated when patients with damage to the VMPFC were shown to display a compromised ability to engage emotions and experience feelings in complex personal and social situations, despite performing normally on many neuropsychological tests (including those of memory, language, and perception) and demonstrating a preserved intelligence (Tranel, Bechara, & Damasio, 2000). The nature of these deficits, coupled with the fact that they could not be accounted for by disruption in the availability of social knowledge, inability to apply logic to such knowledge, or general deficits in attention or language, led to the development of the "somatic marker hypothesis" (Damasio, 1994; Damasio, Tranel, & Damasio, 1991); a systems-level neuroanatomical and cognitive framework of decision making.

The key premise of the somatic marker hypothesis is that deficits in bioregulatory responses explain the pattern of change in social conduct and decision making capacity often seen in patients with VMPFC damage. The proposition is that many of the processes involved in the operation of decision making, including the experience of emotion and feeling, are expressed predominantly, although not exclusively, through changes in the representation of body states. The idea of distinct autonomic patterns of activity being associated with particular emotions and that the perception of these bodily changes is what constitutes the subjective experience of emotion is not new (Cannon, 1927; Ekman, Levenson, & Frieson, 1983; James, 1884). However, the somatic marker hypothesis expands on original work through its discussion of a neural network, including structures within the VMPFC that are seen as central to experiencing emotions. Damasio (Damasio, 1994; Damasio et al., 1991) proposes that these networks promote associations between each other that are specific for various classes of complex stimuli that encompass a given situation and a range of internal states of the individual. Exposure to a member of that class of stimuli will evoke a conscious feeling. These internal states are referred to as "somatic" in that they are represented in the brain as transient changes in activity in somatosensory maps in a large range of structures, including the brainstem, hypothalamus, and cerebral cortex. Consequently, when an individual re-experiences a particular class of complex stimuli, the systems within the VMPFC that developed the initial associations trigger the accompanying, and most appropriate, somatic state and hence emotion. This reactivation process can be achieved either through a "body-loop", in which the soma actually changes in response to the activation, or via an "as-if-body-loop", in which the body is bypassed, and reactivation signals are relayed directly to the somatosensory structures where the appropriate response pattern is then adopted. Each of these mechanisms occurs either overtly (consciously), where the somatic state operates as an alarm or incentive signal alerting the individual to the cost or benefit of a particular option-outcome decision, or covertly (nonconsciously), where the somatic state constitutes a biasing signal that influences cognitive processing by facilitating appetitive or avoidance behaviour.

Somatic markers are therefore thought to improve performance by providing biasing or incentive signals that remove options from consideration that may be less optimal and that allow more favourable option-outcome pairs to be rapidly endorsed. Consequently, an absence of somatic markers may result in a range of response options and outcomes becoming equally available, forcing individuals to respond by a decision making strategy that is slow and laborious due to consideration of many potential alternatives and a lack of consideration of previous experience. This may be manifest in untimely, inaccurate, and unfavourable decision making, often becoming random or impulsive.

Abnormal decision making has been reported in many neuropsychiatric disorders, including mania, substance abuse, and personality disorders (Rahman et al., 2001). Support for its involvement in unipolar depression comes from recent research using a computerized decision making task (Rogers et al., 1999a) with both adult (Murphy et al., 2001; Rahman et al., 2001) and first-episode adolescent populations (Kyte, Goodyer, & Sahakian, 2004). In this task, the participants are required to decide, in terms of colour, in which box the computer has hidden a yellow token (a red box or a blue box, with ratios of each colour changing across trials from $6:4$ through to $9:1$). Once they have made their decision, they must then place a bet depending on how confident they are that they have chosen the correct colour. Possible bets either begin low and increase (ascend condition), or begin high and decrease (descend condition), and in each case, if the correct choice is made, the participants win the points they were willing to bet. If the wrong decision is made, they lose the points they bet. In an attempt to model most closely real-life decision making, three features of this task are of interest: decision making behaviour across a range of contingencies (manipulation of the ratio of red to blue boxes across trials), individual efficiency (allowing participants to decide for themselves how many of their points they wish to bet), and impulsivity versus genuine risk-taking behaviour (offering bets in both ascend and descend conditions). From this conceptual framework, three principal measures are derived: (1) speed of decision making—how long it takes to decide which colour box is hiding the token; (2) quality of decision making—how much of the time the subject chooses the most likely outcome; (3) risk adjustment—the rate at which a subject increases the percentage of available bets in response to more favourable ratios of red to blue (that is, $9:1$ versus $6:4$).

In adult patients with unipolar depression, administration of this task has resulted in reports of suboptimal decision making characterized by a protracted time to make decisions, and the employment of less responsive betting strategies as indicated by the allocation of an inappropriate number of points to a given decision (Murphy et al., 2001; Rahman, Robbins, & Sahakian, 1999; Rogers et al., 1999a; Rubinsztein, Michael, Paykel, & Sahakian, 2000). Ability to make decisions that are likely to produce the desired outcome, however, appears to be less impaired (Murphy et al., 2001), indicating that adults with unipolar depression remain able to effectively encode information about the likelihood of a reward response and make decisions accordingly.

Using the same task, adolescents experiencing first-episode unipolar depression also displayed a preserved ability to make decisions that were likely to produce the desired outcome (Kyte et al., 2004), as well as displaying suboptimal decision making in the form of an inappropriate allocation of resources (that is, betting a large proportion of their points on a decision with an unfavourable outcome), although to a greater extent than seen in previous adult populations (Beats et al., 1996; Corwin, Peselow, Feenan, Rotrosen, & Fieve, 1990; Elliott et al., 1996, 1997). Although this may be consistent with the notion that adolescents are more inclined to take risks than older populations, when combined with results that indicated higher bets made overall in descend conditions (where bets begin high and decrease) than in ascend conditions (where bets begin low and increase), the pattern becomes more consistent with that of a tendency to be impulsive (that is, a failure to consider, analyse, and reflect before engaging in a response, leading adolescents with recent, first-episode unipolar depression to choose bets early in both conditions). Although impulsivity is a feature of normal development, it can be both functional and dysfunctional (Dickman, 1990) and has been reported as an important dimension of clinical depression (Corruble, Damy, & Guelfi, 1999). A task of further development research is to disaggregate the effects of development on the expected level of impulsivity (for example, by age, pubertal stage, or some physiological index of developmental change) in order to examine the unique contribution of illness to task performance at different stages in the life cycle.

Although increases in impulsivity may serve as some explanation of the patterns of suboptimal decision making profiles reported in unipolar depression, a number of other neuropsychological processes have also been implicated. These include hyposensitivity to reward (the prospect of a large immediate gain outweighing any prospect of future loss), insensitivity to punishment (prospect of a large loss not overriding any prospect of gain), and insensitivity to future consequences (behaviour always guided by immediate prospects) (Bechara, Damasio, & Damasio, 2000a). Additionally, depressed individuals may display compromised decision making as a result of an inability to resolve effectively two competing response options (Rogers et al., 1999b), a loss of ability to ponder over different courses of action (Tranel, Bechara, & Damasio, 2000), or a degree of cognitive (rather than behavioural) impulsivity (Bechara et al., 2000b). We know very little about the development influences on these alternative psychological components of decision making and therefore cannot determine whether individuals with unipolar depression at differing points in the life cycle are more or less likely to demonstrate these impairments.

The neural basis of decision making

Studies based not only on the somatic marker hypothesis of decision making (Bechara, Tranel, Damasio, & Damasio, 1996; Bechara, Damasio, Tranel, & Anderson, 1998; Bechara, Damasio, & Damasio, 2000a) but also on behavioural (Bechara, Damasio, Damasio, & Anderson, 1994; Bechara et al., 1996, 1997) and functional imaging studies (Elliott, Rees, & Dolan, 1999; Rogers et al., 1999b) implicate a key role for the VMPFC/OFC in decision making. Overall, it has been suggested that the complexities of the decision making process are mediated by a large-scale system involving both cortical *and* subcortical structures, including the amygdala, somatosensory/insular cortices, and peripheral nervous system, that subserve a range of psychological features, including impulse control, risk taking, evaluative processes, and emotion processing (Bechara et al., 2000a; Tranel et al., 2000), all of which are proposed components of decision making.

The OFC in particular has been associated with encoding information that is used to guide goal-directed behaviour (Schoenbaum, Chiba, & Gallagher, 1998). It is thought to be particularly important when decisions have to be made in the context of limited contextual information, in assisting the identification of an optimal response (Rahman et al., 2001), and in reinforcement and incentive motivation (Damasio, 1995), presumably through its rich interconnections with limbic structures.

A specific candidate as a source of information to the inferior PFC is the amygdala. This region of the brain is thought to be particularly important in the creation of biases within the decision making process (Bechara, Damasio, Damasio, & Lee, 1999), largely through its role in emotion regulation and its contribution to emotional processing. Damage, therefore, is thought to compromise ability to sufficiently experience the emotional aspects of a situation, thereby precluding the enactment of somatic states and thus preventing patients from deliberating decisions and considering their future consequences. This is supported by reports of patients with damage to the amygdala demonstrating poor judgement and decision making in social behaviour (Tranel & Hyman, 1990), and it may be important, given the putative emotional basis of depression.

Similarly, patients with damage to the OFC have been seen to exhibit profound difficulties with their emotional reactions to sensory stimuli, as well as problems with self-conduct, personality changes, difficulties in situations of social interaction, and problems in making everyday decisions (Stuss & Benson, 1986). Patients with damage to the VMPFC exhibit similar profiles of deficits in executive processing, including inability to initiate, organize, and conduct normal activities, decreased spontaneity, and poor decision making, often resulting in the break-up of relationships, financial difficulties, and perseverative activities (Anderson, Damasio, Tranel, & Damasio, 1992). These occur in the absence of the marked cognitive deficits that have been reported to occur within patients with more DLPFC damage.

Behavioural inhibition and biases in unipolar depression

Inhibitory control is another central cognitive process that is contained within the range of executive functions of the cognitive system (Schacter & Logan, 1990), and has a critical role in social cognition through influencing the interrelated components of reasoning, planning, and the appropriate control of behaviour. In addition to using such executive control to choose, construct, execute, and maintain optimal strategies in a given situation, people must also be able to inhibit strategies that become inappropriate when their goals or task demands alter or errors occur. In order to keep behaviour coherent, therefore, it is necessary that relevant actions are allowed to continue while other potential but also irrelevant actions are inhibited. Defiant inhibitory control may, therefore, have psychopathological consequences.

In line with this, Plaisted and Sahakian (1997) proposed the "inhibition hypothesis", which was developed in response to reports that patients with frontal lobe damage display deficits in behavioural inhibition in relation to salient social scenarios, but not when tested on *abstract* scenarios (Saver & Damasio, 1991). Derived from the well-established notion that damage to the PFC often results in a loss of inhibitory control over inappropriate responses to a current situation (Dias et al., 1996; Milner, 1963; Dias, Robbins, & Roberts, 1997), this hypothesis suggests that deficits in behavioural inhibition can be characterized by an inability of PFC inhibitory mechanisms to suppress inappropriate behaviours elicited by cues from the immediate environment. Such disinhibition would prevent the selection of alternative and more appropriate action plans which are governed by more long-term goals, leaving behaviour to become dominated by the *immediate* emotional evaluation of the environment. The result is that reactions are based purely on the experience of associated emotions, and that behaviour is unconstrained by the regard for social norms, often, therefore, seeming inappropriate. Thus, patients with deficits in social cognition respond to immediate but not future social situations, accounting for the finding of specificity to real life compared to abstract situations.

In a sense, such emotionally based, behaviourally disinhibited reactions may be seen as a form of impulsivity; a failure to fully consider, analyse, and reflect before engaging in a particular behaviour. As previously discussed within the context of decision making, impulsivity is a feature of normal behaviour that can be both functional and dysfunctional (Dickman, 1990), and has often been reported as a feature of a number of psychiatric disorders, including depression (Corruble et al., 1999). In the example of behavioural inhibition, however, the role of impulsivity may depend upon the subtype of disorder, as suggested by reports of an impaired ability to inhibit behavioural responses in an affective go, no-go task in adults with bipolar disorder, yet a preserved ability in adults with unipolar depression (Murphy et al., 1999). In addition, disruption in inhibitory control may be more relevant to unipolar depression when considered in relation to emotional as opposed to cognitive processing. In support of this, depressed patients have been shown to exhibit a bias in their processing for negative affective stimuli in both adult (Murphy et al., 1999) and adolescent (Kyte et al., 2004) populations.

Suggestions of such mood-congruent processing biases are among the most robust findings in neuropsychological studies of depression (Bradley, Mogg, & Miller, 1996; Mogg, Bradley, & Williams, 1995; Williams, Watts, MacLeod, & Matthews, 1997) and are central to several of the cognitive theories of the disorder discussed previously (Beck, 1967, 1976; Bower, 1981). Indeed, there is evidence for such a bias among adolescents with no lifetime history of unipolar depression, suggesting that such a process may indeed be a true cognitive vulnerability for subsequent affective disorders (Kelvin, Goodyer, Teasdale, & Brechin, 1999)

The neural basis of behavioural inhibition and biases

Inhibition of movement is thought to be one of the principal roles of the PFC, with specific regions being shown to be important in tasks requiring inhibitory control in both animal (Iversen & Mishkin, 1970; Petrides, 1986) and human neuropsychological and imaging studies (Drewe, 1975; Elliott, Rubinsztein, Sahakian, & Dolan, 2000; Malloy, Birhlr, & Duffy, 1993; Perret, 1964).

Originally, it was believed that inhibitory control was a function residing exclusively within the VMPFC (Fuster, 1989; Mishkin, 1964). However, closer examination of the neuroanatomy of behavioural inhibition, together with converging evidence from electrophysiological and neuropsychological studies, has shown that the ability to suppress inappropriate prepotent response tendencies is an intrinsic property of the PFC as a whole. Within this recently established framework, current evidence focuses specifically on ventral and orbital regions (Dias et al., 1996, 1997; Roberts & Wallis, 2000), although others have included other areas, such as the sulcus principalis (Diamond & Goldman-Rakic, 1989) and dorsolateral regions (Casey et al., 1997).

The OFC, in particular, has received a great deal of attention with regard to its role in inhibitory control and the control of emotionality (Damasio et al., 1991; Mishkin, 1964). Evidence for the former is derived largely from experimental lesion studies, in which monkeys with damage to the OFC have shown disrupted performance in tasks requiring inhibition of a prepotent response tendency (Iversen & Mishkin, 1970). Evidence for the latter is derived from studies in which patients with damage to this region have displayed changes in their emotional and social behaviour (Eslinger & Damasio, 1985; Phineas Gage—Harlow, 1868). Specifically, regions within both the

OFC and the VMPFC have shown differences in activation in depressed patients when compared with controls, as well as during induction of sad mood in controls (Drevets & Raichle, 1995).

Collectively, reports of patients with damage to the OFC are often characterized by features including behavioural disinhibition and impulsivity (Diamond & Goldman-Rakic, 1989; Hornak, Rolls, & Wade, 1996; Rolls, Hornak, Wade, & McGrath, 1994), compromised abilities in focusing attention (Godefroy & Rousseaux, 1996), and biases in attentional processing (Dias et al., 1996, 1997). However, it is important to acknowledge that many patients exhibiting similar disturbances in their emotional and social behaviour often have damage to their medial PFC. This implies that behavioural features such as inhibition are not solely a function of the OFC. Rather it would seem that individual regions within the PFC can be differentiated on the basis of the kinds of information that are processed and the functions or operations that are performed within such a context.

In line with this, both the OFC and the VMPFC have been proposed to be part of a double dissociation in which these distinct regions carry out independent but complementary forms of cognitive processing, culminating in the experience of inhibitory control (Dias et al., 1996, 1997). Loss of inhibitory control with regard to its affective component has been attributed to lesions or damage within the OFC/VMPFC in marmosets, resulting in an impaired ability to alter behaviour in response to changes in the emotional significance of stimuli. In contrast, attentional selection difficulties (higher-order shifting of attention between features) have been associated with lesions within the lateral PFC (Dias et al., 1996, 1997; Roberts & Wallis, 2000).

With regard specifically to the presence of mood-congruent biases in processing, studies have reported an association with attenuated neural responses in the ventral cingulate and posterior orbitofrontal cortices when comparing emotional with neutral targets, and with elevated responses specific to sad targets in the rostral anterior cingulate extending to the anterior medial PFC (Elliott et al., 2002). The same study also showed depressed adults to display a differential neural response to emotional (particularly sad) distractors in the lateral OFC. This finding complements findings with regard to overall performance on the affective go, no-go task (Kyte et al., in press; Murphy et al., 1999) in implicating the VMPFC and the OFC in behavioural inhibition within an emotional context, and suggesting these same areas to be sensitive to the presence of depression.

Social cognition, executive functions, and responding to adversity

If individuals with depression experience weakness in their social cognition, as implied by research reporting executive deficits in unipolar depression, modulating the mood-congruent effects of experiences within their social world (that is, the experience of adversity) may also be inefficient and result in impaired behavioural responses (in the form of coping styles), further exacerbating the individual's vulnerability to the development and maintenance of disorder. Currently, little is known about the putative role that executive processes may play in the context of coping with social environments and adversity (Goodyer, 2002). However, given that some of the principal characteristics of executive functions are to construct, execute, and maintain optimal response patterns, a tentative account aimed at generating hypotheses suggests that the action and outcome of an experience in the social world of an individual may be determined, at least in part, by the combined processes of attention, behavioural inhibition, and decision making, via their effects on social coping styles. In other words, the social behaviour of individuals with depression may be compromised not only directly as a consequence of executive deficits, but also indirectly via the effect of these deficits on other social processes such as coping (Kyte, 2003). This idea can be conceptualized as in Figure 9.1.

Alternatively, this idea can be considered within the framework of there being three levels of processing: (1) selective and sustained attention + behavioural inhibition = construction phase; (2) choice and action = execution phase; (3) outcome = maintenance phase (Kyte, 2003). The implication is that disruption in one or a combination of these individual phases may result in interference in optimal behavioural responses and may contribute to the development of psychopathology. At the very least, it is thought that disruption in these executive processes is likely to interfere with optimal responses in a manner so as to produce behaviour that is characterized by behavioural rigidity (perseveration) (Milner, 1963), extreme distractibility (Shallice, 1988), inability to maintain goal-directed behaviour (Baddeley, 1986), prevention of selecting the most appropriate or alternative action plans (Murphy et al., 1999, 2001), impaired shifting of attention and response (Downes, Roberts, Sahakian, Evenden, Morris, & Robbins, 1989; Owen et al., 1992; Owen, Downes, Sahakian, Polkey, & Robbins, 1990), suboptimal decision making (Rogers et al., 1999a), and diminished opportunity for adaptive coping (Kyte, 2003).

Social coping

Coping styles can be defined as the pattern of response to external demand events (Billings & Moos, 1984; McCrae, 1984), whose function is to ameliorate potentially undesirable outcomes such as anxiety or depression. As a construct, coping is concerned with achieving several aims, including the reduction of the degree of harm and emotional distress while enhancing the prospects of recovery, maintaining a positive self-image, and developing resilience to negative events (Cohen & Lazarus, 1979). In an attempt to achieve these aims, several different behavioural options may be considered, ranging from seeking advice to listening to music or reading a book, depending

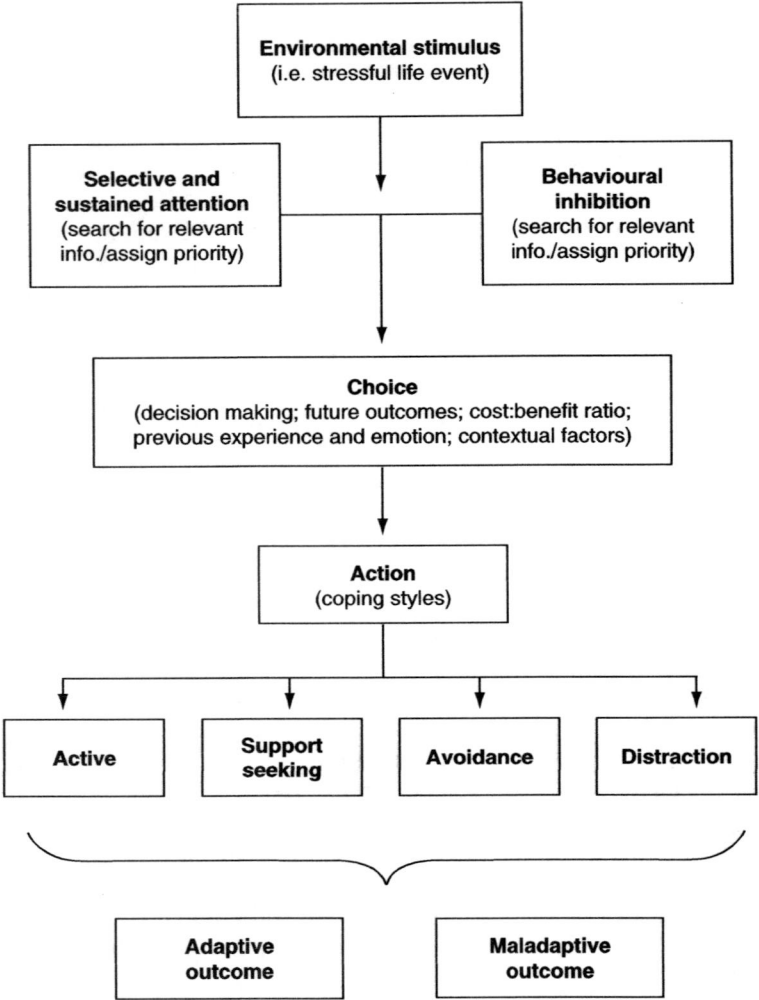

Figure 9.1 Action and outcome of a social experience and the role of executive functions.

on the characteristics of the situation (that is, degree of perceived controllability) and of the individual concerned (that is, temperament and problem solving ability). Generally speaking, options in social coping are likely to fall into two central categories; one in which strategies provide immediate relief, but at the cost of being only short-term solutions (that is, behavioural or cognitive distraction/avoidance), and another in which attempts are made to alter the actual or mental representations of the situation and therefore maintain a substantially longer-term solution (that is, active strategies).

Social coping and unipolar depression

The relationship between coping styles and unipolar depression is neither simple nor necessarily direct, although the manner in which adversity is appraised and responded to is thought to be important in the onset, maintenance, and outcome of the disorder. Individual characteristics of unipolar depression thought to influence both the selection of specific coping strategies and their perceived efficiency and perhaps, therefore, their subsequent use (Zeidner & Saklofske, 1996) include social features, such as the tendency to perceive a greater percentage of life events as undesirable and stressful (Billings, Cronkite, & Moos, 1983); cognitive features, such as low mood and self-preoccupation (Endler & Parker, 1990), disrupted skills in problem solving (Nezu, 1986), a view of oneself as an inefficient problem solver (Mayo & Tanaka-Matsumi, 1993), and a tendency to feel less in control of one's circumstances (Mirowsky & Ross, 1990); and executive features, such as a difficulty in making decisions (Coyne, Aldwin, & Lazarus, 1981).

Both adults and adolescents with unipolar depression have been shown to require more information prior to deciding on a coping response, as well as having social coping styles that are characterized by emotion-focused or avoidance coping (Compas, Malcarne, & Fondacaro, 1988; Kyte, 2003; McNaughton, Patterson, Irwin, & Grant, 1992; Perrez & Reicherts, 1992; Saklofske, 1993; Zeidner, 1994). Such strategies may provide immediate relief from the negative emotional arousal provoked, but would fail to provide a longer-term solution, making the individual vulnerable to repeated exposure to similar stressors. Alternatively, problem-focused or active coping would require an external focus, skill in identifying and defining problem situations, and access to a range of appropriate strategies that provide longer-term solutions through management of both the actual stressor and the emotional reaction elicited by the experience (Zeidner & Saklofske, 1996). Consequently, such strategies have been associated with fewer psychological problems (Ayers, Sandler, West, & Roosa, 1990; Sandler, Tein, & West, 1994).

The neural basis of responding to adversity

The neural models of individual executive functions and specific psychological mechanisms that are involved in the processing of and responding to social life events and difficulties have been associated with discrete brain regions within the limbic-cortical circuitry. Studies in this area have been concerned with having participants think about specific autobiographical experiences, thereby engaging episodic event memory processes containing affective valent personal material. This cognitive manipulation can be brought about directly through instruction or indirectly through inducing dysphoric mood. The latter method has been used to show that adolescents with no past history of unipolar depression but with an increased temperamental risk of affective disorders display an increased level of negative self-description when mildly dysphoric compared to controls with no such temperamental risk (Kelvin et al., 1999). This form of experiment has been translated for use in association with neuroimaging to determine the neural characteristics that are activated after affective challenge or cognitive manipulation (that is, directly asking participants to recall events without recourse to specific mood induction). For example, recognizing the emotional tone of a social experience has been associated with activation primarily within the amygdala (Calder, Lawrence, & Young, 2001; Thomas et al., 2001). Processing affect-related meanings of life events appears to be mediated by the medial PFC functioning as the executive component of limbic-cortical activity (Teasdale et al., 1999). The neural basis for evaluating, organizing, and consolidating the meaning of environmental stimuli in declarative memory has been shown to be a function of the hippocampus (Eichenbaum, 1999). Finally, establishing the degree of difficulty of inductive inference from external stimuli appears to be preferentially associated with activation within the OFC (Goel & Dolan, 2000).

Conclusions

This chapter has outlined current knowledge of the associations between social cognition and unipolar depression. Over the next decade, we can expect continuing refinement of the affective-cognitive tasks for use in functional neuroimaging studies to determine the neural correlates that underpin mental processes in both normal adults, and those at high risk of or those suffering from unipolar depression (Elliott et al., 2002). The findings to date indicate that there is no single brain area or processing component that is the key to the vulnerability to unipolar depression. Rather, a coherence of brain systems, involved in the recognition of, processing of, and response formation to emotionally meaningful stimuli from the environment, is required to prevent inefficient mental functions. Exactly how these neural systems operate to process affectively valent information is slowly emerging, but we remain relatively ignorant of the precise psychological processes whose failure to function will result in depressive disorders. It seems highly likely that fully integrated social and performance functions are needed for mental competence, and that it is the breakdown in one or more components involved in processing environmental stimuli that may result in unipolar depression. Furthermore, it seems possible, even probable, that social cognitive impairments vary according to the nature of the depression. Thus, we should not assume that social cognitive impairments are likely to be the same in first-episode versus recurrent disorders, in younger versus older individuals, or in those at high versus low risk of psychopathology. Although studies into the development of neuropsychological processes have begun (Kyte et al., in press, Luciana & Nelson, 1998; Nelson, Thomas, de Haan, & Wewerka, 1998), we know little about the individual variations in social cognitive processing in the population at large, or how these critical mental processes evolve with development.

It is important that we determine the similarities and differences in the nature and characteristics of unipolar depression that occur across the lifespan (Goodyer, 2003). We also have yet to characterize which social cognitive processing abnormalities predict the onset of an episode, and to distinguish between sporadic and recurrent or familial and nonfamilial disorders. Unipolar depression is one of the most disabling illnesses not only among mental disorders but also in comparison with the cost and consequences to public health of diseases such as cancer and cardiovascular disease. Characterizing the intermediate psychological phenotype and its neural processes is an important and achievable objective for the early part of the twenty-first century.

References

Abas, M. A., Sahakian, B. J., & Levy, R. (1990). Neuropsychological deficits and CT scan changes in elderly depressives. *Psychological Medicine*, 20, 507–520.

Abramson, L. Y., Seligman, M. E. P., & Teasdale, J. D. (1978). Learned helplessness in humans: Critique and formulation. *Journal of Abnormal Psychology*, 87, 49–74.

Adolphs, R. (2001). The neurobiology of social cognition. *Current Opinion in Neurobiology*, 11, 231–239.

Adolphs, R. (2003). Cognitive neuroscience of human social behaviour. *Nature Reviews Neuroscience*, 4, 165–178.

American Psychiatric Association. (1994). *Diagnostic and statistical manual for mental and behavioural disorders*, Vol. 4. Washington, DC: APA.

Anderson, S. W., Damasio, H., Tranel, D., & Damasio, A. R. (1992). Cognitive sequelae of focal lesions in ventromedial frontal lobe. *Journal of Clinical and Experimental Neuropsychology*, 14, 83.

Angold, A., Costello, E. J., & Erkanli, A. (1999). Comorbidity. *Journal of Child Psychology, Psychiatry, and Allied Disciplines*, 40, 57–87.

Ayers, T. S., Sandler, I. N., West, S. G., & Roosa, M. W. (1990). *Assessment of children's coping behaviours: Testing alternative models of children's coping*. Paper presented at the American Psychological Association, Boston, MA.

Baddeley, A. D. (1986). *Working memory*. Oxford: Clarendon Press.

Beats, B. C., Sahakian, B. J., & Levy, R. (1996). Cognitive performance in tests sensitive to frontal lobe dysfunction in the elderly depressed. *Psychological Medicine*, 26, 591–603.

Bechara, A., Damasio, A. R., Damasio, H., & Anderson, S. W. (1994). Insensitivity to future consequences following damage to human prefrontal cortex. *Cognition*, 50, 7–15.

Bechara, A., Tranel, D., Damasio, H., & Damasio, A. R. (1996). Failure to respond autonomically to anticipated future outcomes following damage to prefrontal cortex. *Cerebral Cortex*, 6, 215–225.

Bechara, A., Damasio, H., Tranel, D., & Damasio, A. R. (1997). Deciding advantageously before knowing the advantageous strategy. *Science*, 275, 1293–1295.

Bechara, A., Damasio, H., Tranel, D., & Anderson, S. W. (1998). Dissociation of working memory from decision making within the human prefrontal cortex. *Journal of Neuroscience, 18*, 428–437.

Bechara, A., Damasio, H., Damasio, A. R., & Lee, G. P. (1999). Different contributions of the human amygdala and ventromedial prefrontal cortex to decision making. *Journal of Neuroscience, 1*, 5473–5481.

Bechara, A., Damasio, A., & Damasio, A. R. (2000a). Emotion, decision making and the orbitofrontal cortex. *Cerebral Cortex, 10*, 295–307.

Bechara, A., Tranel, D., & Damasio, H. (2000b). Characterisation of the decision making deficit of patients with ventromedial prefrontal cortex lesions. *Brain, 123*, 2189–2202.

Beck, A. T. (1967). *Depression: Clinical, experimental and theoretical aspects.* New York: Harper and Row.

Beck, A. T. (1976). *Cognitive therapy and the emotional disorders.* New York: International Universities Press.

Bench, C. J., Friston, K. L., Brown, R. G., & Scott, L. C. (1992). The anatomy of melancholia: Focal abnormalities of cerebral blood flow in unipolar depression. *Psychological Medicine, 22*, 607–615.

Billings, A. G., Cronkite, R. C., & Moos, R. H. (1983). Social environmental factors in unipolar depression: Comparisons of depressed patients and non-depressed controls. *Journal of Abnormal Psychology, 92*, 119–133.

Billings, A. G., & Moos, R. H. (1984). Coping, stress and social resources among adults with unipolar depression. *Journal of Personality and Social Psychology, 46*, 877–891.

Borkowska, A., & Rybakowski, J. K. (2001). Neuropsychological frontal tests indicate that bipolar depressed patients are more impaired than unipolar. *Bipolar Disorders, 3*, 88–94.

Bower, G. H. (1981). Mood and memory. *American Psychologist, 36*, 129–148.

Bradley, B. P., Mogg, K., & Miller, N. (1996). Implicit memory bias a clinical and non-clinical depression. *Behaviour Research and Therapy, 34*, 865–879.

Brown, R. G., Scott, L. C., Bench, C. J., & Dolan, R. J. (1994). Cognitive function in depression: Its relationship to the presence and severity of intellectual decline. *Psychological Medicine, 24*, 829–849.

Bush, G., Whalen, P. J., Rosen, B. R., McInerney, S. C., & Jenike, M. A. (1998). The emotional counting Stroop paradigm: An interference task specialized for functional neuroimaging validation study with functional MRI. *Human Brain Mapping, 6*, 270–282.

Calder, A., Lawrence, A. D., & Young, A. W. (2001). Neuropsychology of fear and loathing. *Nature, 2*, 351–363.

Cannon, W. B. (1927). The James–Lange theory of emotions: A critical examination and an alternative theory. *American Journal of Psychology, 39*, 106–124.

Casey, B. J., Trainor, R. J., Orendi, J. L., Schbert, A. B., Nystrom, L. E., Giedd, J. N., et al. (1997). A developmental functional MRI study of prefrontal activation during performance of a go/no-go task. *Journal of Cognitive Neuroscience, 9*, 835–847.

Cassidy, F., Ahearn, E. P., & Carroll, B. J. (2001). Substance abuse in bipolar disorder. *Bipolar Disorders, 3*, 181–188.

Cohen, F., & Lazarus, R. (1979). Coping with the stresses of illness. In G. C. Stone, F. Cohen, & N. E. Alder (Eds.), *Health Psychology: A handbook* (pp. 217–254). San Francisco: Jossey-Bass.

Compas, B. E., Malcarne, V., & Fondacaro, K. M. (1988). Coping with stressful events in older children and adolescents. *Journal of Consulting and Clinical Psychology*, 56, 405–411.

Corruble, E., Damy, C., & Guelfi, J. D. (1999). Impulsivity: a relevant dimension in depression regarding suicide attempts? *Journal of Affective Disorders*, 53, 211–215.

Corwin, J., Peselow, E., Feenan, K., Rotrosen, J., & Fieve, R. (1990). Disorders of decision in affective disease: An effect of B-adrenergic dysfunction? *Biological Psychiatry*, 27, 813–833.

Costello, E. J., Angold, A., Burns, B. J., Stangl, D. K., Tweed, D. L., Erkanli, A., et al. (1996). The Great Smoky Mountains Study of Youth. Goals, design, methods, and the prevalence of DSM-III-R disorders. *Archives of General Psychiatry*, 53, 1129–1136.

Costello, E. J., Angold, A., & Keeler, G. P. (1999). Adolescent outcomes of childhood disorders: The consequences of severity and impairment. *Journal of the American Academy of Child and Adolescent Psychiatry*, 38, 121–128.

Coyne, J. C., Aldwin, C., & Lazarus, R. S. (1981). Depression and coping in stressful episodes. *Journal of Abnormal Psychology*, 90, 439–447.

Craik, F. I. M., Moroz, T. M., Moscovitch, M., Stuss, D. T., Winocur, G., & Tulving, E. (1999). In search of the self: A positron emission tomography investigation. *Psychological Science*, 10, 26–34.

Damasio, A. R. (1994). *Descartes' error*. New York: Putnam Press.

Damasio, A. R. (1995). *Descartes' error: Emotion, reason and the human brain*. London: Picador.

Damasio, A. R., Tranel, D., & Damasio, H. (1990). Individuals with sociopathic behaviour caused by frontal damage fail to respond automatically to social stimuli. *Behavioural Brain Research*, 4, 81–94.

Damasio, A. R., Tranel, D., & Damasio, H. (1991). Somatic markers and the guidance of behaviour: Theory and preliminary testing. In H. S. Levin, H. M. Eisenberg, & A. L. Benton (Eds.), *Frontal lobe function and dysfunction* (pp. 217–229). New York: Oxford University Press.

Decety, J., & Grezes, J. (1999). Neural mechanisms subserving the perception of human actions. *Trends in Cognitive Science*, 3, 172–178.

D'Esposito, M., Postle, B. R., Ballard, D., & Lease, J. (1999). Maintenance versus manipulation of information held in working memory: An event-related fMRI study. *Brain and Cognition*, 41, 66–86.

Diamond, A., & Goldman-Rakic, P. S. (1989). Comparison of human infants and rhesus monkeys on Piaget's A-not-B task: Evidence for dependence on dorsolateral prefrontal cortex. *Experimental Brain Research*, 74, 24–40.

Dias, R., Roberts, A. C., & Robbins, T. W. (1996). Dissociation in prefrontal cortex of affective and attentional shifts. *Nature*, 380, 69–72.

Dias, R., Robbins, T. W., & Roberts, A. C. (1997). Dissociable forms of inhibitory controls within the prefrontal cortex with an analog of the WCST: Restriction to novel situations and independence from "on-line" processing. *Journal of Neuroscience*, 17, 9285–9297.

Dickman, S. J. (1990). Functional and dysfunctional impulsivity: Personality and cognitive correlates. *Journal of Personality and Social Psychology*, 58, 95–102.

Dolan, R. J., Bench, C. J., Brown, R. G., Scott, L. C., & Frackowiak, R. S. J. (1994). Neuropsychological dysfunction in depression: The relationship to regional cerebral blood flow. *Psychological Medicine*, 24, 849–857.

Downes, J. J., Roberts, A. C., Sahakian, B. J., Evenden, J. L., Morris, R. G., &

Robbins, T. W. (1989). Impaired extra-dimensional shift performance in medicated and unmedicated Parkinson's disease: Evidence for a specific attentional dysfunction. *Neuropsychologia, 27*, 1329–1343.

Drevets, W. C. (2000). Neuroimaging studies of mood disorders. *Biological Psychiatry, 48*, 813–829.

Drevets, W. C. (2001). Neuroimaging and neuropathological studies of depression: Implications for the cognitive-emotional features of mood disorders. *Current Opinion in Neurobiology, 11*, 240–249.

Drevets, W. C. Videen, T. O., Price, J. L., Preskorn, S. H., Carmichael, S. T., & Raichle, M. E. (1992). A functional anatomical study of unipolar depression. *Journal of Neuroscience, 12*, 3628–3641.

Drevets, W. C., & Raichle, M. E. (1995). Positron emission tomographic imaging studies of human emotional disorders. In M. S. Gazzaniga (Ed.), *The cognitive neurosciences* (pp. 1153–1164). Cambridge, MA: MIT Press.

Drevets, W. C., Price, J. L., Simpson, J. R., Todd, R. D., Reich, T., & Vannier, M. (1997). Subgenual prefrontal cortex abnormalities in mood disorders. *Nature, 386*, 824–827.

Drewe, E. A. (1975). Go/no-go learning after frontal lobe lesions in humans. *Cortex, 11*, 8–16.

Duncan, J. (1986). Disorganisation of behaviour after frontal lobe damage. *Cognitive Neuropsychology, 3*, 271–290.

Eichenbaum, H. (1999). The hippocampus and mechanisms of declarative memory. *Behaviour and Brain Research, 103*, 123–133.

Ekman, P., Levenson, R. W., & Frieson, W. C. (1983). Autonomic nervous system activity distinguishes among emotions. *Science, 221*, 1208–1210.

Elliott, R., Sahakian, B. J., McKay, A. P., Herrod, J. J., Robbins, T. W., & Paykel, E. S. (1996). Neuropsychological impairment in unipolar depression: The influence of perceived failure on subsequent performance. *Psychological Medicine, 26*, 975–989.

Elliott, R., Baker, S. C., Rogers, R. D., O'Leary, D. A., Paykel, E. S., Frith, C. D., et al. (1997). Prefrontal dysfunction in depressed patients performing a complex planning task: A study using positron emission tomography. *Psychological Medicine, 27*, 931–942.

Elliott, R., Rees, G., & Dolan, R. J. (1999). Ventromedial prefrontal cortex mediates guessing. *Neuropsychologia, 37*, 403–411.

Elliott, R., Rubinsztein, J. S., Sahakian, B. J., & Dolan, R. J. (2000). Selective attention to emotional stimuli in a verbal go/no-go task: An fMRI study. *Neuroreport, 11*, 1739–1744.

Elliott, R., Rubinsztein, J. S., Sahakian, B. J., & Dolan, R. J. (2002). The neural basis of mood-congruent processing biases in depression. *Archives of General Psychiatry, 59*, 597–604.

Ellis, H. C., & Ashbrook, P. W. (1988). Resource allocation model of the effects of depressed mood states on memory. In K. Fiedler & J. Forgas (Eds.), *Affect, cognition and social behaviour* (pp. 25–43). Toronto: Hogrefe.

Endler, N. S., & Parker, J. D. (1990). State and trait anxiety, depression and coping styles. *Australian Journal of Psychology, 42*, 207–220.

Eslinger, P. J., & Damasio, A. R. (1985). Severe disturbance of higher cognition after bilateral frontal lobe ablation: Patient EVR. *Neurology, 35*, 1731–1741.

Franke, P., Maier, W., Hardt, J., Frieboes, R., Lichtermann, D., & Hain, C. (1993).

Assessment of frontal lobe functioning in schizophrenia and unipolar depression. *Psychopathology, 26,* 76–84.
Fuster, J. M. (1989). *The prefrontal cortex.* New York: Raven Press.
Godefroy, O., & Rousseaux, M. (1996). Divided and focused attention in patients with lesions of the prefrontal cortex. *Brain and Cognition, 30,* 155–174.
Goel, V., & Dolan, R. J. (2000). Anatomical segregation of component processes in an inductive inference task. *Journal of Cognitive Neuroscience, 12,* 110–119.
Goodwin, G. W. (1997). Neuropsychological and neuroimaging evidence for the involvement of the frontal lobes in depression. *Journal of Psychopharmacology, 11,* 115–122.
Goodyer, I. M. (2002). Social adversity and mental functions in adolescents at high risk of psychopathology. Position paper and suggested framework for future research. *British Journal of Psychiatry, 181,* 383–386.
Goodyer, I. M. (2003). *Unipolar depression: A lifespan perspective.* Oxford: Oxford University Press.
Goodyer, I. M., Herbert, J., Secher, S. M., & Pearson, J. (1997). Short-term outcome of major depression. I. Co-morbidity and severity at presentation as predictors of persistent disorder. *Journal of the American Academy of Child and Adolescent Psychiatry, 36,* 179–187.
Goodyer, I. M., Herbert, J., Tamplin, A., & Altham, P. M. (2000). First episode major depression in adolescents: Affective, cognitive and endocrine characteristics of risk status and predictors of onset. *British Journal of Psychiatry, 176,* 142–149.
Grady, C. L., & Keightley, M. L. (2002). Studies of altered social cognition in neuropsychiatric disorders using functional neuroimaging. *Canadian Journal of Psychiatry, 47,* 327–336.
Gunnar, M. R., & Donzella, B. (2002). Social regulation of the cortisol levels in early human development. *Psychoneuroendocrinology, 27,* 199–220.
Gusnard, D. A., Akbudak, E., Shulman, G. L., & Raichle, M. E. (2001). Medial prefrontal cortex and self-referential mental activity: Relation to a default mode of brain function. *Proceedings of the National Academy of Sciences of the USA, 98,* 4259–4264.
Harlow, J. M. (1868). Recovery from the passage of an iron bar through the head. *Publications of the Massachusetts Medical Society (Boston), 2,* 327–346.
Harrington, R., Fudge, H., Rutter, M., Pickles, A., & Hill, J. (1991). Adult outcomes of childhood and adolescent depression. II. Links with antisocial disorders. *Journal of the American Academy of Child and Adolescent Psychiatry, 30,* 434–439.
Harrington, R. C., & Dubicka, B. (2001). Natural history of mood disorders in children and adolescents. In I. M. Goodyer (Ed.), *The depressed child and adolescent* (pp. 311–343). Cambridge: Cambridge University Press.
Hasher, L., & Zacks, R. T. (1979). Automatic and effortful processes in memory. *Journal of Experimental Psychology: General, 108,* 356–388.
Haxby, J. V., Horwitz, B., Ungerleider, L. G., Maisog, J. M., Pietrini, P., & Grady, C. L. (1994). The functional organisation of human extrastriate cortex: A PET-rCBF study of selective attention to faces and locations. *Journal of Neuroscience, 14,* 6336–6353.
Hazell, P., O'Connell, D., Heathcote, D., Robertson, J., & Henry, D. (1995). Efficacy of tricyclic drugs in treating child and adolescent depression. *British Medical Journal, 310,* 897–901.
Hoffman, E. A., & Haxby, J. V. (2000). Distinct representations of eye gaze and

identity in the distributed human neural system for face perception. *Nature Neuroscience, 3*, 80–84.

Hornak, J., Rolls, E. T., & Wade, D. (1996). Face and voice expression identification in patients with emotional and behavioural changes following ventral frontal lobe damage. *Neuropsychologia, 34*, 247–261.

Ilsley, J. E., Moffoot, A. P. R., & O'Carroll, R. E. (1995). An analysis of memory dysfunction in unipolar depression. *Journal of Affective Disorders, 35*, 1–9.

Iversen, S. D., & Mishkin, M. (1970). Perseverative interference in monkeys following selective lesions of the interior prefrontal convexity. *Experimental Brain Research, 11*, 376–386.

James, W. (1884). What is an emotion? *Mind, 9*, 188–205.

Kaufman, J., & Ryan, N. (1999). The neurobiology of child and adolescent depression. In D. Charney, E. Nestler, & B. Bunny (Eds.), *The neurobiological foundation of mental illness* (pp. 810–822). New York: Oxford University Press.

Kaufman, J., Martin, A., King, R. A., & Charney, D. (2001). Are child-, adolescent-, and adult-onset depression one and the same disorder? *Biological Psychiatry, 49*, 980–1001.

Keller, M. B., Ryan, N. D., Strober, M., Klein, R. G., Kutcher, S. P., Birmaher, B., et al. (2001). Efficacy of paroxetine in the treatment of adolescent major depression: A randomized, controlled trial. *Journal of the American Academy of Child and Adolescent Psychiatry, 40*, 762–772.

Kelvin, R. G., Goodyer, I. M., Teasdale, J. D., & Brechin, D. (1999). Latent negative self-schema and high emotionality in well adolescents at risk for psychopathology. *Journal of Child Psychology and Psychiatry, 40*, 959–968.

Kendler, K. S., Thornton, L. M., & Gardner, C. O. (2000). Stressful life events and previous episodes in the etiology of major depression in women: An evaluation of the "kindling" hypothesis. *American Journal of Psychiatry, 157*, 1243–1251.

Kendler, K., Thornton, L. M., & Gardner, C. O. (2001). Genetic risk, number of previous depressive episodes, and stressful life events in predicting onset of major depression. *American Journal of Psychiatry, 158*, 582–586.

Kovacs, M. (1996). Presentation and course of major depressive disorder during childhood and later years of the life span. *Journal of the American Academy of Child and Adolescent Psychiatry, 35*, 705–715.

Kyte, Z. A. (2003). *Executive abilities and social coping in adolescents with and without first episode unipolar depression*. Ph.D. thesis, Department of Psychiatry, University of Cambridge.

Kyte, Z. A., Goodyer, I. M., & Sahakian, B. J. (2004). Selected executive skills in adolescents with recent first episode major depression. *Journal of Child Psychology and Psychiatry, 45*.

Le Doux, J. E. (1996). *The emotional brain: The mysterious underpinnings of emotional life*. New York: Simon and Schuster.

Le Doux, J. E. (2000). The amygdala and emotion: A view through fear. In J. P. Aggleton (Ed.), *The amygdala. A functional analysis* (pp. 289–310). Oxford: Oxford University Press.

Lewinsohn, P. M., Allen, N. B., Seeley, J. R., & Gotlib, I. H. (1999). First onset versus recurrence of depression: Differential processes of psychosocial risk. *Journal of Abnormal Psychology, 102*, 483–489.

Luciana, M., & Nelson, C. A. (1998). The functional emergence of prefrontallyguided working memory systems in four-to-eight-year-old children. *Neuropsychologia, 36*, 273–293.

Luciana, M., Lindeke, L., Georgieff, M., Mills, M., & Nelson, C. A. (1999). Neurobehavioural evidence for working memory deficits in school-aged children with histories of prematurity. *Developmental Medicine and Child Neurology, 41*, 521–533.

Lupien, S. J., Nair, N. P., Brier, S., Maheu, F., Tu, M. T., Lemay, M., et al. (1999). Increased cortisol levels and impaired cognition in human ageing: Implication for depression and dementia in later life. *Review of Neuroscience, 10*, 117–139.

Lupien, S. J., King, S., Meaney, M. J., & McEwen, B. S. (2001). Can poverty get under your skin? Basal cortisol levels and cognitive function in children from low and high socioeconomic status. *Development and Psychopathology, 13*, 653–676.

Lupien, S. J., Wilkinson, C. W., Briere, S., Menard, C., Ng Ying Kin, N. M., & Nair, N. P. (2002a). The modulatory effects of corticosteroids on cognition: Studies in young human populations. *Psychoneuroendocrinology, 27*, 401–416.

Lupien, S. J., Wilkinson, C. W., Briere, S., Ng Ying Kin, N. M., Meaney, M. J., & Nair, N. P. (2002b). Acute modulation of aged human memory by pharmacological manipulation of glucocorticoids. *Journal of Clinical Endocrinology and Metabolism, 87*, 3798–3807.

Malloy, P., Birhlr, A., & Duffy, J. (1993). The orbitomedial frontal syndrome. *Archives of Clinical Neuropsychology, 8*, 185–201.

Mayberg, H. S., Brannan, S. K., Mahurin, R. K., Jerabek, P. A., Brickman, J. S., & Tekell, J. L. (1997). Cingulate function in depression: A potential predictor of treatment response. *Neuroreport, 8*, 1057–1061.

Mayberg, H. S., Liotti, M., Brannan, S. K., McGinnis, S., Mahurin, R. K., & Jerabek, P. A. (1998). Disease and state-specific effects of mood challenge on rCBF. *NeuroImage, 7*, S901.

Mayberg, H. S., Liotti, M., Brannan, S. K., McGinnis, S., Mahurin, R. K., Jerabek, P. A., et al. (1999). Reciprocal limbic-cortical function and negative mood: Converging PET findings in depression and normal sadness. *American Journal of Psychiatry, 156*, 675–682.

Mayo, V. D., & Tanaka-Matsumi, J. (1993). *Emotion versus problem-focused approaches to an interpersonal problem by depressives*. Paper presented at 101st Annual Convention of the American Psychological Association, Toronto, Canada.

McCrae, R. R. (1984). Situational determinants of coping responses: Loss, threat and challenge. *Journal of Personality and Social Psychology, 46*, 919–928.

McNaughton, M. E., Patterson, T. L., Irwin, M. R., & Grant, I. (1992). The relationship of life adversity, social support and coping to hospitalization with unipolar depression. *Journal of Nervous and Mental Disease, 180*, 491–497.

Miller, W. R. (1975). Psychological deficits in depression. *Psychological Bulletin, 82*, 238–260.

Milner, B. (1963). Effects of different brain lesions on card sorting. *Archives of Neurology, 9*, 90–100.

Mirowsky, J., & Ross, C. (1990). Control or defence? Depression and the sense of control: Good and bad outcomes. *Journal of Health and Social Behaviour, 31*, 71–86.

Mishkin, M. (1964). Perseveration of control sets after frontal lesions in monkeys. In J. M. Warren & K. Akert (Eds.), *The frontal granular cortex and behaviour* (pp. 219–294). New York: McGraw-Hill.

Mogg, K., Bradley, B. P., & Williams, R. (1995). Attentional bias in anxiety and depression: The role of awareness. *British Journal of Clinical Psychology, 34*, 17–36.

Murphy, F. C., Sahakian, B. J., Rubinsztein, J. S., Michael, A., Rogers, R. D., Robbins, T. W. et al. (1999). Emotional bias and inhibitory control processes in mania and depression. *Psychological Medicine, 29*, 1307–1321.

Murphy, F. C., Rubinsztein, J. S., Michael, A., Rogers, R. D., Robbins, T. W., Paykel, E. S., et al. (2001). Decision making cognition in mania and depression. *Psychological Medicine, 31*, 679–693.

Nelson, C. A., Thomas, K. M., de Haan, M., & Wewerka, S. S. (1998). Delayed recognition memory in infants and adults as revealed by event-related potentials. *International Journal of Psychophysiology, 29*, 145–165.

Newcomer, J. W., Selke, G., Melson, A. K., Hershey, T., Craft, S., Richards, K., et al. (1999). Decreased memory performance in healthy humans induced by stress-level cortisol treatment. *Archives of General Psychiatry, 56*, 527–533.

Nezu, A. M. (1986). Efficacy of a social problem solving therapy approach for unipolar depression. *Journal of Consulting and Clinical Psychology, 54*, 196–202.

Owen, A. M., Downes, J. J., Sahakian, B. J., Polkey, C. E., & Robbins, T. W. (1990). Planning and spatial working memory following frontal lobe lesions in man. *Neuropsychologia, 28*, 1021–1034.

Owen, A. M., James, M., Leigh P. N., Summers, B. A., Marsden, C. D., Quinn, N. P., et al. (1992). Fronto-striatal cognitive deficits at different stages of Parkinson's disease. *Brain, 115*, 1727–1751.

Pandya, D. N., & Yeterian, E. H. (1996). Comparison of prefrontal architecture and connections. *Philosophical Transactions of the Royal Society of London. Series B: Biological Sciences, 29*, 1423–1432.

Pardo, J. V., Pardo, P. J., Janer, K. W., & Raichle, M. E. (1990). The anterior cingulated cortex mediates processing selection in the Stroop attentional conflict paradigm. *Proceedings of the National Academy of Sciences of the USA, 87*, 256–259.

Paus, T., Petrides, M., Evans, A. C., & Meyer, E. (1993). Role of the human anterior cingulated cortex in the control of oculomotor, manual, and speech responses: A positron emission tomography study. *Journal of Neurophysiology, 70*, 453–469.

Pennington, B. F., & Ozonoff, S. (1996). Executive function and developmental neuropsychopathology. *Journal of Child Psychology and Psychiatry, 36*, 51–87.

Perret, E. (1964). The left frontal lobe of man and the suppression of habitual responses in verbal categorical behaviour. *Neuropsychologia, 12*, 323–330.

Perrez, M., & Reicherts, M. (1992). Depressed people coping with aversive situations. In *Stress, coping and health: A situation-behaviour approach: Theory, methods and applications* (pp. 103–111). Seattle, WA: Hogrefe & Huber.

Petrides, M. (1986). The effect of periarcuate lesions in the monkey on the performance of symmetrically and asymmetrically reinforced visual and auditory go, no-go tasks. *Journal of Neuroscience, 6*, 2054–2063.

Plaisted, K. C., & Sahakian, B. J. (1997). Dementia of frontal lobe type—living in the here and now. *Ageing and Mental Health, 1*, 293–295.

Post, R. M. (1992). Transduction of psychosocial stress into the neurobiology of recurrent affective disorder. *American Journal of Psychiatry, 149*, 999–1010.

Post, R. M., Weiss, S. R. B., Leverich, G. S., George, M. S., Frye, M., & Ketter, T. A. (1996). Developmental psychobiology of cyclic affective illness: Implications for early therapeutic intervention. *Development and Psychopathology, 8*, 273–305.

Price, J. L. (1999). Prefrontal cortical networks related to visceral function and mood. *Annals of the New York Academy of Science, 877*, 383–396.

Puce, A., Allison, T., Bentin, S., Gore, J. C., & McCarthy, G. (1998). Temporal cortex

activation in humans viewing eye and mouth movements. *Journal of Neuroscience*, *18*, 2188–2199.
Purcell, R., Maruff, P., Kyrios, M., & Pantelis, C. (1997). Neuropsychological function in young patients with unipolar major depression. *Psychological Medicine*, *27*, 1277–1285.
Rahman, S., Robbins, T. W., & Sahakian, B. J. (1999). Comparative cognitive neuropsychological studies of frontal lobe function: Implications for therapeutic strategies in frontal variant frontotemporal dementia. *Dementia and Geriatric Cognitive Disorders*, *10*(Suppl 1), 15–28.
Rahman, S., Sahakian, B. J., Cardinal, R. N., Rogers, R. D., & Robbins, T. W. (2001). Decision making and neuropsychiatry. *Trends in Cognitive Sciences*, *5*, 271–277.
Rajkowska, G., Miguel-Hidalgo, J. J., Wei, J., Dilley, G., Pittman, S. D., Meltzer, H. Y., et al. (1999). Morphometric evidence for neuronal and glial prefrontal cell pathology in major depression. *Biological Psychiatry*, *45*, 1085–1098.
Reynolds, C. F., Frank, E., & Perel, J. M. (1999). Nortryptiline and interpersonal psychotherapy as maintenance therapies for recurrent major depression: A randomized controlled trial in patients older than 59 years. *Journal of the American Medical Association*, *281*, 39–45.
Roberts, A. C. & Wallis, J. D. (2000). Inhibitory control and affective processing in the prefrontal cortex: Neuropsychological studies in the common marmoset. *Cerebral Cortex*, *10*, 252–262.
Rogers, R. D., Everitt, B. J., Baldacchino, A., Blackshaw, A. J., Swainson, R., Wynne, K., et al. (1999a). Dissociable deficits in the decision making cognition of chronic amphetamine abusers, opiate abusers, patients with focal damage to prefrontal cortex, and tryptophan-depleted normal volunteers: Evidence for monoaminergic mechanisms. *Neuropsychopharmacology*, *20*, 322–339.
Rogers, R. D., Owen, A. M., Middleton, H. C., Williams, E. J., Pickard, J. D., Sahakian, B. J., et al. (1999b). Choosing between small, likely rewards and large, unlikely rewards activates inferior and orbital prefrontal cortex. *Journal of Neuroscience*, *20*, 9029–9038.
Rolls, E. T., Hornak, J., Wade, D., & McGrath, J. (1994). Emotion-related learning in patients with social and emotional changes associated with frontal lobe damage. *Journal of Neurology, Neurosurgery and Psychiatry*, *57*, 1518–1524.
Rubinsztein, J. S., Michael, A., Paykel, E. S., & Sahakian, B. J. (2000). Cognitive impairment in remission in bipolar affective disorder. *Psychological Medicine*, *30*, 1025–1036.
Saklofske, D. H. (1993). The position of N with non-clinical groups. *Proceedings of the 6th Meeting of the International Society for the Study of Individual Differences, Baltimore* (p. 32).
Sandler, I. N., Tein, J.-Y., & West, S. G. (1994). Coping, stress and the psychological symptoms of children of divorce: A cross-sectional and longitudinal study. *Child Development*, *65*, 1744–1763.
Sapolsky, R. M. (2000). The possibility of neurotoxicity in the hippocampus in major depression: A primer on neuron death. *Biological Psychiatry*, *48*, 755–765.
Saver, J. L., & Damasio, A. R. (1991). Preserved access and processing of social knowledge in a patient with acquired sociopathy due to ventromedial frontal damage. *Neuropsychologia*, *29*, 1241–1249.
Schacter, R., & Logan, G. D. (1990). Impulsivity and inhibitory control in normal

development and childhood psychopathology. *Developmental Psychology*, 26, 710–720.
Schoenbaum, G., Chiba, A. A., & Gallagher, M. (1998). Orbitofrontal cortex and basolateral amygdala encode expected outcomes during learning. *Nature Neuroscience*, 1, 155–159.
Seligman, M. E. P. (1975). *Helplessness*. San Francisco: Freeman.
Shallice, T. (1988). Information processing models of consciousness. In A. J. Marcel & E. Bisiach (Eds.), *Consciousness in contemporary science* (pp. 305–333). Oxford: Oxford University Press.
Stuss, D. T., & Benson, D. F. (1986). *The frontal lobes*. New York: Raven Press.
Tamminga, C. A. (2000). Images in neuroscience: Executive function. *American Journal of Psychiatry*, 157, 3.
Taylor, S. F., Liberson, I., Fig, L. M., Decker, L. R., Minoshima, S., & Koeppe, R. A. (1998). The effect of emotional content on visual recognition memory: A PET activation study. *NeuroImage*, 8, 188–197.
Teasdale, J. D. (1983). Negative thinking in depression: Cause, effect or reciprocal relationship? *Advances in Behaviour Research and Therapy*, 5, 3–26.
Teasdale, J. D. (1988). Cognitive vulnerability to persistent depression. *Cognition and Emotion*, 2, 247–274.
Teasdale, J. D., & Dent, J. (1987). Cognitive vulnerability to depression: An investigation of two hypotheses. *British Journal of Clinical Psychology*, 26, 113–126.
Teasdale, J. D., & Barnard, P. J. (1993). *Affect, cognition and change: Remodelling depressive thought*. Hillsdale, NJ: Lawrence Erlbaum Associates, Inc.
Teasdale, J. D., Howard, R. J., Cox, S. G., Ha, Y., Brammer, M. J., Williams, S. C. R., et al. (1999). Functional MRI study of the cognitive generation of affect. *American Journal of Psychiatry*, 156, 209–215.
Thomas, K., Drevets, W. C., Whalen, P., Eccard, C. H., Dahl, R. E., Ryan, N. D., et al. (2001). Amygdala response to facial expression in children and adults. *Biological Psychiatry*, 49, 309–316.
Tranel, D., & Hyman, B. T. (1990). Neuropsychological correlates of bilateral amygdala damage. *Archives of Neurology*, 47, 349–355.
Tranel, D., Bechara, A., & Damasio, A. R. (2000). Decision making and the somatic marker hypothesis. In M. S. Gazzaniga (Ed.), *The cognitive neurosciences* (2nd Ed., pp. 1047–1106). Cambridge, MA: MIT Press.
Veiel, H. O. F. (1997). A preliminary profile of neuropsychological deficits associated with unipolar depression. *Journal of Clinical and Experimental Neuropsychology*, 19, 587–603.
Whalen, P. J., Rauch, S. L., Etcoff, N. L., McInerney, S. C., Lee, M. B., & Jenike, M. A. (1998). Masked presentations of emotional facial expressions modulate amygdala activity without explicit knowledge. *Journal of Neuroscience*, 18, 411–418.
Williams, J. M. G., Watts, F. N., MacLeod, C., & Matthews, A. (1997). *Cognitive psychology and emotional disorders* (2nd Ed.). Chichester, UK: Wiley.
Zajonc, R. B. (1984). On the primacy of affect. *American Psychologist*, 39, 117–123.
Zeidner, M. (1994). Personal and contextual determinants of coping and anxiety in an evaluative situation: A prospective study. *Personality and Individual Differences*, 16, 899–918.
Zeidner, M., & Saklofske, D. (1996). Adaptive and maladaptive coping. In M. Zeider & N. S. Endler (Eds.), *Handbook of coping* (pp. 505–531). New York: Wiley.

10 The neurobiology of antisocial behaviour and psychopathy

R. James R. Blair

Summary

This chapter considers neurobiological influences on threat/frustration-based reactive aggressions and goal-directed instrumental aggression. Reactive aggression is mediated by a dedicated subcortical neural system that humans share with other mammalian species. It is suggested that this system is modulated by the amygdala and regions of the orbital and medial frontal cortex, and that dysfunction within these structures can dysregulate the individual's response to threat. Instrumental aggression is goal-directed motor activity: the aggression is used to achieve a particular goal such as obtaining another individual's money or increasing status within a group. Remarkable levels of instrumental aggression are displayed by individuals with psychopathy. Various models of instrumental aggression/psychopathy will be considered. However, it will be suggested that only the integrated emotion systems (IES) approach can account for the emergence of this disorder.

Introduction

There is considerable concern about the level of antisocial behaviour in society. More than three million violent crimes are committed in the USA annually (Reiss, Miczek, & Roth, 1994), 20,000 of these involving murder by gunfire (*Source book of Criminal Justice Statistics Online*, 1998). A disproportionately large number of these antisocial acts are committed by a relatively small number of individuals (Farrington, 1995).

In this chapter, neurobiological influences on the level of antisocial behaviour will be considered. However, before this can be done, two distinctions must be made. The first is that between reactive and instrumental aggression (Barratt, Stanford, Dowdy, Liebman, & Kent, 1999; Barratt, Stanford, Kent, & Felthous, 1997; Berkowitz, 1993; Linnoila et al., 1983). In reactive aggression (also referred to as affective aggression), a frustrating or threatening event triggers the aggressive act and frequently also induces anger. Importantly, the aggression is initiated without regard for any potential goal (for example, gaining the victim's possessions or increasing status within the hierarchy). In contrast, instrumental aggression (also referred to as proactive aggression) is purposeful and goal directed. The aggression is used instrumentally to achieve a specific desired goal such as obtaining the victim's possessions or to increase status within a group hierarchy (Berkowitz, 1993). Bullying is an example of instrumental aggression and, unsurprisingly, individuals who engage in bullying behaviours, frequently engage in other forms of instrumental antisocial behaviour in other contexts (Roland & Idsoe, 2001).

A second distinction that should be drawn is that between conventional and moral antisocial behaviour (Blair, 1995; Smetana, 1993; Turiel, 1983). Conventional transgressions do not result in harm to others but disrupt social order and frequently involve violations of expectations of behaviour according to social hierarchy (such as public nudity, subordinates putting their feet on the desk of their boss, or a child talking in class). Moral transgressions are acts which result in harm to others (such as hitting another individual or stealing another's property). The distinction between conventional and moral transgressions is important, as there is considerable reason to believe that the neurocognitive architectures regulating moral and conventional transgressions are separable (Blair, 2001). In particular, the neurocognitive architecture regulating reactive aggression is thought to be involved in regulating conventional transgressions, while the neurocognitive architecture regulating instrumental aggression is thought to be involved in regulating moral transgressions.

Both the distinctions between reactive and instrumental aggression and conventional and moral transgressions have been criticized (Bushman & Anderson, 2001; Shweder, Mahaptra, & Miller, 1987). However, considerable data show that there are two relatively separable populations of aggressive individuals. First, there are individuals who present with solely reactive aggression. Such individuals are particularly indifferent to conventional rules and do not modulate their behaviour according to the status of the individuals with which they are interacting. Individuals with lesions that include the orbital frontal cortex may present with elevated levels of reactive aggression (Anderson, Bechara, Damasio, Tranel, & Damasio, 1999; Blair & Cipolotti, 2000; Grafman, Schwab, Warden, Pridgen, & Brown, 1996). In addition, individuals with impulsive aggressive disorder can present with elevated levels of reactive aggression (Best, Williams, & Coccaro, 2002; Coccaro, 1998).

The second group of individuals present with elevated levels of both instrumental and reactive aggression. Such individuals are particularly indifferent to moral transgressions and show little indication of guilt or empathy with their victims. Individuals with psychopathy present with highly elevated levels of both instrumental and reactive aggression (Cornell et al., 1996; Williamson, Hare, & Wong, 1987). Psychopathy is a developmental disorder that presents across the lifespan (Harpur & Hare, 1994); children and adults with the disorder present with similar symptomatology. In childhood and adolescence, psychopathic tendencies are identified principally by the use of either the Antisocial Process Screening Device (Frick & Hare, 2001) or the Psychopathy Checklist: Youth Version (Forth, Kosson, & Hare, in press; Kosson, Cyterski, Steuerwald, Neumann, & Walker-Matthews, 2002). In adulthood, psychopathy is identified though use of the Psychopathy Checklist–Revised (Hare, 1991). While content differences exist between the measures, all index a similar syndrome involving both affective-interpersonal (such as lack of empathy and guilt) and behavioural components (such as criminal activity and poor behavioural controls) (Frick, O'Brien, Wootton, & McBurnett, 1994; Harpur, Hare, & Hakstian, 1989).

It should be noted that classifications of psychopathy are not synonymous with diagnoses of conduct disorder (CD) or antisocial personality disorder (APD) (American Psychiatric Association, 1994). The psychiatric diagnoses of CD and APD are poorly specified. For example, no distinction is made between the forms of aggression the individual may present with. Because of this imprecision, a highly heterogeneous sample can receive the diagnosis. Indeed, the diagnostic rate of CD is 16% of boys in mainstream education (American Psychiatric Association, 1994) and over 80% for APD in adult forensic institutions (Hart & Hare, 1996). Unsurprisingly, therefore, diagnoses of CD and APD are relatively uninformative regarding an individual's prognosis. This is in sharp contrast to the classification of psychopathy, which is highly predictive of a patient's future behaviour (Hare, 1991).

The distinctions between reactive and instrumental aggression and conventional and moral transgressions have been almost totally ignored by neurocognitive models of antisocial behaviour/psychopathy (Damasio, 1994; Davidson, Putnam, & Larson, 2000; Lykken, 1995; Moffitt, 1993a; Newman, 1998; Patrick, Cuthbert, & Lang, 1994; Raine, 2002a). However, it is almost certain that the neurocognitive architectures mediating these forms of aggression/transgression are dissociable and, indeed, that dysfunction in these dissociable architectures can result in different pathologies (Blair, 2001).

This chapter will begin with a discussion of the neurobiology of reactive aggression before concluding by considering the neurobiology of instrumental aggression. Five theories will be critiqued. These are the frontal lobe hypotheses (Gorenstein, 1991; Moffitt, 1993a, 1993b; Raine, 2002a, 2002b), the response set modulation hypothesis (Newman 1998; Patterson & Newman, 1993), the dysfunctional fear hypotheses (Fowles, 1988; Lykken, 1995; Patrick, 1994), the empathy-based violence inhibition mechanism (VIM) model (Blair, 1995), and the new integrated emotional systems model (Blair, 2003b, 2003c).

Neurobiology of reactive aggression

Considerably more is known about the neurobiology of reactive than instrumental aggression. Reactive aggression is mediated by a dedicated neural system that humans share with other mammalian species (Gregg &

Siegel, 2001; Panksepp, 1998). It runs from medial amygdaloidal areas downward, largely via the stria terminalis, to the medial hypothalamus, and from there to the dorsal half of the periaqueductal grey (PAG). It is organized in a hierarchical manner such that aggression evoked from the amygdala is dependent on the functional integrity of the medial hypothalamus and PAG, but that aggression evoked from the PAG is not dependent on the functional integrity of the amygdala (Bandler, 1988; Gregg & Siegel, 2001; Panksepp, 1998). This system mediates the animal's response to threat. At low levels of stimulation, from a distant threat, the animal will freeze. At higher levels, from a closer threat, the animal will attempt to escape the environment. At higher levels still, when the threat is very close and escape is impossible, the animal will display reactive aggression (Blanchard, Blanchard, & Takahashi, 1977).

Both the amygdala and orbital frontal cortex modulate this neural system (Gregg & Siegel, 2001; Panksepp, 1998). However, the ways in which they modulate this neural system are likely to differ (Blair, 2004). The amygdala responds to reinforcing as well as aversive stimuli (Everitt, Cardinal, Hall, Parkinson, & Robbins, 2000). This suggests that the amygdala would be in a position to both upgrade (as a response to an aversive stimulus) and downgrade (as a response to an appetitive stimulus) the responsiveness of the subcortical systems that respond to threat. This suggestion receives support from the startle reflex literature. The basic startle reflex is also mediated by the subcortical systems that respond to threat. The magnitude of the startle reflex can be altered by the presence of visual or auditory primes that occur shortly before the startle stimulus. Thus, the presence of an aversive threat prime augments the magnitude of the startle reflex relative to neutral primes, while appetitive visual primes reduce the magnitude of the startle reflex (Lang, Bradley, & Cuthbert, 1990). This modulation is achieved by the operation of the amygdala on the subcortical systems that respond to threat and which generate the reflex (Angrilli et al., 1996; Campeau & Davis, 1995; Davis, 2000; Funayama, Grillon, Davis, & Phelps, 2001).

Lesions of the amygdala can either increase or decrease the probability of reactive aggression. Thus, bilateral amygdalectomies have been reported to decrease aggressive behaviour in 70–76% of cases (Ramamurthi, 1988). However, very severe amygdalar atrophy is found in a significant subgroup of aggressive patients with temporal lobe epilepsy (van Elst, Woermann, Lemieux, Thompson, & Trimble, 2000). Moreover, unilateral damage to the central nucleus of the amygdala in cats increases the expression of reactive aggression (Zagrodzka, Hedberg, Mann, & Morrison, 1998). At first glance, these data appear problematic; lesions to the same neural region can have opposite effects. However, if we assume that the amygdala can both up- and downgrade the functioning of the subcortical threat systems, the data become less surprising. Amygdala lesions could reduce the probability of reactive aggression in threatening circumstances because the threatening cues would no longer activate the subcortical threat systems through the amygdala.

However, amygdala lesions could also increase the probability of reactive aggression more generally. The amygdala lesion would prevent the suppression of reactive aggression as a function of amygdala activation by appetitive stimuli in the environment. Thus, potentially, amygdala lesions may either increase or decrease the probability of reactive aggression according to the contextual parameters (aversive/appetitive) the animal is exposed to.

Considerable data suggest that the frontal cortex, in particular, the ventromedial and orbital frontal cortex, is involved in the modulation of the subcortical threat systems that mediate reactive aggression (Anderson et al., 1999; Grafman et al., 1996; Gregg & Siegel, 2001; Panksepp, 1998; Pennington & Bennetto, 1993). Thus, damage to the ventromedial frontal and orbital frontal cortex is associated with increased risk of the display of reactive aggression in humans whether the lesion occurs in childhood or adulthood (Anderson et al., 1999; Grafman et al., 1996; Pennington & Bennetto, 1993). In addition, a series of neuroimaging studies have revealed reduced frontal functioning in patients presenting with reactive aggression (Goyer et al., 1994; Soderstrom, Tullberg, Wikkelso, Ekholm, & Forsman, 2000; Volkow & Tancredi, 1987; Volkow et al., 1995). Interestingly, this reduced frontal functioning is not observed in patients presenting with predominantly instrumental aggression (Raine et al., 1998a). This is consistent with neuropsychological data indicating that individuals with psychopathy who present with marked levels of instrumental aggression do not present with poor performance on general measures of dorsolateral or medial frontal lobe functioning (Kandel & Freed, 1989; LaPierre, Braun, & Hodgins, 1995; Mitchell, Colledge, Leonard, & Blair, 2002).

The orbital frontal cortex is involved in at least two processes that have been hypothesized to modulate the subcortical systems mediating reactive aggression. The first is response reversal: the computation of expectations of reward, identifying whether these expectations have been violated, and reversing responding if they have (Cools, Clark, Owen, & Robbins, 2002; Rolls, 2000). Frustration has long been linked to the display of reactive aggression (Berkowitz, 1993). Frustration occurs after the initiation of a behaviour to achieve an expected reward and the subsequent absence of this reward. The orbital frontal cortex is involved in the expectation-violation computations necessary to induce frustration. It can therefore be suggested that the orbital frontal cortex may increase neuronal activity in the subcortical systems mediating reactive aggression under conditions when an expected reward has not been achieved, and suppress neuronal activity when the expected reward is achieved.

The second process is social response reversal (SRR) (Blair, 2001; Blair & Cipolotti, 2000). This position stresses the role of social cues in modulating social behaviour (Blair, 2001; Blair & Cipolotti, 2000). Thus, angry expressions, in particular, are known to curtail the behaviour of others in situations where social conventional rules or expectations have been violated (Averill, 1982). The main neural region implicated in SRR is the lateral orbital frontal cortex (in particular, Brodmann's area [BA] 47) (Blair, 2001; Blair & Cipolotti, 2000). Neuroimaging work has shown this area to be activated by negative emotional expressions; in particular, anger but also fear and disgust (Blair, Morris, Frith, Perrett, & Dolan, 1999; Kesler-West et al., 2001; Sprengelmeyer, Rausch, Eysel, & Przuntek, 1998). This region of the lateral orbital frontal cortex has also been shown to respond when the individual him/herself is angry (Dougherty et al., 1999). Patients with orbital frontal cortex lesions are impaired in the ability to recognize facial expressions, particularly anger (Blair & Cipolotti, 2000; Hornak, Rolls, & Wade, 1996). Moreover, patients with orbital frontal cortex lesions are impaired in identifying anger-inducing conventional transgressions (Blair & Cipolotti, 2000; Stone, Baron-Cohen, & Knight, 1998; Stone, Cosmides, Tooby, Kroll, & Knight, 2002). Interestingly, recent neuroimaging data have shown that the same region of the lateral orbitofrontal cortex (BA 47) that responds to angry expressions also responds to conventional transgressions (Berthoz, Armony, Blair, & Dolan, 2002).

According to the position, the lateral orbital frontal cortex is involved in modulating the individual's social behaviour particularly as a function of the position in the dominance hierarchy of any people with whom the individual is interacting. Thus, for example, the angry expression of an individual higher in the dominance hierarchy will suppress reactive aggression or inappropriate social behaviour and lead to alterations in current instrumental behaviour. In contrast, the angry expression of an individual lower in the dominance hierarchy will lead to activation of the subcortical circuitry for reactive aggression. In line with this suggestion, primates with intact orbital frontal cortex will vent their rage on more submissive animals and avoid confrontations with more dominant ones following neural stimulation of brainstem threat circuitry (Alexander & Perachio, 1973). However, patients with orbital frontal cortex lesions may show heightened levels of reactive aggression, and, if they do, this aggression is not tempered by considerations of the hierarchical status of the other (Blair & Cipolotti, 2000; Grafman et al., 1996; Pennington & Bennetto, 1993).

On a related note, Leary (Leary & Meadows, 1991; Leary, Landel, & Patton, 1996) and others (Gilbert, 1997; Keltner, 1995; Keltner & Buswell, 1997; Miller, 1996) have suggested that embarrassment serves an important social function by signalling appeasement to others. The basic idea is that embarrassment serves to aid the restoration of relationships after social conventional transgressions (Keltner & Buswell, 1997). There is a good deal of empirical evidence to support this "appeasement" or remedial function of embarrassment from studies of both humans and nonhuman primates (for reviews, see Gilbert, 1997; Keltner & Anderson, 2000; Keltner & Buswell, 1997; Leary & Meadows, 1991). In line with the suggestions of the SRR hypothesis, patients with orbital frontal cortex lesions present with impaired attributions of embarrassment to story protagonists (Blair & Cipolotti, 2000).

Neurobiology of instrumental aggression

Instrumental aggression is goal-directed motor activity; the aggression is used to achieve a particular goal such as obtaining another individual's money or increasing status within a group. Indeed, most forms of antisocial behaviour (shoplifting, fraud, theft, and robbery) are instrumental, goal-directed behaviours. As such, when an individual is engaged in instrumental aggression, he/she is likely to be recruiting the same cortical neural systems as any other goal-directed motor programme. In brief, these neural systems would include the temporal cortex, to represent the object, and striatal and premotor cortical neurons to implement the actual behaviour (Passingham & Toni, 2001). Thus, when considering models of the neurobiology of instrumental aggression, we should be considering whether the model explains why an individual might be particularly predisposed to engage in heightened levels of this form of instrumental behaviour.

Individuals with psychopathy present with high levels of instrumental aggression (Cornell et al., 1996; Williamson et al., 1987). We will therefore consider existing models of psychopathy to be models explaining the heightened incidence of instrumental aggression in this population. The models we will consider are the frontal lobe dysfunction hypotheses (Gorenstein, 1991; Moffitt, 1993a, 1993b; Raine, 2002a, 2002b), the response set modulation hypothesis (Newman, 1998; Patterson & Newman 1993), the dysfunctional fear hypotheses (Fowles, 1988; Lykken, 1995; Patrick, 1994), and the development of the empathy-based violence inhibition mechanism (VIM) model, the new integrated emotion systems (IES) model (Blair, 1995, 2003b, 2003c).

The frontal lobe dysfunction hypothesis

Frontal lobe and consequent executive dysfunction has long been related to antisocial behaviour (Barratt, 1994; Gorenstein, 1982; Moffitt, 1993a; Raine, 1997, 2002a). Indeed, there is ample evidence that individuals with antisocial behaviour show impaired performance on measures of executive functioning (for reviews of this literature, see Kandel & Freed, 1989; Moffitt, 1993b; Morgan & Lilienfeld, 2000; Pennington & Ozonoff, 1996). Moreover, as noted above, a series of brain-imaging studies of aggressive individuals have supported the suggestion of reduced frontal functioning in aggressive individuals (Raine, Buchsbaum, & LaCasse, 1997; Raine et al., 1994; Raine, Lencz, Bihrle, LaCasse, & Colletti, 2000; Raine et al., 1998a; Raine, Phil, Stoddard, Bihrle, & Buchsbaum, 1998b; Volkow & Tancredi, 1987; Volkow et al., 1995).

However, it is important to note that the frontal lobe positions are rather underspecified. Thus, the frontal cortex corresponds to almost half of the cortex (Fuster, 1980) and has been implicated in a variety of putative processes (Baddeley & Della Sala, 1998; Burgess & Shallice, 1996; Luria, 1966; Pennington & Ozonoff, 1996; Roberts, Robbins, & Weiskrantz, 1998).

However, the frontal lobe positions typically do not distinguish between different regions of the prefrontal cortex, between different forms of executive function or, at the behavioural level, between reactive and instrumental aggression. Moreover, the frontal lobe positions usually fail to provide any detailed cognitive account as to why damage to functions mediated by the frontal cortex should lead to an increased risk of aggression.

The neuropsychological literature examining the relationship between frontal dysfunction and antisocial behaviour has, to a very large extent, concentrated on the use of tasks that index executive functions commonly linked to the dorsolateral prefrontal cortex (Kandel & Freed, 1989; Moffitt, 1993b; Morgan & Lilienfield, 2000; Pennington & Ozonoff, 1996). This literature has found that general antisocial populations show impaired performance on these measures of executive functioning (for reviews of this literature see Kandel & Freed, 1989; Moffitt, 1993b; Morgan & Lilienfield, 2000; Pennington & Ozonoff, 1996). However, individuals with psychopathy, a population notable for their level of instrumental aggression, fail to show executive dysfunction on measures linked to the dorsolateral prefrontal cortex (Kandel & Freed, 1989; LaPierre et al., 1995; Mitchell et al., 2002). This suggests a first refinement of the frontal dysfunction positions; dorsolateral prefrontal cortex dysfunction is not related to the emergence of instrumental aggression. But a second refinement is necessary regarding reactive aggression. The neurological literature strongly suggests that while the orbital and ventromedial frontal cortex is involved in the regulation of (reactive) aggression, the dorsolateral prefrontal cortex is not (Grafman et al., 1996). Yet, antisocial individuals are present with dorsolateral executive dysfunction (Kandel & Freed, 1989; Moffitt, 1993b; Morgan & Lilienfield, 2000; Pennington & Ozonoff, 1996). This suggests that the reactive aggression of these antisocial individuals is related to a cause that affects general frontal cortex development (that is, the dorsolateral prefrontal cortex as well as the orbital and medial frontal cortex). Thus, the association between dorsolateral executive dysfunction and antisocial behaviour would be correlational rather than causal. The greater the degree of apparent dorsolateral executive dysfunction, the more likely regions of orbital and medial frontal cortex involved in the regulation of reactive aggression have also been disrupted.

Thus, in short, the frontal lobe dysfunction positions are not incorrect but rather in need of greater specification. Specifically, a frontal lobe explanation is more appropriate for reactive rather than instrumental aggression. Moreover, while dorsolateral executive dysfunction may be associated with reactive antisocial behaviour, the association is likely to be correlational rather than causal. In contrast, ventralmedial and orbital frontal cortex dysfunction is causally related to a heightened risk of reactive aggression (Anderson et al., 1999; Blair & Cipolotti, 2000; Grafman et al., 1996; Pennington & Bennetto, 1993). To specify at the cognitive level, we would relate the modulation of reactive aggression to systems involved in response reversal and social response reversal. Thus, to develop the frontal lobe hypotheses, we could argue that dysfunction of the ventralmedial and orbital frontal cortex, if it leads to impaired response reversal/social response reversal, will put the individual at increased risk of the presentation of reactive aggression.

The response set modulation hypothesis

An influential model of psychopathy is the response modulation hypothesis of Newman and colleagues (Newman, 1998; Patterson & Newman, 1993). Response modulation involves "a rapid and relatively automatic (i.e., non-effortful or involuntary) shift of attention from the effortful organization and implementation of goal-directed behavior to its evaluation" (Newman et al., 1997). This "brief and highly automatic shift of attention ... enables individuals to monitor and, if relevant, use information that is peripheral to their dominant response set (i.e., deliberate focus of attention")" (Lorenz & Newman, 2002, p. 92). The initial physiological basis of the model (Gorenstein & Newman, 1980) was based on the work of Gray and others on the implications of septohippocampal lesions for emotional learning (Gray, 1971). "In animal studies, deficient response modulation typically involves response perseveration or a tendency to continue some goal-directed behavior (e.g., running down the arm of a maze) despite punishment or frustrative nonreward (i.e., extinction)" (Newman, 1998, p. 85).

It is this proposed reduced automatic processing in individuals with psychopathy that is at the core of Newman's model: "Whereas most people automatically anticipate the consequences of their actions, automatically feel shame for unkind deeds, automatically understand why they should persist in the face of frustration, automatically distrust propositions that seem too good to be true, and are automatically aware of their commitments to others, psychopaths may only become aware of such factors with effort" (Newman, 1998, p. 84). Newman argues that it is not that individuals with psychopathy are incapable of regulating their behaviour, but that self-regulation is more effortful for psychopaths because of the lack of these "relatively automatic processes" to guide actions.

The response set modulation hypothesis is an attention-based model. According to the model, "the impulsivity, poor passive avoidance, and emotion-processing deficits of individuals with psychopathy may all be understood as a failure to process the meaning of information that is peripheral or incidental to their deliberate focus of attention" (Lorenz & Newman, 2002, p. 92).

The response set modulation hypothesis has generated a considerable body of experimental work. Thus, this hypothesis has been used to explain the observed impairment in passive avoidance learning presented by individuals with psychopathy (Newman & Kosson, 1986). Indeed, the most frequently used measure of passive avoidance learning in individuals with psychopathy is the computerized number task introduced by Newman and Kosson (1986). In this task, participants are presented with a series of two-digit numbers, some of which, when responded to, result in reward while others result in punishment (Kosson, Smith, & Newman, 1990; Newman & Kosson, 1986; Newman, Patterson, Howland, & Nichols, 1990). Participants must learn which stimuli, when responded to, result in reward and which result in punishment. In the original investigation using this task, Newman and Kosson (1986) found that individuals with psychopathy committed more passive avoidance errors than comparison individuals. This finding has been consistently replicated (Kosson et al., 1990; Newman & Kosson, 1986; Newman et al., 1990; Thornquist & Zuckerman, 1995).

A second major paradigm introduced by Newman and related to response set modulation is the one-pack, card-playing task (Newman, Patterson, & Kosson, 1987). In this task, the participants have to decide whether to play a card. Initially, the participants' choice to play is always reinforcing; if they play the card, they will win points or money. However, as the participants progress through the pack of cards, their probability of reward decreases. They should terminate their responding before they receive greater levels of punishment than reward. Children with psychopathic tendencies and adult individuals with psychopathy have considerable difficulty with this task; they continue to play the cards even when they are being repeatedly punished and may end up losing all the points that they have gained (Fisher & Blair, 1998; Newman et al., 1987; O'Brien & Frick, 1996).

According to the response set modulation hypothesis, the poor performance of individuals with psychopathy on both the passive avoidance and one-pack, card-playing tasks are related to their inability to shift their attention from their goal of responding to gain reward to the peripheral punishment information. However, the response set modulation hypothesis has also been used to explain data that are not derived from emotional learning tasks. In the lexical decision task, participants are presented with letter strings and must respond when the letter strings presented to them form a word. Healthy individuals respond faster, and show larger event-related potentials (ERPs), over central and parietal sites, to emotional than neutral words (Begleiter, Gross, & Kissin, 1967; Graves, Landis, & Goodglass, 1981). In contrast, individuals with psychopathy fail to show any reaction time or ERP differences between emotional and neutral words (Kiehl, Hare, McDonald, & Brink, 1999; Lorenz & Newman, 2002; Williamson, Harpur, & Hare, 1991). Interestingly, as regards the response set modulation hypothesis, while healthy individuals are faster to respond to high-frequency than low-frequency words, individuals with psychopathy are not (Lorenz & Newman, 2002). According to the response set modulation hypothesis, the absence of emotion and frequency effects on lexical decision performance in individuals with psychopathy is due to their inability to use the peripheral affective or frequency information because of their focus of attention on the dominant response set (deciding whether the stimulus was a word or not).

The response set modulation hypothesis has thus been associated with the development of an assortment of interesting paradigms. However, it is not without difficulties. In particular, while the response-modulation hypothesis is an attentional account, it is unclear to what extent this account is compatible with contemporary models of attention. The currently predominant model of attention is probably the biased competition model (Desimone & Duncan, 1995). According to this model, attention reflects the competition among stimuli for neural representation. This occurs within sensory cortices and can be biased in several ways. One way is by bottom-up, sensory-driven mechanisms, such as stimulus salience. For example, stimuli that are colourful or of high contrast will be at a competitive advantage. But another way is by attentional top-down feedback, which is generated in areas outside the visual cortex. For example, directed attention to a particular location in space facilitates processing of stimuli presented at that location. In this way, even objects that are not physically salient may win the competition and influence ongoing behaviour. In short, an object may become the focus of attention because either it is intrinsically salient or top-down feedback processes bias its processing.

There are two ways to consider the response-modulation hypothesis with respect to this framework. According to the response-modulation hypothesis, the difficulty faced by individuals with psychopathy is that the "relatively automatic processes" are less likely to guide actions. A first way of interpreting this idea within the biased competition model would be to suggest that the impact of bottom-up, sensory-driven mechanisms is reduced in individuals with psychopathy. While such an interpretation makes some interesting novel predictions, such as, for example, that individuals with psychopathy would be less sensitive to pop-out effects of stimulus salience in a visual array, it is less clear that it is in line with the spirit of the response-modulation hypothesis. The hypothesis stresses that the problems for individuals with psychopathy should emerge when they are engaged in goal-directed behaviour. However, reduced functioning of bottom-up, sensory-driven mechanisms would be apparent in behaviour whether the individual was engaged in goal-directed action or not.

The second interpretation of the response-modulation hypothesis makes reference to attentional top-down feedback. According to the biased competition model, the degree to which a stimulus is processed (that is, attended to) is determined by the degree to which it survives the competition process in sensory systems. The degree to which a stimulus that is not the focus of attention survives the competition process is thought to be a function of task load (Lavie, 1995). Under difficult task conditions (high-load conditions), where processing of additional stimuli may fatally disrupt the goal-directed processing of the target stimuli, top-down processes will result in a tight focus on the target stimuli. As a consequence, the representation of the unattended stimuli will be sufficiently suppressed by the target stimuli as to not be processed. In contrast, under less difficult task conditions (low load conditions), where the processing of additional stimuli will not disrupt the goal-directed processing of the target stimuli, the unattended stimuli can survive the competition and be processed. For example, determining whether a centrally presented word stimulus is bisyllabic or not (high-task load) prevents the identification of whether a peripherally presented nontarget stimulus is moving. In contrast, determining whether the centrally presented word stimulus is written in upper or lower case (low-task load) does not (Rees, Frith, & Lavie, 1997).

As regards the response-modulation hypothesis, the suggestion would therefore be that individuals with psychopathy always operate under high-load conditions during goal-directed activity. That is, attention to the target stimuli so suppresses the representation of the unattended stimuli that they are not processed. At first glance, such an interpretation is attractive. It would appear to explain reduced processing of punishment information during goal-directed attention to stimuli associated with reward (Newman & Kosson, 1986; Newman et al., 1987) as well as reduced interference in Stroop-type tasks (Newman, Schmitt, & Voss, 1997).

However, such an interpretation would not explain the lexical decision data (healthy individuals respond faster to emotional than neutral words, while individuals with psychopathy do not). If the stimulus to be identified as a word or not is being attended to (as must be the case to perform the task), then the stimulus should automatically activate the semantic stimuli; this would not be a function of attention, but it would be an inevitable function of the word's associations. The only way that the word should not activate these associations would be independent of an attentional account; that is, if the semantic system of individuals with psychopathy was profoundly impaired. Studies examining semantic priming and semantic impact on Stroop interference all suggest no generalized semantic impairment in individuals with psychopathy (Brinkley, Schmitt, & Newman, manuscript submitted for publication; Peschardt, Mitchell, Leonard, & Blair, manuscript submitted for publication).

Moreover, an attentional account of the impairment seen in individuals with psychopathy in passive avoidance learning and response reversal, as indexed by the one-pack, card-playing task, is only superficially attractive. In the passive-avoidance and response-reversal paradigms (Newman & Kosson, 1986; Newman et al., 1987), the punishment information is presented in the absence of distracting information. According to models of attention (Desimone & Duncan, 1995; Lavie, 1995), it would be difficult to see why this information should not be attended to or processed given the absence of competing stimuli. The fact that the punishment information does not modulate the behaviour of individuals with psychopathy would tend to suggest that they cannot learn from this information, rather than that they cannot attend to this information. Such a suggestion is made by the fear and IES accounts (Blair, 2003b; Fowles, 1988; Lykken, 1995; Patrick et al., 1994).

In short, the response set modulation hypothesis has resulted in the development of an assortment of interesting paradigms. However, at present, the extent to which this attention-driven hypothesis is compatible with contemporary positions on attention is unclear.

The dysfunctional fear hypotheses

One of the main positions regarding the emotional impairment shared by individuals with psychopathy is that there is impairment in the neurophysiological systems modulating fear behaviour (Cleckley, 1976; Eysenck, 1964; Fowles, 1988; Gray, 1987; Lykken, 1995; Mealey, 1995; Patrick, 1994; Trasler, 1973, 1978). For example, Cleckley (1976) wrote: "Within himself [the psychopathic individual] appears almost as incapable of anxiety as of profound remorse" (p. 340). The dysfunctional fear positions all assume that moral socialization is achieved through the use of punishment (Eysenck & Gudjonsson, 1989; Trasler, 1978). In essence, they assume that the healthy individual is frightened by punishment and associates this fear with the action that resulted in the punishment, thus making the individual less likely to engage in the action in the future. The suggestion is that individuals with psychopathy, because they are less aversively aroused by punishment, make weaker associations and thus are more likely to engage in the punished action in the future than healthy individuals.

The variants of the fear-dysfunction hypothesis have generated a considerable body of empirical literature. Indeed, the earliest formal experimental investigations of psychopathy were based on this hypothesis (Lykken, 1957). Thus, the fear-dysfunction positions predict the observed findings of impairment in individuals with psychopathy in aversive conditioning (Flor, Birbaumer, Hermann, Ziegler, & Patrick, 2002; Lykken, 1957), in generating autonomic responses to anticipated threat (Hare, 1982; Ogloff & Wong, 1990), in the augmentation of the startle reflex to visual threat primes (Herpertz et al., 2001; Levenston, Patrick, Bradley, & Lang, 2000), in passive avoidance learning (Lykken, 1957; Newman & Kosson, 1986), and in response reversal (Mitchell et al., 2002; Newman et al., 1987).

Many theorists have thus suggested that reduced anxiety levels lead to the development of antisocial behaviour and psychopathy (Cleckley, 1976; Eysenck, 1964; Gray, 1987; Lykken, 1995; Patrick, 1994; Trasler, 1973). However, in apparent contradiction of this position, there is a consistent body of literature indicating that high levels of antisocial behaviour are associated with heightened levels of anxiety. Thus, there is a well-documented positive correlation between anxiety and antisocial behaviour in children (Pine, Cohen, Cohen, & Brook, 2000; Russo & Beidel, 1993; Zoccolillo, 1992) and adults (Robins, Tipp, & Pryzbeck, 1991). In other words, higher levels of anxiety are associated with higher levels of antisocial behaviour.

This presents yet another conundrum, albeit one that is easily resolved. It is important to consider reactive aggression separately from instrumental aggression. Reactive aggression occurs to a very high level of threat/frustration (Blanchard et al., 1977). Anxiety reflects the activation of neural circuitry involved in the processing of threat (Kagan & Snidman, 1999). In other words, an individual presenting with elevated anxiety is presenting with an elevated threat response and is thus, ceteris paribus, more likely to display reactive aggression to an additional environmental threat or source of frustration. In contrast, according to the dysfunctional fear accounts, there should be an inverse relationship between level of anxiety and incidence of instrumental aggression. As yet, no studies have directly assessed the relationship between anxiety and reactive/instrumental aggression. However, studies have examined the relationship between anxiety and the callous and unemotional and the impulsive and conduct-disordered dimensions of psychopathy (Frick, Lilienfeld, Ellis, Loney, & Silverthorn, 1999; Patrick, 1994; Schmitt & Newman, 1999; Verona, Patrick, & Joiner, 2001). Schmitt and Newman (1999) reported that both the callous and unemotional and the impulsive and conduct-disordered dimensions of psychopathy are independent of level of anxiety. However, this study did not partial out the effects of the level of conduct problems from the effects of the emotional dysfunction. This was unfortunate given the well-documented positive correlation between anxiety and aggression in antisocial populations (Pine et al., 2000; Robins et al., 1991; Russo & Beidel, 1993; Zoccolillo, 1992). Indeed, those studies that did examine the callous and unemotional and the impulsive and conduct-disordered dimensions of psychopathy independently reported that anxiety level is *inversely* associated with the callous and unemotional dimension of psychopathy but *positively* associated with the impulsive and conduct-disordered dimension (Frick et al., 1999; Patrick, 1994; Verona et al., 2001).

However, despite this empirical success, the variants of the fear-dysfunction hypothesis face several problems. First, for the most part, the variants are underspecified at both the cognitive and neural levels. The various authors do not provide many details concerning the computational properties of the fear system. For example, it is difficult to be certain about the range of inputs to any putative fear systems or how the fear system operates in response to these inputs. The only more detailed account of a fear system that has been used in relation to explaining psychopathy is the behavioural inhibition system model (Gray, 1987; Gray & McNaughton, 1996; McNaughton & Gray, 2000). The suggestion here is that there is a unitary fear system, the behavioural inhibition system, which is thought to generate autonomic responses to punished stimuli (through classical conditioning) as well as inhibiting responding after punishment (through instrumental conditioning).

The behavioural inhibition system model does provides us with a putative range of inputs to a fear system and outputs from this system. However, it assumes that there is a unitary fear system, a claim implicit in all the variants of the fear-dysfunction hypothesis. However, and this brings us to the second problem for the fear-dysfunction hypothesis, the empirical literature strongly suggests that there is no single fear system but rather that there are a series of at least partially separable neural systems that are engaged in specific forms of processing that can be subsumed under the umbrella term "fear". For example, aversive conditioning and instrumental learning are two forms of processing that the fear system is thought to be involved in (Lykken, 1995; Patrick, 1994). Yet, the neural circuitries to achieve aversive conditioning and instrumental learning are doubly dissociable (Killcross, Robbins, & Everitt, 1997). Thus, a lesion to the central nucleus of the amygdala will prevent aversive conditioning but still allow instrumental learning to occur. In contrast, a lesion to the basolateral nucleus of the amygdala will prevent instrumental learning but still allow aversive conditioning to occur. Moreover, early amygdala lesions result in a massive reduction of neophobia; the infant monkey is no longer fearful of novel objects. However, the same infant monkeys with amygdala lesions show heightened social phobia; that is, their fear response to another infant monkey is actually heightened (Amaral, 2001; Prather et al., 2001). These findings strongly suggest partially separable "fear" systems: those for aversive conditioning/instrumental learning and for social threats.

The third problem faced by the fear-dysfunction hypotheses is that it is unclear why the fear theories should predict the very high level of antisocial behaviour shown by individuals with psychopathy. The positions usually argue that the individual with psychopathy has failed to be socialized away from antisocial behaviour (Eysenck & Gudjonsson, 1989; Trasler, 1978). However, the assumption that conditioned fear responses play a crucial role in moral socialization has been questioned (Blackburn, 1988; Blair & Morton, 1995). Thus, the developmental literature indicates that moral socialization is not achieved through the formation of conditioned fear responses but rather through the induction and fostering of empathy (Hoffman, 1984). Studies have shown, for example, that moral socialization is better achieved through the use of induction (reasoning that draws children's attention to the effects of their misdemeanours on others and increases empathy) than through harsh, authoritarian or power-assertive parenting practices which rely on the use of punishment (Baumrind, 1971, 1983; Hoffman & Saltzstein, 1967). Indeed, it has been suggested that while empathy facilitates moral socialization, fear actually hinders it (Hoffman, 1994). Thus, a review of a large number of studies of disciplinary methods concluded that punishment-based power assertion had an adverse effect on moral socialization regardless of age (Brody & Shaffer, 1982).

In addition, according to conditioning theory and data, the conditioned stimulus (CS) that is associated with the unconditioned stimulus (US) is the CS that most consistently predicts the US (Dickinson, 1980). To achieve socialization through aversive conditioning, it would therefore be crucial to ensure that the relevant CS (a representation of the transgression activity that the caregiver is attempting to ensure the child will find aversive) consistently predicts the US (the caregiver's hitting the child). However, this is very difficult to achieve. In houses using punishment-based techniques, the punishment is rarely contiguous with the performance of the transgression. This means that the desired CS rarely predicts the US of the caregiver's punishment. Instead, the CS predicting the US is more likely to the individual who delivers the US. Thus, in these households, aversive conditioning may occur, but the US–CS association will be physical pain and a particular parent, rather than physical pain and antisocial behaviour. Indeed, in households using punishment-based techniques, the punished child frequently does not show fear of committing transgressions (the poorly predictive CS) but does show fear of the person who is likely to punish them (the highly predictive CS) (Hoffman, 1994).

A fourth problem faced by the fear positions is also related to the idea embedded in the fear positions, that socialization should be achieved through punishment. If healthy individuals learn to avoid antisocial behaviour because of fear of punishment, it must be assumed that the healthy child judge all rules/transgressions in a similar way. In other words, if we learn to avoid talking in class and hitting other individuals because we are punished when we commit these actions, there is no reason for us to distinguish between these two transgressions. However, as noted above, healthy, developing children make a distinction between moral (victim-based) and conventional (social order-based) transgressions from the age of 36 months (Smetana, 1981, 1985, 1993). In other words, children do not judge all transgressions in an identical fashion. Instead, they distinguish those transgressions that result in harm to another from those that simply cause social disorder.

Thus, in conclusion, while the fear positions have generated a considerable body of data, it remains unclear why fear impairment should result in the development of psychopathy.

The violence inhibition mechanism (VIH) model

The importance of empathy for moral socialization was one of the reasons for the development of the VIH model of psychopathy and moral development (Blair, 1995; Blair, Jones, Clark, & Smith, 1997). At its simplest, the VIM was thought to be a system that, when activated by distress cues (the sad and fearful expressions of others), results in increased autonomic activity, attention, and activation of the brainstem threat response system (usually resulting in freezing) (Blair, 1995). The VIM was thought to be activated whenever distress cues are displayed. It was not thought to be reliant upon contextual information about ongoing violence for activation. In line with the model, the display of distress cues has been found to result in the inhibition of not only aggression (Perry & Perry, 1974) but also nonviolent disputes over property ownership (Camras, 1977) and sexual activity (Chaplin, Rice, & Harris, 1995).

The main focus of the model was to describe the cognitive prerequisites for moral development. According to the model, moral socialization occurs through the pairing of the activation of the mechanism by distress cues with representations of the act that caused the distress cues (Blair, 1995). Through association, these representations of moral transgressions become triggers for the mechanism. Thus, the appropriately developing child initially finds the pain of others aversive and then, through socialization, the thoughts of acts that cause pain to others aversive. It is proposed that individuals with psychopathy have had disruption to this system such that representations of acts that cause harm to others do not become triggers for the VIM (Blair, 1995).

One early index of appropriate moral socialization, and thus the developmental integrity of the VIM, is the demonstration by the child of the moral/conventional distinction mentioned above. Children with psychopathic tendencies and adults with psychopathy present with severe difficulties in distinguishing moral and conventional transgressions (Blair, 1995, 1997; Blair, Jones, Clark, & Smith, 1995; Blair, Monson, & Frederickson, 2001; for related work with children with behaviour disorder and conduct disorder, see Arsenio & Fleiss, 1996; Nucci & Herman, 1982). In addition, and in line with the VIM position, psychopathic adults show reduced comprehension of situations likely to induce guilt, although they show appropriate comprehension of happiness, sadness, and even complex emotions such as embarrassment (Blair et al., 1995). Finally, and as a direct prediction of the model, psychopathic adults and children with psychopathic tendencies show reduced autonomic activity to the sadness and fear of others (Aniskiewicz, 1979; Blair, 1999; Blair et al., 1997; House & Milligan, 1976).

However, while the original VIM model could provide an account of the emergence of instrumental antisocial behaviour in individuals with psychopathy and while it did generate a variety of predictions that have been empirically confirmed, it faced a serious difficulty; it could not account for the data associated with the response set modulation and fear hypotheses. Moreover, it could not account for data on the effect of the interaction of temperament and socialization practice on the development of moral development/conscience. Kochanska has stressed the role of fearfulness as the important temperamental factor (Kochanska, 1993, 1997). Indeed, she and others have found fearful children to show higher levels of moral development/conscience by a variety of measures (Asendorpf & Nunner-Winkler, 1992; Kochanska, 1997; Kochanska, De Vet, Goldman, Murray, & Putman, 1994; Rothbart, Ahadi, & Hershey, 1994). In addition, Kochanska has stressed that different socialization practices may promote moral development in children with different temperaments (Kochanska, 1993, 1997). In line with this, she found that, for fearful children, gentle maternal discipline promoted moral/conscience development. In contrast, for "fearless" children, alternative socialization practices, presumably capitalizing on mother–child positive orientation (secure attachment and maternal responsiveness), promoted the development of conscience (Kochanska, 1997).

The fact that the VIM model provides an incomplete account has resulted in an expansion of the model at both the cognitive and neural levels: the integrated emotion systems (IES) model.

The integrated emotion systems (IES) model

The IES model is an initial attempt to develop a more detailed model of amygdala-cortical interactions (Blair, 2003b, 2003c, 2004). With respect to psychopathy, the suggestion is that psychopathy is linked to early amygdala dysfunction (Blair, 2001, 2002; Blair et al., 1999; Patrick, 1994). In line with this suggestion, individuals with psychopathy have been found to present with reduced amygdaloid volume relative to comparison individuals (Tiihonen et al., 2000), and reduced amygdala activation during emotional memory (Kiehl et al., 2001) and aversive conditioning tasks (Veit et al., 2002). Moreover, functions that recruit the amygdala, such as aversive conditioning and instrumental learning, the augmentation of startle reflex by visual threat primes, and arousal to the anticipation of punishment, are all impaired in individuals with psychopathy (Blair, 2001); see also below. Of course, it should be noted that other structures, such as the orbital frontal cortex, which are interconnected with the amygdala, may also be affected (Damasio, 1994; LaPierre et al., 1995; Mitchell et al., 2002; Raine, 2002a).

The IES model is depicted in Figure 10.1. The amygdala is crucially involved in the formation of stimulus–reward and stimulus–punishment associations (Baxter & Murray, 2002). In the IES model, this is represented by the two modules of nonlinear, computational units, with one module representing the amygdala and one model representing sensory regions (such as the auditory, visual, and temporal cortex). This represents a simplified version of a model of aversive conditioning (Armony, Servan-Schreiber, Romanski, Cohen, & LeDoux, 1997). However, in the current model, the connections between the units in the different modules are reciprocal, reflecting the interconnections of the amygdala with cortical regions (Amaral, Price, Pitkanen, & Carmichael, 1992). The strength of the connections between units in the different modules increases through Hebbian learning (Hebb, 1949). Recent data at the cellular level confirm this characterization of learning within the amygdala as Hebbian (Blair, Schafe, Bauer, Rodrigues, & LeDoux, 2001).

There are at least three possible explanations of the amygdala dysfunction shown by individuals with psychopathy. First, there could be reduced nociceptive (US) input to the amygdala. This would result in reduced activation of the amygdala neurons and thus prevent learning. Secondly, the amygdala neurons of individuals with psychopathy may be hyporesponsive; that is, less likely to fire than the amygdala neurons of comparison individuals to a given level of input. This would again interfere with learning. Thirdly, there might be some cellular property of the amygdala neurons of individuals with psychopathy such that they are less capable of Hebbian learning irrespective of their level of activation. While these explanations give rise to slightly different predictions, they are unlikely to be disentangled in the near future. However, functionally, their impact would be similar. The amygdala's capacity to perform aversive conditioning would be detrimentally affected.

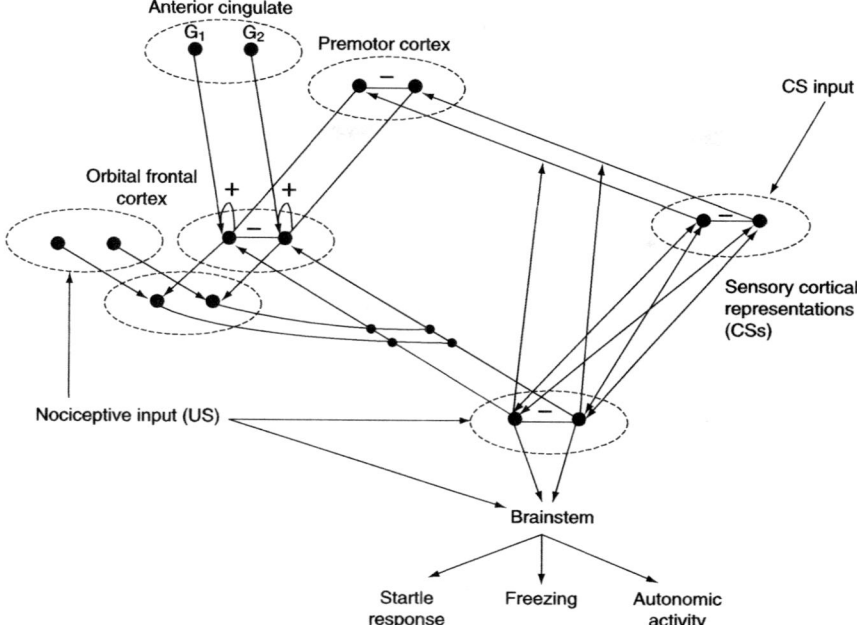

Figure 10.1 The sensory cortex (auditory, visual, and temporal cortex) and the hippocampus allow the representation of conditioned stimuli. Contiguous activation of representations of conditioned stimuli in the sensory cortex and amygdala activation by an unconditioned stimulus will increase the connections between the two representations through Hebbian learning, allowing the CS to activate the brainstem even if the US is not present. Expectations of reinforcement/punishment transmitted from the amygdala to the medial orbital frontal cortex allow resolution if more than one motor response option has been activated. Goal representations also modulate this processing. It is suggested that there are comparator units in lateral orbital that would detect mismatches between expectations of reinforcement (provided by the amygdala units) and actual reinforcement (the nociceptive input). When activated, these would disrupt the connections (weights) between amygdala units and orbital frontal cortex units as a function of the degree of the previous strength of these connection weights.

An impairment in aversive conditioning has been confirmed on several occasions (Flor et al., 2002; Hare & Quinn, 1971; Lykken, 1957). Moreover, recent neuroimaging work has demonstrated reduced amygdala activation in individuals with psychopathy during aversive conditioning (Veit et al., 2002). Following the VIM position, the IES model considers the sadness and fearfulness of others to be aversive unconditioned stimuli (Blair, 1995, 2003a). In line with this suggestion, functional imaging studies have shown, with a few exceptions (Kesler-West et al., 2001), that fearful and sad expressions all modulate amygdala activity (Baird et al., 1999; Blair et al., 1999; Breiter et al.,

1996; Drevets, Lowry, Gautier, Perrett, & Kupfer, 2000; Morris et al., 1996; Phillips et al., 1997, 1998; Schneider, Gur, Gur, & Muenz, 1994). Moreover, in line with the amygdala-dysfunction hypothesis, individuals with psychopathy show pronounced impairment in processing sad and fearful facial and vocal expressions (Aniskiewicz, 1979; Blair, Colledge, Murray, & Mitchell, 2001; Blair et al., 1997, 2002).

Words, like any other stimuli, can become aversive and appetitive CSs if they are paired with either aversive or appetitive USs. Thus, "murder" is an aversive CS and "love" is an appetitive CS. Such affective word stimuli generate a neural response within the amygdala (Hamann & Mao, 2002). In line with the amygdala-dysfunction hypothesis developed here, while individuals with psychopathy show autonomic responses to unpleasant or fearful experiences they have been asked to imagine, individuals with psychopathy do not (Patrick et al., 1994).

As illustrated in Figure 10.1, the interconnections of the amygdala with cortical regions are reciprocal (Amaral et al., 1992). Thus, activation of the amygdala by a linguistic CS, such as the word "murder", will subsequently result in increased activation of the representation of this linguistic CS because of reciprocal activation from the amygdala. In short, emotional words are more salient than neutral words, ceteris paribus, because of these reciprocal connections and are thus likely to be processed more rapidly. It is these interconnections, according to the IES model, that drive the emotion facilitation effect in lexical decision tasks. Dysfunction in the formation of these interconnections in individuals with psychopathy leads to their lack of facilitation for emotional words in the lexical decision task.

The amygdala, and particularly the basolateral nucleus of the amygdala, is known to be implicated in instrumental learning, including passive avoidance learning (Ambrogi Lorenzini, Baldi, Bucherelli, Sacchetti, & Tassoni, 1999; Everitt et al., 2000; Killcross et al., 1997; LeDoux, 2000). Within the IES model, three additional modules of nonlinear, identical computational units are used to describe instrumental learning. The first of these corresponds to units coding motor responses and includes the premotor cortex and basal ganglia. The second corresponds to units coding expectation of reward/punishment (medial orbital frontal cortex). These expectations are provided by the amygdala. The suggestion is that units in the medial orbital frontal cortex receive information in order to solve response competition on the basis not only of the activation of premotor units but also of expectations of reinforcement provided by the amygdala. In addition, they receive input from units from the third module, possibly involving the anterior cingulate, representing desired goal states. The suggestion is that reinforcer devaluation (Baxter, Parker, Lindner, Izquierdo, & Murray, 2000; Gallagher, McMahan, & Schoenbaum, 1999) would reduce potential activation of the corresponding units in the orbital frontal cortex. This would reduce the probability that a response associated with these units would be chosen; the units involved would be less likely to win out in competition with other units that had not been associated with reinforcer devaluation.

Amygdala lesions impair instrumental learning, including passive avoidance learning (Ambrogi Lorenzini et al., 1999; Everitt et al., 2000; Killcross et al., 1997; LeDoux, 2000). In line with the suggestion that individuals with psychopathy present with amygdala dysfunction, individuals with psychopathy present with marked impairment on measures of instrumental (Fine et al., manuscript submitted for publication) and, in particular, passive avoidance learning (Budhani, Johnston, & Blair, manuscript in preparation; Newman & Kosson, 1986; Newman & Schmitt, 1998; Thornquist & Zuckerman, 1995).

Response reversal involves changing a response to a stimulus as a function of a change in contingency; that is, learning to withhold a response that is now punished though previously it had been rewarded (Rolls, 1997). The reversal is the crucial component here; individuals must reverse their response to a stimulus. Response reversal is thus not involved in the passive avoidance task (Newman & Kosson, 1986) where the individual simply learns to respond to some stimuli and withhold responses to others, but never to reverse the response to a stimulus. There is a considerable neuropsychological and neuroimaging literature demonstrating that the orbital frontal cortex is crucially involved in response reversal (Cools et al., 2002; Rahman, Sahakian, Hodges, Rogers, & Robbins, 1999; Rolls, Hornak, Wade, & McGrath, 1994).

Within the IES model, it is suggested that there are comparator units in the lateral orbital cortex that would detect mismatches between expectations of reinforcement (provided by the amygdala units) and actual reinforcement (the nociceptive input). When activated, these would disrupt the connections (weights) between amygdala units and orbital frontal cortex units as a function of the degree of the previous strength of these connection weights. Thus, under conditions where reinforcement had been a certainty and the connection weights were high, there would be considerable disruption. Under conditions where the reinforcement contingency was less obvious and the connection weights were lower, there would be less disruption. This disruption process would allow another unit to develop the new expectation of reinforcement associated with the changed contingency to the stimulus and thus allow faster response reversal.

Within the model, the known role of the orbital frontal cortex in response reversal (Cools et al., 2002; Dias, Robbins, & Roberts, 1996; Rolls et al., 1994) is seen as a function of the degree to which there is a mismatch between the expectation of reinforcement, provided by the amygdala to the orbital frontal cortex, and the presence of reinforcement. This suggests that if there is dysfunction in either the amygdala or orbital frontal cortex or the connections between the amygdala and orbital frontal cortex, response reversal will be detrimentally affected. Moreover, the greater the degree of dysfunction, the more difficult it will be for the individual to identify the contingency change.

Children with psychopathic tendencies and adult individuals with psychopathy show comparably impaired performance on measures of amygdala functioning such as passive avoidance (Newman & Kosson, 1986; Newman, Widom, & Nathan, 1985), the processing of fearful expressions (Blair, Colledge, Murray, & Mitchell, 2001b), and aversive conditioning (Lykken, 1957; Raine, Venables, & Williams, 1996). However, there is less clear evidence that children with psychopathic tendencies show comparably impaired performance on measures requiring the orbital frontal cortex such as response reversal. Newman's card-playing task (Newman et al., 1987) involves response reversal; the participant learns to play the card for reward but then must extinguish this response, as, proceeding through the pack of cards, the probability of reward decreases successively. Both children with psychopathic tendencies and adult individuals with psychopathy show marked impairment in this task (Fisher & Blair, 1998; Newman et al., 1987; O'Brien & Frick, 1996). However, another paradigm, the intradimensional extradimensional (ID-ED) task, also includes response reversal; the participants must reverse their responding from the object that, when responded to, had elicited reward but that now elicits punishment. While adult individuals with psychopathy show notable impairment in response reversal on this task (Mitchell et al., 2002), children with psychopathic tendencies do not (Blair, Colledge, & Mitchell, 2001a). A major difference between these two tasks is in the salience of the contingency change. In the card-playing task, the probability of reinforcement decreases by 10% over every 10 trials. In the ID-ED task, the probability of reinforcement changes from 100% to 0% once the initial learning criterion has been achieved. This indicates that while both children with psychopathic tendencies and adults with psychopathy are impaired in the detection of contingency change, this impairment is markedly greater in the adults with psychopathy. Moreover, this suggests that if we reduce the salience of the contingency change, we should see impairment in the children with psychopathic tendencies and that the degree of impairment will be a function of the salience of the contingency change. This was tested by a probabilistic response-reversal paradigm. Participants were presented with pairs of stimuli. The probability of reward was different across pairs (that is, for pair 1, stimulus 1 was rewarded 100% of the time; for pair 2, stimulus 3 was rewarded 90% of the time, etc.). After a set number of trials, the contingency was reversed (that is, for pair 1, stimulus 2 was rewarded 100% of the time; for pair 2, stimulus 4 was rewarded 90% of the time). While the children with psychopathic tendencies showed no difficulty in reversing their responses for salient contingency changes, they did show significant difficulty as the salience of the contingency change decreased (Budhani et al., in press).

Conclusions

Research into the neurobiology of antisocial behaviour is moving forward with considerable speed. Positions which were competitors a year or so ago now appear complementary, at least after they have been specified in greater detail. Thus, the frontal lobe positions (Gorenstein, 1982; Moffitt, 1993b; Raine, 2002a), while potentially of little relevance to an account of instrumental aggression, are of clear significance to explain some cases of reactive aggression. However, they do require greater specification. It is likely that only dysfunction within the medial and orbital frontal cortex, but not the dorsolateral prefrontal cortex, leads to an increased risk of reactive aggression and only if this dysfunction impairs response reversal and social response reversal.

The IES position (Blair, 2003c) can be considered an extension of the fear and empathy/VIM accounts of instrumental aggression. Both the fear and the VIM positions considered a failure in socialization as the fundamental cause of the instrumental aggression shown by individuals with psychopathy; the individual did not learn to avoid using instrumental aggression to achieve goals (Blair, 1995; Eysenck, 1964; Trasler, 1978). The fundamental difference between these accounts was that while the fear accounts considered punishment the aversive US necessary for socialization, the VIM account considered the fear/sadness of another to be the necessary US. The IES position (Blair, 2003c) integrates these models from the perspective of affective cognitive neuroscience. In line with the parenting literature, the fear/sadness of another is still considered to be the necessary US for socialization (cf. Brody & Shaffer, 1982; Hoffman, 1988). Socialization is achieved through aversive and instrumental learning, as suggested by the fear positions. Aversive and instrumental learning require the amygdala (LeDoux, 1998).

The considerable progress in the neurobiology of antisocial behaviour is likely to result in applied benefits in the very near future. In the short term, we should see neuropsychological assessment batteries targeting systems empirically implicated in antisocial behaviour (that is, tasks indexing the functions of the amygdala, and the medial and orbital frontal cortex). In the medium term, we are likely to see an explosion of treatment possibilities. While psychopathy is currently regarded as untreatable (Hare, 1991), this situation is likely to soon change. An understanding of the basis of the disorder in terms of affective cognitive neuroscience immediately establishes a series of predictions for potential pharmacological treatment.

References

Alexander, M., & Perachio, A. A. (1973). The influence of target sex and dominance on evoked attack in rhesus monkeys. *American Journal of Physical Anthropology*, *38*, 543–547.

Amaral, D. G. (2001). *The amygdaloid complex and the neurobiology of social behaviour*. Paper presented at the Society for Research in Child Development, Minneapolis.

Amaral, D. G., Price, J. L., Pitkanen, A., & Carmichael, S. T. (1992). Anatomical organization of the primate amygdaloid complex. In J. P. Aggleton (Ed.),

The amygdala: Neurobiological aspects of emotion, memory, and mental dysfunction (pp. 1–66). New York: Wiley.

Ambrogi Lorenzini, C. G., Baldi, E., Bucherelli, C., Sacchetti, B., & Tassoni, G. (1999). Neural topography and chronology of memory consolidation: A review of functional inactivation findings. *Neurobiology of Learning and Memory, 71*, 1–18.

American Psychiatric Association (1994) *Diagnostic and statistical manual of mental disorders*. Washington, DC: American Psychiatric Association.

Anderson, S. W., Bechara, A., Damasio, H., Tranel, D., & Damasio, A. R. (1999). Impairment of social and moral behaviour related to early damage in human prefrontal cortex. *Nature Neuroscience, 2*, 1032–1037.

Angrilli, A., Mauri, A., Palomba, D., Flor, H., Birhaumer, N., Sartori, G., et al. (1996). Startle reflex and emotion modulation impairment after a right amygdala lesion. *Brain, 119*, 1991–2000.

Aniskiewicz, A. S. (1979). Autonomic components of vicarious conditioning and psychopathy. *Journal of Clinical Psychology, 35*, 60–67.

Armony, J. L., Servan-Schreiber, D., Romanski, L. M., Cohen, J. D., & LeDoux, J. E. (1997). Stimulus generalization of fear responses: Effects of auditory cortex lesions in a computational model and in rats. *Cerebral Cortex, 7*, 157–165.

Arsenio, W. F., & Fleiss, K. (1996). Typical and behaviourally disruptive children's understanding of the emotion consequences of socio-moral events. *British Journal of Developmental Psychology, 14*, 173–186.

Asendorpf, J. B., & Nunner-Winkler, G. (1992). Children's moral motive strength and temperamental inhibition reduce their immoral behaviour in real moral conflicts. *Child Development, 63*, 1223–1235.

Averill, J. R. (1982). *Anger and aggression: An essay on emotion*. New York: Springer-Verlag.

Baddeley, A., & Della Sala, S. (1998). Working memory and executive control. In A. C. Roberts, T. W. Robbins, & L. Weiskrantz (Eds.), *The prefrontal cortex* (pp. 9–21). New York: Oxford University Press.

Baird, A. A., Gruber, S. A., Fein, D. A., Maas, L. C., Steingard, R. J., Renshaw, P. F., et al. (1999). Functional magnetic resonance imaging of facial affect recognition in children and adolescents. *Journal of the American Academy of Child and Adolescent Psychiatry, 38*, 195–199.

Bandler, R. (1988). Brain mechanisms of aggression as revealed by electrical and chemical stimulation: Suggestion of a central role for the midbrain periaqueductal gray region. In A. N. Epstein & A. R. Morrison (Eds.), *Progress in psychobiology and physiological psychology* (Vol. 14, pp. 135–233). San Diego, CA: Academic Press.

Barratt, E. S. (1994). Impulsiveness and aggression. In J. Monahan & H. Steadman (Eds.), *Violence and mental disorders: Developments in risk assessment* (pp. 61–79). Chicago: University of Chicago Press.

Barratt, E. S., Stanford, M. S., Dowdy, L., Liebman, M. J., & Kent, T. A. (1999). Impulsive and premeditated aggression: A factor analysis of self-reported acts. *Psychiatry Research, 86*, 163–173.

Barratt, E. S., Stanford, M. S., Kent, T. A., & Felthous, A. (1997). Neuropsychological and cognitive psychophysiological substrates of impulsive aggression. *Biological Psychiatry, 41*, 1045–1061.

Baumrind, D. (1971). Current patterns of parental authority. *Developmental Psychology Monographs, 4*, 1–103.

Baumrind, D. (1983). Rejoinder to Lewis's interpretation of parental firm control effects: Are authoritative families really harmonious? *Psychological Bulletin, 94*, 132–142.

Baxter, M. G., & Murray, E. A. (2002). The amygdala and reward. *Nature Reviews Neuroscience, 3*, 563–573.

Baxter, M. G., Parker, A., Lindner, C. C., Izquierdo, A. D., & Murray, E. A. (2000). Control of response selection by reinforcer value requires interaction of amygdala and orbital prefrontal cortex. *Journal of Neuroscience, 20*, 4311–4319.

Begleiter, H., Gross, M. M., & Kissin, B. (1967). Evoked cortical responses to affective visual stimuli. *Psychophysiology, 3*, 336–344.

Berkowitz, L. (1993). *Aggression: Its causes, consequences, and control*. Philadelphia: Temple University Press.

Berthoz, S., Armony, J., Blair, R. J. R., & Dolan, R. (2002). Neural correlates of violation of social norms and embarrassment. *Brain, 125*, 1696–1708.

Best, M., Williams, J. M., & Coccaro, E. F. (2002). Evidence for a dysfunctional prefrontal circuit in patients with an impulsive aggressive disorder. *Proceedings of the National Academy of Sciences of the USA, 99*, 8448–8453.

Blackburn, R. (1988). On moral judgements and personality disorders: The myth of psychopathic personality revisited. *British Journal of Psychiatry, 153*, 505–512.

Blair, H. T., Schafe, G. E., Bauer, E. P., Rodrigues, S. M., & LeDoux, J. E. (2001). Synaptic plasticity in the lateral amygdala: A cellular hypothesis of fear conditioning. *Learning and Memory, 8*, 229–242.

Blair, R. J., Colledge, E., & Mitchell, D. G. (2001a). Somatic markers and response reversal: Is there orbitofrontal cortex dysfunction in boys with psychopathic tendencies? *Journal of Abnormal Child Psychology, 29*, 499–511.

Blair, R. J., Colledge, E., Murray, L., & Mitchell, D. G. (2001b). A selective impairment in the processing of sad and fearful expressions in children with psychopathic tendencies. *Journal of Abnormal Child Psychology, 29*, 491–498.

Blair, R. J., Mitchell, D. G., Richell, R. A., Kelly, S., Leonard, A., Newman, C., & Scott, S. K. (2002). Turning a deaf ear to fear: Impaired recognition of vocal affect in psychopathic individuals. *Journal of Abnormal Psychology, 111*, 682–686.

Blair, R. J. R. (1995). A cognitive developmental approach to morality: Investigating the psychopath. *Cognition, 57*, 1–29.

Blair, R. J. R. (1997). Moral reasoning in the child with psychopathic tendencies. *Personality and Individual Differences, 22*, 731–739.

Blair, R. J. R. (1999). Responsiveness to distress cues in the child with psychopathic tendencies. *Personality and Individual Differences, 27*, 135–145.

Blair, R. J. R. (2001). Neuro-cognitive models of aggression, the antisocial personality disorders and psychopathy. *Journal of Neurology, Neurosurgery and Psychiatry, 71*, 727–731.

Blair, R. J. R. (2002). A neuro-cognitive model of the psychopathic individual. In M. Ron (Ed.), *Disorders of brain and mind II* (pp. 400–420). Cambridge: Cambridge University Press.

Blair, R. J. R. (2003a). Facial expressions, their communicatory functions and neuro-cognitive substrates. *Philosophical Transactions of the Royal Society of London. Series B: Biological Sciences, 358*(1431), 561–572.

Blair, R. J. R. (2003b). Neurobiological basis of psychopathy. *British Journal of Psychiatry, 182*, 5–7.

Blair, R. J. R. (2003c). A neurocognitive model of the psychopathic individual. In

M. A. Ron & T. W. Robbins (Eds.), *Disorders of brain and mind II* (pp. 400–420). Cambridge: Cambridge University Press.

Blair, R. J. R. (2004). The roles of orbital frontal cortex in the modulation of antisocial behavior. *Brain and Cognition, 55*, 198–208.

Blair, R. J. R., & Cipolotti, L. (2000). Impaired social response reversal: A case of "acquired sociopathy". *Brain, 123*, 1122–1141.

Blair, R. J. R., Jones, L., Clark, F., & Smith, M. (1995). Is the psychopath "morally insane"? *Personality and Individual Differences, 19*, 741–752.

Blair, R. J. R., Jones, L., Clark, F., & Smith, M. (1997). The psychopathic individual: A lack of responsiveness to distress cues? *Psychophysiology, 34*, 192–198.

Blair, R. J. R., Monson, J., & Frederickson, N. (2001). Moral reasoning and conduct problems in children with emotional and behavioural difficulties. *Personality and Individual Differences, 31*, 799–811.

Blair, R. J. R., Morris, J. S., Frith, C. D., Perrett, D. I., & Dolan, R. (1999). Dissociable neural responses to facial expressions of sadness and anger. *Brain, 122*, 883–893.

Blair, R. J. R., & Morton, J. (1995). Putting cognition into sociopathy. *Brain and Behavioral Science, 18*, 548.

Blair, R. J. R., Sellars, C., Strickland, I., Clark, F., Williams, A. O., Smith, M., & Jones, L. (1995). Emotion attributions in the psychopath. *Personality and Individual Differences, 19*, 431–437.

Blanchard, R. J., Blanchard, D. C., & Takahashi, L. K. (1977). Attack and defensive behaviour in the albino rat. *Animal Behaviour, 25*, 197–224.

Breiter, H. C., Etcoff, N. L., Whalen, P. J., Kennedy, W. A., Rauch, S. L., Buckner, R. L., et al. (1996). Response and habituation of the human amygdala during visual processing of facial expression. *Neuron, 17*, 875–887.

Brinkley, C. A., Schmitt, W. A., & Newman, J. P. (manuscript submitted for publication). An empirical test of the semantic processing deficit in psychopathic offenders.

Brody, G. H., & Shaffer, D. R. (1982). Contributions of parents and peers to children's moral socialisation. *Developmental Review, 2*, 31–75.

Budhani, S., & Blair, R. J. R. (in press). Response reversal and children with psychopathic tendencies: Success is a function of salience of contingency change. *Journal of Child Psychology and Psychiatry*.

Budhani, S., Johnston, K., & Blair, R. J. R. (manuscript in preparation). Passive avoidance learning in boys with psychopathic tendencies: Effects of attention deficit/hyperactivity disorder, memory load and level of punishment/reward. *Journal of Abnormal Child Psychology*.

Burgess, P. W., & Shallice, T. (1996). Response suppression, initiation and strategy use following frontal lobe lesions. *Neuropsychologia, 34*, 263–272.

Bushman, B. J., & Anderson, C. A. (2001). Is it time to pull the plug on the hostile versus instrumental aggression dichotomy? *Psychological Review, 108*, 273–279.

Campeau, S., & Davis, M. (1995). Involvement of the central nucleus and basolateral complex of the amygdala in fear conditioning measured with fear-potentiated startle in rats trained concurrently with auditory and visual conditioned stimuli. *Journal of Neuroscience, 15*(3 Pt 2), 2301–2311.

Camras, L. A. (1977). Facial expressions used by children in a conflict situation. *Child Development, 48*, 1431–1435.

Chaplin, T. C., Rice, M. E., & Harris, G. T. (1995). Salient victim suffering and the sexual responses of child molesters. *Journal of Consulting and Clinical Psychology*, *63*, 249–255.

Cleckley, H. M. (1976). *The mask of sanity* (5th ed.). St Louis, MO: Mosby.

Coccaro, E. F. (1998). Impulsive aggression: A behavior in search of clinical definition. *Harvard Review of Psychiatry*, *5*, 336–339.

Cools, R., Clark, L., Owen, A. M., & Robbins, T. W. (2002). Defining the neural mechanisms of probabilistic reversal learning using event-related functional magnetic resonance imaging. *Journal of Neuroscience*, *22*, 4563–4567.

Cornell, D. G., Warren, J., Hawk, G., Stafford, E., Oram, G., & Pine, D. (1996). Psychopathy in instrumental and reactive violent offenders. *Journal of Consulting and Clinical Psychology*, *64*, 783–790.

Damasio, A. R. (1994). *Descartes' error: Emotion, rationality and the human brain*. New York: Putnam (Grosset Books).

Davidson, R. J., Putnam, K. M., & Larson, C. L. (2000). Dysfunction in the neural circuitry of emotion regulation—a possible prelude to violence. *Science*, *289*, (5479), 591–594.

Davis, M. (2000). The role of the amygdala in conditioned and unconditioned fear and anxiety. In J. P. Aggleton (Ed.), *The amygdala: A functional analysis* (pp. 289–310). Oxford: Oxford University Press.

Desimone, R., & Duncan, J. (1995). Neural mechanisms of selective visual attention. *Annual Review of Neuroscience*, *18*, 193–222.

Dias, R., Robbins, T. W., & Roberts, A. C. (1996). Dissociation in prefrontal cortex of affective and attentional shifts. *Nature*, *380*, 69–72.

Dickinson, A. (1980). *Contemporary animal learning theory*. Cambridge: Cambridge University Press.

Dougherty, D. D., Shin, L. M., Alpert, N. M., Pitman, R. K., Orr, S. P., Lasko, M., et al. (1999). Anger in healthy men: A PET study using script-driven imagery. *Biological Psychiatry*, *46*, 466–472.

Drevets, W. C., Lowry, T., Gautier, C., Perrett, D. I., & Kupfer, D. J. (2000). Amygdalar blood flow responses to facially expressed sadness. *Biological Psychiatry*, *47*(8S), 160S.

Everitt, B. J., Cardinal, R. N., Hall, J., Parkinson, J. A., & Robbins, T. W. (2000). Differential involvement of amygdala subsystems in appetitive conditioning and drug addiction. In J. P. Aggleton (Ed.), *The amygdala: A functional analysis* (pp. 289–310). Oxford: Oxford University Press.

Eysenck, H. J. (1964). *Crime and personality*. London: Routledge & Kegan Paul.

Eysenck, H. J., & Gudjonsson, G. H. (1989). *The causes and cures of criminality*. London: Plenum Press.

Farrington, D. P. (1995). The Twelfth Jack Tizaard Memorial Lecture: The development of offending and antisocial behaviour from childhood: Key findings from the Cambridge study in delinquent development. *Journal of Child Psychology and Psychiatry*, *360*, 929–964.

Fine, C., Richell, R. A., Mitchell, D. G. V., Newman, C., Lumsden, J., & Blair, R. J. R. (manuscript submitted for publication). Instrumental learning and response reversal: The involvement of the amygdala and orbital frontal cortex and implications for psychopathy.

Fisher, L., & Blair, R. J. R. (1998). Cognitive impairment and its relationship to psychopathic tendencies in children with emotional and behavioural difficulties. *Journal of Abnormal Child Psychology*, *26*, 511–519.

Flor, H., Birbaumer, N., Hermann, C., Ziegler, S., & Patrick, C. J. (2002). Aversive Pavlovian conditioning in psychopaths: Peripheral and central correlates. *Psychophysiology, 39*, 505–518.

Forth, A. E., Kosson, D. S., & Hare, R. D. (in press). *The Psychopathy Checklist: Youth Version*. Toronto: Multi-Health Systems.

Fowles, D. C. (1988). Psychophysiology and psychopathy: A motivational approach. *Psychophysiology, 25*, 373–391.

Frick, P. J., & Hare, R. D. (2001). *The antisocial process screening device*. Toronto: Multi-Health Systems.

Frick, P. J., Lilienfeld, S. O., Ellis, M., Loney, B., & Silverthorn, P. (1999). The association between anxiety and psychopathy dimensions in children. *Journal of Abnormal Child Psychology, 27*, 383–392.

Frick, P. J., O'Brien, B. S., Wootton, J. M., & McBurnett, K. (1994). Psychopathy and conduct problems in children. *Journal of Abnormal Psychology, 103*, 700–707.

Funayama, E. S., Grillon, C., Davis, M., & Phelps, E. A. (2001). A double dissociation in the affective modulation of startle in humans: Effects of unilateral temporal lobectomy. *Journal of Cognitive Neuroscience, 13*, 721–729.

Fuster, J. M. (1980). *The prefrontal cortex*. New York: Raven Press.

Gallagher, M., McMahan, R. W., & Schoenbaum, G. (1999). Orbitofrontal cortex and representation of incentive value in associative learning. *Journal of Neuroscience, 19*, 6610–6614.

Gilbert, P. (1997). The evolution of social attractiveness and its role in shame, humiliation, guilt and therapy. *British Journal of Medical Psychology, 70*, 113–147.

Gorenstein, E. E. (1982). Frontal lobe functions in psychopaths. *Journal of Abnormal Psychology, 91*, 368–379.

Gorenstein, E. E. (1991). A cognitive perspective on antisocial personality. In P. A. Magaro (Ed.), *Cognitive bases of mental disorders* (pp. 100–133). Newbury Park, CA: Sage.

Goyer, P. F., Andreason, P. J., Semple, W. E., Clayton, A. H., King, A. C., Compton-Toth, B. A., et al. (1994). Positron-emission tomography and personality disorders. *Neuropsychopharmacology, 10*, 21–28.

Grafman, J., Schwab, K., Warden, D., Pridgen, B. S., & Brown, H. R. (1996). Frontal lobe injuries, violence, and aggression: A report of the Vietnam head injury study. *Neurology, 46*, 1231–1238.

Graves, R., Landis, T., & Goodglass, H. (1981). Laterality and sex differences for visual recognition of emotional and non-emotional words. *Neuropsychologia, 19*, 95–102.

Gray, J. A. (1971). *The psychology of fear and stress*. London: Weidenfeld & Nicolson.

Gray, J. A. (1987). *The psychology of fear and stress* (2nd ed.). Cambridge: University of Cambridge Press.

Gray, J. A., & McNaughton, N. (1996). The neuropsychology of anxiety: Reprise. *Nebraska Symposium on Motivation, 43*, 61–134.

Gregg, T. R., & Siegel, A. (2001). Brain structures and neurotransmitters regulating aggression in cats: implications for human aggression. *Progress in Neuro-Psychopharmacology and Biological Psychiatry, 25*, 91–140.

Hamann, S., & Mao, H. (2002). Positive and negative emotional verbal stimuli elicit activity in the left amygdala. *Neuroreport, 13*, 15–19.

Hare, R. D. (1982). Psychopathy and physiological activity during anticipation of an aversive stimulus in a distraction paradigm. *Psychophysiology, 19*, 266–271.

Hare, R. D. (1991). *The Hare Psychopathy Checklist–Revised*. Toronto: Multi-Health Systems.

Hare, R. D., & Quinn, M. J. (1971). Psychopathy and autonomic conditioning. *Journal of Abnormal Psychology, 77*, 223–235.

Harpur, T. J., & Hare, R. D. (1994). Assessment of psychopathy as a function of age. *Journal of Abnormal Psychology, 103*, 604–609.

Harpur, T. J., Hare, R. D., & Hakstian, A. R. (1989). Two-factor conceptualization of psychopathy: Construct validity and assessment implications. *Psychological Assessment: A Journal of Consulting and Clinical Psychology, 1*, 6–17.

Hebb, D. O. (1949). *The organization of behavior*. New York: Wiley.

Herpertz, S. C., Werth, U., Lukas, G., Qunaibi, M., Schuerkens, A., Kunert, H. J., et al. (2001). Emotion in criminal offenders with psychopathy and borderline personality disorder. *Archives of General Psychiatry, 58*, 737–745.

Hoffman, M. L. (1984). Empathy, its limitations, and its role in a comprehensive moral theory. In J. Gewirtz & W. Kurtines (Eds.), *Morality, moral development, and moral behavior* (pp. 283–302). New York: Wiley.

Hoffman, M. L. (1988). Moral development. In M. Bornstein & M. Lamb (Eds.), *Developmental psychology: An advanced textbook* (pp. 497–548). Hillsdale, NJ: Lawrence Erlbaum Associates, Inc.

Hoffman, M. L. (1994). Discipline and internalisation. *Developmental Psychology, 30*, 26–28.

Hoffman, M. L., & Saltzstein, H. D. (1967). Parent discipline and the child's moral development. *Journal of Personality and Social Psychology, 5*, 45–57.

Hornak, J., Rolls, E. T., & Wade, D. (1996). Face and voice expression identification in patients with emotional and behavioural changes following ventral frontal damage. *Neuropsychologia, 34*, 247–261.

House, T. H., & Milligan, W. L. (1976). Autonomic responses to modeled distress in prison psychopaths. *Journal of Personality and Social Psychology, 34*, 556–560.

Kagan, J., & Snidman, N. (1999). Early childhood predictors of adult anxiety disorders. *Biological Psychiatry, 46*, 1536–1541.

Kandel, E., & Freed, D. (1989). Frontal lobe dysfunction and antisocial behavior: a review. *Journal of Clinical Psychology, 45*, 404–413.

Keltner, D. (1995). Signs of appeasement: Evidence for the distinct displays of embarrassment, amusement, and shame. *Journal of Personality and Social Psychology, 68*, 441–454.

Keltner, D., & Anderson, C. (2000). Saving face for Darwin: The functions and uses of embarrassment. *Current Directions in Psychological Science, 9*, 187–192.

Keltner, D., & Buswell, B. N. (1997). Embarrassment: Its distinct form and appeasement functions. *Psychological Bulletin, 122*, 250–270.

Kesler-West, M. L., Andersen, A. H., Smith, C. D., Avison, M. J., Davis, C. E., Kryscio, R. J., et al. (2001). Neural substrates of facial emotion processing using fMRI. *Cognitive Brain Research, 11*, 213–226.

Kiehl, K. A., Hare, R. D., McDonald, J. J., & Brink, J. (1999). Semantic and affective processing in psychopaths: An event-related potential (ERP) study. *Psychophysiology, 36*, 765–774.

Kiehl, K. A., Smith, A. M., Hare, R. D., Mendrek, A., Forster, B. B., Brink, J., et al. (2001). Limbic abnormalities in affective processing by criminal psychopaths as revealed by functional magnetic resonance imaging. *Biological Psychiatry, 50*, 677–684.

Killcross, S., Robbins, T. W., & Everitt, B. J. (1997). Different types of fear-conditioned behaviour mediated by separate nuclei within amygdala. *Nature*, *388*, 377–380.

Kochanska, G. (1993). Toward a synthesis of parental socialization and child temperament in early development of conscience. *Child Development*, *64*, 325–347.

Kochanska, G. (1997). Multiple pathways to conscience for children with different temperaments: From toddlerhood to age 5. *Developmental Psychology*, *33*, 228–240.

Kochanska, G., De Vet, K., Goldman, M., Murray, K., & Putman, P. (1994). Maternal reports of conscience development and temperament in young children. *Child Development*, *65*, 852–868.

Kosson, D. S., Cyterski, T. D., Steuerwald, B. L., Neumann, C. S., & Walker-Matthews, S. (2002). The reliability and validity of the psychopathy checklist: Youth version (PCL:YV) in nonincarcerated adolescent males. *Psychological Assessment*, *14*, 97–109.

Kosson, D. S., Smith, S. S., & Newman, J. P. (1990). Evaluating the construct validity of the psychopathy construct in blacks: A preliminary investigation. *Journal of Abnormal Psychology*, *99*, 250–259.

Lang, P. J., Bradley, M. M., & Cuthbert, B. N. (1990). Emotion, attention, and the startle reflex. *Psychological Review*, *97*, 377–398.

LaPierre, D., Braun, C. M. J., & Hodgins, S. (1995). Ventral frontal deficits in psychopathy: Neuropsychological test findings. *Neuropsychologia*, *33*, 139–151.

Lavie, N. (1995). Perceptual load as a necessary condition for selective attention. *Journal of Experimental Psychology: Human Perception and Performance*, *21*, 451–468.

Leary, M. R. Landel, J. L., & Patton, K. M. (1996). The motivated expression of embarrassment following a self-presentational predicament. *Journal of Personality*, *64*, 619–637.

Leary, M. R., & Meadows, S. (1991). Predictors, elicitors, and concomitants of social blushing. *Journal of Personality and Social Psychology*, *60*, 254–262.

LeDoux, J. (1998). *The emotional brain*. New York: Weidenfeld & Nicolson.

LeDoux, J. E. (2000). The amygdala and emotion: A view through fear. In J. P. Aggleton (Ed.), *The amygdala: A functional analysis* (pp. 289–310). Oxford: Oxford University Press.

Levenston, G. K., Patrick, C. J., Bradley, M. M., & Lang, P. J. (2000). The psychopath as observer: Emotion and attention in picture processing. *Journal of Abnormal Psychology*, *109*, 373–386.

Linnoila, M., Virkkunen, M., Scheinin, M., Nuutila, A., Rimon, R., & Goodwin, F. K. (1983). Low cerebrospinal fluid 5-hydroxy indoleacetic acid concentration differentiates impulsive from nonimpulsive violent behavior. *Life Sciences*, *33*, 2609–2614.

Lorenz, A. R., & Newman, J. P. (2002). Deficient response modulation and emotion processing in low-anxious Caucasian psychopathic offenders: Results from a lexical decision task. *Emotion*, *2*, 91–104.

Luria, A. (1966). *Higher cortical functions in man*. New York: Basic Books.

Lykken, D. T. (1957). A study of anxiety in the sociopathic personality. *Journal of Abnormal and Social Psychology*, *55*, 6–10.

Lykken, D. T. (1995). *The antisocial personalities*. Hillsdale, NJ: Lawrence Erlbaum Associates, Inc.

McNaughton, N., & Gray, J. A. (2000). Anxiolytic action on the behavioural inhibition system implies multiple types of arousal contribute to anxiety. *Journal of Affective Disorders, 61*, 161–176.

Mealey, L. (1995). The sociobiology of sociopathy: An integrated evolutionary model. *Behavioral and Brain Sciences, 18*, 523–599.

Miller, R. S. (1996). *Embarrassment: Poise and peril in everyday life.* New York: Guilford.

Mitchell, D. G. V., Colledge, E., Leonard, A., & Blair, R. J. R. (2002). Risky decisions and response reversal: Is there evidence of orbitofrontal cortex dysfunction in psychopathic individuals? *Neuropsychologia, 40*, 2013–2022.

Moffitt, T. E. (1993a). Adolescence-limited and life-course-persistent antisocial behavior: A developmental taxonomy. *Psychological Review, 100*, 674–701.

Moffitt, T. E. (1993b). The neuropsychology of conduct disorder. *Development and Psychopathology, 5*, 135–152.

Morgan, A. B., & Lilienfield, S. O. (2000). A meta-analytic review of the relation between antisocial behavior and neuropsychological measures of executive function. *Clinical Psychology Review, 20*, 113–136.

Morris, J. S., Frith, C. D., Perrett, D. I., Rowland, D., Young, A. W., Calder, A. J., et al. (1996). A differential response in the human amygdala to fearful and happy facial expressions. *Nature, 383*, 812–815.

Newman, J. P. (1998). Psychopathic behaviour: An information processing perspective. In D. J. Cooke, A. E. Forth, & R. D. Hare (Eds.), *Psychopathy: Theory, research and implications for society* (pp. 81–105). Dordrecht, The Netherlands: Kluwer.

Newman, J. P., & Kosson, D. S. (1986). Passive avoidance learning in psychopathic and nonpsychopathic offenders. *Journal of Abnormal Psychology, 95*, 252–256.

Newman, J. P., Patterson, C. M., Howland, E. W., & Nichols, S. L. (1990). Passive avoidance in psychopaths: The effects of reward. *Personality and Individual Differences, 11*, 1101–1114.

Newman, J. P., Patterson, C. M., & Kosson, D. S. (1987). Response perseveration in psychopaths. *Journal of Abnormal Psychology, 96*, 145–148.

Newman, J. P., & Schmitt, W. A. (1998). Passive avoidance in psychopathic offenders: A replication and extension. *Journal of Abnormal Psychology, 107*, 527–532.

Newman, J. P., Schmitt, W. A., & Voss, W. D. (1997). The impact of motivationally neutral cues on psychopathic individuals: Assessing the generality of the response modulation hypothesis. *Journal of Abnormal Psychology, 106*, 563–575.

Newman, J. P., Widom, C. S., & Nathan, S. (1985). Passive avoidance in syndromes of disinhibition: Psychopathy and extraversion. *Journal of Personality and Social Psychology, 48*, 1316–1327.

Nucci, L. P., & Herman, S. (1982). Behavioral disordered children's conceptions of moral, conventional, and personal issues. *Journal of Abnormal Child Psychology, 10*, 411–425.

O'Brien, B. S., & Frick, P. J. (1996). Reward dominance: Associations with anxiety, conduct problems, and psychopathy in children. *Journal of Abnormal Child Psychology, 24*, 223–240.

Ogloff, J. R., & Wong, S. (1990). Electrodermal and cardiovascular evidence of a coping response in psychopaths. *Criminal Justice and Behaviour, 17*, 231–245.

Panksepp, J. (1998). *Affective neuroscience: The foundations of human and animal emotions.* New York: Oxford University Press.

Passingham, R. E., & Toni, I. (2001). Contrasting the dorsal and ventral visual systems: Guidance of movement versus decision making. *NeuroImage, 14*(1 Pt 2), S125–131.

Patrick, C. J. (1994). Emotion and psychopathy: Startling new insights. *Psychophysiology, 31*, 319–330.

Patrick, C. J., Cuthbert, B. N., & Lang, P. J. (1994). Emotion in the criminal psychopath: Fear image processing. *Journal of Abnormal Psychology, 103*, 523–534.

Patterson, C. M., & Newman, J. P. (1993). Reflectivity and learning from aversive events: Toward a psychological mechanism for the syndromes of disinhibition. *Psychological Review, 100*, 716–736.

Pennington, B. F., & Bennetto, L. (1993). Main effects or transaction in the neuropsychology of conduct disorder? Commentary on "The neuropsychology of conduct disorder". *Development and Psychopathology, 5*, 153–164.

Pennington, B. F., & Ozonoff, S. (1996). Executive functions and developmental psychopathology. *Journal of Child Psychology and Psychiatry, 37*, 51–87.

Perry, D. G., & Perry, L. C. (1974). Denial of suffering in the victim as a stimulus to violence in aggressive boys. *Child Development, 45*, 55–62.

Peschardt, K. S., Mitchell, D. G., Leonard, A., & Blair, R. J. R. (manuscript submitted for publication). Impaired affective priming in psychopathic individuals.

Phillips, M. L., Young, A. W., Scott, S. K., Calder, A. J., Andrew, C., Giampietro, V., et al. (1998). Neural responses to facial and vocal expressions of fear and disgust. *Proceedings of the Royal Society of London. Series B: Biological Sciences, 265* (1408), 1809–1817.

Phillips, M. L., Young, A. W., Senior, C., Brammer, M., Andrews, C., Calder, A. J., et al. (1997). A specified neural substrate for perceiving facial expressions of disgust. *Nature, 389*, 495–498.

Pine, D. S., Cohen, E., Cohen, P., & Brook, J. S. (2000). Social phobia and the persistence of conduct problems. *Journal of Child Psychology and Psychiatry, 41*, 657–665.

Prather, M. D., Lavenex, P., Mauldin-Jourdain, M. L., Mason, W. A., Capitanio, J. P., Mendoza, S. P., et al. (2001). Increased social fear and decreased fear of objects in monkeys with neonatal amygdala lesions. *Neuroscience, 106*, 653–658.

Rahman, S., Sahakian, B. J., Hodges, J. R., Rogers, R. D., & Robbins, T. W. (1999). Specific cognitive deficits in mild frontal variant frontotemporal dementia. *Brain, 122*, 1469–1493.

Raine, A. (1997). *The psychopathology of crime*. New York: Academic Press.

Raine, A. (2002a). Annotation: The role of prefrontal deficits, low autonomic arousal, and early health factors in the development of antisocial and aggressive behavior in children. *Journal of Child Psychology and Psychiatry, 43*, 417–434.

Raine, A. (2002b). Biosocial studies of antisocial and violent behavior in children and adults: A review. *Journal of Abnormal Child Psychology, 30*, 311–326.

Raine, A., Buchsbaum, M. S., & LaCasse, L. (1997). Brain abnormalities in murderers indicated by positron emission tomography. *Biological Psychiatry, 42*, 495–508.

Raine, A., Buchsbaum, M. S., Stanley, J., Lottenberg, S., Abel, L., & Stoddard, J. (1994). Selective reductions in prefrontal glucose metabolism in murderers. *Biological Psychiatry, 15*, 365–373.

Raine, A., Lencz, T., Bihrle, S., LaCasse, L., & Colletti, P. (2000). Reduced prefrontal gray matter volume and reduced autonomic activity in antisocial personality disorder. *Archives of General Psychiatry, 57*, 119–127.

Raine, A., Meloy, J. R., Birhle, S., Stoddard, J., LaCasse, L., & Buchsbaum, M. S. (1998a). Reduced prefrontal and increased subcortical brain functioning assessed

using positron emission tomography in predatory and affective murderers. *Behaviour Science and Law, 16,* 319–332.
Raine, A., Phil, D., Stoddard, J., Bihrle, S., & Buchsbaum, M. (1998b). Prefrontal glucose deficits in murderers lacking psychosocial deprivation. *Neuropsychiatry, Neuropsychology, and Behavioral Neurology, 11,* 1–7.
Raine, A., Venables, P. H., & Williams, M. (1996). Better autonomic conditioning and faster electrodermal half-recovery time at age 15 years as possible protective factors against crime at age 29 years. *Developmental Psychology, 32,* 624–630.
Ramamurthi, B. (1988). Stereotactic operation in behaviour disorders. Amygdalotomy and hypothalamotomy. *Acta Neurochirurgica, Supplementum (Wien), 44,* 152–157.
Rees, G., Frith, C. D., & Lavie, N. (1997). Modulating irrelevant motion perception by varying attentional load in an unrelated task. *Science, 278* (5343), 1616–1619.
Reiss, A. J., Miczek, K. A., & Roth, J. A. (1994). *Understanding and preventing violence* (Vol. 2. *Biobehavioral influences*). Washington, DC: National Academy Press.
Roberts, A. C., Robbins, T. W., & Weiskrantz, L. (1998). *The prefrontal cortex: Executive and cognitive functions.* Oxford: Oxford University Press.
Robins, L. N., Tipp, J., & Pryzbeck, T. (1991). Antisocial personality. In L. N. Robins & D. A. Regier (Eds.), *Psychiatric disorders in North America.* New York: Free Press.
Roland, E., & Idsoe, T. (2001). Aggression and bullying. *Aggressive Behavior, 27,* 446–462.
Rolls, E. T. (1997). The orbitofrontal cortex. *Philosophical Transactions of the Royal Society of London. Series B: Biological Sciences, 351,* 1433–1443.
Rolls, E. T. (2000). The orbitofrontal cortex and reward. *Cerebral Cortex, 10,* 284–294.
Rolls, E. T., Hornak, J., Wade, D., & McGrath, J. (1994). Emotion-related learning in patients with social and emotional changes associated with frontal lobe damage. *Journal of Neurology, Neurosurgery and Psychiatry, 57,* 1518–1524.
Rothbart, M., Ahadi, S., & Hershey, K. L. (1994). Temperament and social behaviour in children. *Merrill-Palmer Quarterly, 40,* 21–39.
Russo, M. F., & Beidel, D. C. (1993). Co-morbidity of childhood anxiety and externalizing disorders: Prevalence, associated characteristics, and validation issues. *Clinical Psychology Review, 14,* 199–221.
Schmitt, W. A., & Newman, J. P. (1999). Are all psychopathic individuals low-anxious? *Journal of Abnormal Psychology, 108,* 353–358.
Schneider, F., Gur, R. C., Gur, R. E., & Muenz, L. R. (1994). Standardized mood induction with happy and sad facial expression. *Psychiatry Research, 51,* 19–31.
Shweder, R. A., Mahaptra, M., & Miller, J. G. (1987). Culture and moral development. In J. Kagan & S. Lamb (Eds.), *The emergence of morality in young children* (pp. 1–82). Chicago: University of Chicago Press.
Smetana, J. G. (1981). Preschool children's conceptions of moral and social rules. *Child Development, 52,* 1333–1336.
Smetana, J. G. (1985). Preschool children's conceptions of transgressions: The effects of varying moral and conventional domain-related attributes. *Developmental Psychology, 21,* 18–29.
Smetana, J. G. (1993). Understanding of social rules. In M. Bennett (Ed.), *The child as psychologist: An introduction to the development of social cognition* (pp. 111–141). New York: Harvester Wheatsheaf.
Soderstrom, H., Tullberg, M., Wikkelso, C., Ekholm, S., & Forsman, A. (2000). Reduced regional cerebral blood flow in non-psychotic violent offenders. *Psychiatry Research, 98,* 29–41.

Source book of criminal justice statistics online (1998). Washington, DC, Department of Justice, Bureau of Justice Statistics. www.albany.edu/sourcebook. Retrieval date 2002.

Sprengelmeyer, R., Rausch, M., Eysel, U. T., & Przuntek, H. (1998). Neural structures associated with the recognition of facial basic emotions. *Proceedings of the Royal Society of London. Series B: Biological Sciences*, 265, 1927–1931.

Stone, V. E., Baron-Cohen, S., & Knight, R. T. (1998). Frontal lobe contributions to theory of mind. *Journal of Cognitive Neuroscience*, 10, 640–656.

Stone, V. E., Cosmides, L., Tooby, J., Kroll, N., & Knight, R. T. (2002). Selective impairment of reasoning about social exchange in a patient with bilateral limbic system damage. *Proceedings of the National Academy of Sciences of the USA*, 99, 11531–11536.

Thornquist, M. H., & Zuckerman, M. (1995). Psychopathy, passive-avoidance learning and basic dimensions of personality. *Personality and Individual Differences*, 19, 525–534.

Tiihonen, J., Hodgins, S., Vaurio, O., Laakso, M., Repo, E., Soininen, H., et al. (2000). Amygdaloid volume loss in psychopathy. *Society for Neuroscience Abstracts*, 2017.

Trasler, G. (1978). Relations between psychopathy and persistent criminality—methodological and theoretical issues. In R. D. Hare & D. Schalling (Eds.), *Psychopathic behaviour: Approaches to research*. Chichester, UK: Wiley.

Trasler, G. B. (1973). Criminal behaviour.. In H. J. Eysenck (Ed.), *Handbook of abnormal psychology*. London: Pitman.

Turiel, E. (1983). *The development of social knowledge: Morality and convention*. Cambridge: Cambridge University Press.

van Elst, L. T., Woermann, F. G., Lemieux, L., Thompson, P. J., & Trimble, M. R. (2000). Affective aggression in patients with temporal lobe epilepsy: A quantitative MRI study of the amygdala. *Brain*, 123(Pt 2), 234–243.

Veit, R., Flor, H., Erb, M., Hermann, C., Lotze, M., Grodd, W., et al. (2002). Brain circuits involved in emotional learning in antisocial behavior and social phobia in humans. *Neuroscience Letters*, 328, 233–236.

Verona, E., Patrick, C. J., & Joiner, T. E. (2001). Psychopathy, antisocial personality, and suicide risk. *Journal of Abnormal Psychology*, 110, 462–470.

Volkow, N. D., & Tancredi, L. (1987). Neural substrates of violent behaviour. A preliminary study with positron emission tomography. *British Journal of Psychiatry*, 151, 668–673.

Volkow, N. D., Tancredi, L. R., Grant, C., Gillespie, H., Valentine, A., Mullani, N., et al. (1995). Brain glucose metabolism in violent psychiatric patients: A preliminary study. *Psychiatry Research*, 61, 243–253.

Williamson, S., Hare, R. D., & Wong, S. (1987). Violence: Criminal psychopaths and their victims. *Canadian Journal of Behavioral Science*, 19, 454–462.

Williamson, S., Harpur, T. J., & Hare, R. D. (1991). Abnormal processing of affective words by psychopaths. *Psychophysiology*, 28, 260–273.

Zagrodzka, J., Hedberg, C. E., Mann, G. L., & Morrison, A. R. (1998). Contrasting expressions of aggressive behavior released by lesions of the central nucleus of the amygdala during wakefulness and rapid eye movement sleep without atonia in cats. *Behavioral Neuroscience*, 112, 589–602.

Zoccolillo, M. (1992). Co-occurrence of conduct disorder and its adult outcomes with depressive and anxiety disorders: A review. *Journal of the American Academy of Child and Adolescent Psychiatry*, 31, 547–556.

Index

Accidental versus intentional actions 134
Action perception 81–105
Acquired sociopathy 174
Aggression
   Anti-social personality disorder 291–313
   Instrumental aggression 291, 297, 303–304
   Reactive aggression 291, 293–296, 298–299, 303
Amygdala
   Accessory basal nucleus 23
   Amygdala theory of autism 246–247
   Anatomy 21
   Basolateral nucleus 21
   Central nucleus 23
   Decision-making and 273–274
   Electrophysiology 38
   Emotion and 29–31, 163–166
   Face perception and 160
   Lateral nucleus 21
   Social behaviour and 25–26, 32–37, 62
   Social cognition and 45–46, 158, 175–176
Anger 163
Anhedonia 258
Animacy 158
Anterior cingulate cortex
   Anatomy 25
   Social behaviour and 44–45
   Social cognition and 46–47
Anti-social personality disorder 291–313
Attention-getting behaviours 130–131
Argument by analogy 146–147

Autism 239–249
   Empathizing and 243–245
   Eye contact 243
   Foetal testosterone and 248
   Gaze following 248
   Neurobiology of 246–248
   Social brain 242, 246–247
   Systematizing and 242
   Theory of mind and 242

Basal forebrain 64, 69–70
Basolateral nucleus of the amygdale 21
Bee-eaters 129
Behavioural flexibility 59–76
   Social behaviour and 76
Behavioural inhibition 32–37, 242
   Depression 274–275
   Neural basis 275–276
Biconditional discrimination task 71–75
Biological motion 179–180
Birds
   Corvids 61, 116, 128–129, 137
   Raven 128–129, 139
   Western scrub-jay 128–129, 137, 144–147

Cache protection strategies 128–129
   Social cognition and 129
   Visual perspective-taking and 129
   Knowledge attribution and 137
   Experience projection and 144
   Tactical deception and 139
Capgras syndrome 212
Capuchin monkeys 127, 137, 140–141
Chimpanzees 116, 121–125, 127–128, 130–136, 138–142, 144–147

Decision-making
   Amygdala and 273–274

Depression and 265, 269–273
　Prefrontal cortex and 273–274
Depression, unipolar 257–281
　Development 259–261
　Differential activation hypothesis 263–264
　Learned helplessness theory 262–263
　Negative cognitive triad 261–263
　Stress sensitization model 264
　Social cognition and brain 264, 266–267
Disgust 163
Dolphins 116
Domestic dogs 116, 125–126
Domestic cats 126
Domestic pigs 137–138
Domestication of social cognition 125–126
Dominance hierarchy
　Chimpanzees 116
　Humans 292, 296
　Monkeys 20, 29–30
Dorsolateral prefrontal cortex 23–24

Electrophysiology
　Actions and space 88–92, 98
　Gaze 84–88
　Faces 84
　Hidden objects 102–105
　Implied motion 93–98
　Intention movements 88
　Limb articulation 86–88, 94, 96
　Mirror neurons 144–145
　Walking 86, 92–98
Elephants 116
Embarassment 296
Emotion 19, 241
Empathizing 242–246
Empathy 1, 175, 220
　Mirror neurons and 144–145
Enculturation 123
Episodic memory 198, 207, 279–280
Evolution
　Social brain 115
　Social cognition 115–147
　Social intelligence 116–117
Experience projection 143
Executive control
　Depression 268–269
Eye witness identification 215

Face perception
　Emotion and 160
　Facial expressions and 160
　Fusiform face area 160, 213–215
　Fusiform gyrus 158–160
　Identity 160
　Person-related judgements 171–173
　Prosopagnosia 212–214, 240
　Racial judgements 170–171
False belief task 117–118, 138, 141–143, 173–175, 246
Fear 163
　Amygdala and 162
Foetal testosterone
　Brain development 248
Folk physics 241
Food competition task 61–62, 127–128, 141
Frontotemporal dementia 218
Fusiform face area. *See* Face perception.

GABA 39
Gambling task 270–273
Gaze alternation 131–132
Gaze discrimination 85–86, 120–126
Goal-directedness 162, 179–180
Gorillas 123–131

Happy 163
Hippocampus 205
Horses 116, 126

Imitation 1
Inferotemporal cortex & learning 68
Intention-reading 133–135
Intentionality 116
Intentional stance 118–119
IQ 241
Instrumental aggression
　Frontal lobe dysfunction hypothesis 297–299
　Integrated emotion systems model 308–312
　Neural basis 297
　Response set modulation hypothesis 299–303
　Violence inhibition mechanism 306–307
Intentional communication 130–133
Intervening variables 118–120

Joint attention 245

Killer whales 116
Kluver-Bucy syndrome 26–29, 31, 38, 43–44, 62
Knowledge attribution 135–138
Knower-guesser paradigm 135–136

Left frontal operculum
  Emotion and 168–169
Left-hemisphere
  Mental states and 177
Level-1 perspective-taking 123–126
Level-2 perspective-taking 126–129
Lions 116

Machiavellian intelligence 116
Medial prefrontal cortex 23–24, 178–179
Memory
  Episodic memory 198
  Recognition memory 69
Mirror neurons
  Cognitive empathy and 144–145
  Electrophysiology 104–105
  Role taking and 144
  Simulation theory and 105, 144, 169, 177
  Moral cognition 1, 221
  Prefrontal cortex and 182

Object-choice paradigm 123–126, 133
Object-reward associations 62, 64–66, 68, 70–71, 76
Orangutans 134, 141–142
Orbitofrontal cortex
  Anatomy 23–24
  Behavioural flexibility 65–67
  Emotion 167
  Faces 41
  Motivational value 63, 65, 71
  Response selection 41–43
  Social behaviour and 40
  Social cognition and 46, 174

Pain, experience of 205–206
Parrots 116
Peripheral feeding hypothesis 128
Personality 170
Placebos
  Ventromedial prefrontal cortex 211
Pointing 126, 132
  Proto-declarative pointing 132–133
  Proto-imperative pointing 132–133
Premotor cortex (F5) 102–105
Prosopagnosia 212–214, 240

Psychology
  Social 60, 195–224

Reinforcer devaluation task 64–66
Right-hemisphere
  Emotion and 167–168
  Theory of mind and 176
Role-taking 143–144

Sally-Anne task 141, 173
Sadness 163
Schizophrenia 1, 59
Self-awareness
  Neural correlates 205–206
  Neurocognitive processes 206–208
Self-control 208
Self-recognition
  Contextual factors 203–204
  Neural correlates 199–201
  Neurocognitive processes 201–203
Simulation theory of mind 105, 143–145, 163
Social behaviour, primate 20
Social brain 115–117, 265–266
Social cognition 1, 115–147, 157, 175
Social cognitive neuroscience 1–14
Social intelligence 116
Social response reversal 295
Somatic markers 174, 270–271
  Prefrontal cortex and 201–203
Somatosensory cortex 183
Squirrel monkeys 140
Stress 61
Stroop task 210
Superior temporal sulcus (STS) 213–218
  Anatomy 82
  Action recognition and 81–107, 161, 179–181, 213, 218
  Electrophysiology 83–84, 124
  Face perception and 160–162
Surprise 163

Tactical deception 116, 138
  Alliances 116
  Reconciliation 116
Temporal cortex
  Contextual factors 219–221
  Neural correlates 217
  Neurocognitive processes 217–219
Temporopolar cortex
  Anatomy 24
  Social behaviour and 43
  Social cognition and 46

Theory of mind 117–147, 157, 173–180, 216–221
   Arguments against ToM 145–147
   Informational 135–143
   Motivational 133–135
   Perceptual 120–130
Triangulation 146

Ventromedial prefrontal cortex
   Theory of mind and 175
Visual co-orienting 120–121
Visual perspective-taking 126–129, 136, 207

Wada test 199
Wason card selection task 181